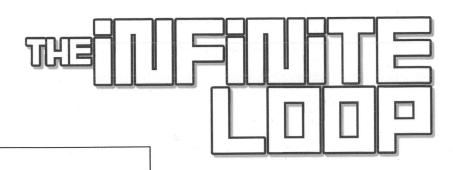

THE INFINITE LOOP

Written and Lettered by
PIERRICK COLINET

Illustrated and Colored by
ELSA CHARRETIER

Special thanks to Katchoo Scarletinred, Nicolas Bannister, Nick Meylaender, Mahmud Asrar, Charlie Adlard, Gerald Parel, Laurent Lefeuvre, and Tom Colinet.

Ted Adams, CEO & Publisher
Greg Goldstein, President & COO
Robbie Robbins, EVP/Sr. Graphic Artist
Chris Ryall, Chief Creative Officer/Editor-in-Chief
Matthew Ruzicka, CPA, Chief Financial Officer
Alan Payne, VP of Sales
Dirk Wood, VP of Marketing
Lorelei Bunjes, VP of Digital Services
Jeff Webber, VP of Digital Publishing & Business Development

www.IDWPUBLISHING.com
IDW founded by Ted Adams, Alex Garner, Kris Oprisko, and Robbie Robbins

Facebook: **facebook.com/idwpublishing**
Twitter: **@idwpublishing**
YouTube: **youtube.com/idwpublishing**
Tumblr: **tumblr.idwpublishing.com**
Instagram: **instagram.com/idwpublishing**

Originally published as THE INFINITE LOOP issues #1-6.

THE iNFiNiTE LOOP

Color Flats by ROSE CITRON

Series Edited by SARAH GAYDOS

Cover by ELSA CHARRETIER & NICOLAS BANNISTER

Collection Edits by JUSTIN EISINGER and ALONZO SIMON

Collection Design by CLAUDIA CHONG

THE INFINITE LOOP

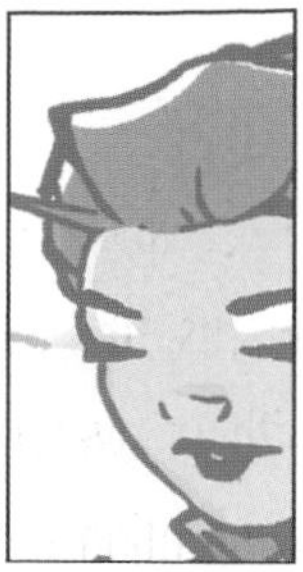

In many ways I am the worst possible person to write this preface.

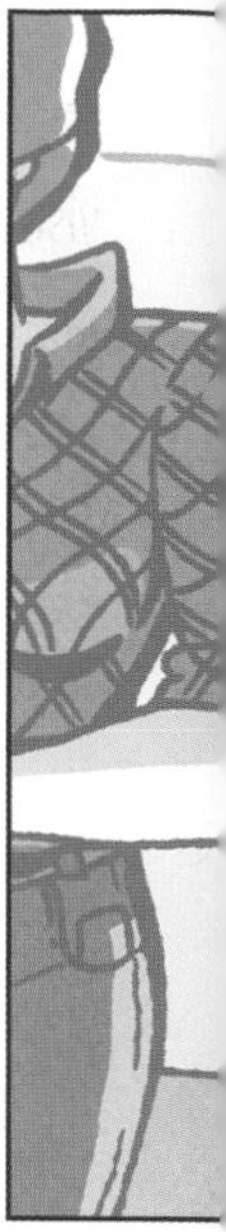

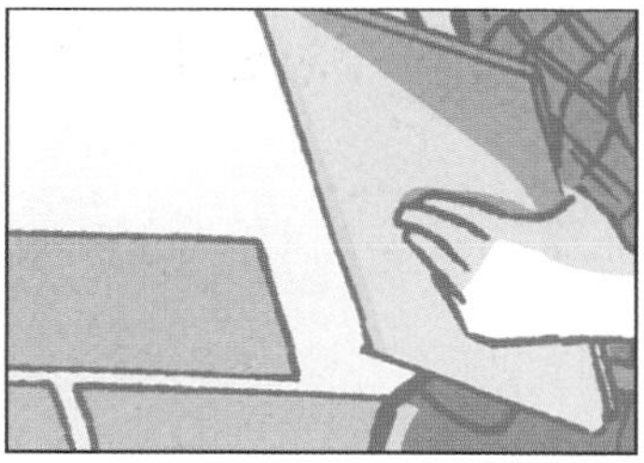

Though I am ridiculously fond of stories that deal with alternate reality, the fact of the matter is that time travel—and thus an "infinite loop" most of all!—makes my head spin. I can never quite hang on to the story threads and all their many consequences to make sense of things. But then this story that is very much about time travel is also not about time travel at all, and so in that way, I am perhaps a perfect fit to talk about why it's so beautiful and inspiring independent of all its cool sci-fi elements.

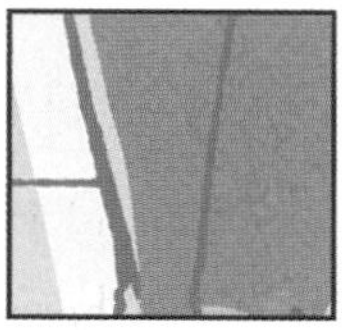

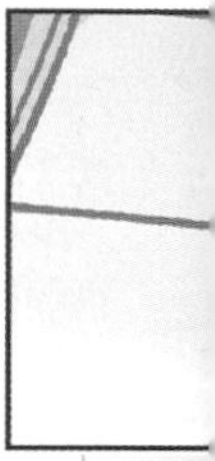

All of my favorite stories are stories that have both a lovely engaging surface and also many fascinating layers underneath that surface, and so it is with *The Infinite Loop*, a story that on the surface is very much about the tricky business of time travel but when you scratch the pretty surface is really about freedom. All kinds of facets of freedom are explored in *The Infinite Loop*—the freedom to be different, the freedom to make your own choices, the freedom to be who you know you are, the freedom to follow your happiness—especially when that happiness comes in the form of pursuit of love. But none of those facets matter, really. All that matters is the freedom bit, because if you have that bit, then you have it all. It's why freedom as a concept is so very important and so often misunderstood. To have freedom is to have EVERYTHING. And to be missing it, is to have NOTHING. Because if you don't have it completely and totally, then you never know what is going to be taken from you next, or what you might not ever even get to imagine, get to discover, get to be.

It's no surprise, given the themes and messages in their story that co-creators Pierrick Colinet and Elsa Charretier carved their own path in the rather unforgiving comics market to bring this book to life. *The Infinite Loop* is a total labor of love—first funded through a wildly successful French Kickstarter campaign before finding a home with publishers both overseas and in the U.S.—and you can feel that love on every page. Elsa Charretier's smooth, clean, open, and confident style that embraces fighting dinosaurs and girls falling in love in equal measure pairs beautifully with Pierrick Colinet's simple, modern words, that have just enough poetry to lend some weight and gravity to the stylized glossy pop visuals without overwhelming them. And let it just be said, comics creators pursuing a non-traditional path of publication to get their story out there is a particularly fitting origin for a book filled with the idea of fighting with everything you've got and refusing to give up no matter what obstacles are presented. It's nice when things all come together, isn't it?

The use of "anomalies" in *The Infinite Loop* is especially resonant as most of us reading this book live in a time and place, where despite a lot of obvious freedoms that we take for granted, a whole lot of people in the world are often considered "anomalies" and themselves not accorded the same rights and freedoms that the rest of us just expect. Presenting "anomalies" here as something beautiful and important and complex while also something that has been frequently misunderstood or cast aside, sends a powerful message through its metaphors. It also speaks to valuable lessons we'd all do well to learn—lessons about what comes next in life, about how you can't bother quantifying and limiting freedoms because there will always be a next level—one that has probably always been there, but which you are just becoming aware of, or don't yet understand. It's why even more than being a love story this will always be a story about freedom—the metaphors and lessons in *The Infinite Loop* simply go too deep for it to just be about romantic love. And that's a great thing because even if you cannot relate to romantic love, we can all relate to freedom. It's a basic tenet hardwired into us. The pursuit of it will drive us to the greatest possible highs and put us in conflict with the most disturbing lows, all in the name of being free to make our own choices. It's what the simple-minded and ignorant never understand about whatever the latest political issue is—the issue at hand doesn't really matter at all—it's the basic freedoms **behind** the issue that matters. It's the freedom for that issue to be whatever it needs to be, an ever changing tapestry as people and the world they live in evolve.

The Infinite Loop is all about that evolution.

Kelly Thompson
New York, NY

Kelly Thompson is the author of the novels The Girl Who Would Be King *and* Storykiller, *writer of the comic* Jem and The Holograms, *co-writer of* Captain Marvel and The Carol Corps, *and writer/co-creator of the graphic novel* Heart In A Box.

Art by
ELSA CHARRETIER & NICOLAS BANNISTER

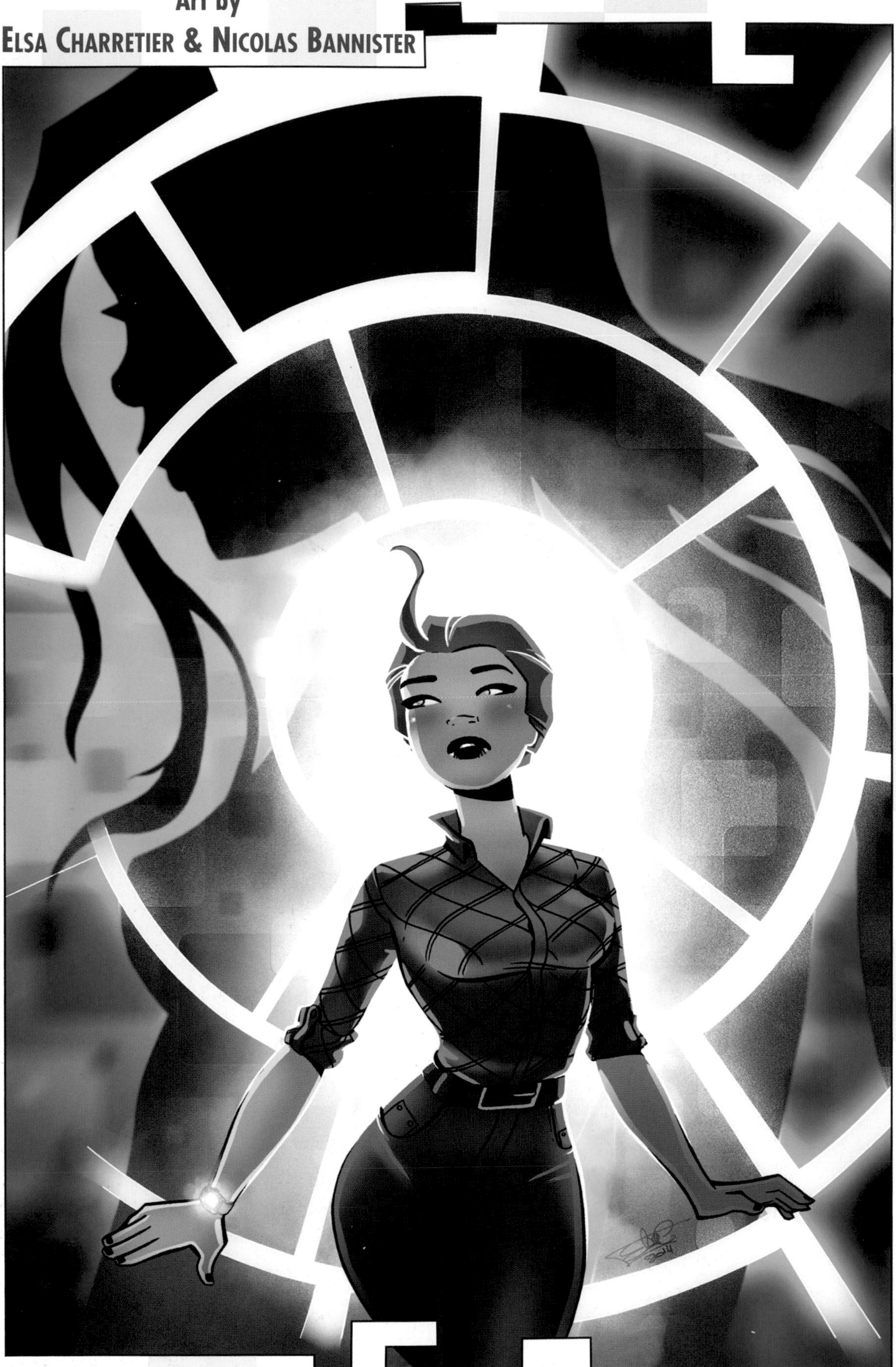

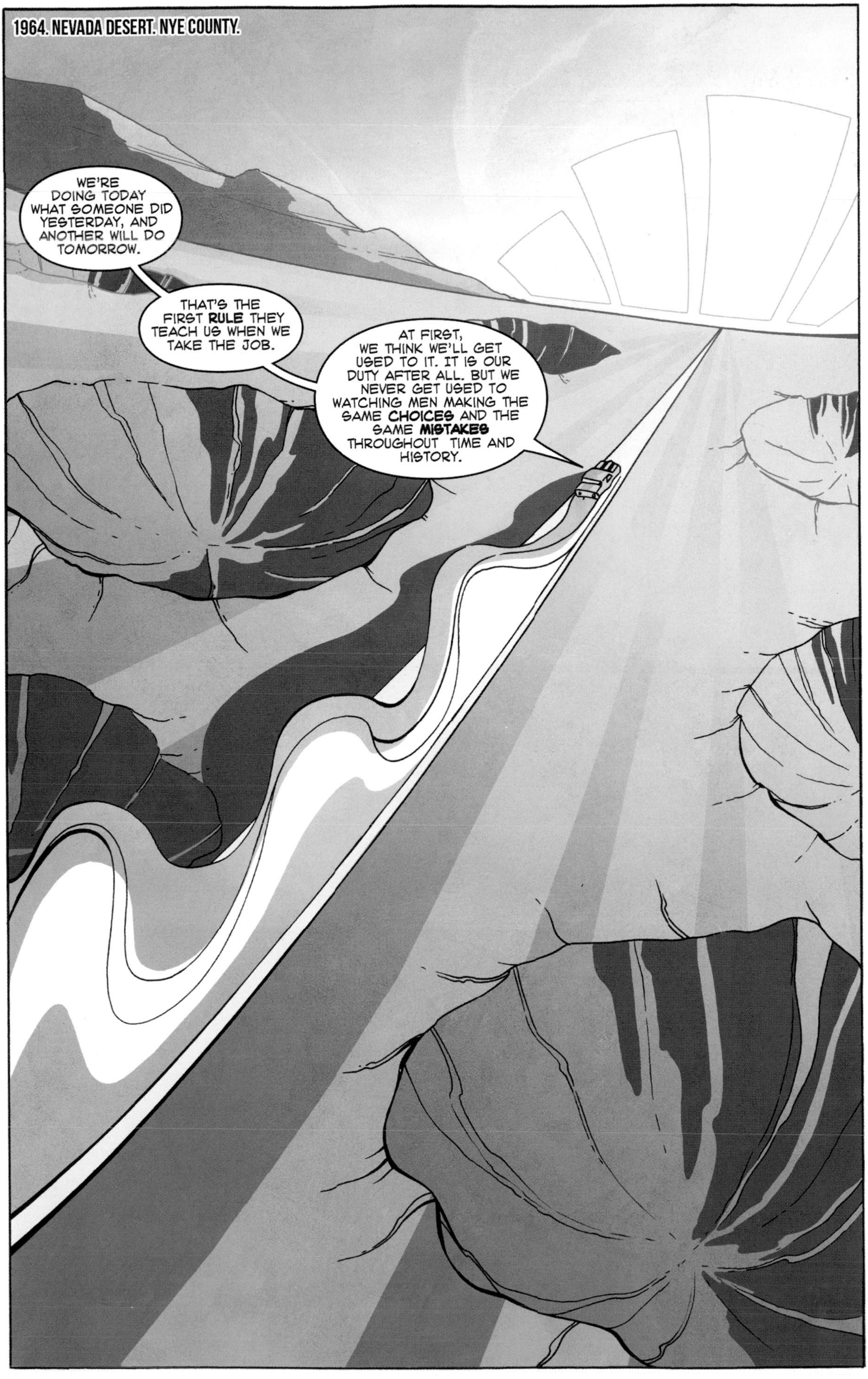
1964. NEVADA DESERT. NYE COUNTY.
WE'RE DOING TODAY WHAT SOMEONE DID YESTERDAY, AND ANOTHER WILL DO TOMORROW.
THAT'S THE FIRST RULE THEY TEACH US WHEN WE TAKE THE JOB.
AT FIRST, WE THINK WE'LL GET USED TO IT. IT IS OUR DUTY AFTER ALL. BUT WE NEVER GET USED TO WATCHING MEN MAKING THE SAME CHOICES AND THE SAME MISTAKES THROUGHOUT TIME AND HISTORY.

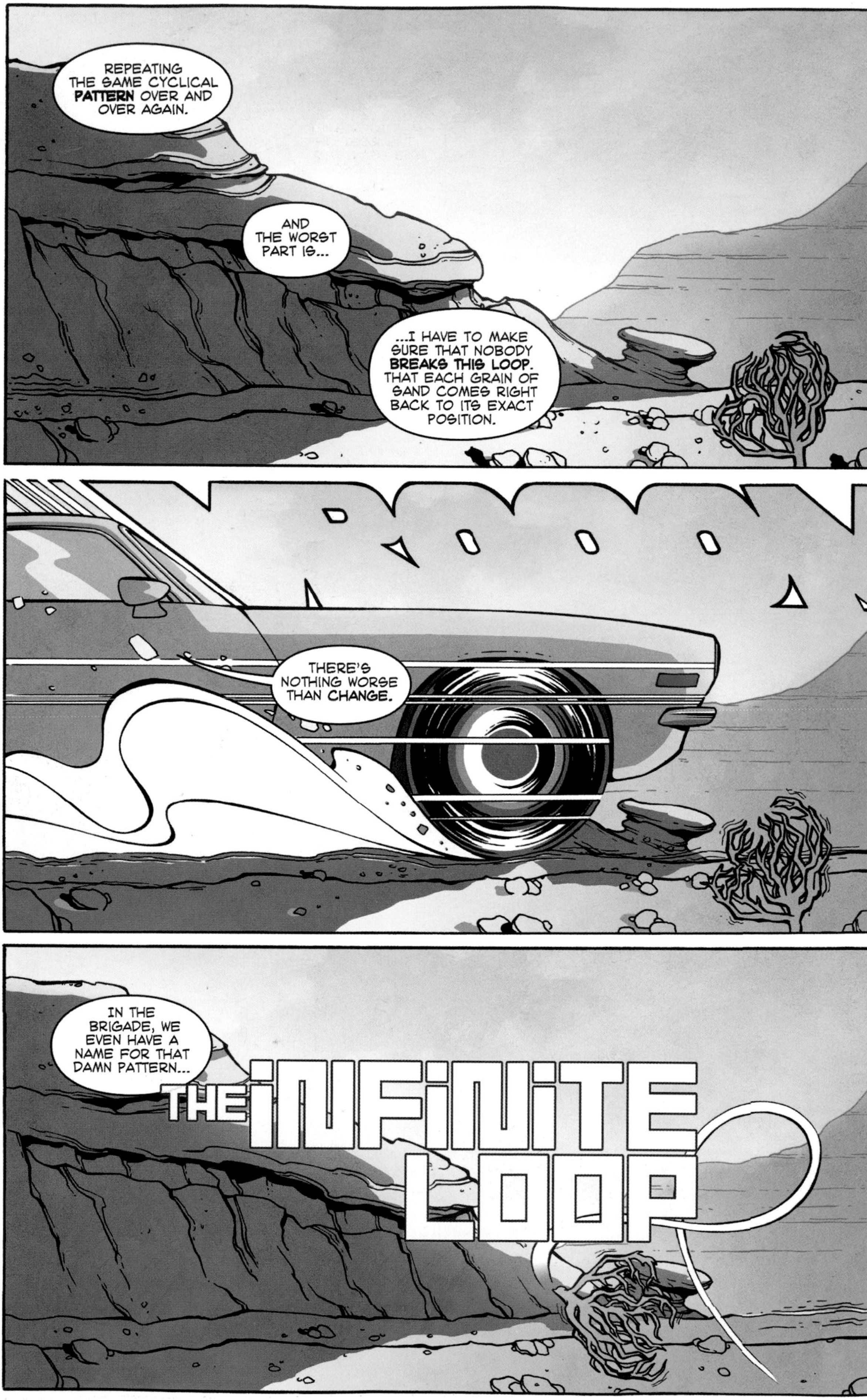
REPEATING THE SAME CYCLICAL PATTERN OVER AND OVER AGAIN.
AND THE WORST PART IS...
...I HAVE TO MAKE SURE THAT NOBODY BREAKS THIS LOOP. THAT EACH GRAIN OF SAND COMES RIGHT BACK TO ITS EXACT POSITION.
THERE'S NOTHING WORSE THAN CHANGE.
IN THE BRIGADE, WE EVEN HAVE A NAME FOR THAT DAMN PATTERN...
THE INFINITE LOOP

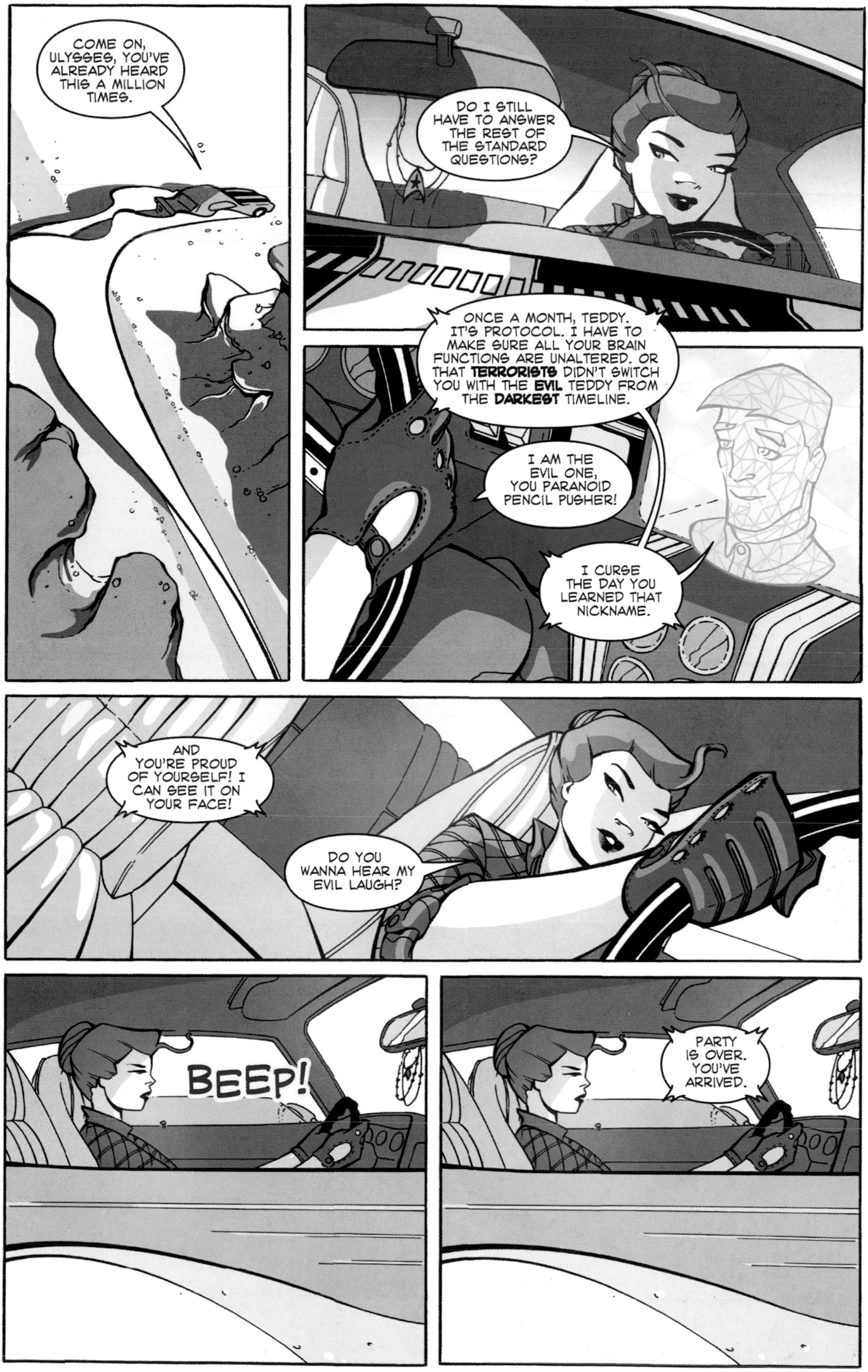
COME ON, ULYSSES, YOU'VE ALREADY HEARD THIS A MILLION TIMES.
DO I STILL HAVE TO ANSWER THE REST OF THE STANDARD QUESTIONS?
ONCE A MONTH, TEDDY. IT'S PROTOCOL. I HAVE TO MAKE SURE ALL YOUR BRAIN FUNCTIONS ARE UNALTERED. OR THAT **TERRORISTS** DIDN'T SWITCH YOU WITH THE **EVIL** TEDDY FROM THE **DARKEST** TIMELINE.
I AM THE EVIL ONE, YOU PARANOID PENCIL PUSHER!
I CURSE THE DAY YOU LEARNED THAT NICKNAME.
AND YOU'RE PROUD OF YOURSELF! I CAN SEE IT ON YOUR FACE!
DO YOU WANNA HEAR MY EVIL LAUGH?
BEEP!
PARTY IS OVER. YOU'VE ARRIVED.

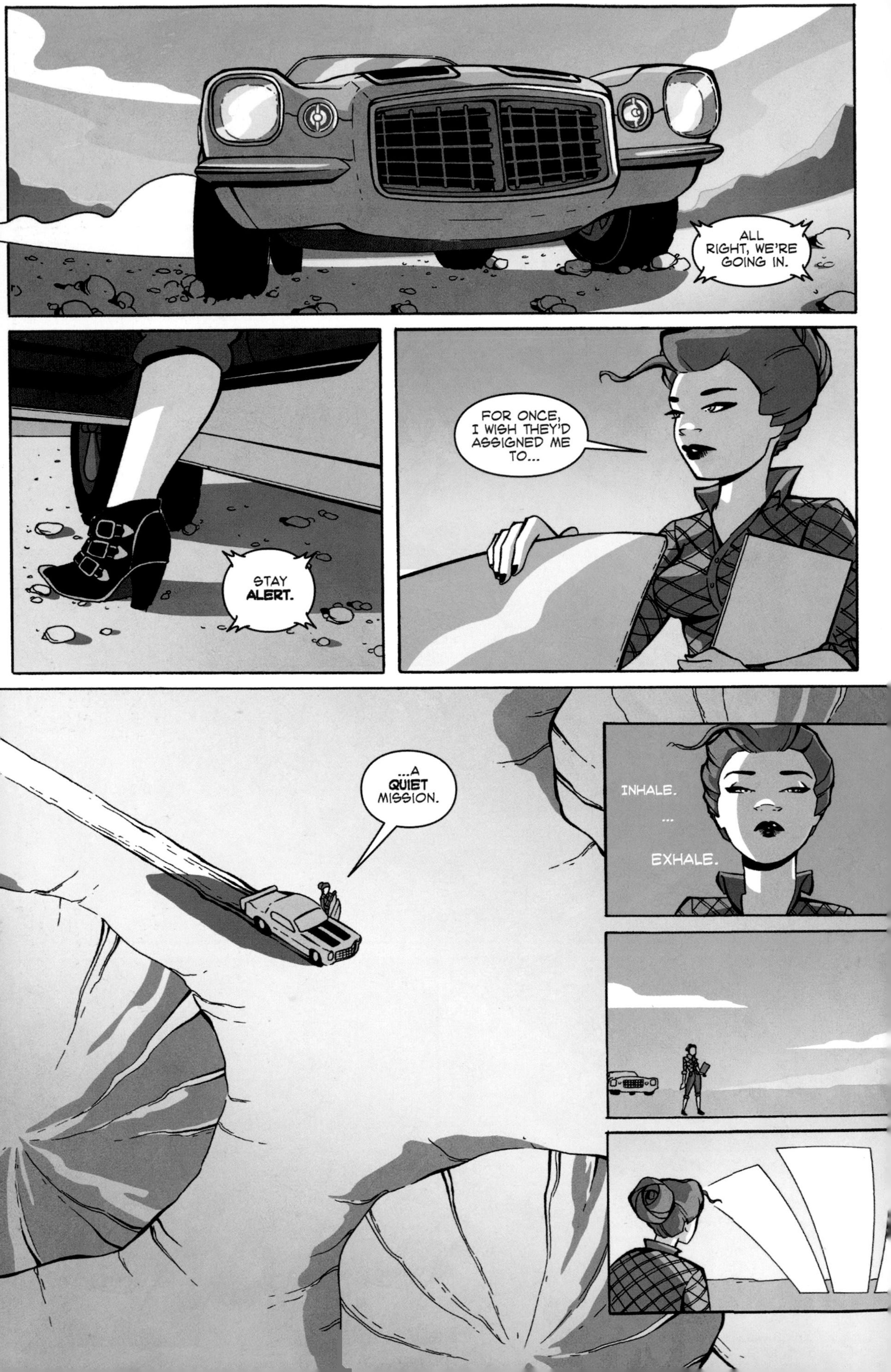
ALL RIGHT, WE'RE GOING IN.
STAY ALERT.
FOR ONCE, I WISH THEY'D ASSIGNED ME TO...
...A QUIET MISSION.
INHALE.
...
EXHALE.

YOU LOOK EXHAUSTED. WHAT'S WRONG?

I'VE JUST GOT BACK FROM 1809. THE TRIP WAS A KILLER.

THE TIME PARADOX **FORGERS** TRIED TO INTERFERE WITH ABRAHAM LINCOLN'S BIRTH...

...FOR THE THOUSANDTH TIME THIS YEAR.

THESE TERRORISTS LOVE TO PLAY WITH LINCOLN. SUCH A DRAG.

THEY'RE REAL ARTISTS, BELIEVE ME. THE **MATERIAL ANOMALIES** AFFECTED SEVERAL DECADES.

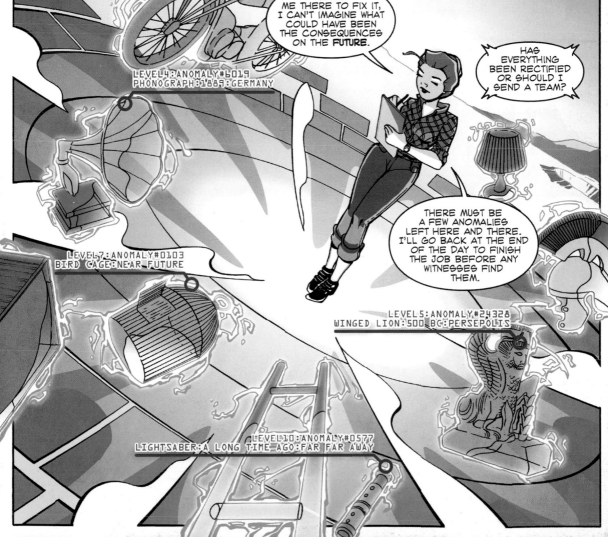

WITHOUT ME THERE TO FIX IT, I CAN'T IMAGINE WHAT COULD HAVE BEEN THE CONSEQUENCES ON THE **FUTURE**.

LEVEL 4: ANOMALY #6019
PHONOGRAPH: 1889: GERMANY

HAS EVERYTHING BEEN RECTIFIED OR SHOULD I SEND A TEAM?

THERE MUST BE A FEW ANOMALIES LEFT HERE AND THERE. I'LL GO BACK AT THE END OF THE DAY TO FINISH THE JOB BEFORE ANY WITNESSES FIND THEM.

LEVEL 7: ANOMALY #0103
BIRD CAGE: NEAR FUTURE

LEVEL 5: ANOMALY #24328
WINGED LION: 500 BC: PERSEPOLIS

LEVEL 10: ANOMALY #0577
LIGHTSABER: A LONG TIME AGO: FAR FAR AWAY

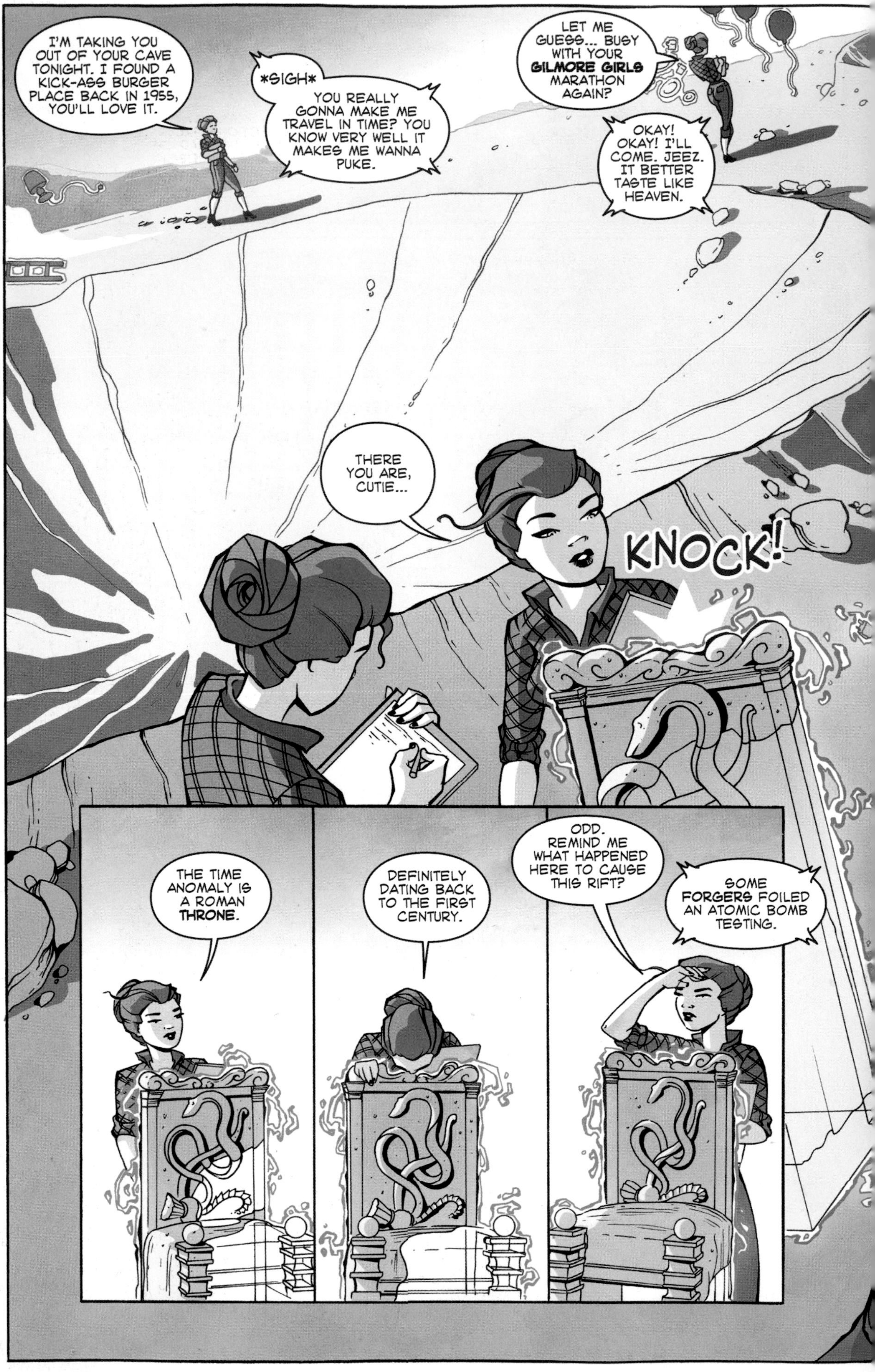
I'M TAKING YOU OUT OF YOUR CAVE TONIGHT. I FOUND A KICK-ASS BURGER PLACE BACK IN 1955, YOU'LL LOVE IT.
SIGH
YOU REALLY GONNA MAKE ME TRAVEL IN TIME? YOU KNOW VERY WELL IT MAKES ME WANNA PUKE.
LET ME GUESS... BUSY WITH YOUR GILMORE GIRLS MARATHON AGAIN?
OKAY! OKAY! I'LL COME. JEEZ. IT BETTER TASTE LIKE HEAVEN.
THERE YOU ARE, CUTIE...
KNOCK!
THE TIME ANOMALY IS A ROMAN THRONE.
DEFINITELY DATING BACK TO THE FIRST CENTURY.
ODD. REMIND ME WHAT HAPPENED HERE TO CAUSE THIS RIFT?
SOME FORGERS FOILED AN ATOMIC BOMB TESTING.

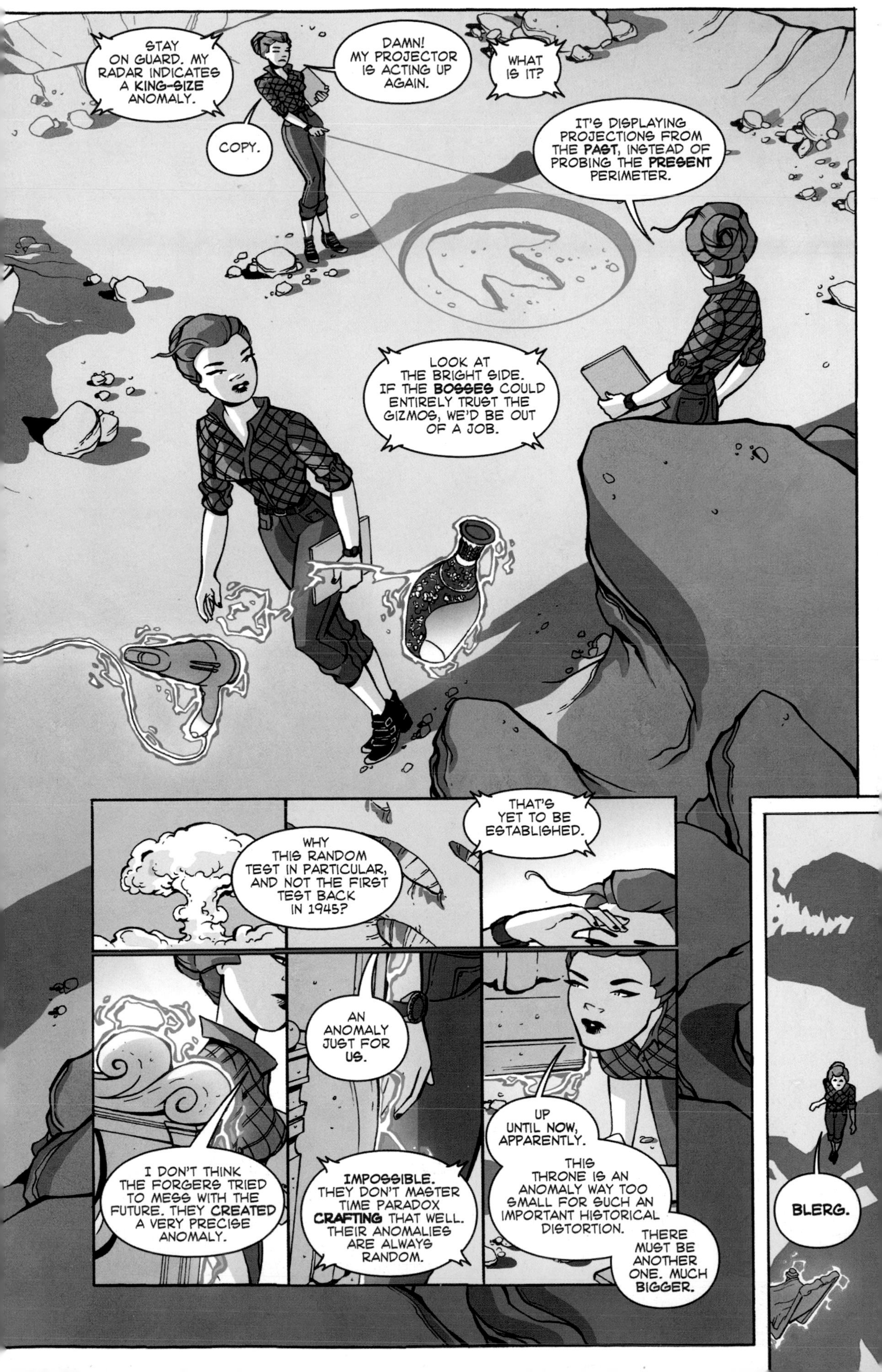
STAY ON GUARD. MY RADAR INDICATES A **KING-SIZE** ANOMALY.
COPY.
DAMN! MY PROJECTOR IS ACTING UP AGAIN.
WHAT IS IT?
IT'S DISPLAYING PROJECTIONS FROM THE **PAST**, INSTEAD OF PROBING THE **PRESENT** PERIMETER.
LOOK AT THE BRIGHT SIDE. IF THE **BOSSES** COULD ENTIRELY TRUST THE GIZMOS, WE'D BE OUT OF A JOB.
WHY THIS RANDOM TEST IN PARTICULAR, AND NOT THE FIRST TEST BACK IN 1945?
THAT'S YET TO BE ESTABLISHED.
I DON'T THINK THE FORGERS TRIED TO MESS WITH THE FUTURE. THEY **CREATED** A VERY PRECISE ANOMALY.
AN ANOMALY JUST FOR **US**.
IMPOSSIBLE. THEY DON'T MASTER TIME PARADOX **CRAFTING** THAT WELL. THEIR ANOMALIES ARE ALWAYS RANDOM.
UP UNTIL **NOW**, APPARENTLY.
THIS THRONE IS AN ANOMALY WAY TOO SMALL FOR SUCH AN IMPORTANT HISTORICAL DISTORTION.
THERE MUST BE ANOTHER ONE. MUCH BIGGER.
BLERG.

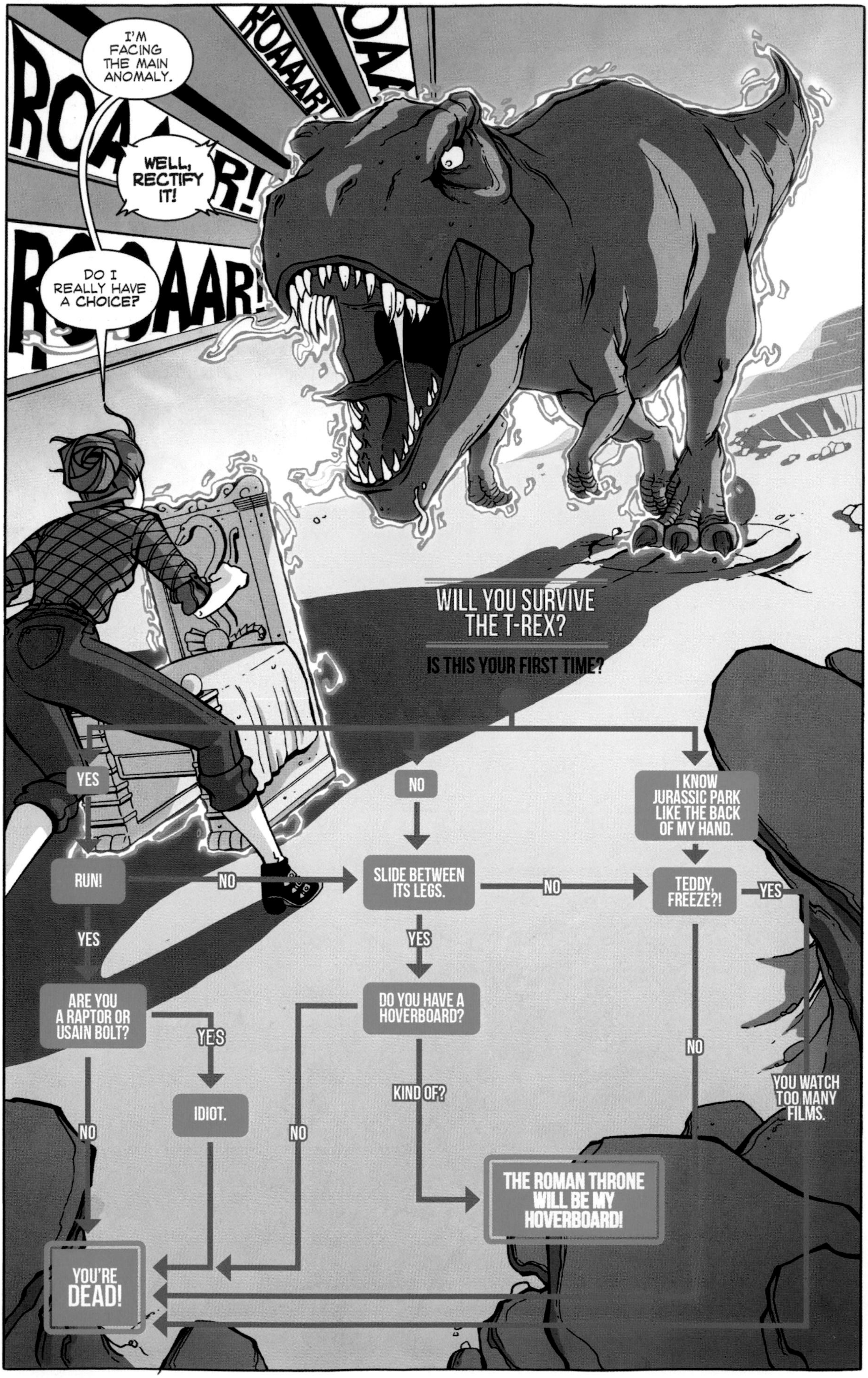

I'M FACING THE MAIN ANOMALY.
WELL, RECTIFY IT!
DO I REALLY HAVE A CHOICE?
ROAAAR!
ROAAR!
ROAAARR!
ROOAAR!
WILL YOU SURVIVE THE T-REX?
IS THIS YOUR FIRST TIME?
YES
NO
I KNOW JURASSIC PARK LIKE THE BACK OF MY HAND.
RUN!
NO
SLIDE BETWEEN ITS LEGS.
NO
TEDDY, FREEZE?!
YES
YES
YES
ARE YOU A RAPTOR OR USAIN BOLT?
YES
DO YOU HAVE A HOVERBOARD?
NO
IDIOT.
KIND OF?
NO
YOU WATCH TOO MANY FILMS.
NO
NO
THE ROMAN THRONE WILL BE MY HOVERBOARD!
YOU'RE DEAD!

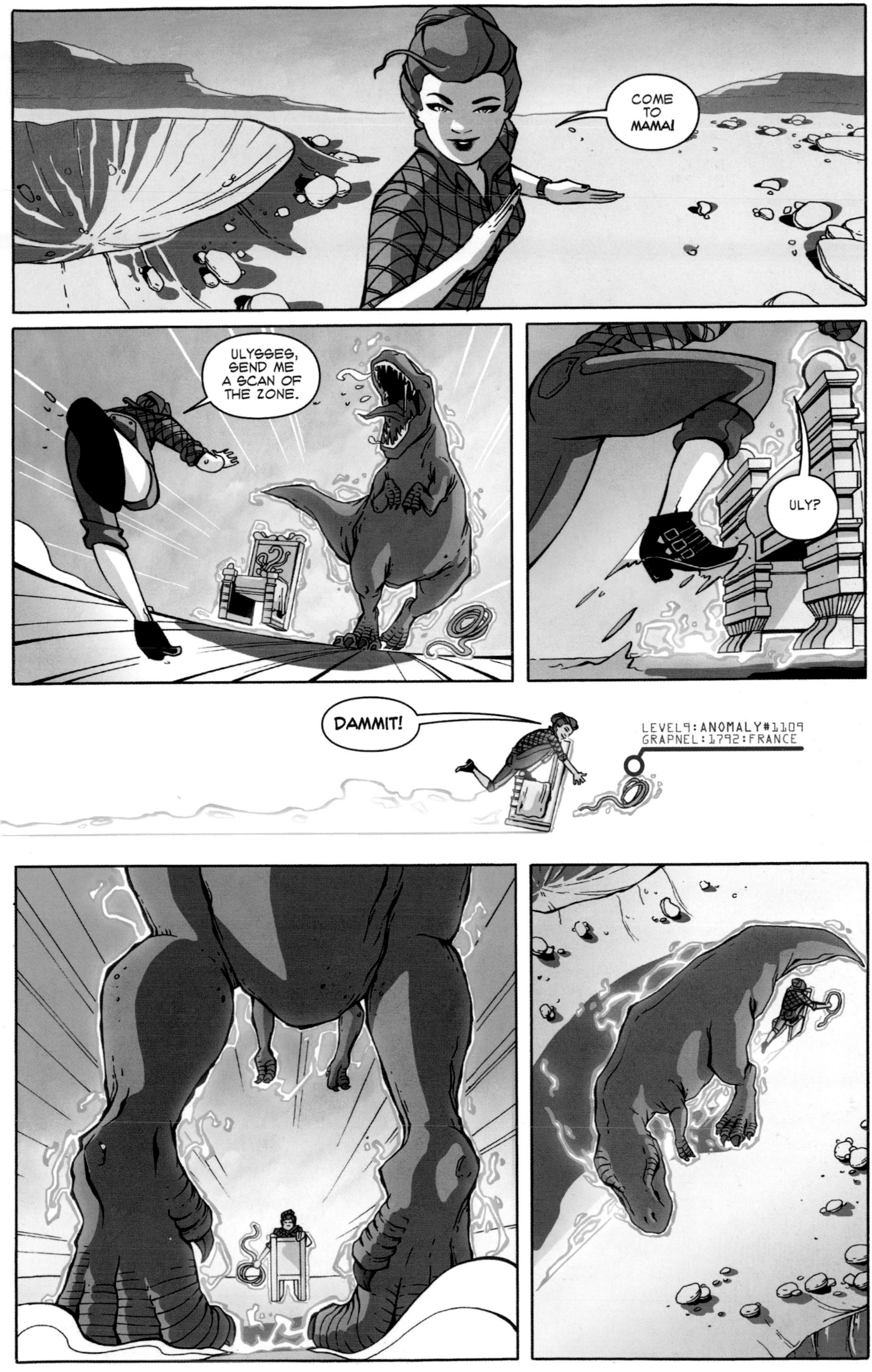
COME TO MAMA!
ULYSSES, SEND ME A SCAN OF THE ZONE.
ULY?
DAMMIT!
LEVEL9:ANOMALY#1109
GRAPNEL:1792:FRANCE

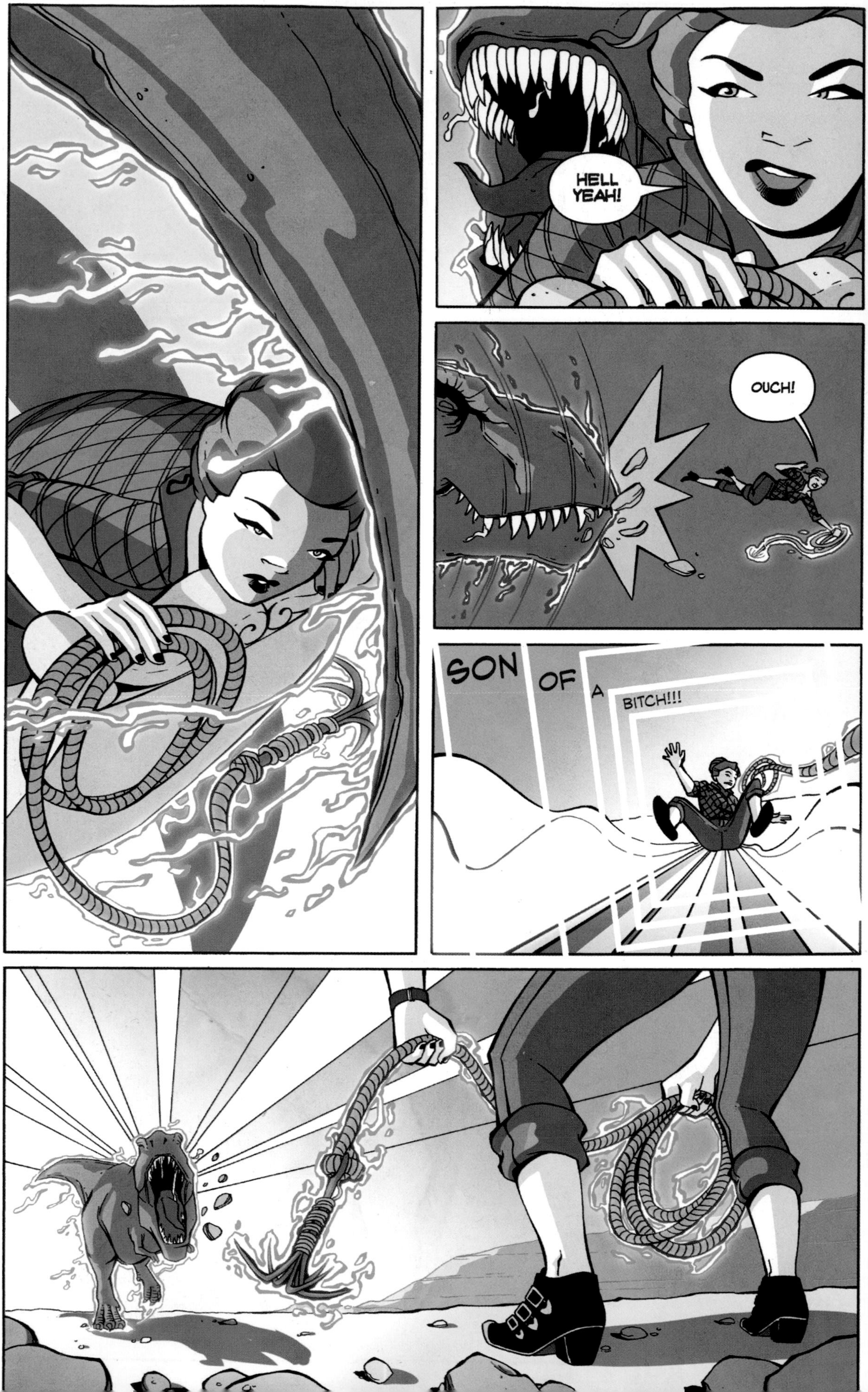
HELL YEAH!
OUCH!
SON OF A BITCH!!!

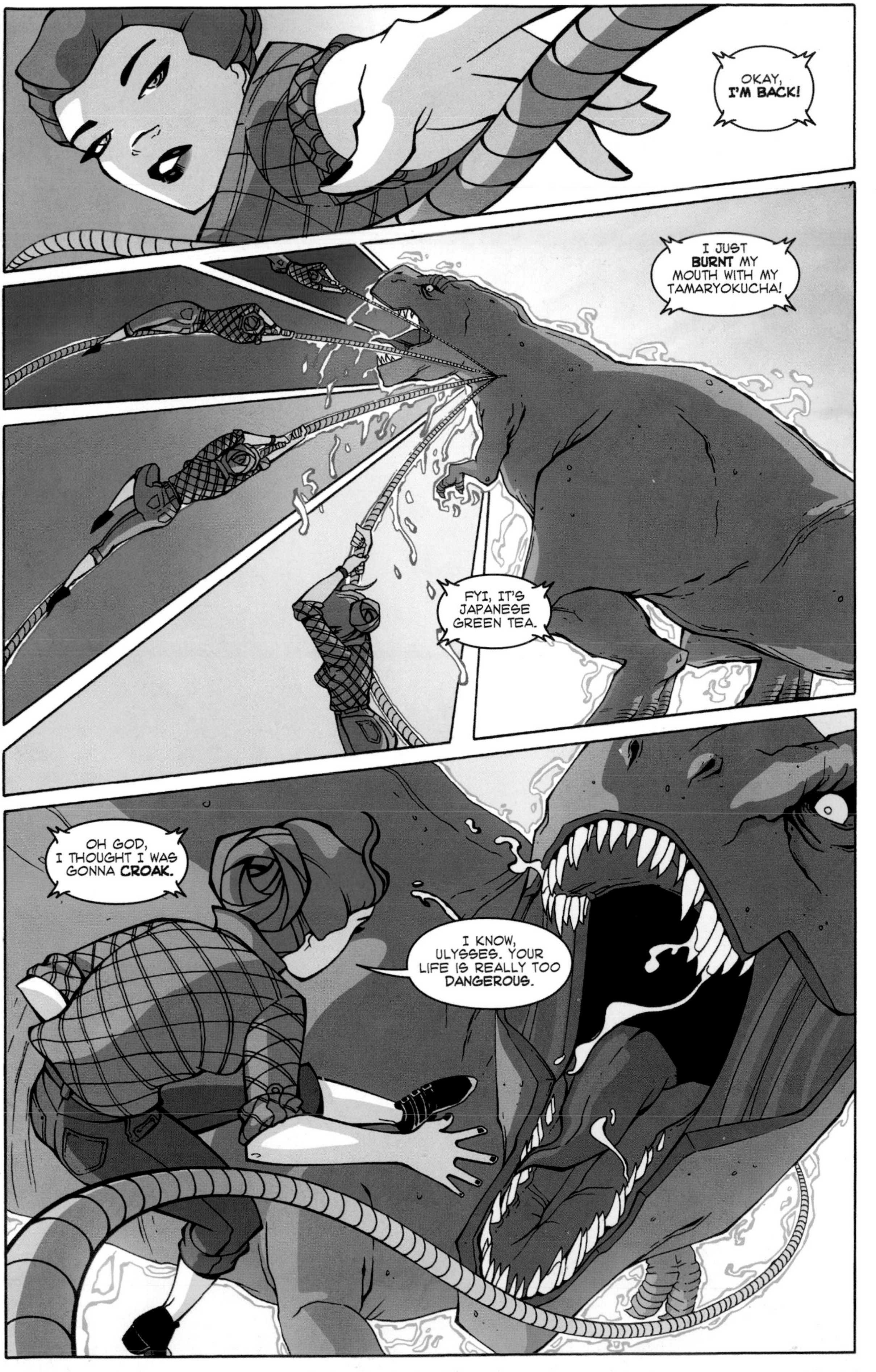
OKAY, I'M BACK!
I JUST BURNT MY MOUTH WITH MY TAMARYOKUCHA!
FYI, IT'S JAPANESE GREEN TEA.
OH GOD, I THOUGHT I WAS GONNA CROAK.
I KNOW, ULYSSES. YOUR LIFE IS REALLY TOO DANGEROUS.

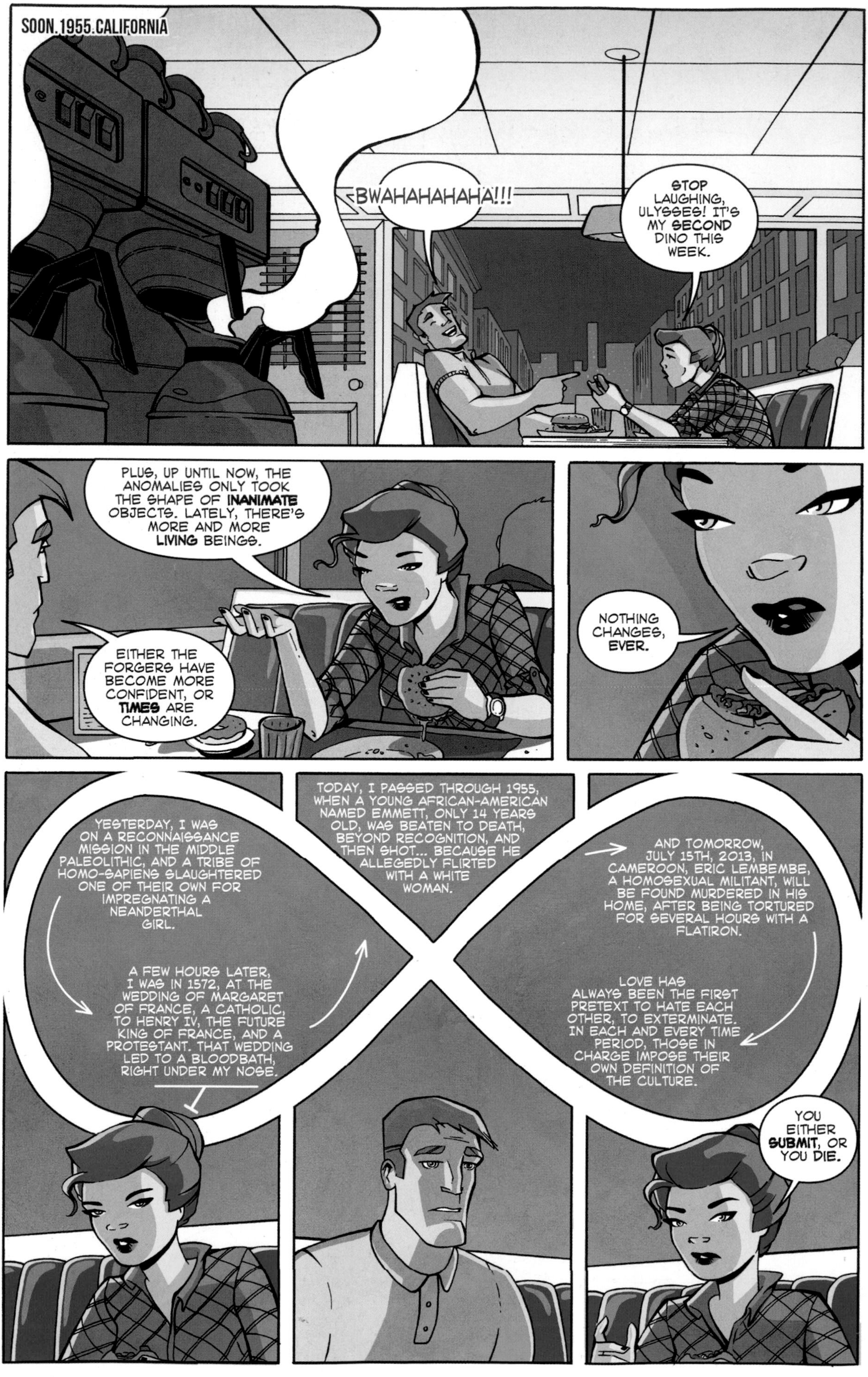
SOON.1955.CALIFORNIA
BWAHAHAHAHA!!!
STOP LAUGHING, ULYSSES! IT'S MY SECOND DINO THIS WEEK.
PLUS, UP UNTIL NOW, THE ANOMALIES ONLY TOOK THE SHAPE OF INANIMATE OBJECTS. LATELY, THERE'S MORE AND MORE LIVING BEINGS.
EITHER THE FORGERS HAVE BECOME MORE CONFIDENT, OR TIMES ARE CHANGING.
NOTHING CHANGES, EVER.
YESTERDAY, I WAS ON A RECONNAISSANCE MISSION IN THE MIDDLE PALEOLITHIC, AND A TRIBE OF HOMO-SAPIENS SLAUGHTERED ONE OF THEIR OWN FOR IMPREGNATING A NEANDERTHAL GIRL.
A FEW HOURS LATER, I WAS IN 1572, AT THE WEDDING OF MARGARET OF FRANCE, A CATHOLIC, TO HENRY IV, THE FUTURE KING OF FRANCE, AND A PROTESTANT. THAT WEDDING LED TO A BLOODBATH, RIGHT UNDER MY NOSE.
TODAY, I PASSED THROUGH 1955, WHEN A YOUNG AFRICAN-AMERICAN NAMED EMMETT, ONLY 14 YEARS OLD, WAS BEATEN TO DEATH, BEYOND RECOGNITION, AND THEN SHOT... BECAUSE HE ALLEGEDLY FLIRTED WITH A WHITE WOMAN.
AND TOMORROW, JULY 15TH, 2013, IN CAMEROON, ERIC LEMBEMBE, A HOMOSEXUAL MILITANT, WILL BE FOUND MURDERED IN HIS HOME, AFTER BEING TORTURED FOR SEVERAL HOURS WITH A FLATIRON.
LOVE HAS ALWAYS BEEN THE FIRST PRETEXT TO HATE EACH OTHER, TO EXTERMINATE. IN EACH AND EVERY TIME PERIOD, THOSE IN CHARGE IMPOSE THEIR OWN DEFINITION OF THE CULTURE.
YOU EITHER SUBMIT, OR YOU DIE.

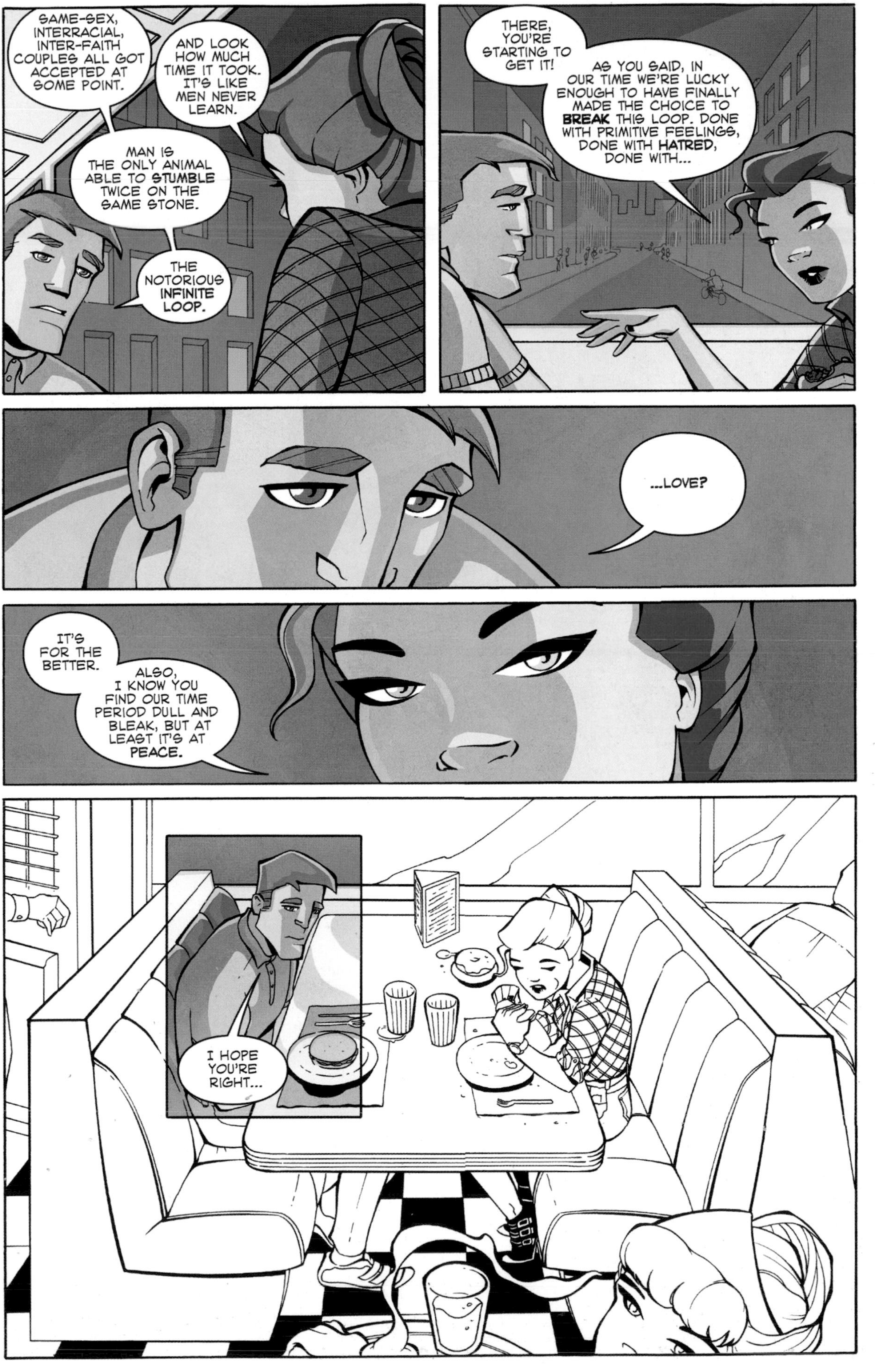
SAME-SEX, INTERRACIAL, INTER-FAITH COUPLES ALL GOT ACCEPTED AT SOME POINT.
AND LOOK HOW MUCH TIME IT TOOK. IT'S LIKE MEN NEVER LEARN.
MAN IS THE ONLY ANIMAL ABLE TO **STUMBLE** TWICE ON THE SAME STONE.
THE NOTORIOUS **INFINITE LOOP.**
THERE, YOU'RE STARTING TO GET IT!
AS YOU SAID, IN OUR TIME WE'RE LUCKY ENOUGH TO HAVE FINALLY MADE THE CHOICE TO **BREAK** THIS LOOP. DONE WITH PRIMITIVE FEELINGS, DONE WITH **HATRED**, DONE WITH...
...LOVE?
IT'S FOR THE BETTER.
ALSO, I KNOW YOU FIND OUR TIME PERIOD DULL AND BLEAK, BUT AT LEAST IT'S AT **PEACE.**
I HOPE YOU'RE RIGHT...

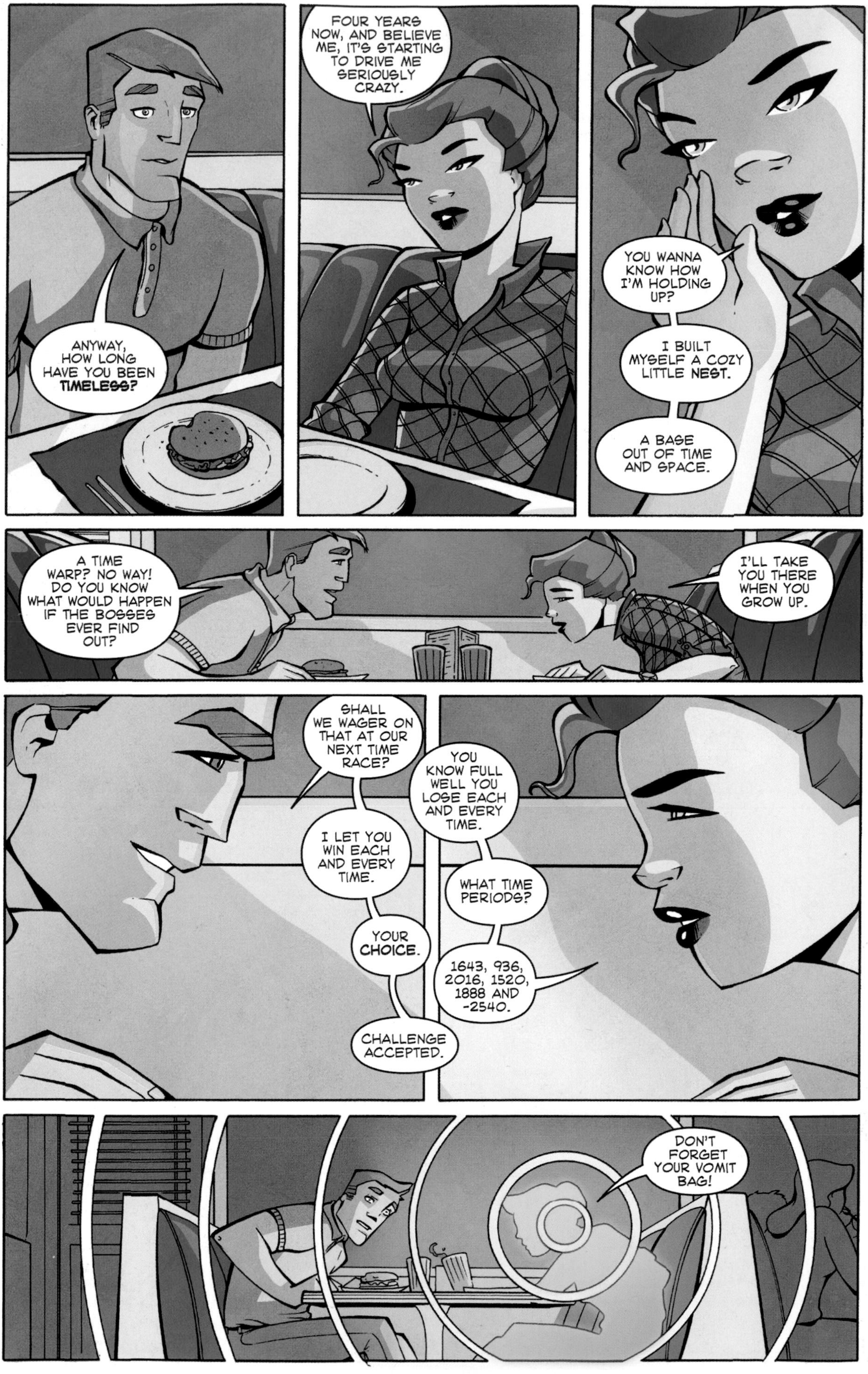
ANYWAY, HOW LONG HAVE YOU BEEN TIMELESS?
FOUR YEARS NOW, AND BELIEVE ME, IT'S STARTING TO DRIVE ME SERIOUSLY CRAZY.
YOU WANNA KNOW HOW I'M HOLDING UP?
I BUILT MYSELF A COZY LITTLE NEST.
A BASE OUT OF TIME AND SPACE.
A TIME WARP? NO WAY! DO YOU KNOW WHAT WOULD HAPPEN IF THE BOSSES EVER FIND OUT?
I'LL TAKE YOU THERE WHEN YOU GROW UP.
SHALL WE WAGER ON THAT AT OUR NEXT TIME RACE?
YOU KNOW FULL WELL YOU LOSE EACH AND EVERY TIME.
I LET YOU WIN EACH AND EVERY TIME.
WHAT TIME PERIODS?
YOUR CHOICE.
1643, 936, 2016, 1520, 1888 AND -2540.
CHALLENGE ACCEPTED.
DON'T FORGET YOUR VOMIT BAG!

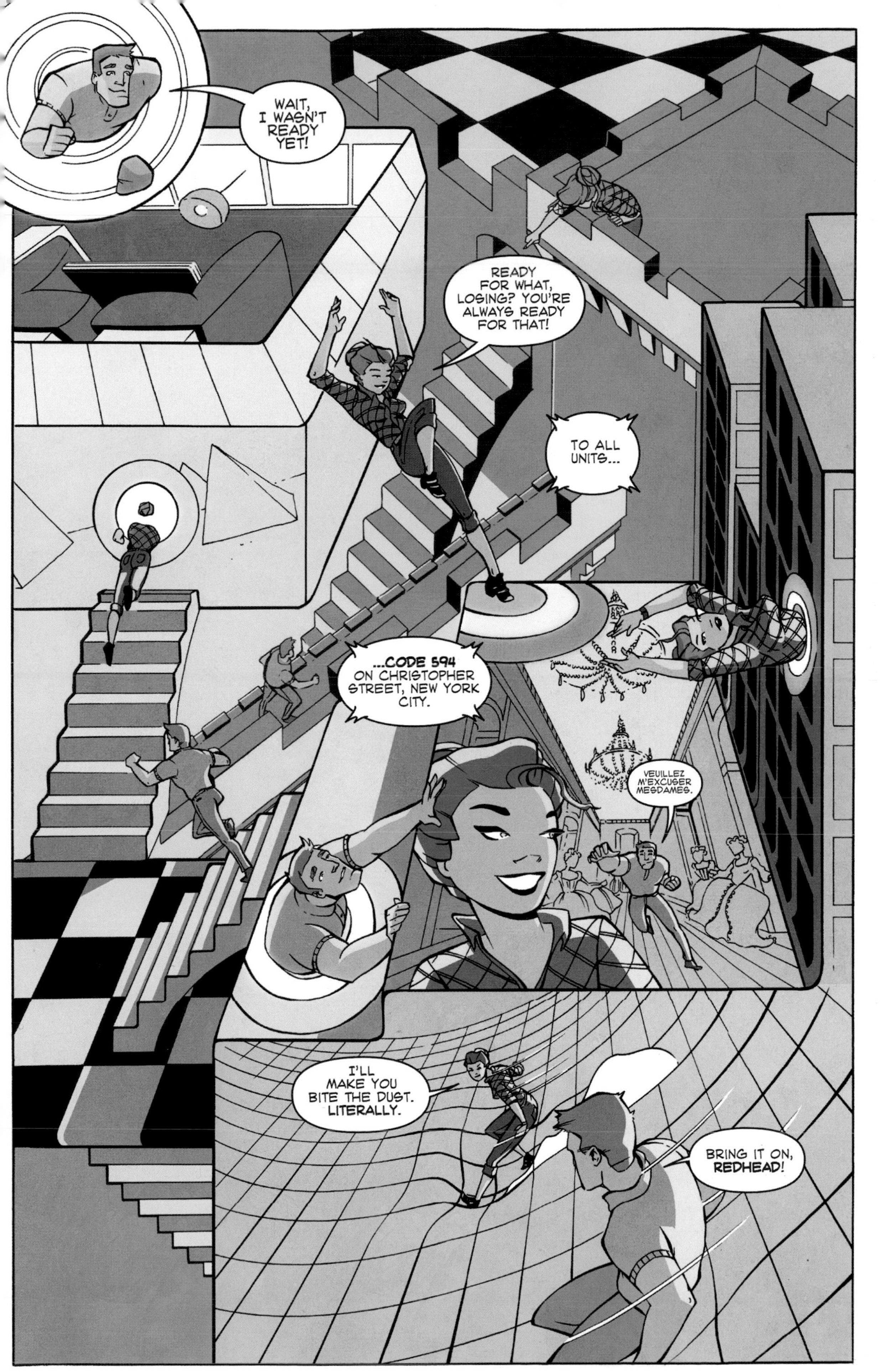
WAIT, I WASN'T READY YET!
READY FOR WHAT, LOSING? YOU'RE ALWAYS READY FOR THAT!
TO ALL UNITS...
...CODE 594 ON CHRISTOPHER STREET, NEW YORK CITY.
VEUILLEZ M'EXCUSER MESDAMES.
I'LL MAKE YOU BITE THE DUST. LITERALLY.
BRING IT ON, REDHEAD!

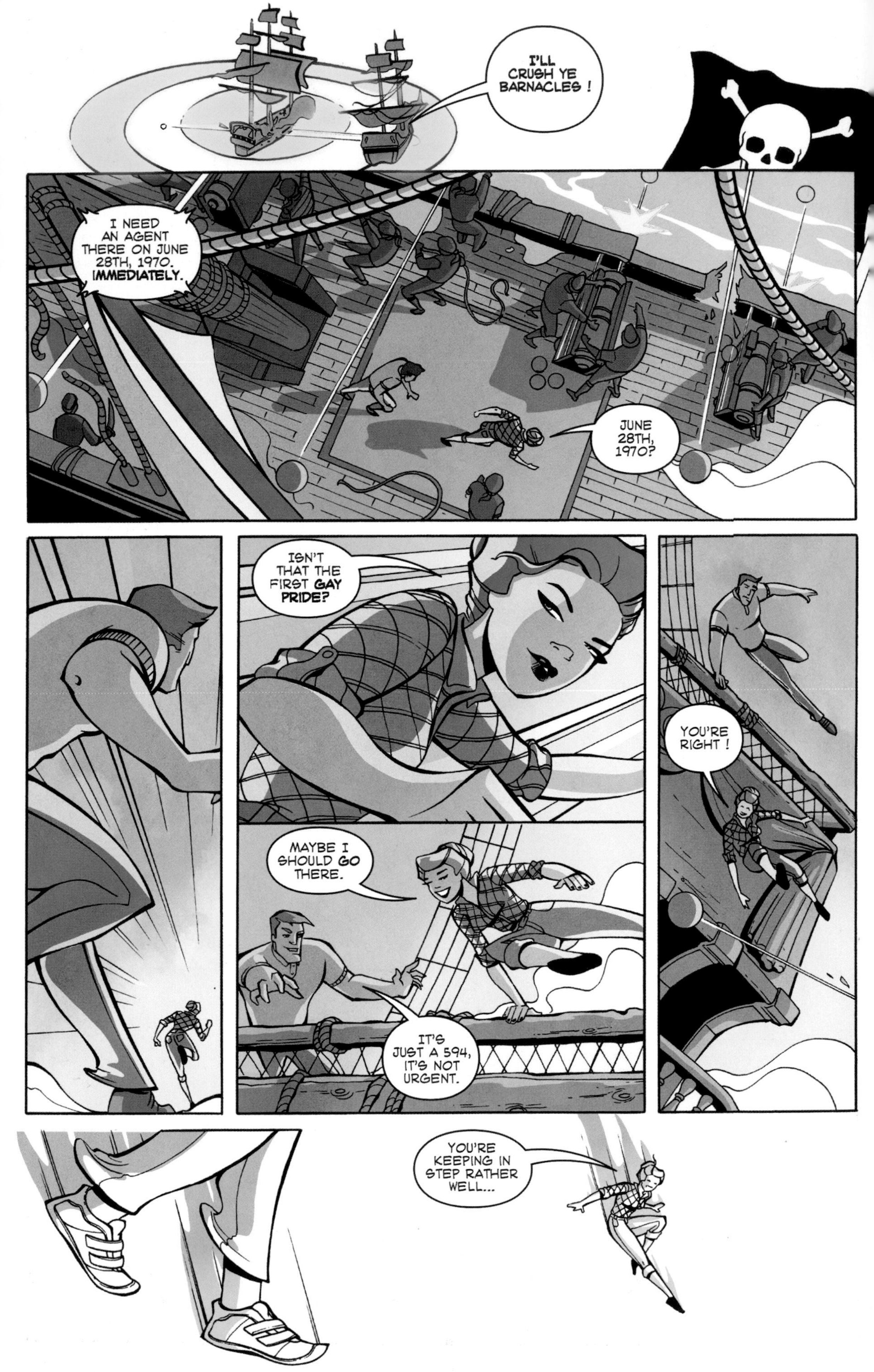
I'LL CRUSH YE BARNACLES !
I NEED AN AGENT THERE ON JUNE 28TH, 1970. IMMEDIATELY.
JUNE 28TH, 1970?
ISN'T THAT THE FIRST GAY PRIDE?
MAYBE I SHOULD GO THERE.
IT'S JUST A 594, IT'S NOT URGENT.
YOU'RE RIGHT !
YOU'RE KEEPING IN STEP RATHER WELL...

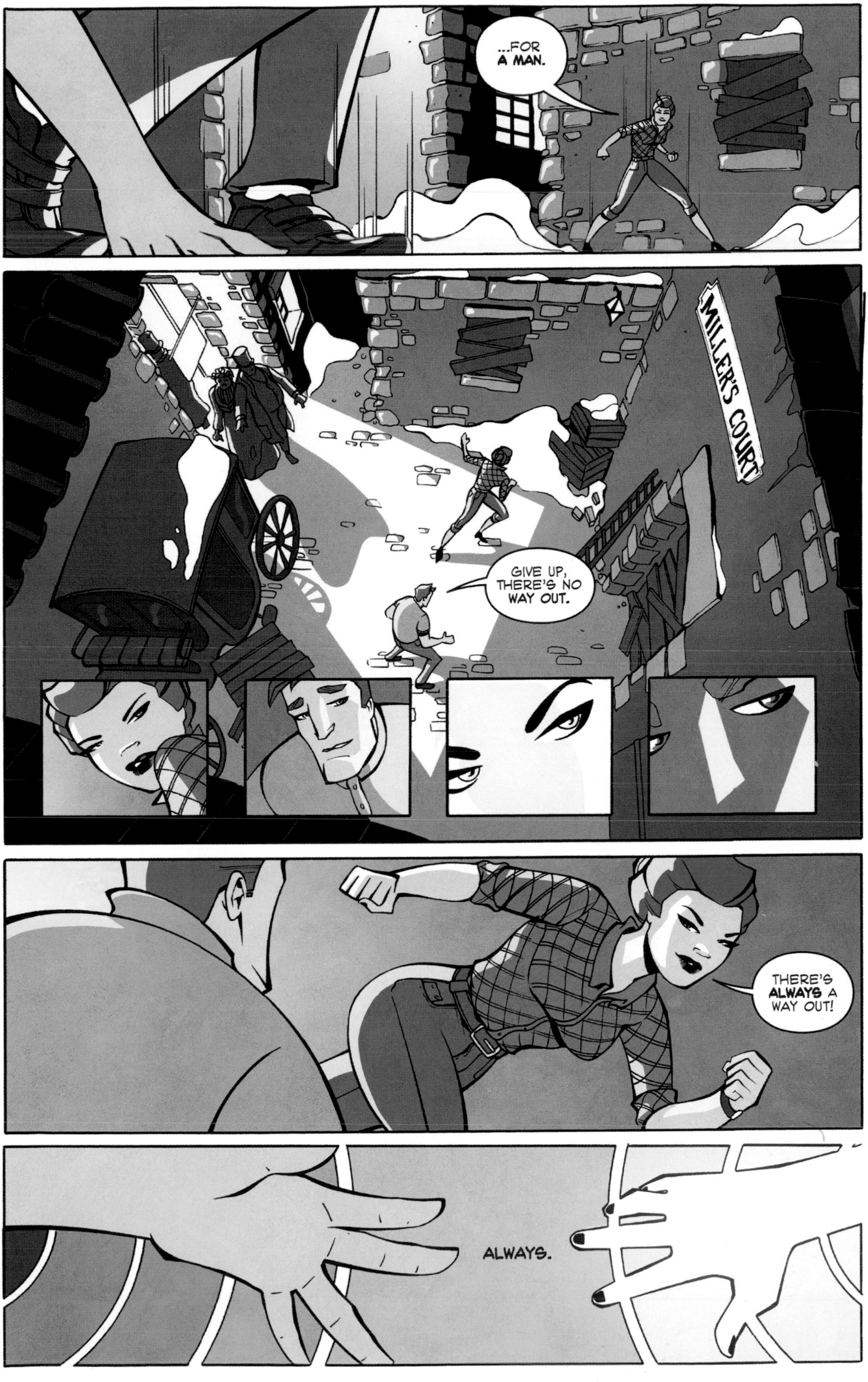

...FOR A MAN.
MILLER'S COURT
GIVE UP, THERE'S NO WAY OUT.
THERE'S ALWAYS A WAY OUT!
ALWAYS.

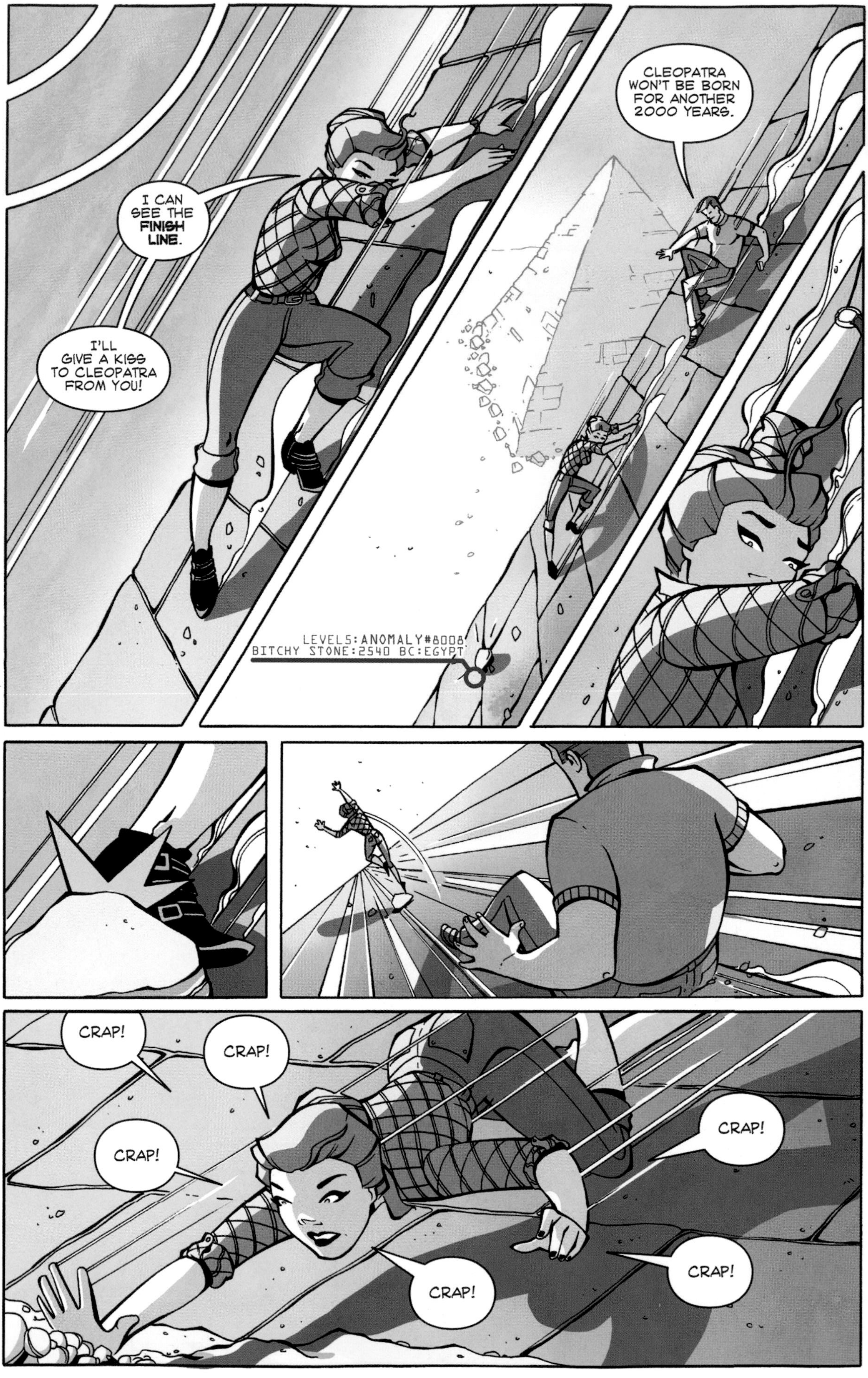
I CAN SEE THE FINISH LINE.
I'LL GIVE A KISS TO CLEOPATRA FROM YOU!
LEVELS:ANOMALY#8008
BITCHY STONE:2540 BC:EGYPT
CLEOPATRA WON'T BE BORN FOR ANOTHER 2000 YEARS.
CRAP!
CRAP!
CRAP!
CRAP!
CRAP!
CRAP!

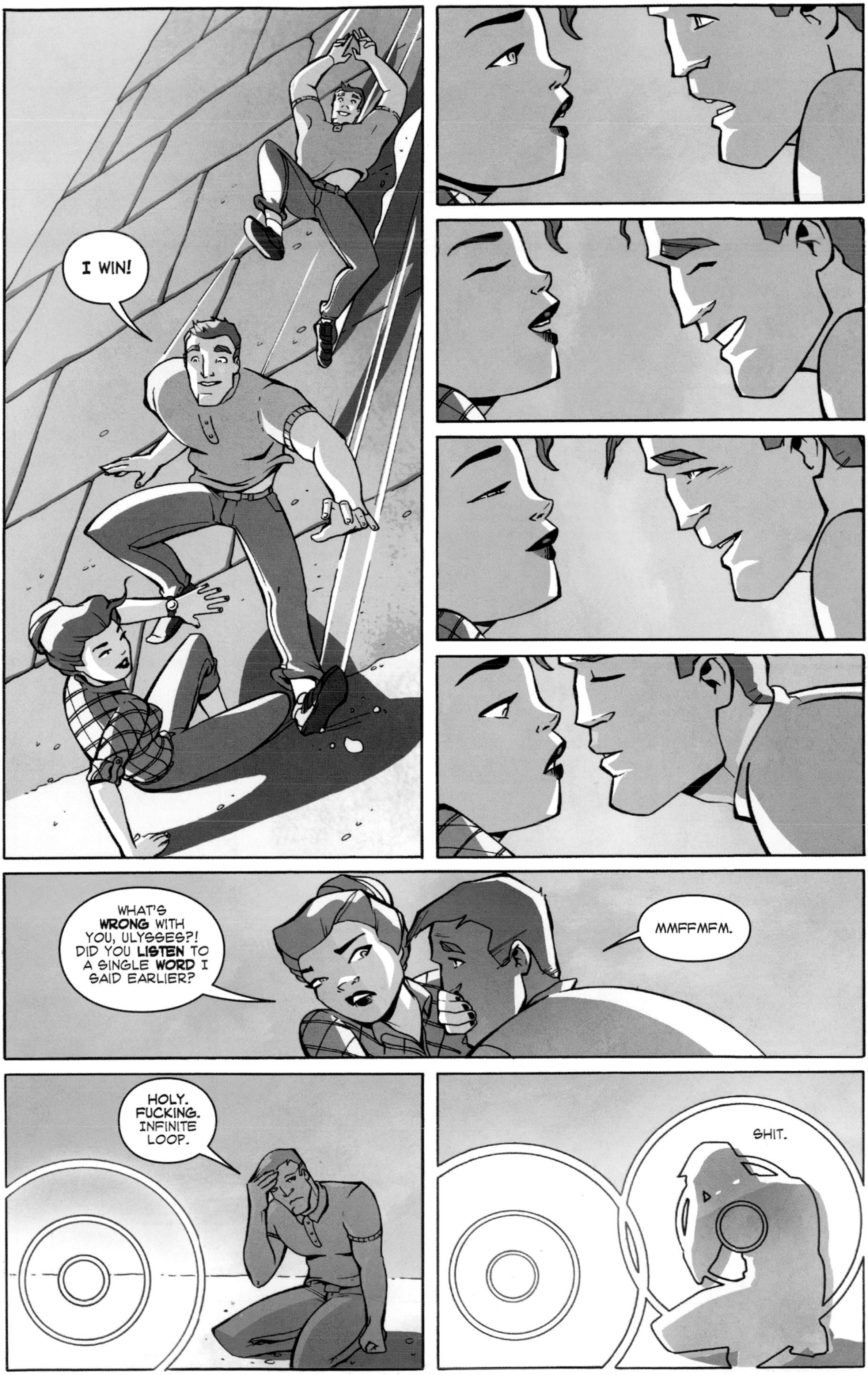
I WIN!
WHAT'S WRONG WITH YOU, ULYSSES?! DID YOU LISTEN TO A SINGLE WORD I SAID EARLIER?
MMFFMFM.
HOLY. FUCKING. INFINITE LOOP.
SHIT.

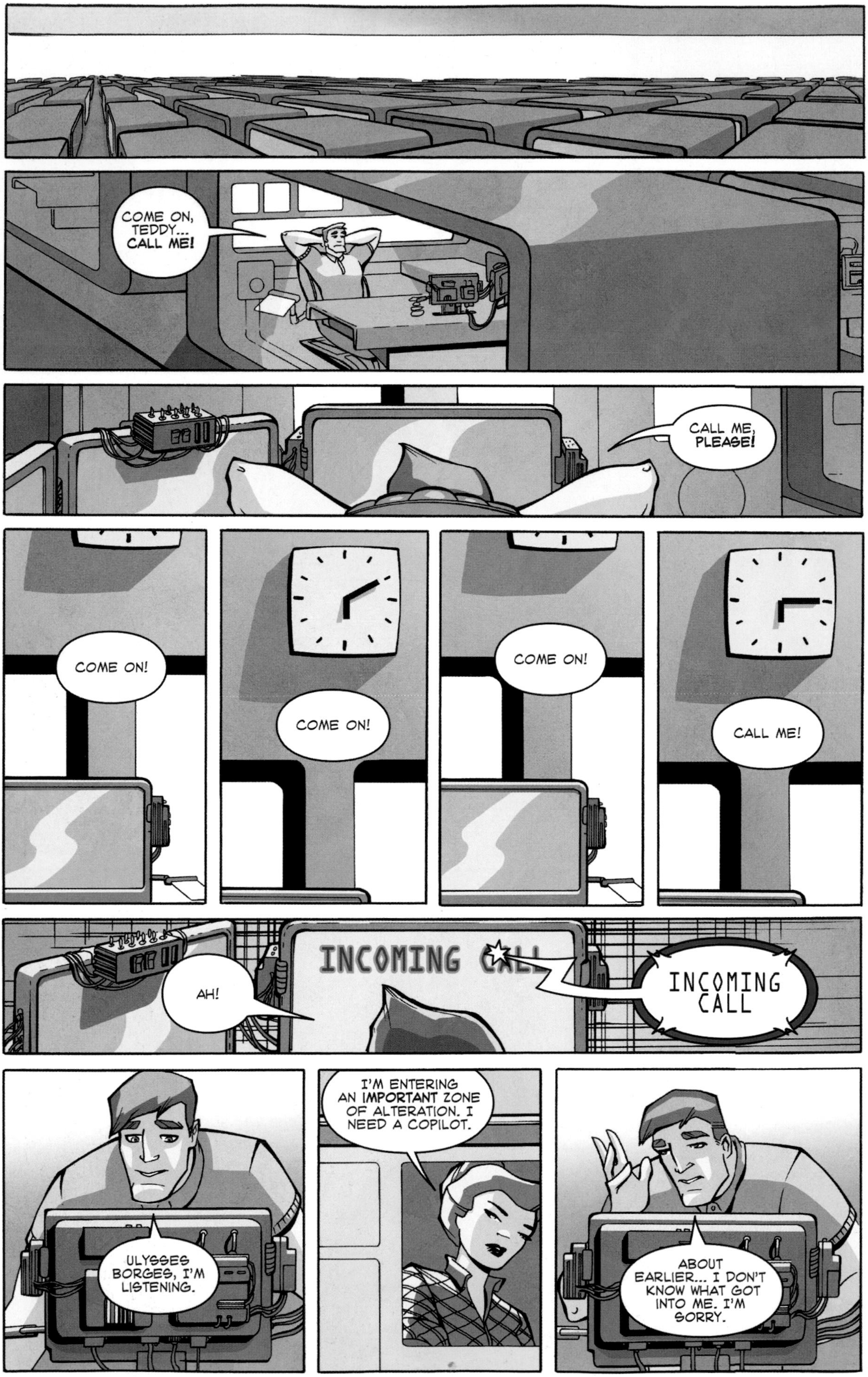
COME ON, TEDDY... CALL ME!
CALL ME, PLEASE!
COME ON!
COME ON!
COME ON!
CALL ME!
INCOMING CALL
AH!
INCOMING CALL
ULYSSES BORGES, I'M LISTENING.
I'M ENTERING AN IMPORTANT ZONE OF ALTERATION. I NEED A COPILOT.
ABOUT EARLIER... I DON'T KNOW WHAT GOT INTO ME. I'M SORRY.

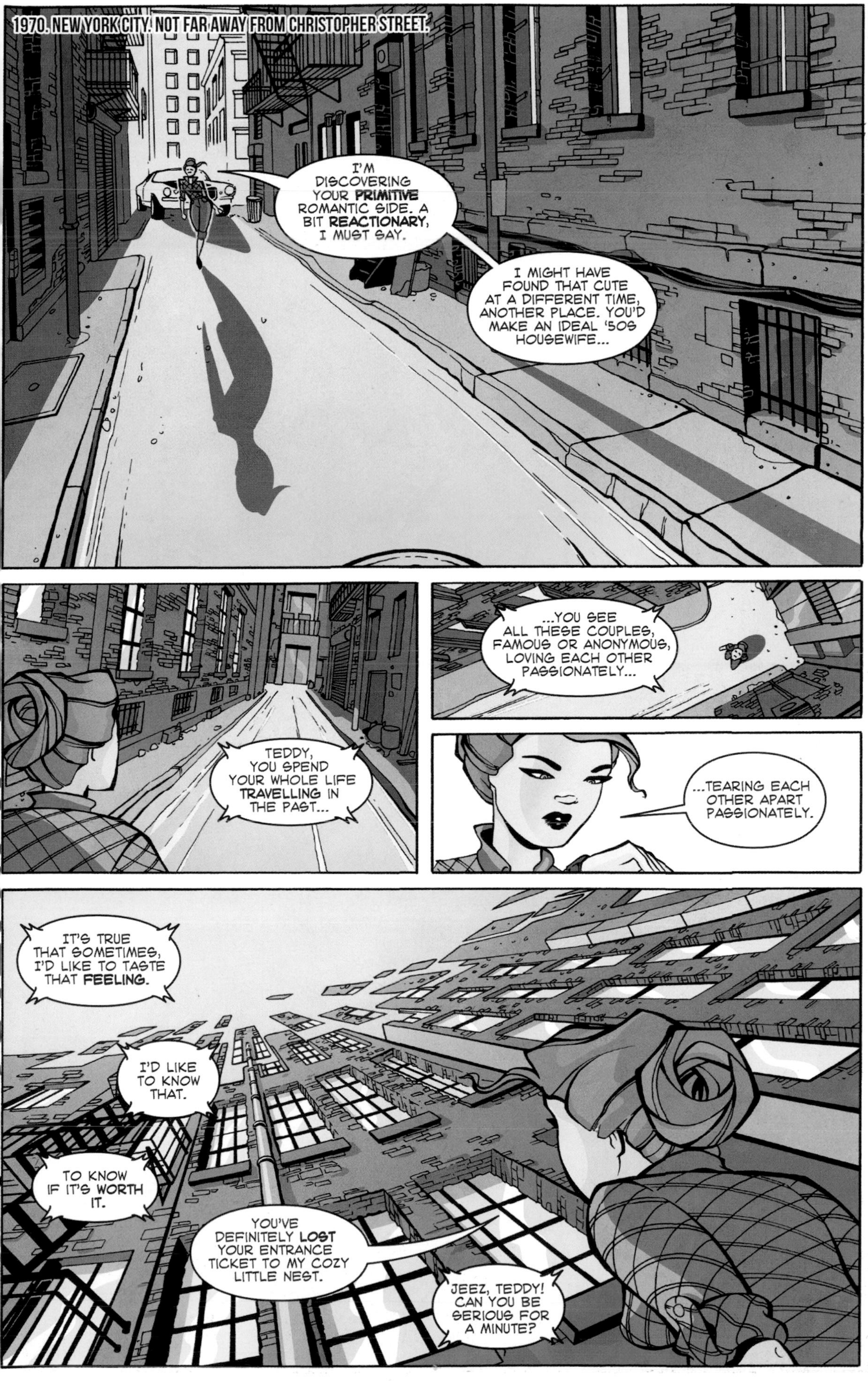
1970. NEW YORK CITY. NOT FAR AWAY FROM CHRISTOPHER STREET.
I'M DISCOVERING YOUR PRIMITIVE ROMANTIC SIDE. A BIT REACTIONARY, I MUST SAY.
I MIGHT HAVE FOUND THAT CUTE AT A DIFFERENT TIME, ANOTHER PLACE. YOU'D MAKE AN IDEAL '50S HOUSEWIFE...
TEDDY, YOU SPEND YOUR WHOLE LIFE TRAVELLING IN THE PAST...
...YOU SEE ALL THESE COUPLES, FAMOUS OR ANONYMOUS, LOVING EACH OTHER PASSIONATELY...
...TEARING EACH OTHER APART PASSIONATELY.
IT'S TRUE THAT SOMETIMES, I'D LIKE TO TASTE THAT FEELING.
I'D LIKE TO KNOW THAT.
TO KNOW IF IT'S WORTH IT.
YOU'VE DEFINITELY LOST YOUR ENTRANCE TICKET TO MY COZY LITTLE NEST.
JEEZ, TEDDY! CAN YOU BE SERIOUS FOR A MINUTE?

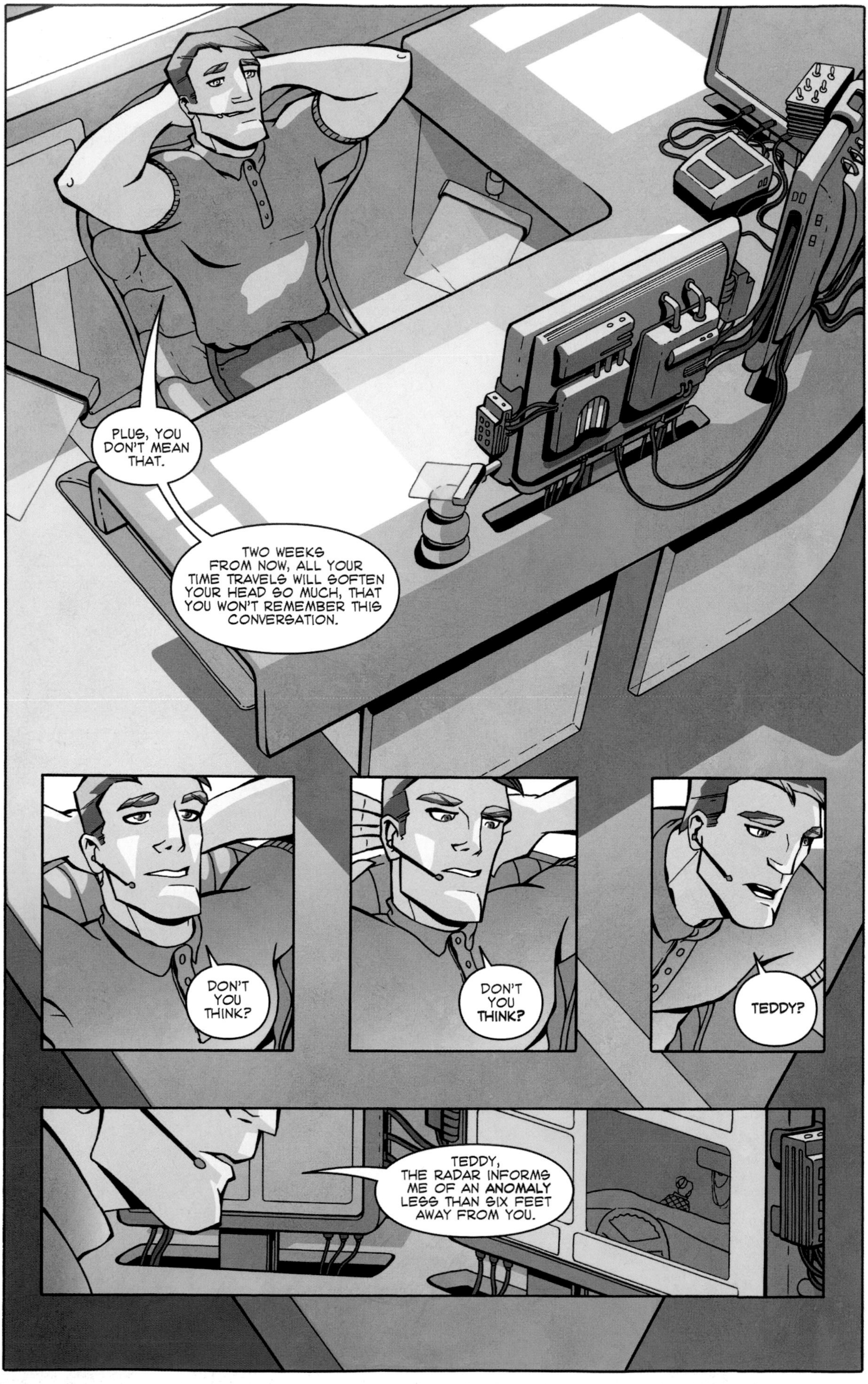
PLUS, YOU DON'T MEAN THAT.
TWO WEEKS FROM NOW, ALL YOUR TIME TRAVELS WILL SOFTEN YOUR HEAD SO MUCH, THAT YOU WON'T REMEMBER THIS CONVERSATION.
DON'T YOU THINK?
DON'T YOU THINK?
TEDDY?
TEDDY, THE RADAR INFORMS ME OF AN ANOMALY LESS THAN SIX FEET AWAY FROM YOU.

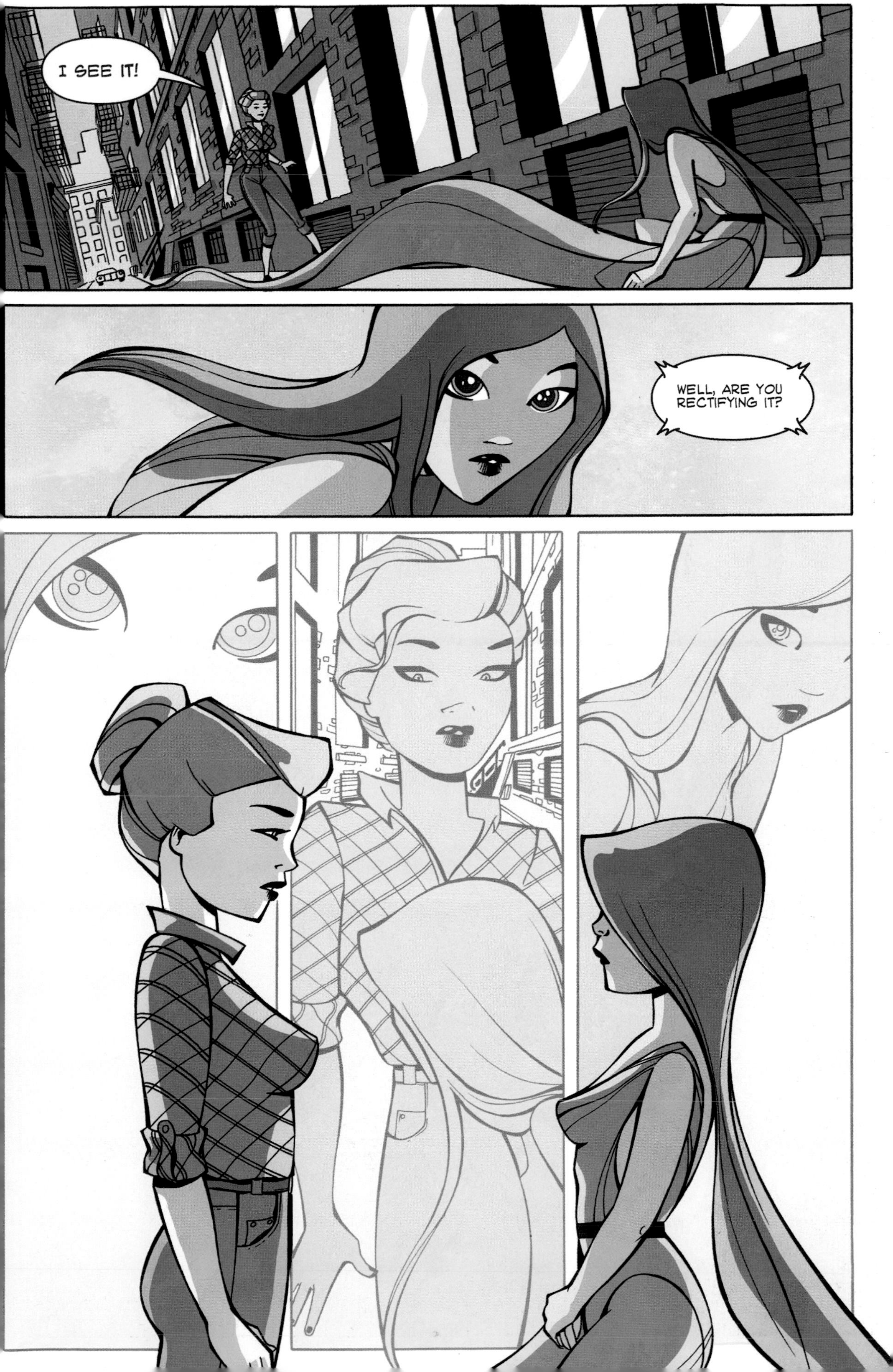
I SEE IT!
WELL, ARE YOU RECTIFYING IT?

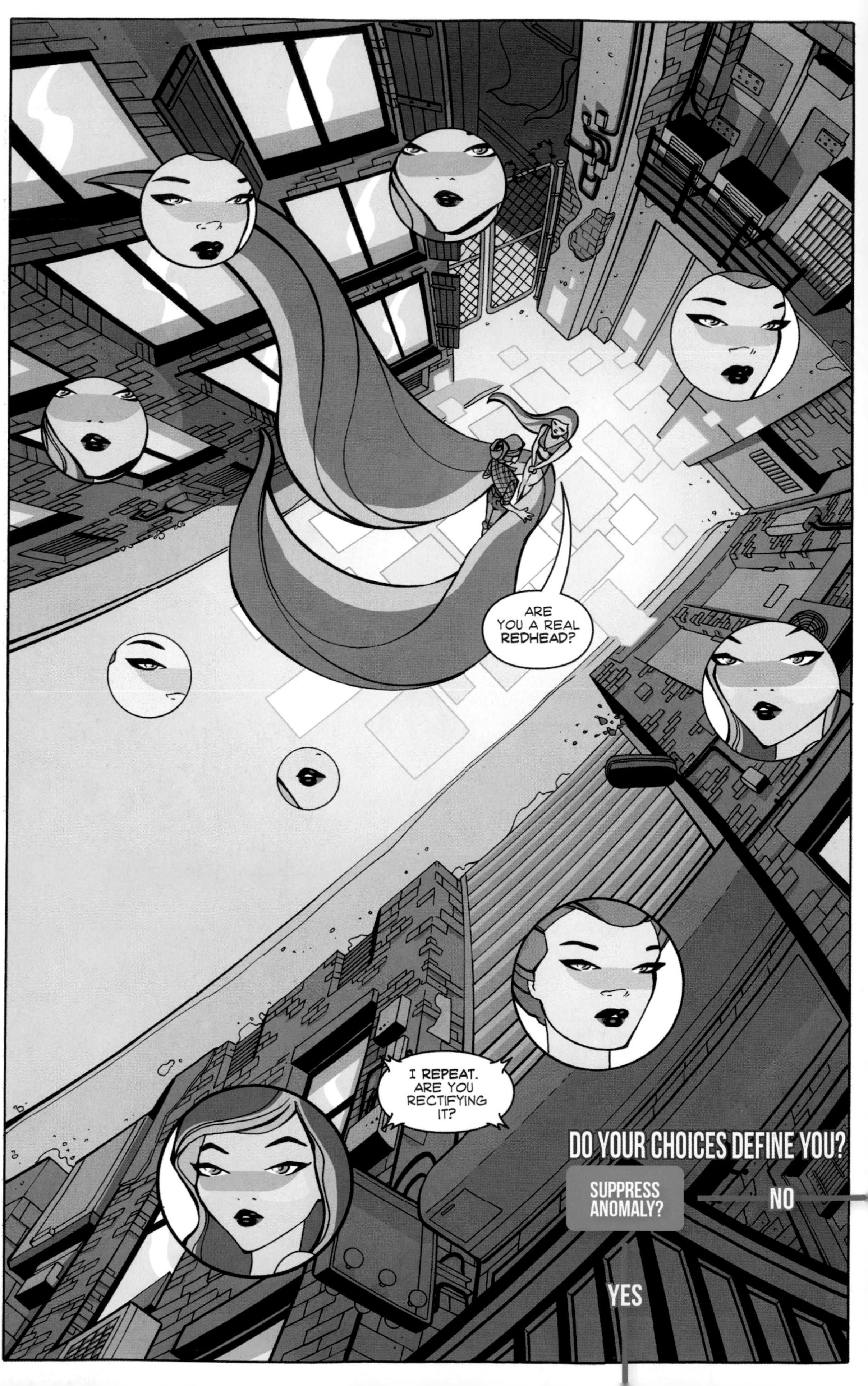
ARE YOU A REAL REDHEAD?
I REPEAT. ARE YOU RECTIFYING IT?
DO YOUR CHOICES DEFINE YOU?
SUPPRESS ANOMALY?
NO
YES

Art by STEPHANIE HANS

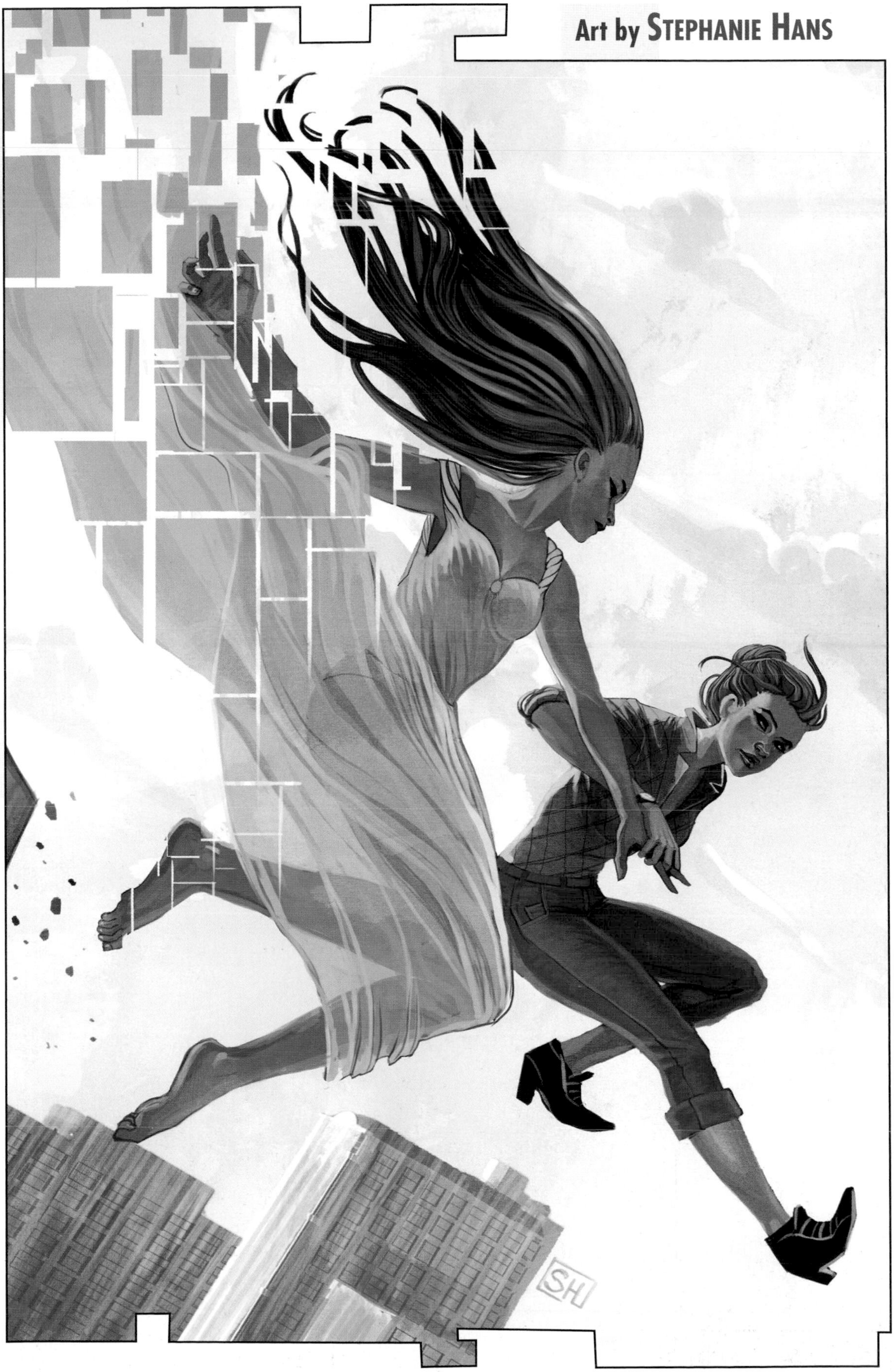
SH

Art by ELSA CHARRETIER

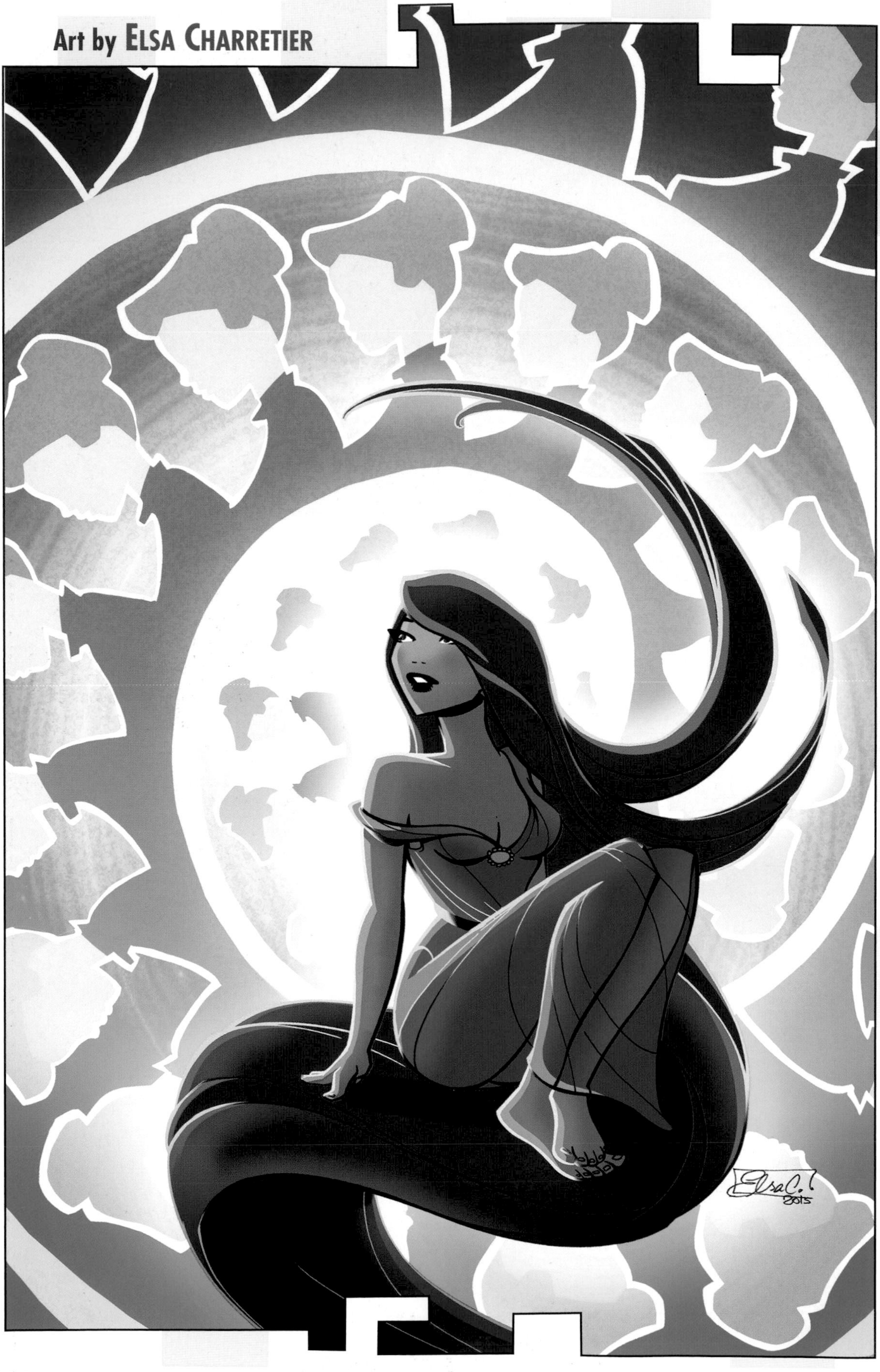
Elsa C.!
2015

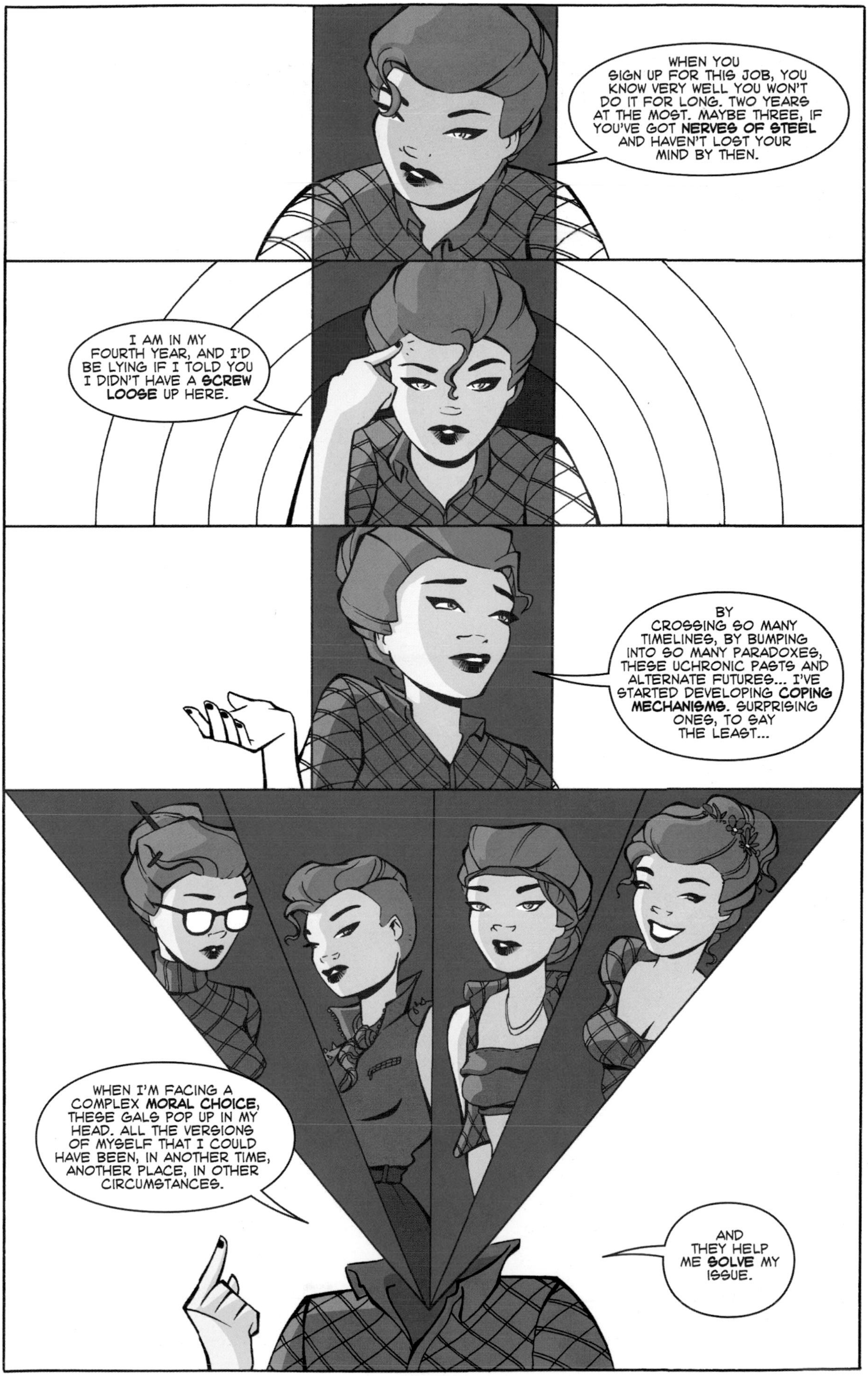
WHEN YOU SIGN UP FOR THIS JOB, YOU KNOW VERY WELL YOU WON'T DO IT FOR LONG. TWO YEARS AT THE MOST. MAYBE THREE, IF YOU'VE GOT **NERVES OF STEEL** AND HAVEN'T LOST YOUR MIND BY THEN.
I AM IN MY FOURTH YEAR, AND I'D BE LYING IF I TOLD YOU I DIDN'T HAVE A **SCREW LOOSE** UP HERE.
BY CROSSING SO MANY TIMELINES, BY BUMPING INTO SO MANY PARADOXES, THESE UCHRONIC PASTS AND ALTERNATE FUTURES... I'VE STARTED DEVELOPING **COPING MECHANISMS**. SURPRISING ONES, TO SAY THE LEAST...
WHEN I'M FACING A COMPLEX **MORAL CHOICE**, THESE GALS POP UP IN MY HEAD. ALL THE VERSIONS OF MYSELF THAT I COULD HAVE BEEN, IN ANOTHER TIME, ANOTHER PLACE, IN OTHER CIRCUMSTANCES.
AND THEY HELP ME **SOLVE** MY ISSUE.

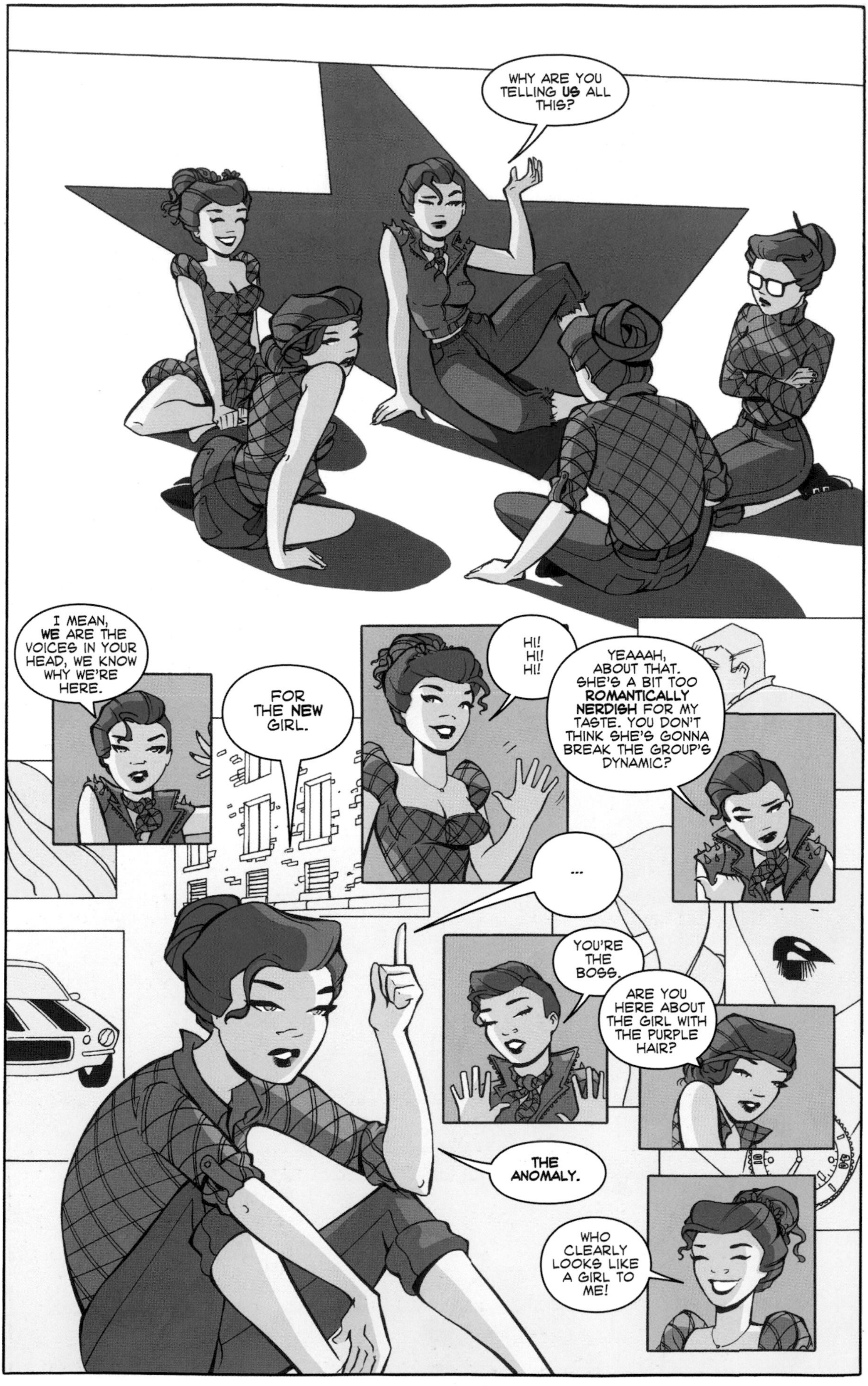
WHY ARE YOU TELLING US ALL THIS?
I MEAN, WE ARE THE VOICES IN YOUR HEAD, WE KNOW WHY WE'RE HERE.
FOR THE NEW GIRL.
HI! HI! HI!
YEAAAH, ABOUT THAT. SHE'S A BIT TOO ROMANTICALLY NERDISH FOR MY TASTE. YOU DON'T THINK SHE'S GONNA BREAK THE GROUP'S DYNAMIC?
...
YOU'RE THE BOSS.
ARE YOU HERE ABOUT THE GIRL WITH THE PURPLE HAIR?
THE ANOMALY.
WHO CLEARLY LOOKS LIKE A GIRL TO ME!

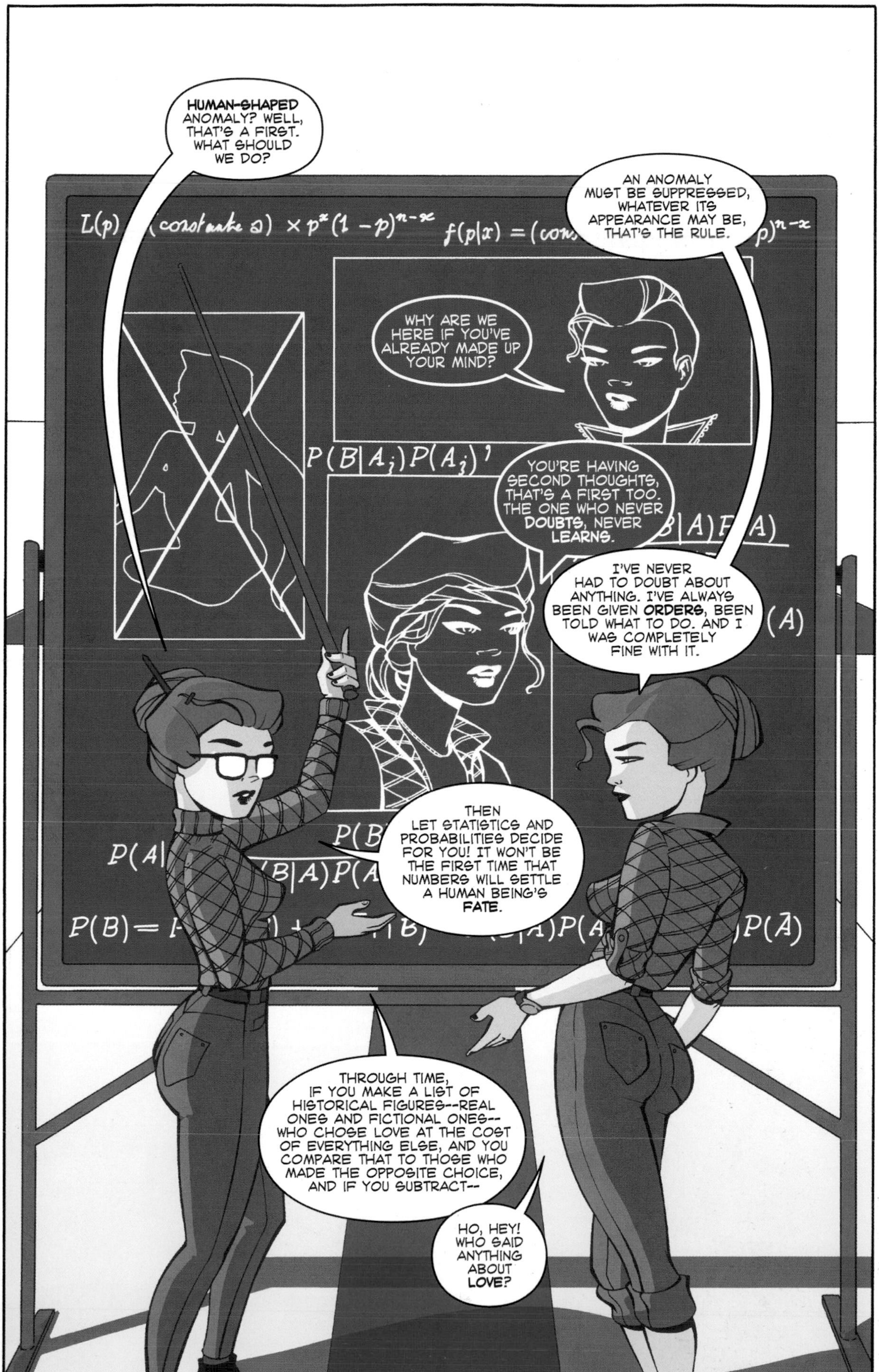
HUMAN-SHAPED ANOMALY? WELL, THAT'S A FIRST. WHAT SHOULD WE DO?
AN ANOMALY MUST BE SUPPRESSED, WHATEVER ITS APPEARANCE MAY BE, THAT'S THE RULE.
WHY ARE WE HERE IF YOU'VE ALREADY MADE UP YOUR MIND?
YOU'RE HAVING SECOND THOUGHTS, THAT'S A FIRST TOO. THE ONE WHO NEVER DOUBTS, NEVER LEARNS.
I'VE NEVER HAD TO DOUBT ABOUT ANYTHING. I'VE ALWAYS BEEN GIVEN ORDERS, BEEN TOLD WHAT TO DO. AND I WAS COMPLETELY FINE WITH IT.
THEN LET STATISTICS AND PROBABILITIES DECIDE FOR YOU! IT WON'T BE THE FIRST TIME THAT NUMBERS WILL SETTLE A HUMAN BEING'S FATE.
THROUGH TIME, IF YOU MAKE A LIST OF HISTORICAL FIGURES--REAL ONES AND FICTIONAL ONES--WHO CHOSE LOVE AT THE COST OF EVERYTHING ELSE, AND YOU COMPARE THAT TO THOSE WHO MADE THE OPPOSITE CHOICE, AND IF YOU SUBTRACT--
HO, HEY! WHO SAID ANYTHING ABOUT LOVE?

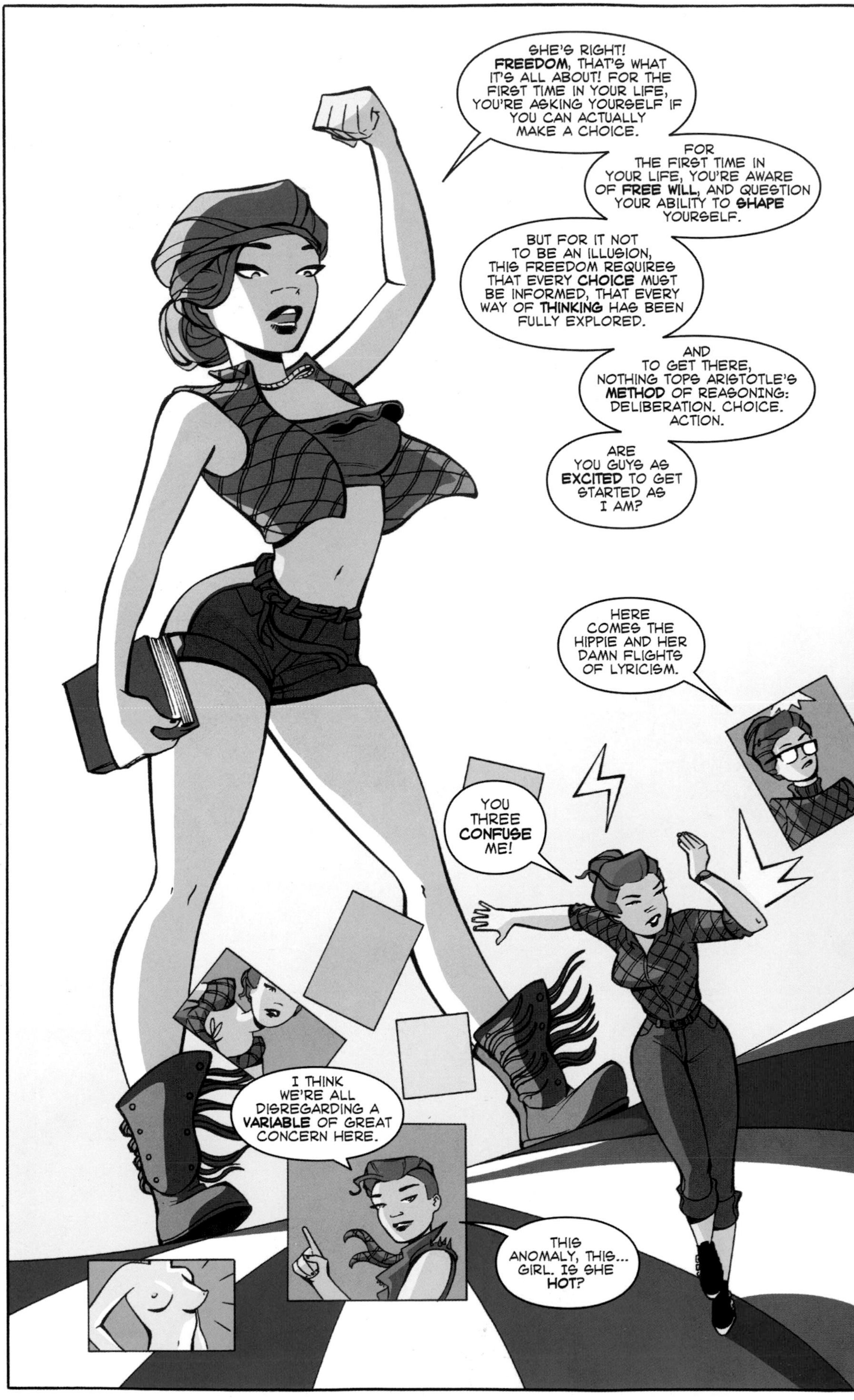
SHE'S RIGHT! FREEDOM, THAT'S WHAT IT'S ALL ABOUT! FOR THE FIRST TIME IN YOUR LIFE, YOU'RE ASKING YOURSELF IF YOU CAN ACTUALLY MAKE A CHOICE.
FOR THE FIRST TIME IN YOUR LIFE, YOU'RE AWARE OF FREE WILL, AND QUESTION YOUR ABILITY TO SHAPE YOURSELF.
BUT FOR IT NOT TO BE AN ILLUSION, THIS FREEDOM REQUIRES THAT EVERY CHOICE MUST BE INFORMED, THAT EVERY WAY OF THINKING HAS BEEN FULLY EXPLORED.
AND TO GET THERE, NOTHING TOPS ARISTOTLE'S METHOD OF REASONING: DELIBERATION. CHOICE. ACTION.
ARE YOU GUYS AS EXCITED TO GET STARTED AS I AM?
HERE COMES THE HIPPIE AND HER DAMN FLIGHTS OF LYRICISM.
YOU THREE CONFUSE ME!
I THINK WE'RE ALL DISREGARDING A VARIABLE OF GREAT CONCERN HERE.
THIS ANOMALY, THIS... GIRL. IS SHE HOT?

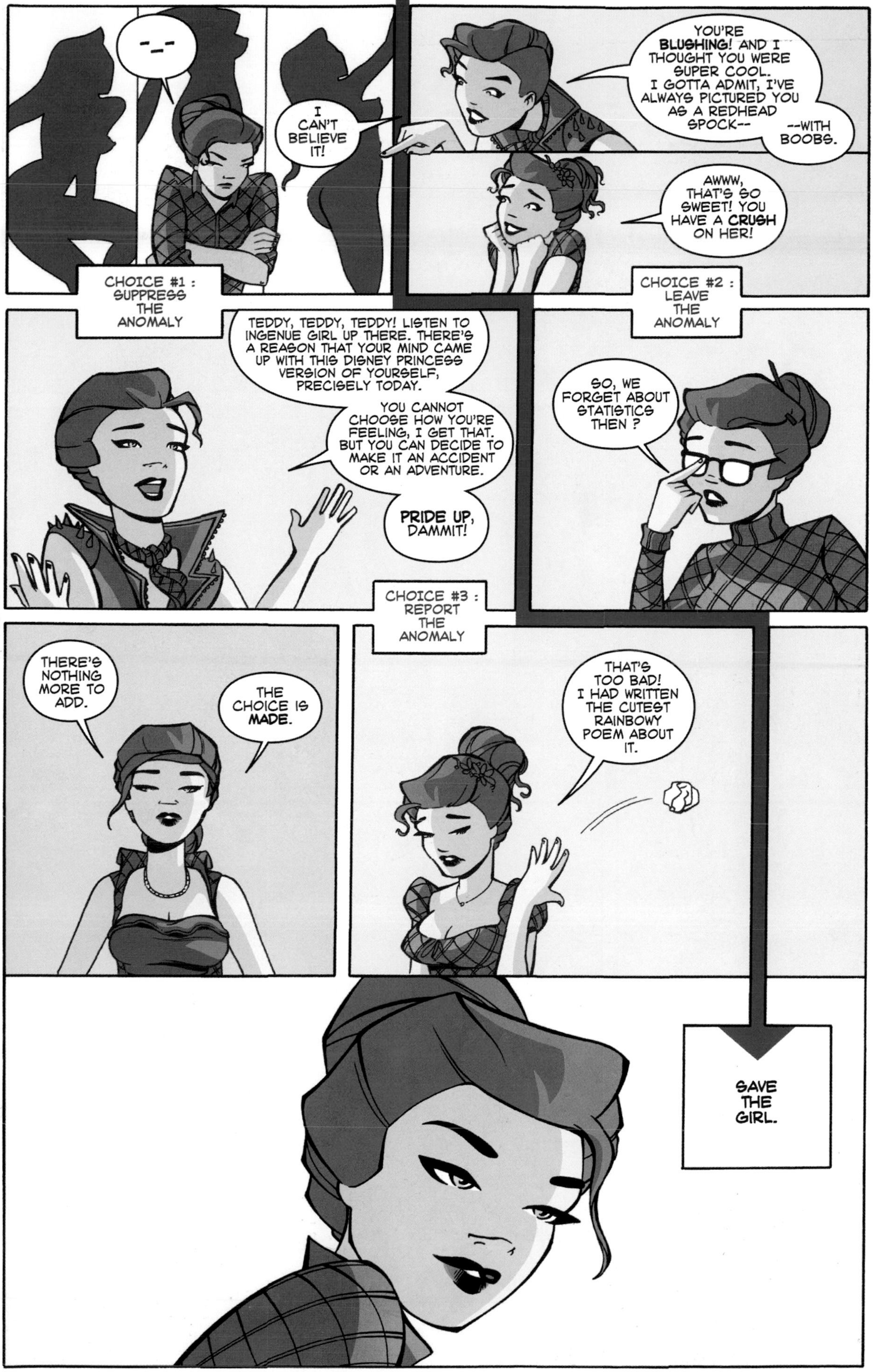

-_-
I CAN'T BELIEVE IT!
YOU'RE BLUSHING! AND I THOUGHT YOU WERE SUPER COOL. I GOTTA ADMIT, I'VE ALWAYS PICTURED YOU AS A REDHEAD SPOCK--
--WITH BOOBS.
AWWW, THAT'S SO SWEET! YOU HAVE A CRUSH ON HER!
CHOICE #1 : SUPPRESS THE ANOMALY
CHOICE #2 : LEAVE THE ANOMALY
TEDDY, TEDDY, TEDDY! LISTEN TO INGENUE GIRL UP THERE. THERE'S A REASON THAT YOUR MIND CAME UP WITH THIS DISNEY PRINCESS VERSION OF YOURSELF, PRECISELY TODAY.
YOU CANNOT CHOOSE HOW YOU'RE FEELING, I GET THAT. BUT YOU CAN DECIDE TO MAKE IT AN ACCIDENT OR AN ADVENTURE.
PRIDE UP, DAMMIT!
SO, WE FORGET ABOUT STATISTICS THEN ?
CHOICE #3 : REPORT THE ANOMALY
THERE'S NOTHING MORE TO ADD.
THE CHOICE IS MADE.
THAT'S TOO BAD! I HAD WRITTEN THE CUTEST RAINBOWY POEM ABOUT IT.
SAVE THE GIRL.

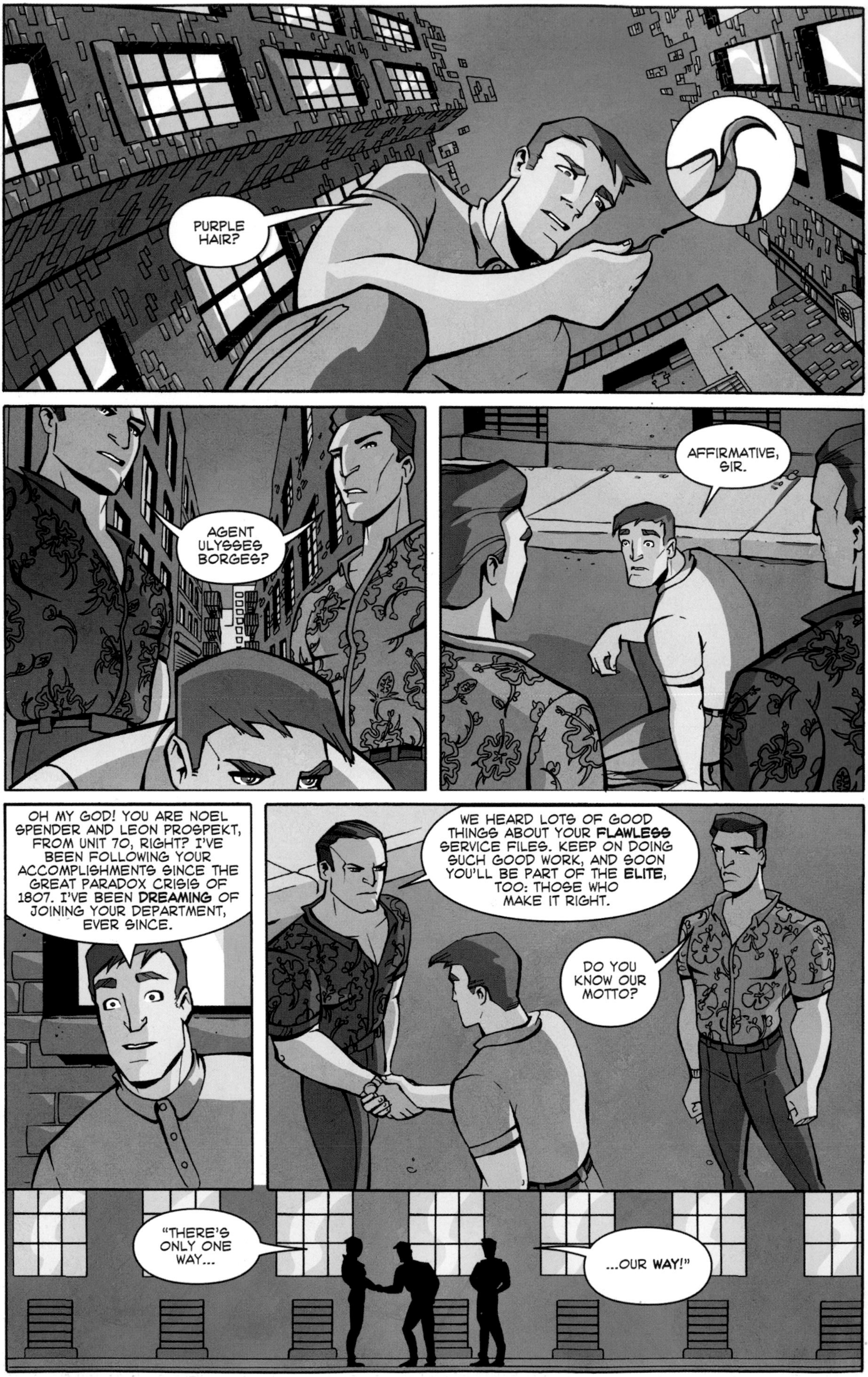
PURPLE HAIR?
AGENT ULYSSES BORGES?
AFFIRMATIVE, SIR.
OH MY GOD! YOU ARE NOEL SPENDER AND LEON PROSPEKT, FROM UNIT 70, RIGHT? I'VE BEEN FOLLOWING YOUR ACCOMPLISHMENTS SINCE THE GREAT PARADOX CRISIS OF 1807. I'VE BEEN DREAMING OF JOINING YOUR DEPARTMENT, EVER SINCE.
WE HEARD LOTS OF GOOD THINGS ABOUT YOUR FLAWLESS SERVICE FILES. KEEP ON DOING SUCH GOOD WORK, AND SOON YOU'LL BE PART OF THE ELITE, TOO: THOSE WHO MAKE IT RIGHT.
DO YOU KNOW OUR MOTTO?
"THERE'S ONLY ONE WAY...
...OUR WAY!"

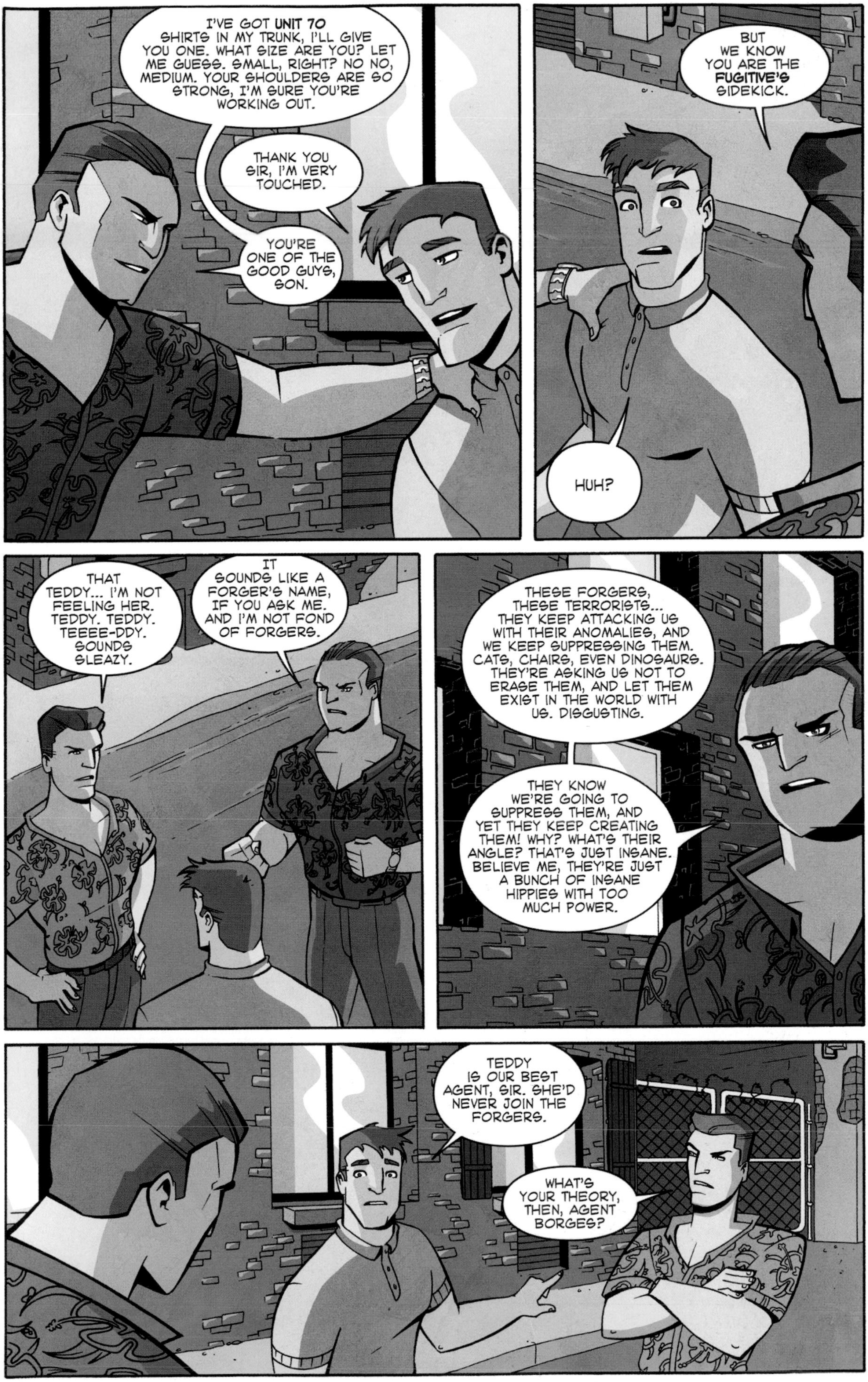
I'VE GOT UNIT 70 SHIRTS IN MY TRUNK, I'LL GIVE YOU ONE. WHAT SIZE ARE YOU? LET ME GUESS. SMALL, RIGHT? NO NO, MEDIUM. YOUR SHOULDERS ARE SO STRONG, I'M SURE YOU'RE WORKING OUT.
THANK YOU SIR, I'M VERY TOUCHED.
YOU'RE ONE OF THE GOOD GUYS, SON.
BUT WE KNOW YOU ARE THE FUGITIVE'S SIDEKICK.
HUH?
THAT TEDDY... I'M NOT FEELING HER. TEDDY. TEDDY. TEEEE-DDY. SOUNDS SLEAZY.
IT SOUNDS LIKE A FORGER'S NAME, IF YOU ASK ME. AND I'M NOT FOND OF FORGERS.
THESE FORGERS, THESE TERRORISTS... THEY KEEP ATTACKING US WITH THEIR ANOMALIES, AND WE KEEP SUPPRESSING THEM. CATS, CHAIRS, EVEN DINOSAURS. THEY'RE ASKING US NOT TO ERASE THEM, AND LET THEM EXIST IN THE WORLD WITH US. DISGUSTING.
THEY KNOW WE'RE GOING TO SUPPRESS THEM, AND YET THEY KEEP CREATING THEM! WHY? WHAT'S THEIR ANGLE? THAT'S JUST INSANE. BELIEVE ME, THEY'RE JUST A BUNCH OF INSANE HIPPIES WITH TOO MUCH POWER.
TEDDY IS OUR BEST AGENT, SIR. SHE'D NEVER JOIN THE FORGERS.
WHAT'S YOUR THEORY, THEN, AGENT BORGES?

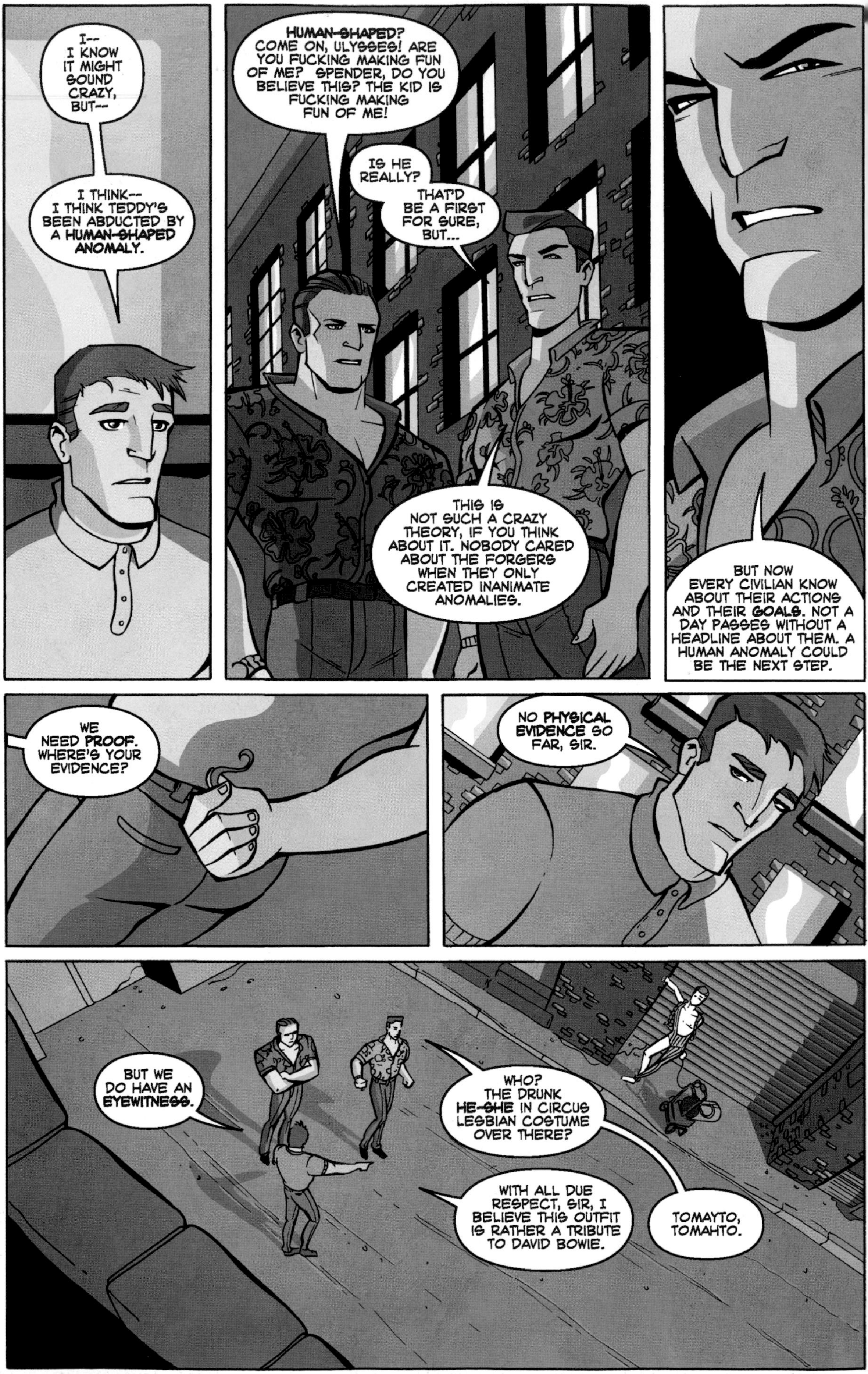
I-- I KNOW IT MIGHT SOUND CRAZY, BUT--
I THINK-- I THINK TEDDY'S BEEN ABDUCTED BY A HUMAN-SHAPED ANOMALY.
HUMAN-SHAPED? COME ON, ULYSSES! ARE YOU FUCKING MAKING FUN OF ME? SPENDER, DO YOU BELIEVE THIS? THE KID IS FUCKING MAKING FUN OF ME!
IS HE REALLY?
THAT'D BE A FIRST FOR SURE, BUT...
THIS IS NOT SUCH A CRAZY THEORY, IF YOU THINK ABOUT IT. NOBODY CARED ABOUT THE FORGERS WHEN THEY ONLY CREATED INANIMATE ANOMALIES.
BUT NOW EVERY CIVILIAN KNOW ABOUT THEIR ACTIONS AND THEIR GOALS. NOT A DAY PASSES WITHOUT A HEADLINE ABOUT THEM. A HUMAN ANOMALY COULD BE THE NEXT STEP.
WE NEED PROOF. WHERE'S YOUR EVIDENCE?
NO PHYSICAL EVIDENCE SO FAR, SIR.
BUT WE DO HAVE AN EYEWITNESS.
WHO? THE DRUNK HE-SHE IN CIRCUS LESBIAN COSTUME OVER THERE?
WITH ALL DUE RESPECT, SIR, I BELIEVE THIS OUTFIT IS RATHER A TRIBUTE TO DAVID BOWIE.
TOMAYTO, TOMAHTO.

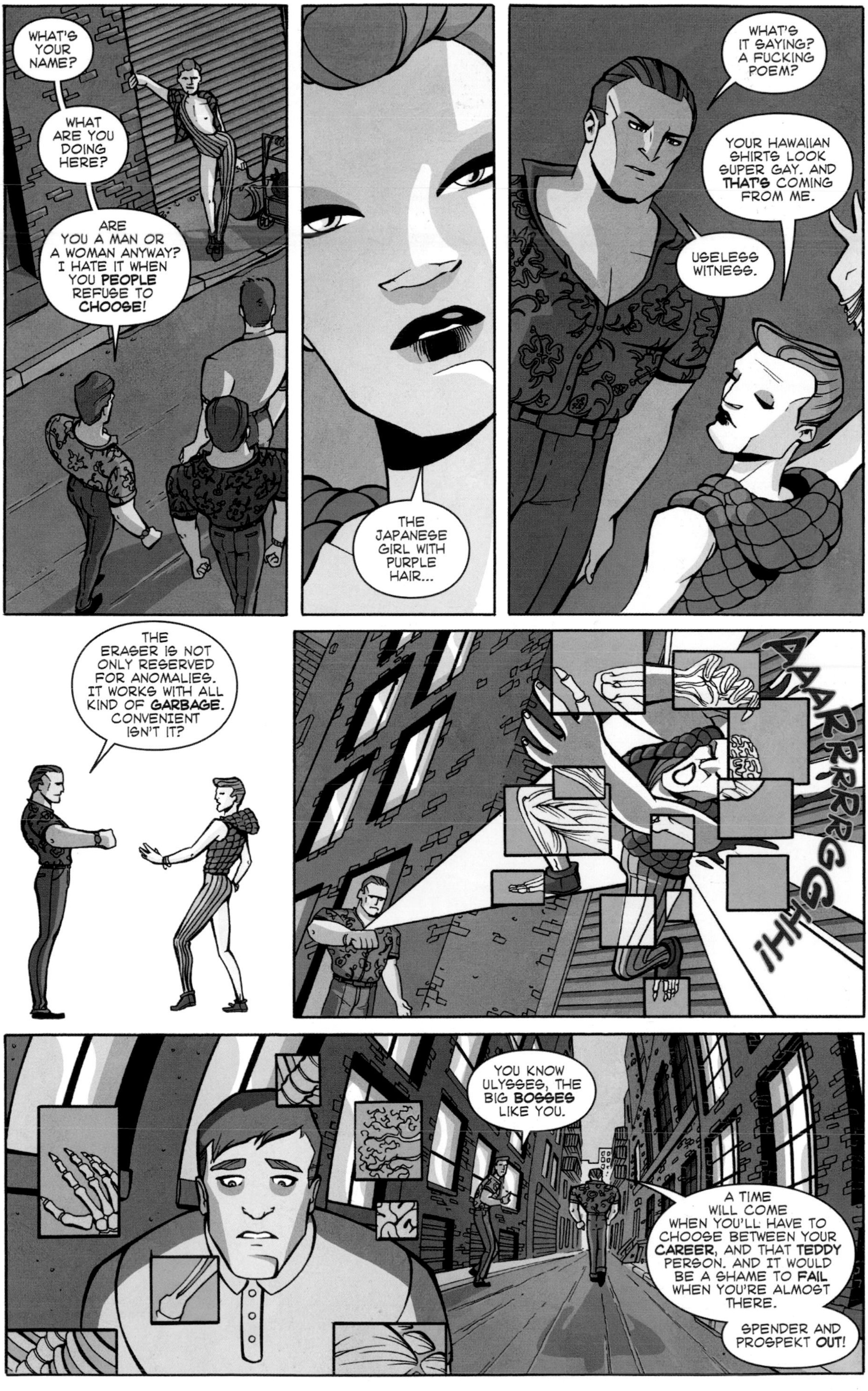

WHAT'S YOUR NAME?
WHAT ARE YOU DOING HERE?
ARE YOU A MAN OR A WOMAN ANYWAY? I HATE IT WHEN YOU PEOPLE REFUSE TO CHOOSE!
THE JAPANESE GIRL WITH PURPLE HAIR...
WHAT'S IT SAYING? A FUCKING POEM?
YOUR HAWAIIAN SHIRTS LOOK SUPER GAY. AND THAT'S COMING FROM ME.
USELESS WITNESS.
THE ERASER IS NOT ONLY RESERVED FOR ANOMALIES. IT WORKS WITH ALL KIND OF GARBAGE. CONVENIENT ISN'T IT?
AAARRRRGGHH!
YOU KNOW ULYSSES, THE BIG BOSSES LIKE YOU.
A TIME WILL COME WHEN YOU'LL HAVE TO CHOOSE BETWEEN YOUR CAREER, AND THAT TEDDY PERSON. AND IT WOULD BE A SHAME TO FAIL WHEN YOU'RE ALMOST THERE.
SPENDER AND PROSPEKT OUT!

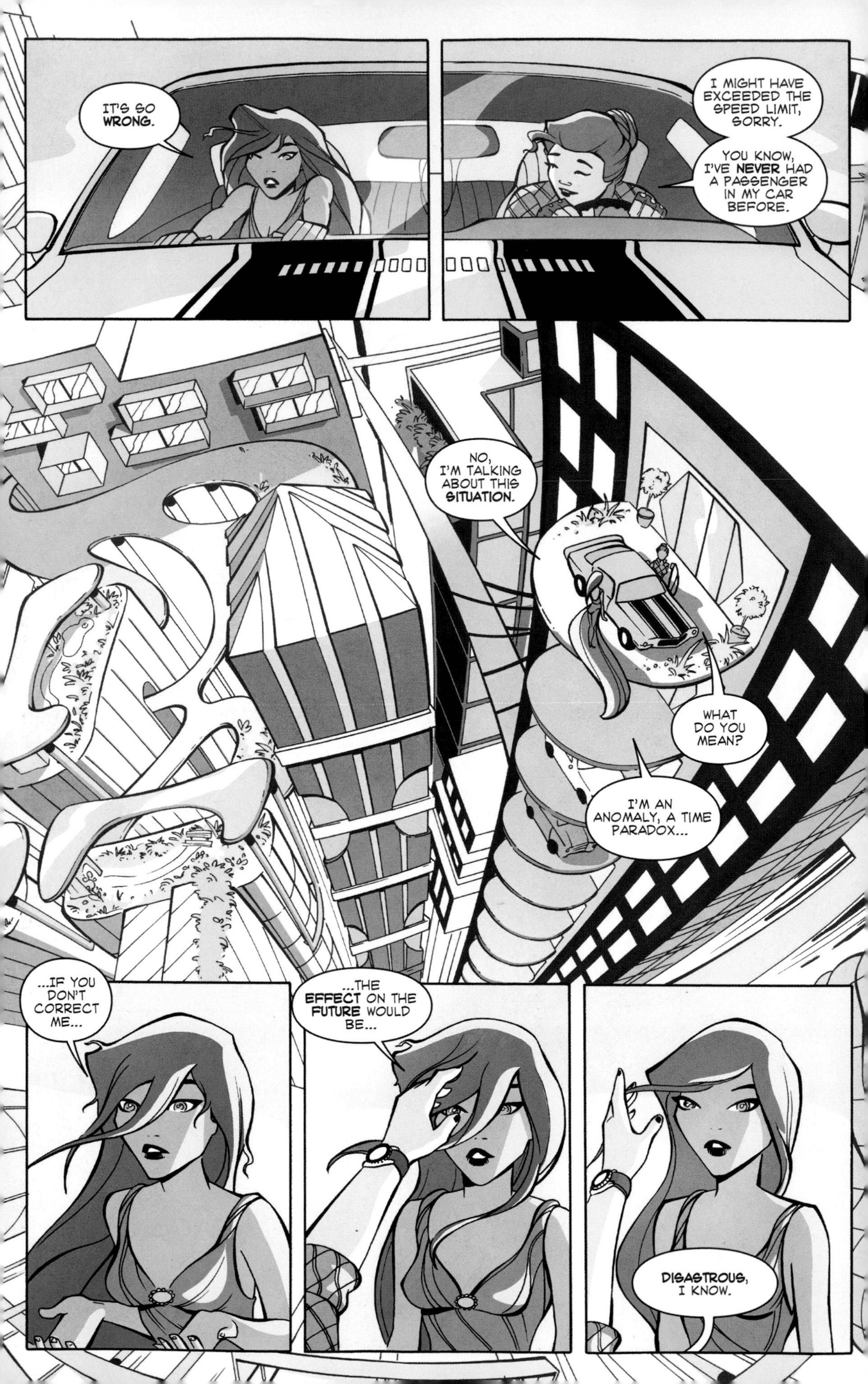
IT'S SO WRONG.
I MIGHT HAVE EXCEEDED THE SPEED LIMIT, SORRY.
YOU KNOW, I'VE NEVER HAD A PASSENGER IN MY CAR BEFORE.
NO, I'M TALKING ABOUT THIS SITUATION.
WHAT DO YOU MEAN?
I'M AN ANOMALY, A TIME PARADOX...
...IF YOU DON'T CORRECT ME...
...THE EFFECT ON THE FUTURE WOULD BE...
DISASTROUS, I KNOW.

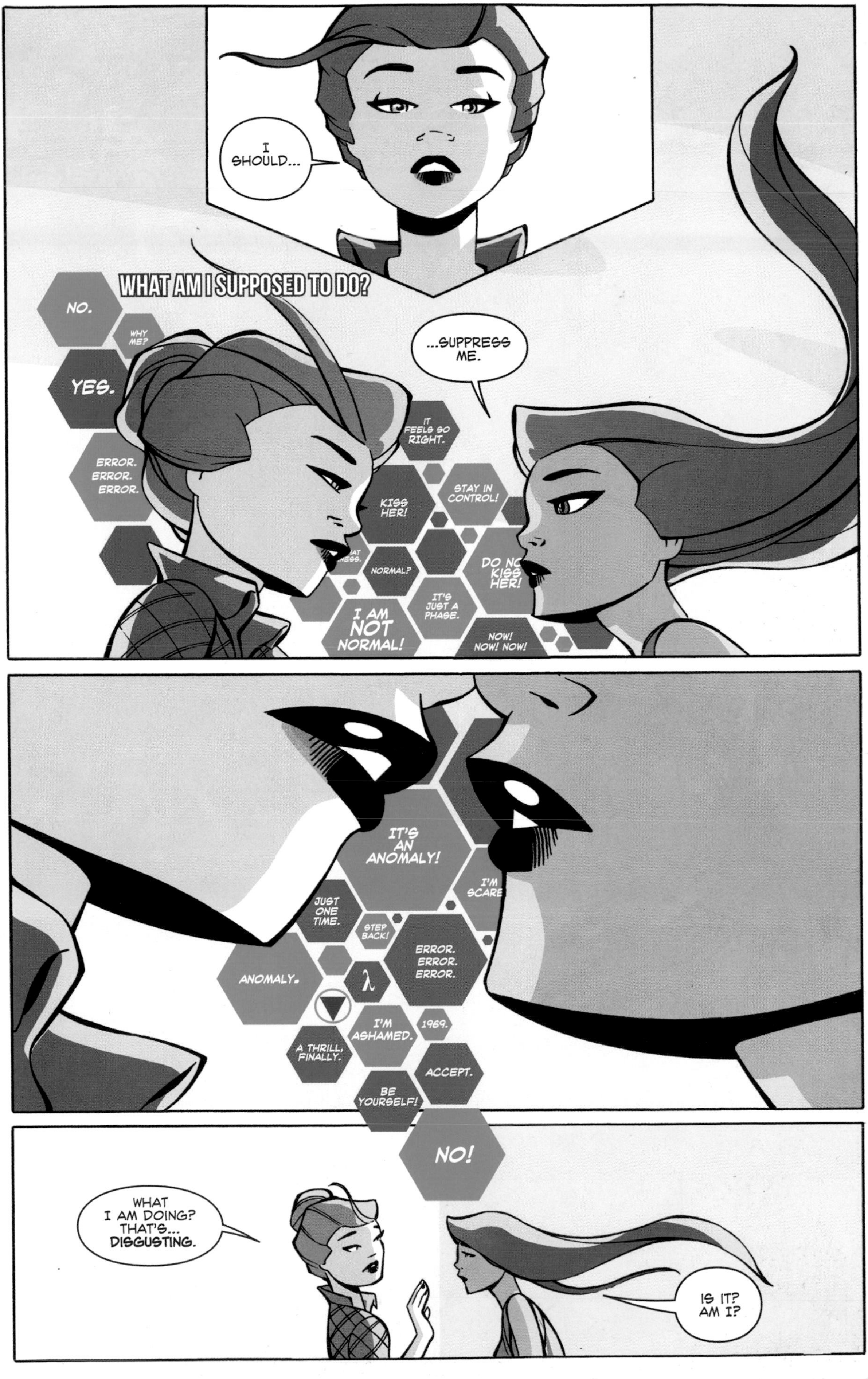
I SHOULD...
WHAT AM I SUPPOSED TO DO?
NO.
WHY ME?
YES.
...SUPPRESS ME.
IT FEELS SO RIGHT.
ERROR. ERROR. ERROR.
KISS HER!
STAY IN CONTROL!
NORMAL?
DO NO KISS HER!
IT'S JUST A PHASE.
I AM NOT NORMAL!
NOW! NOW! NOW!
IT'S AN ANOMALY!
I'M SCARE
JUST ONE TIME.
STEP BACK!
ERROR. ERROR. ERROR.
ANOMALY.
λ
I'M ASHAMED.
1969.
A THRILL, FINALLY.
ACCEPT.
BE YOURSELF!
NO!
WHAT I AM DOING? THAT'S... DISGUSTING.
IS IT? AM I?

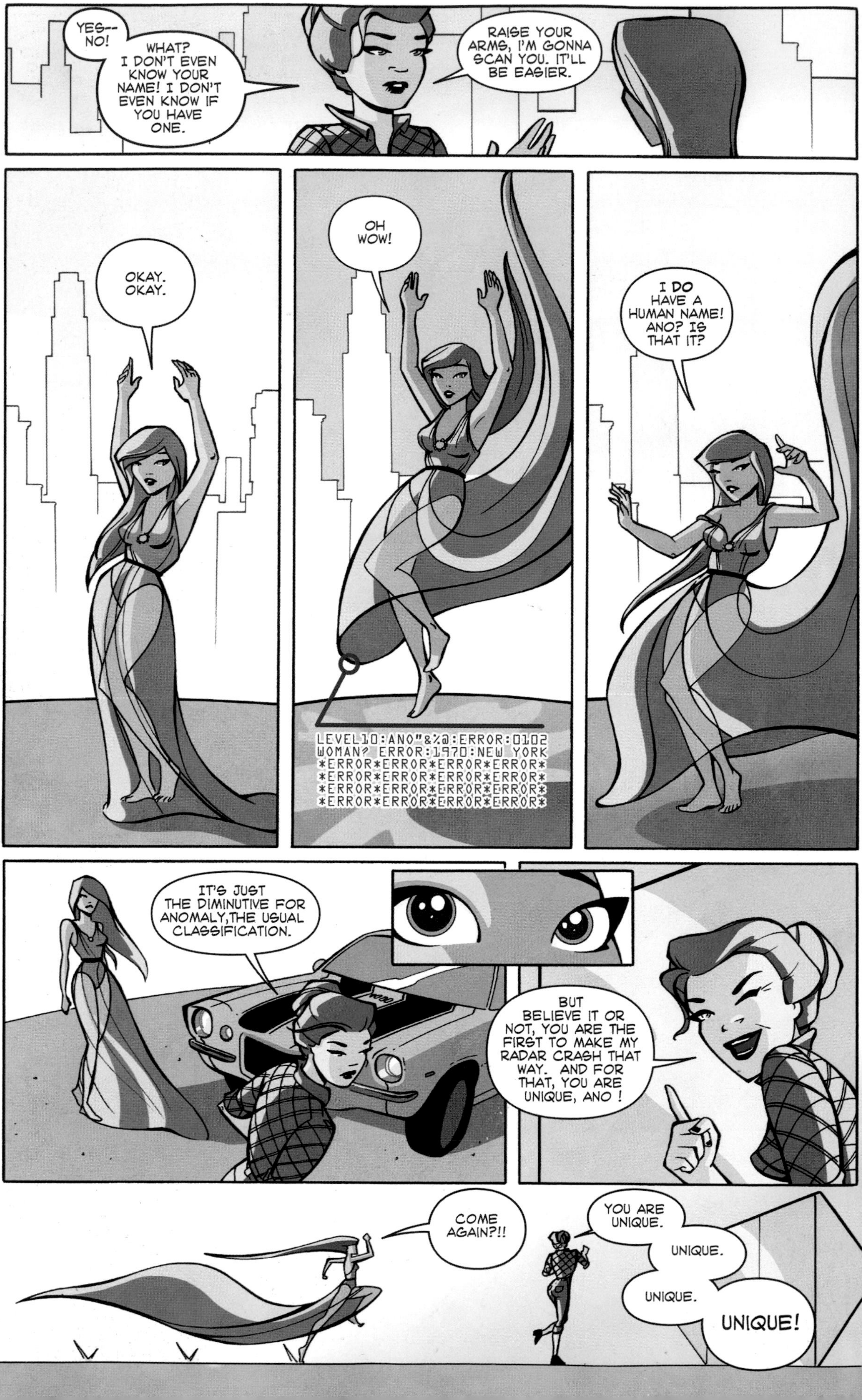
YES-- NO!
WHAT? I DON'T EVEN KNOW YOUR NAME! I DON'T EVEN KNOW IF YOU HAVE ONE.
RAISE YOUR ARMS, I'M GONNA SCAN YOU. IT'LL BE EASIER.
OKAY. OKAY.
OH WOW!
LEVEL10:ANO"&%@:ERROR:0102
WOMAN? ERROR:1970:NEW YORK
*ERROR*ERROR*ERROR*ERROR*
*ERROR*ERROR*ERROR*ERROR*
*ERROR*ERROR*ERROR*ERROR*
*ERROR*ERROR*ERROR*ERROR*
I DO HAVE A HUMAN NAME! ANO? IS THAT IT?
IT'S JUST THE DIMINUTIVE FOR ANOMALY, THE USUAL CLASSIFICATION.
BUT BELIEVE IT OR NOT, YOU ARE THE FIRST TO MAKE MY RADAR CRASH THAT WAY. AND FOR THAT, YOU ARE UNIQUE, ANO !
COME AGAIN?!!
YOU ARE UNIQUE.
UNIQUE.
UNIQUE.
UNIQUE!

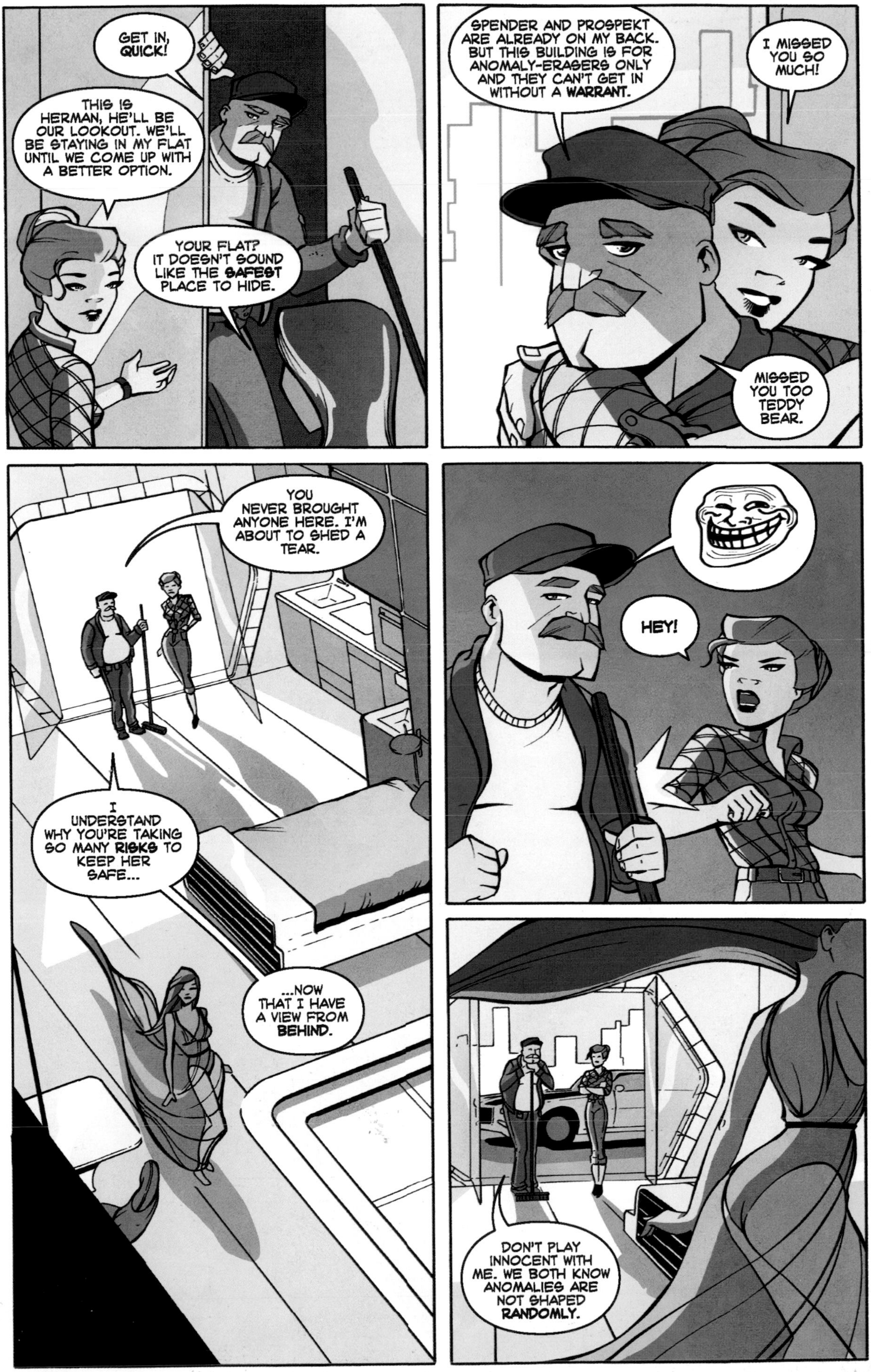
GET IN, QUICK!
THIS IS HERMAN, HE'LL BE OUR LOOKOUT. WE'LL BE STAYING IN MY FLAT UNTIL WE COME UP WITH A BETTER OPTION.
YOUR FLAT? IT DOESN'T SOUND LIKE THE SAFEST PLACE TO HIDE.
SPENDER AND PROSPEKT ARE ALREADY ON MY BACK. BUT THIS BUILDING IS FOR ANOMALY-ERASERS ONLY AND THEY CAN'T GET IN WITHOUT A WARRANT.
I MISSED YOU SO MUCH!
MISSED YOU TOO TEDDY BEAR.
YOU NEVER BROUGHT ANYONE HERE. I'M ABOUT TO SHED A TEAR.
HEY!
I UNDERSTAND WHY YOU'RE TAKING SO MANY RISKS TO KEEP HER SAFE...
...NOW THAT I HAVE A VIEW FROM BEHIND.
DON'T PLAY INNOCENT WITH ME. WE BOTH KNOW ANOMALIES ARE NOT SHAPED RANDOMLY.

HAVE YOU TWO KNOWN EACH OTHER FOR A LONG TIME?

BEFORE HE WAS A JANITOR, HERMAN WAS AN ERASER LIKE ME. HE IS A **LEGEND** IN THE BUSINESS.

IN THE END, IT'S PRETTY MUCH THE SAME JOB: I **CLEAN UP** OTHER PEOPLE'S **MESS.**

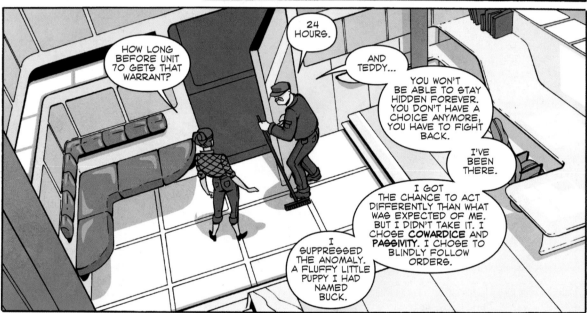

HOW LONG BEFORE UNIT 70 GETS THAT WARRANT?

24 HOURS.

AND TEDDY...

YOU WON'T BE ABLE TO STAY HIDDEN FOREVER. YOU DON'T HAVE A CHOICE ANYMORE, YOU HAVE TO FIGHT BACK.

I'VE BEEN THERE.

I GOT THE CHANCE TO ACT DIFFERENTLY THAN WHAT WAS EXPECTED OF ME. BUT I DIDN'T TAKE IT. I CHOSE **COWARDICE** AND **PASSIVITY.** I CHOSE TO BLINDLY FOLLOW ORDERS.

I SUPPRESSED THE ANOMALY. A FLUFFY LITTLE PUPPY I HAD NAMED BUCK.

I **QUIT** THE NEXT DAY.

ANYWAY, IT'S ALL IN THE **PAST** FOR ME. BUT FOR YOU...

...IT'S YOUR **FUTURE.**

MY FUTURE?

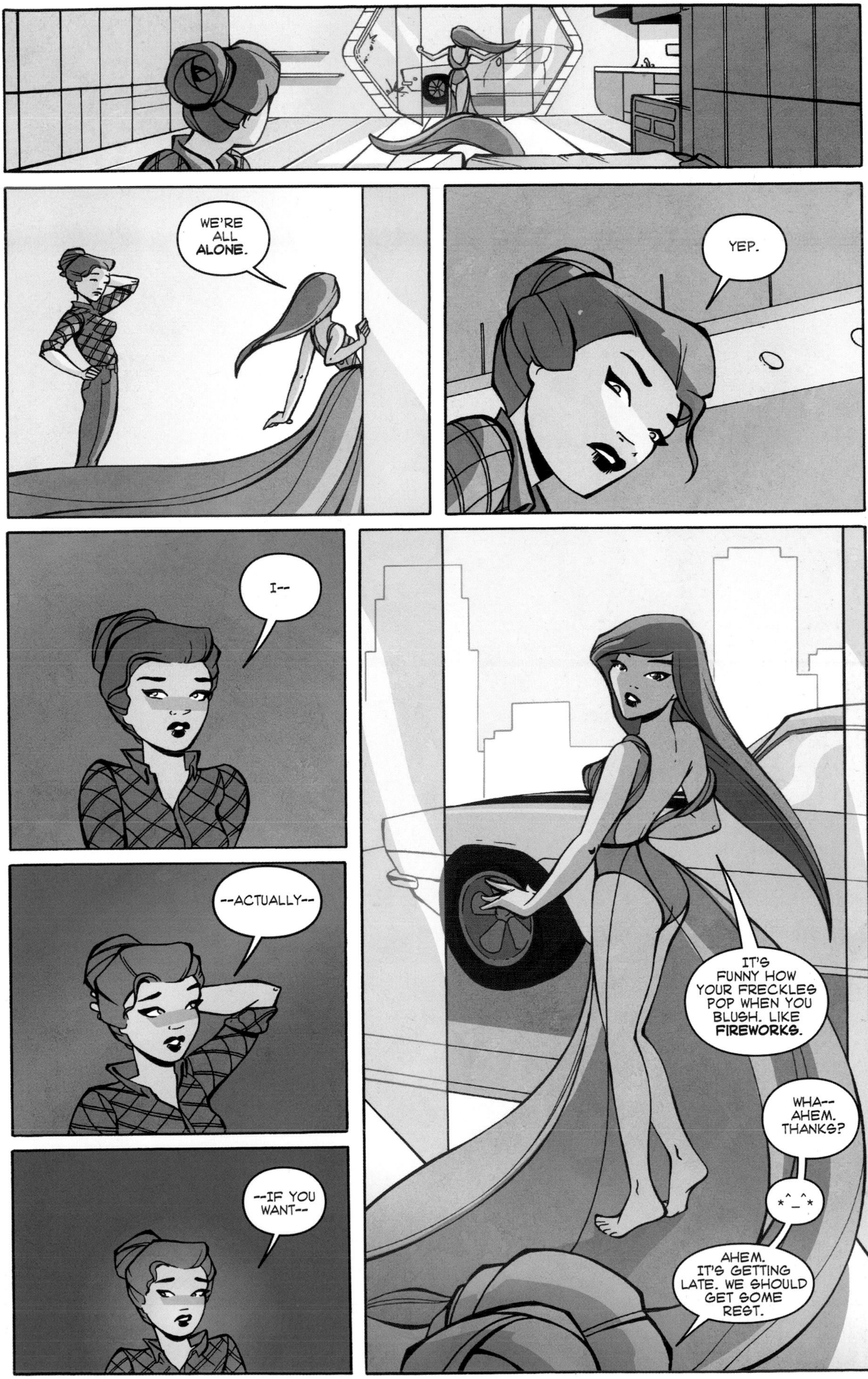
WE'RE ALL ALONE.
YEP.
I--
--ACTUALLY--
--IF YOU WANT--
IT'S FUNNY HOW YOUR FRECKLES POP WHEN YOU BLUSH. LIKE FIREWORKS.
WHA-- AHEM. THANKS?
*^_^*
AHEM. IT'S GETTING LATE. WE SHOULD GET SOME REST.

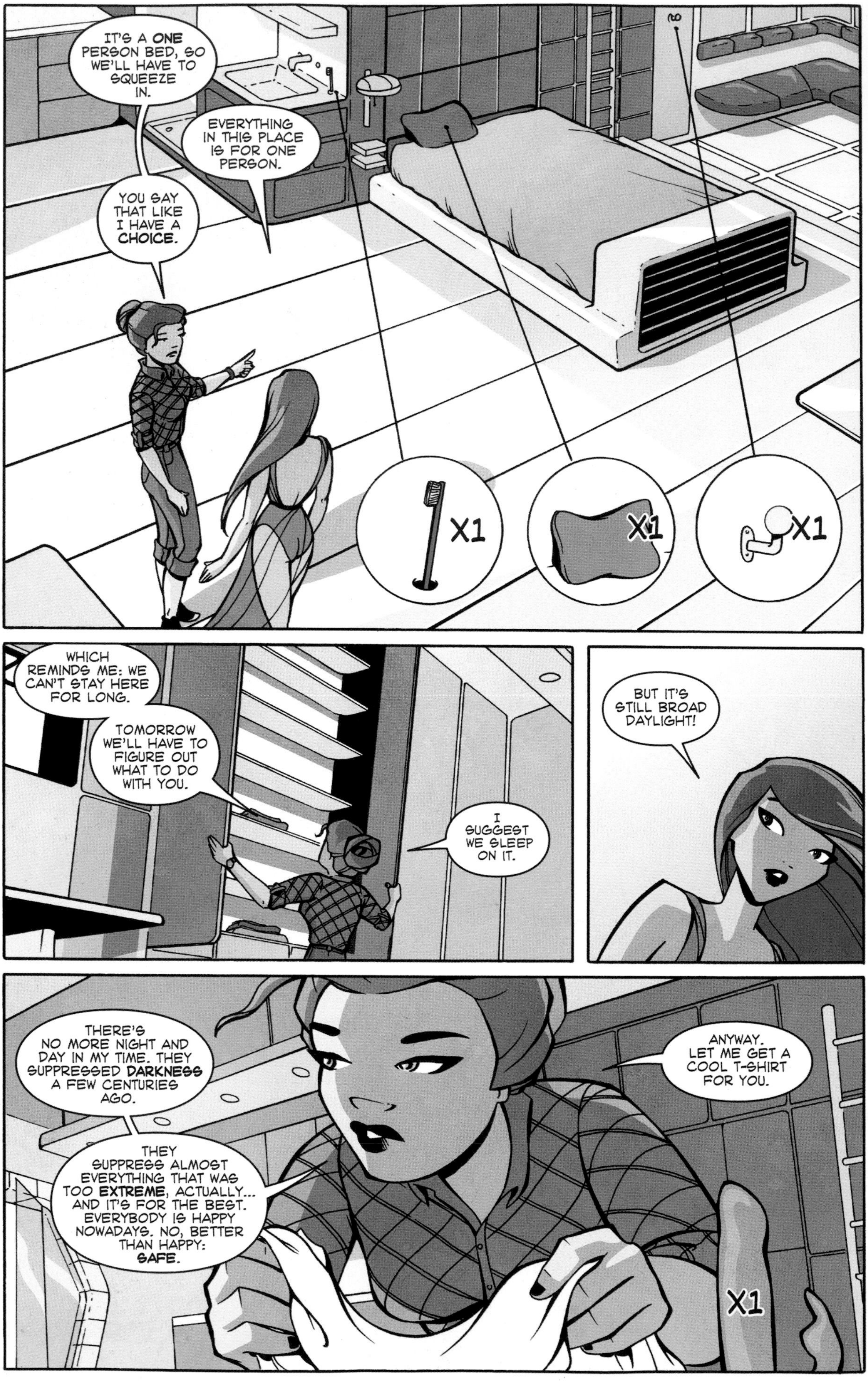
IT'S A ONE PERSON BED, SO WE'LL HAVE TO SQUEEZE IN.
EVERYTHING IN THIS PLACE IS FOR ONE PERSON.
YOU SAY THAT LIKE I HAVE A CHOICE.
X1
X1
X1
WHICH REMINDS ME: WE CAN'T STAY HERE FOR LONG.
TOMORROW WE'LL HAVE TO FIGURE OUT WHAT TO DO WITH YOU.
I SUGGEST WE SLEEP ON IT.
BUT IT'S STILL BROAD DAYLIGHT!
THERE'S NO MORE NIGHT AND DAY IN MY TIME. THEY SUPPRESSED DARKNESS A FEW CENTURIES AGO.
THEY SUPPRESS ALMOST EVERYTHING THAT WAS TOO EXTREME, ACTUALLY... AND IT'S FOR THE BEST. EVERYBODY IS HAPPY NOWADAYS. NO, BETTER THAN HAPPY: SAFE.
ANYWAY. LET ME GET A COOL T-SHIRT FOR YOU.
X1

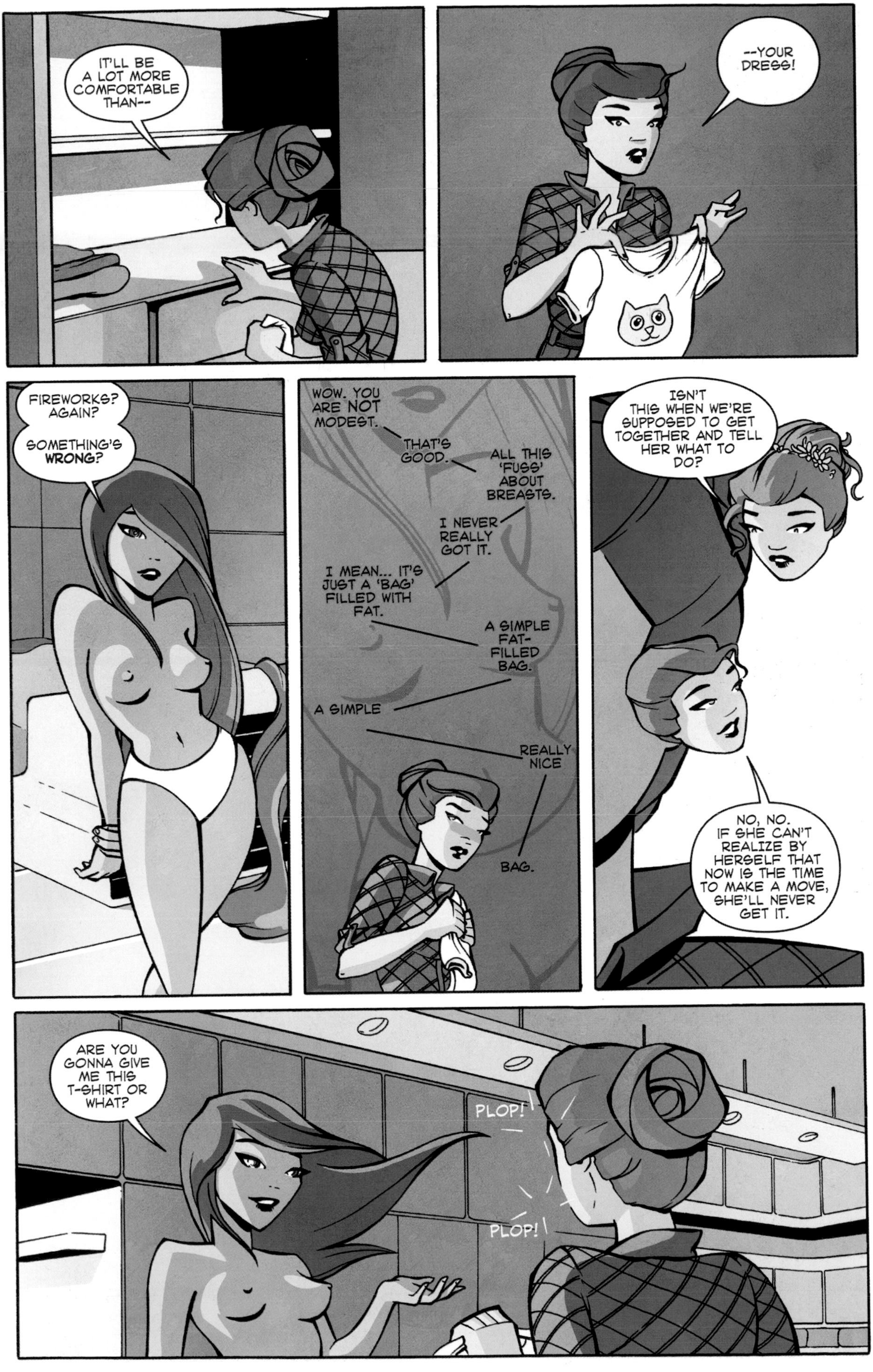
IT'LL BE A LOT MORE COMFORTABLE THAN--
--YOUR DRESS!
FIREWORKS? AGAIN?
SOMETHING'S **WRONG**?
WOW. YOU ARE **NOT** MODEST.
THAT'S GOOD.
ALL THIS 'FUSS' ABOUT BREASTS.
I NEVER REALLY GOT IT.
I MEAN... IT'S JUST A 'BAG' FILLED WITH FAT.
A SIMPLE FAT-FILLED BAG.
A SIMPLE
REALLY NICE
BAG.
ISN'T THIS WHEN WE'RE SUPPOSED TO GET TOGETHER AND TELL HER WHAT TO DO?
NO, NO. IF SHE CAN'T REALIZE BY HERSELF THAT NOW IS THE TIME TO MAKE A MOVE, SHE'LL NEVER GET IT.
ARE YOU GONNA GIVE ME THIS T-SHIRT OR WHAT?
PLOP!
PLOP!

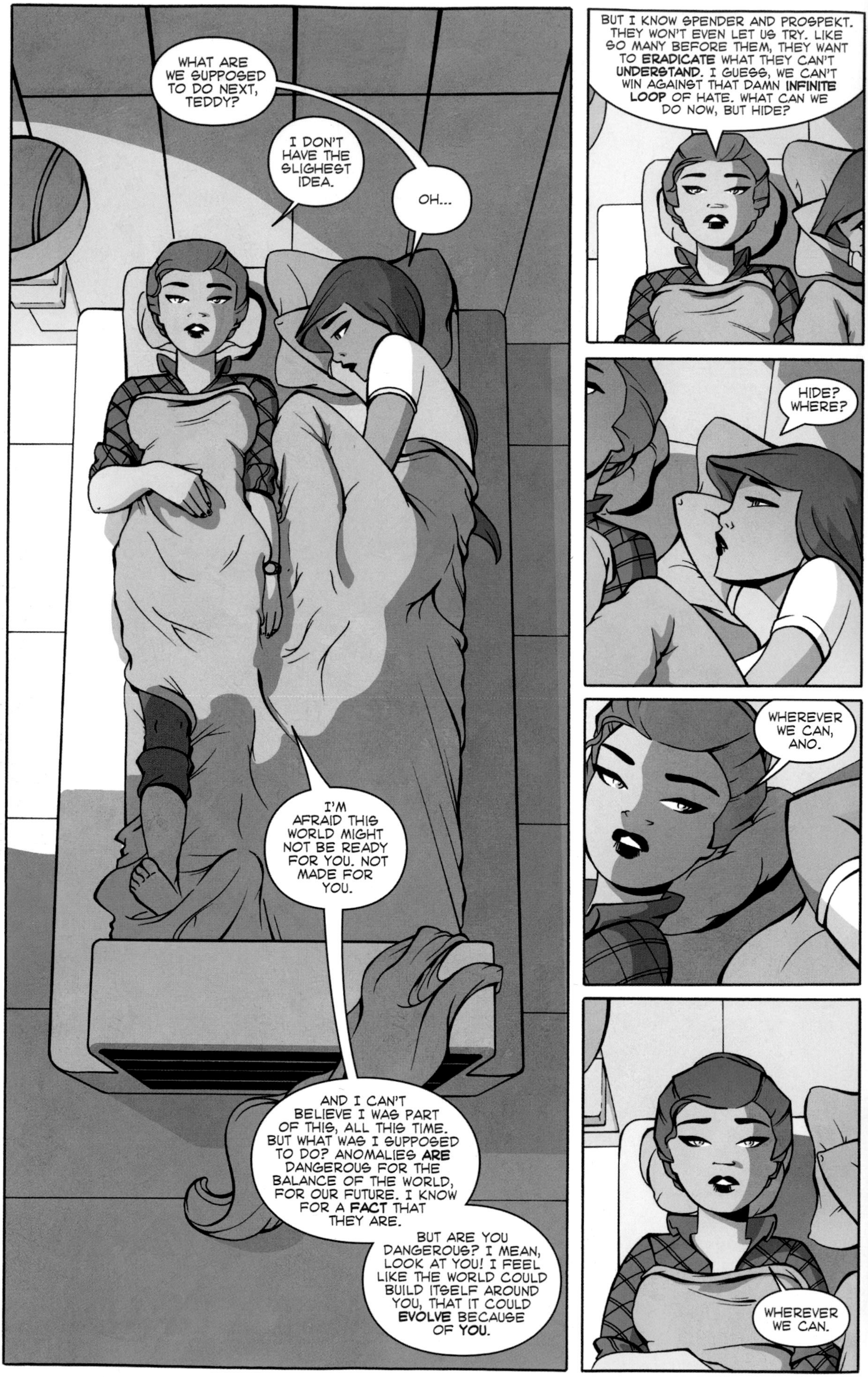
WHAT ARE WE SUPPOSED TO DO NEXT, TEDDY?
I DON'T HAVE THE SLIGHEST IDEA.
OH...
I'M AFRAID THIS WORLD MIGHT NOT BE READY FOR YOU. NOT MADE FOR YOU.
AND I CAN'T BELIEVE I WAS PART OF THIS, ALL THIS TIME. BUT WHAT WAS I SUPPOSED TO DO? ANOMALIES ARE DANGEROUS FOR THE BALANCE OF THE WORLD, FOR OUR FUTURE. I KNOW FOR A FACT THAT THEY ARE.
BUT ARE YOU DANGEROUS? I MEAN, LOOK AT YOU! I FEEL LIKE THE WORLD COULD BUILD ITSELF AROUND YOU, THAT IT COULD EVOLVE BECAUSE OF YOU.
BUT I KNOW SPENDER AND PROSPEKT. THEY WON'T EVEN LET US TRY. LIKE SO MANY BEFORE THEM, THEY WANT TO ERADICATE WHAT THEY CAN'T UNDERSTAND. I GUESS, WE CAN'T WIN AGAINST THAT DAMN INFINITE LOOP OF HATE. WHAT CAN WE DO NOW, BUT HIDE?
HIDE? WHERE?
WHEREVER WE CAN, ANO.
WHEREVER WE CAN.

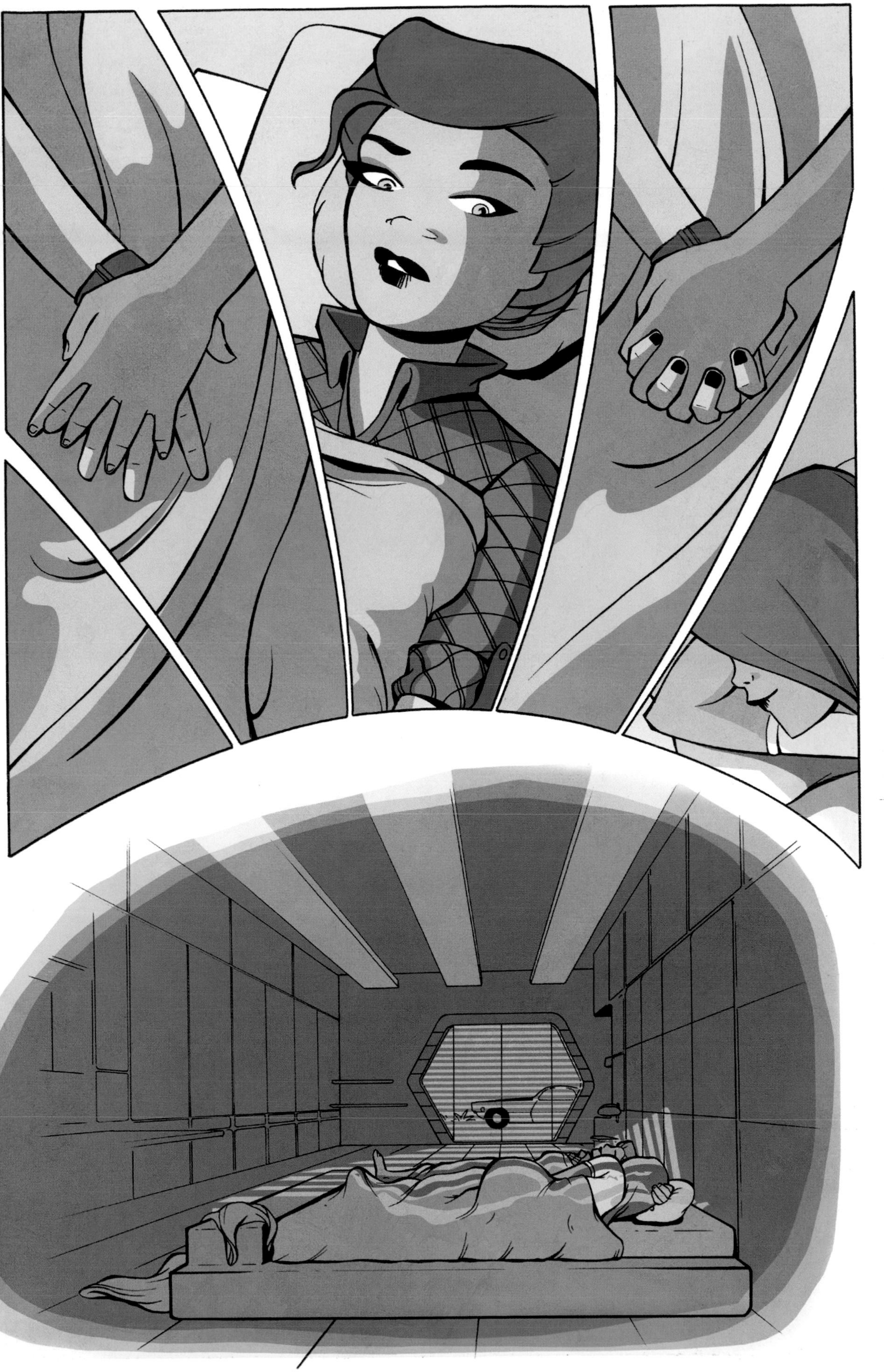

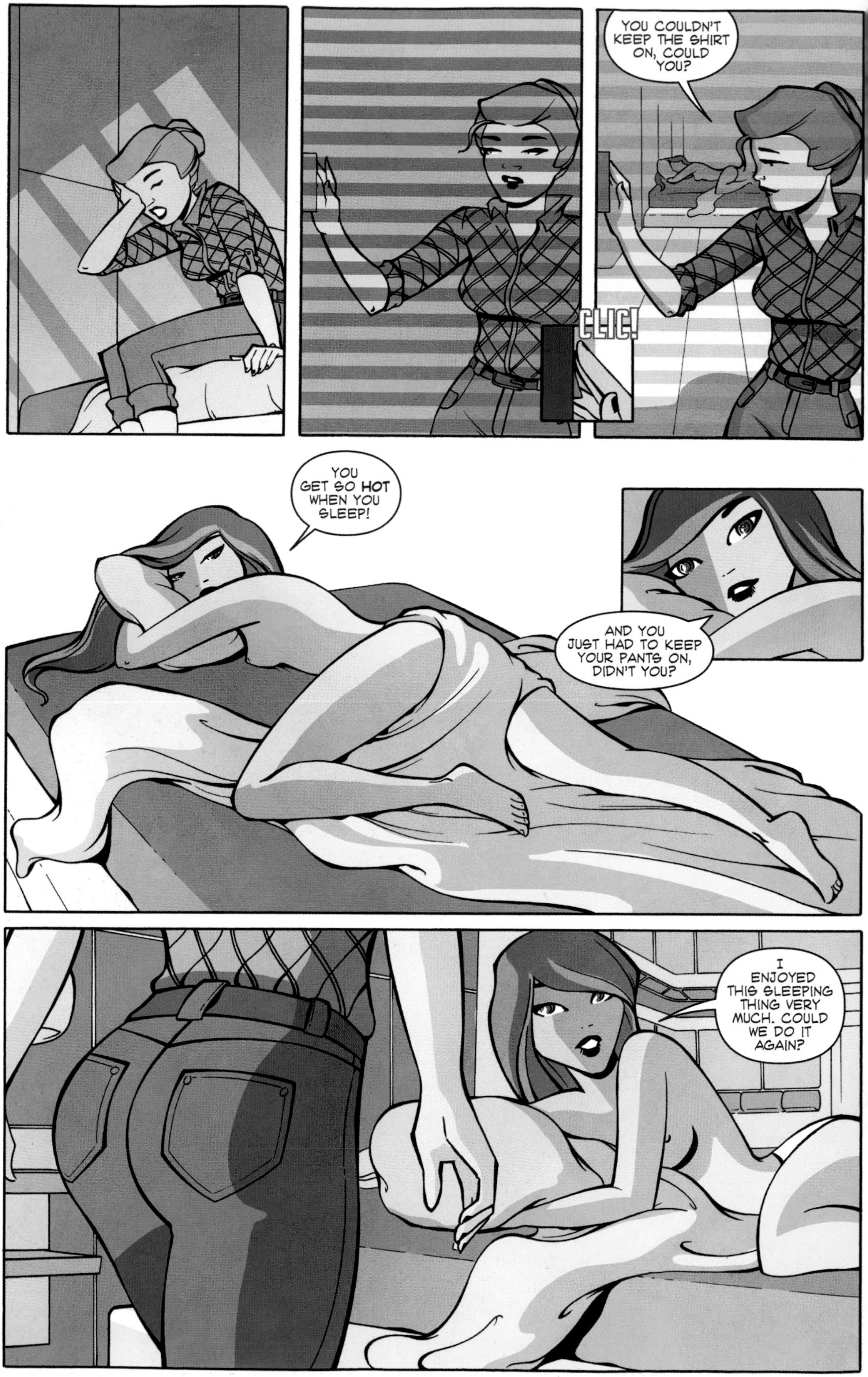
CLIC!
YOU COULDN'T KEEP THE SHIRT ON, COULD YOU?
YOU GET SO HOT WHEN YOU SLEEP!
AND YOU JUST HAD TO KEEP YOUR PANTS ON, DIDN'T YOU?
I ENJOYED THIS SLEEPING THING VERY MUCH. COULD WE DO IT AGAIN?

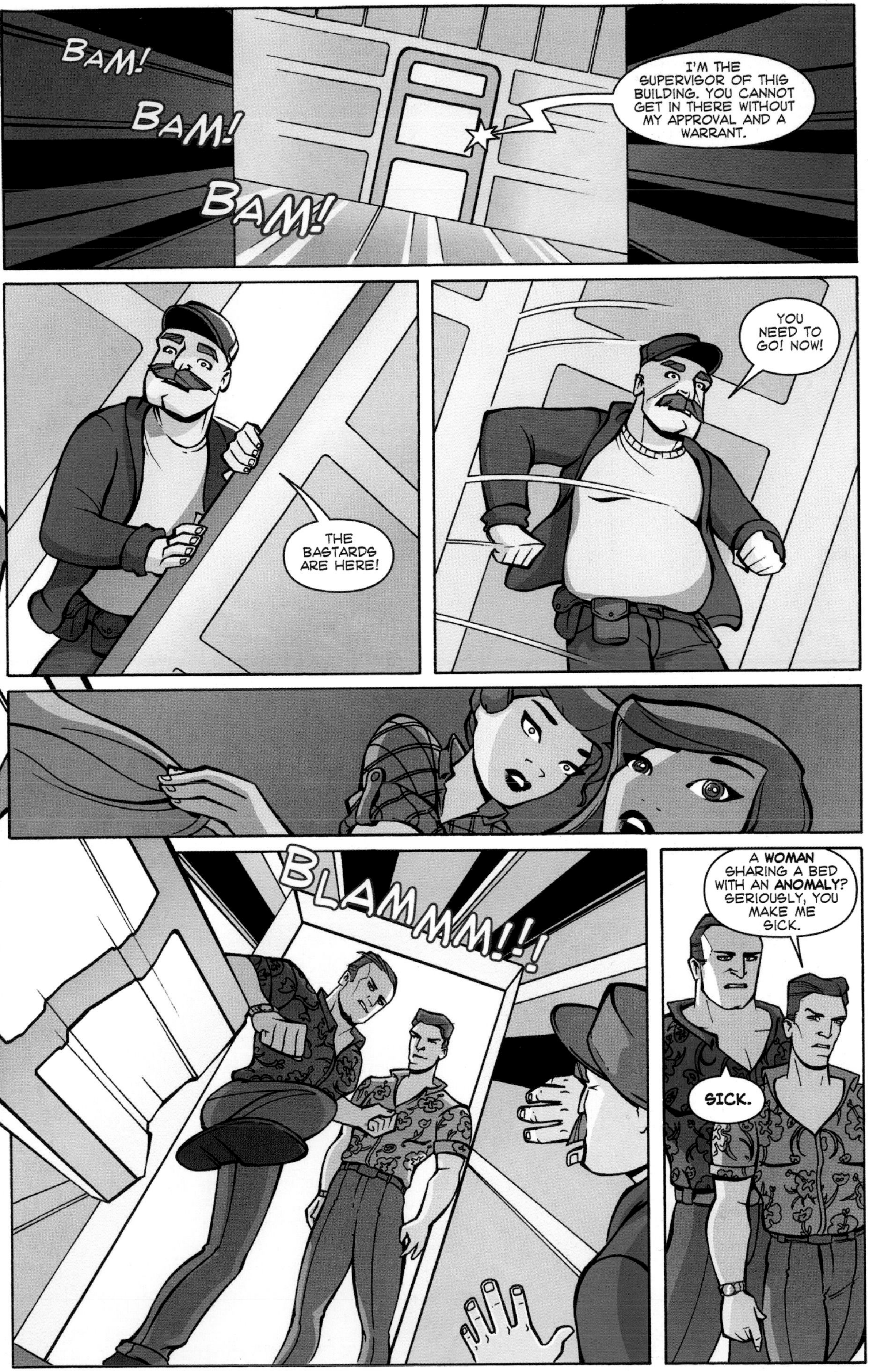
BAM!
BAM!
BAM!
I'M THE SUPERVISOR OF THIS BUILDING. YOU CANNOT GET IN THERE WITHOUT MY APPROVAL AND A WARRANT.
THE BASTARDS ARE HERE!
YOU NEED TO GO! NOW!
BLAMMMM!!!
A WOMAN SHARING A BED WITH AN ANOMALY? SERIOUSLY, YOU MAKE ME SICK.
SICK.

AND YOU'RE OK WITH THIS, HERMAN?

DID YOU GIVE UP ON EVERYTHING I **TAUGHT** YOU, NOEL?

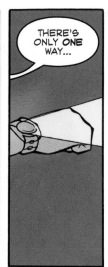

THERE'S ONLY **ONE** WAY...

...OUR WAY!

NOOOOOOO!

RUN TO THE CAR, AND DON'T LOOK BACK.

SONS OF BITCHES!

PROSPEKT, WATCH OUT!

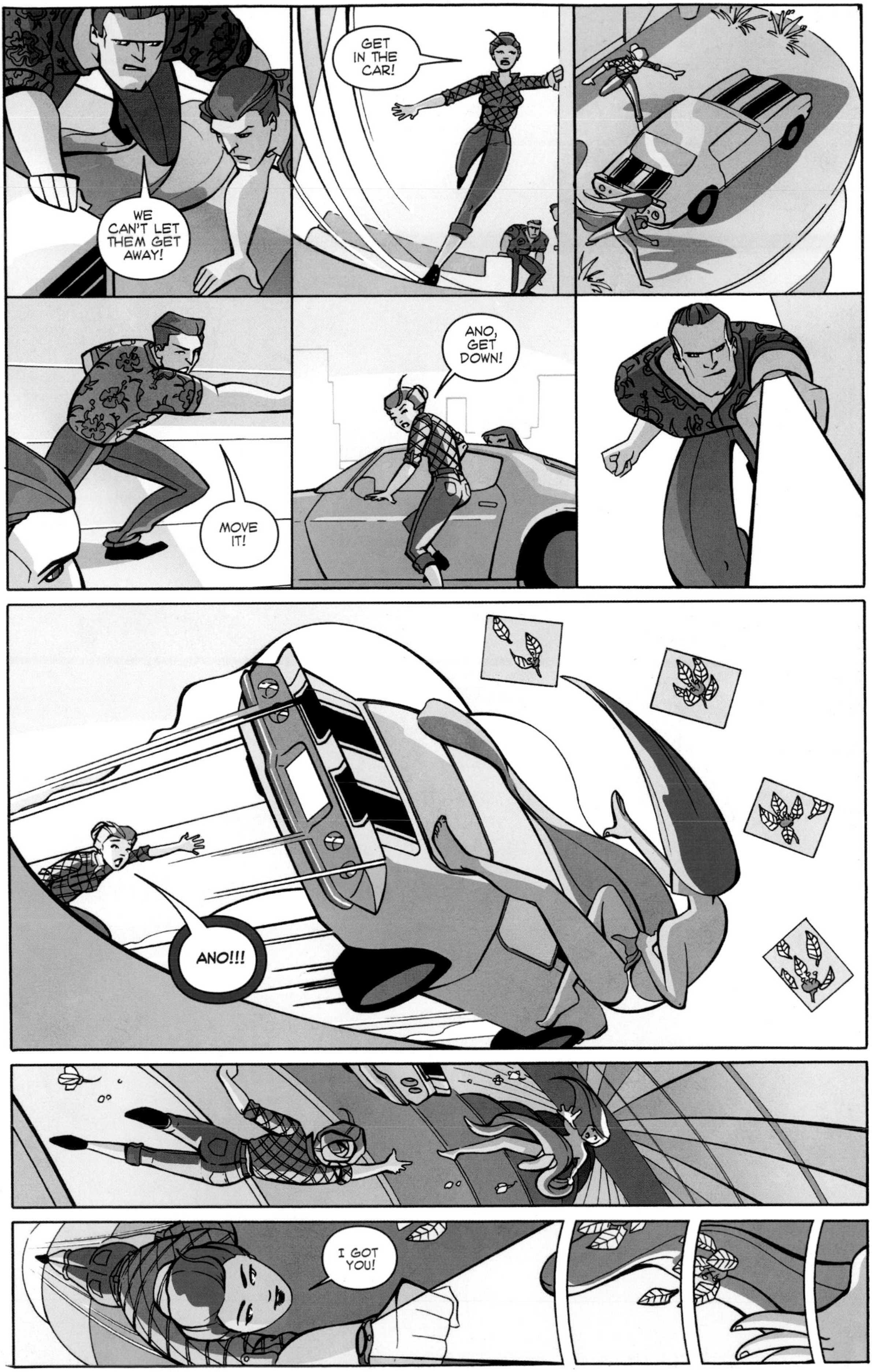
WE CAN'T LET THEM GET AWAY!
GET IN THE CAR!
MOVE IT!
ANO, GET DOWN!
ANO!!!
I GOT YOU!

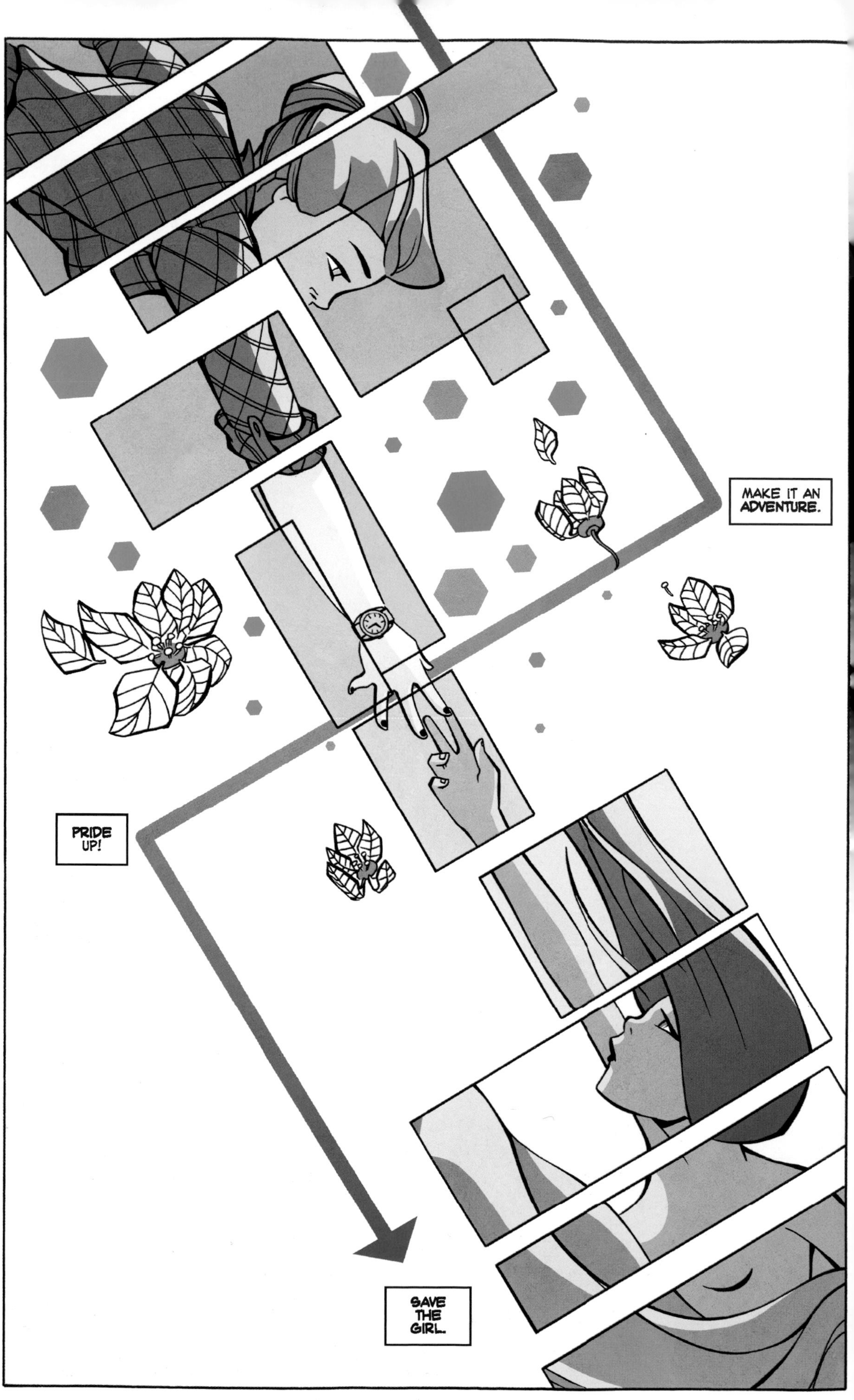
MAKE IT AN ADVENTURE.
PRIDE UP!
SAVE THE GIRL.

Art by **TIM SALE & DAVE STEWART**

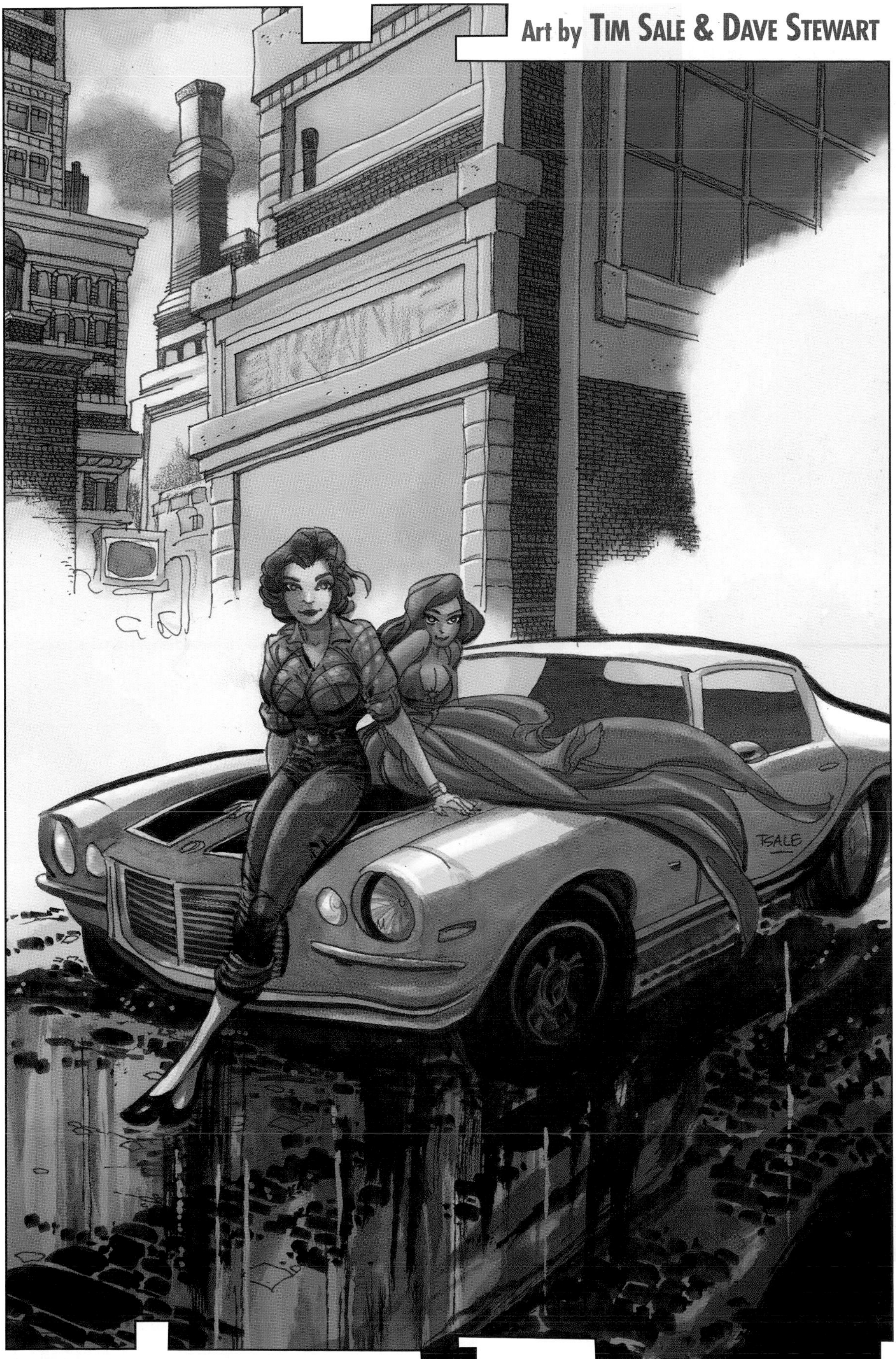

TSALE

Art by ELSA CHARRETIER

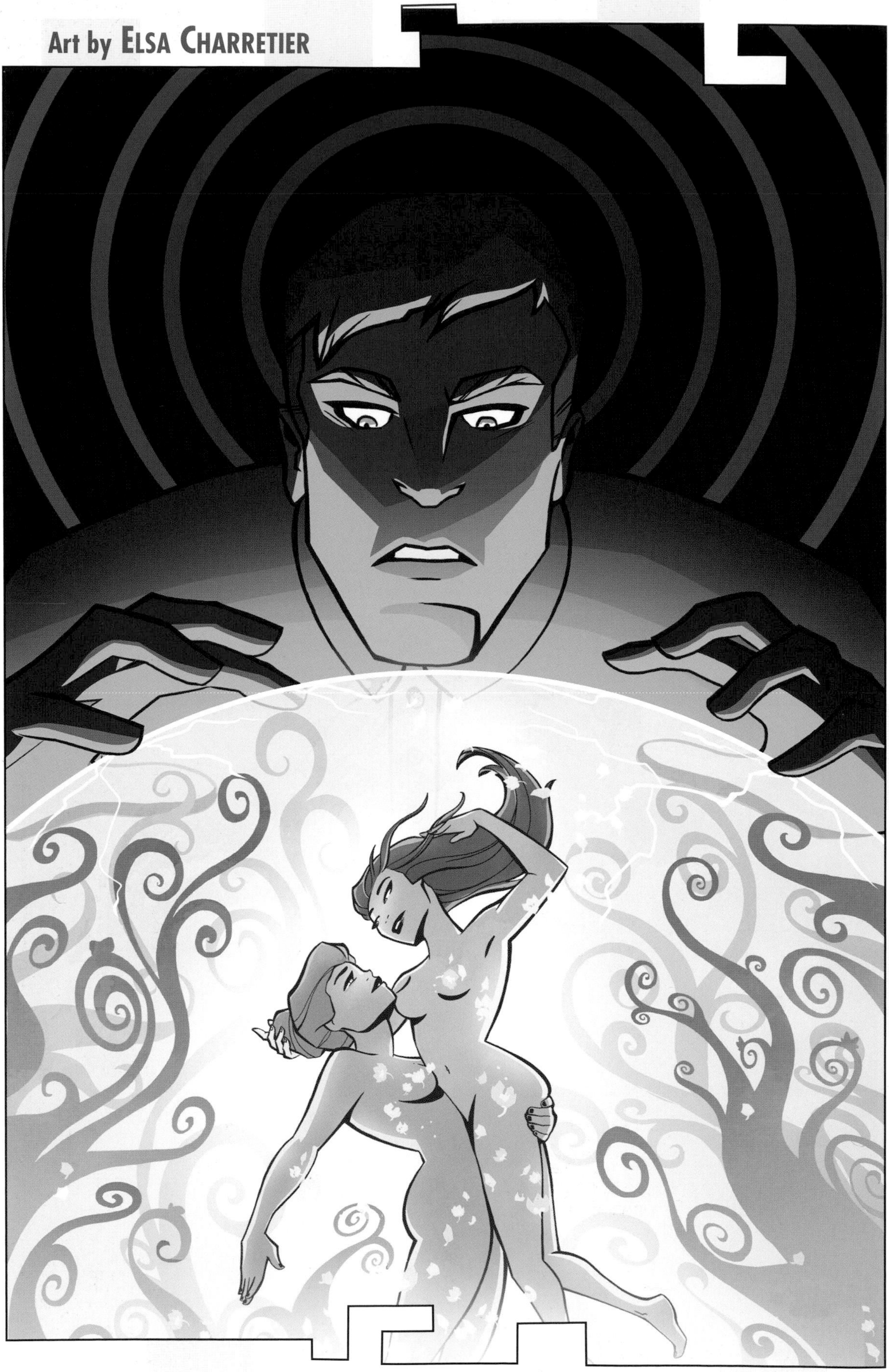

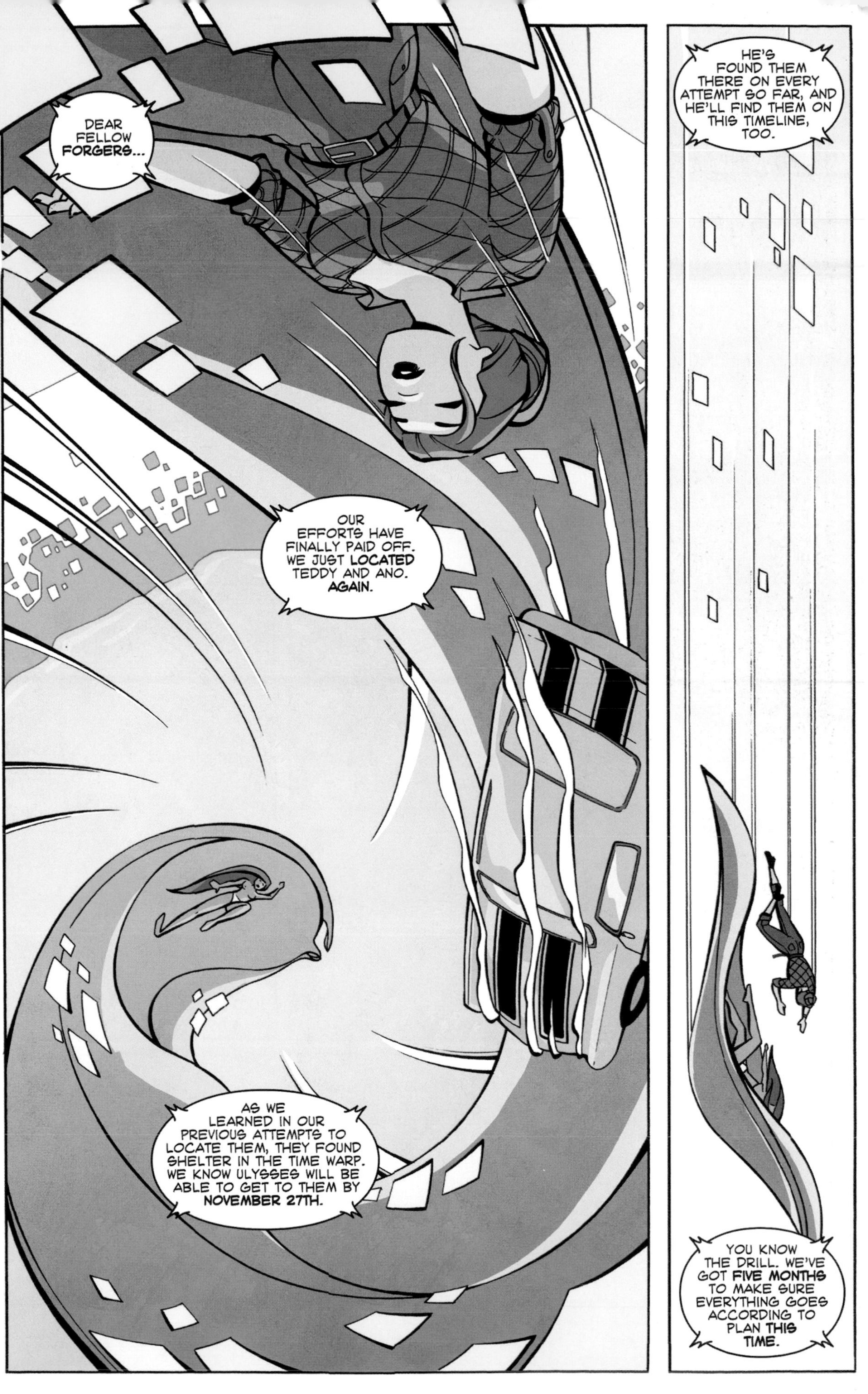
DEAR FELLOW FORGERS...
OUR EFFORTS HAVE FINALLY PAID OFF. WE JUST LOCATED TEDDY AND ANO. AGAIN.
AS WE LEARNED IN OUR PREVIOUS ATTEMPTS TO LOCATE THEM, THEY FOUND SHELTER IN THE TIME WARP. WE KNOW ULYSSES WILL BE ABLE TO GET TO THEM BY NOVEMBER 27TH.
HE'S FOUND THEM THERE ON EVERY ATTEMPT SO FAR, AND HE'LL FIND THEM ON THIS TIMELINE, TOO.
YOU KNOW THE DRILL. WE'VE GOT FIVE MONTHS TO MAKE SURE EVERYTHING GOES ACCORDING TO PLAN THIS TIME.

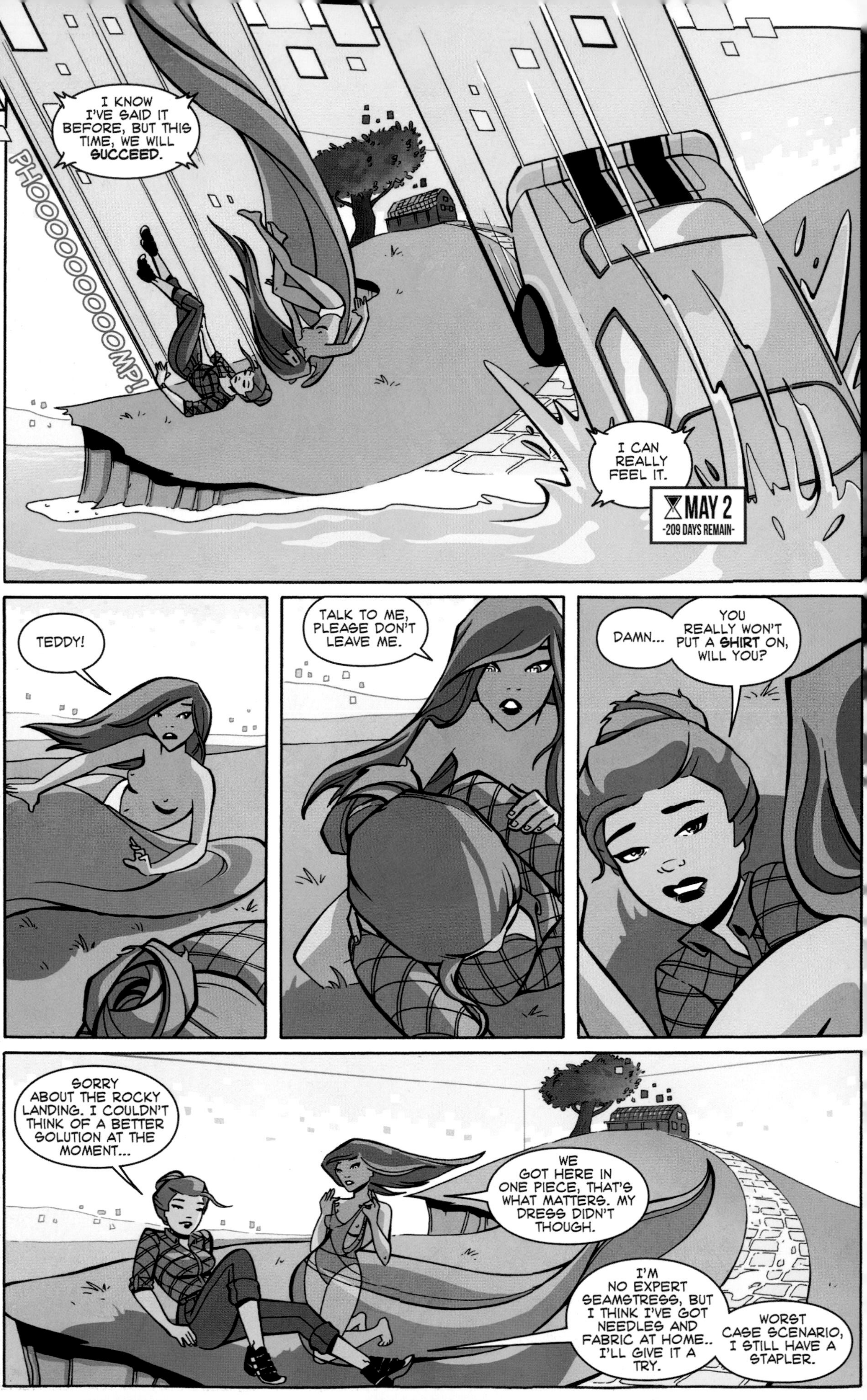
I KNOW I'VE SAID IT BEFORE, BUT THIS TIME, WE WILL SUCCEED.
PHOOOOOOOOOOMP!
I CAN REALLY FEEL IT.
MAY 2
-209 DAYS REMAIN-
TEDDY!
TALK TO ME, PLEASE DON'T LEAVE ME.
DAMN...
YOU REALLY WON'T PUT A SHIRT ON, WILL YOU?
SORRY ABOUT THE ROCKY LANDING. I COULDN'T THINK OF A BETTER SOLUTION AT THE MOMENT...
WE GOT HERE IN ONE PIECE, THAT'S WHAT MATTERS. MY DRESS DIDN'T THOUGH.
I'M NO EXPERT SEAMSTRESS, BUT I THINK I'VE GOT NEEDLES AND FABRIC AT HOME.. I'LL GIVE IT A TRY.
WORST CASE SCENARIO, I STILL HAVE A STAPLER.

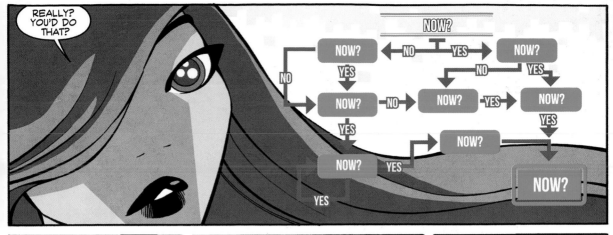

NOW?

NOW? ◄ NO │ YES ► NOW?

NO ► NOW?

NOW? ─NO─► NOW? ─YES─► NOW?

NOW? YES ► NOW?

NOW?

YES

REALLY? YOU'D DO THAT?

WHAT? OKAY... YOU SEEM TO BE QUITE THE STAPLER ENTHUSIAST.

ANO, PLEASE, THIS IS NOT THE RIGHT TIME.

TRUST ME.

YOUR TURN.

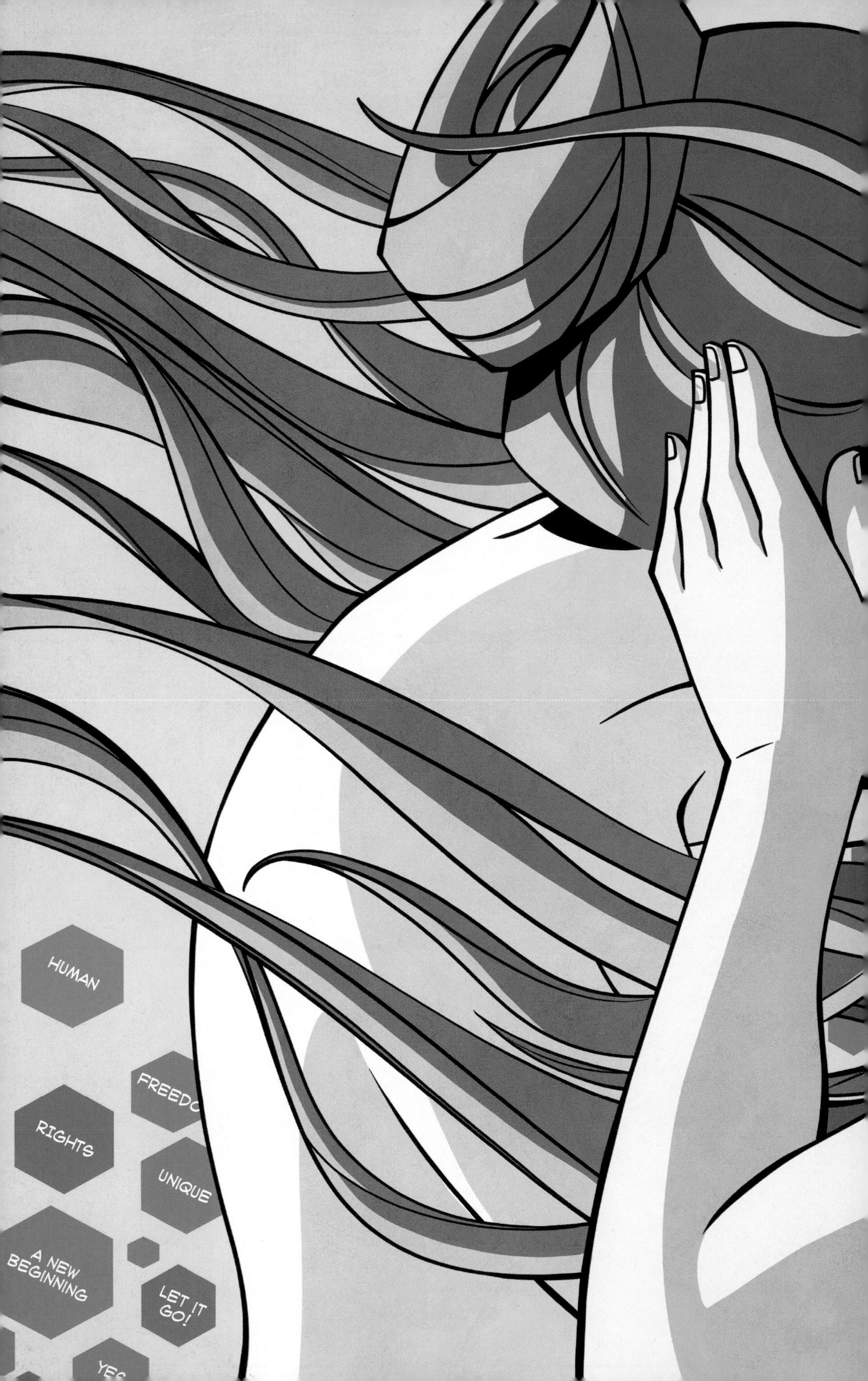
HUMAN
FREEDO
RIGHTS
UNIQUE
A NEW BEGINNING
LET IT GO!

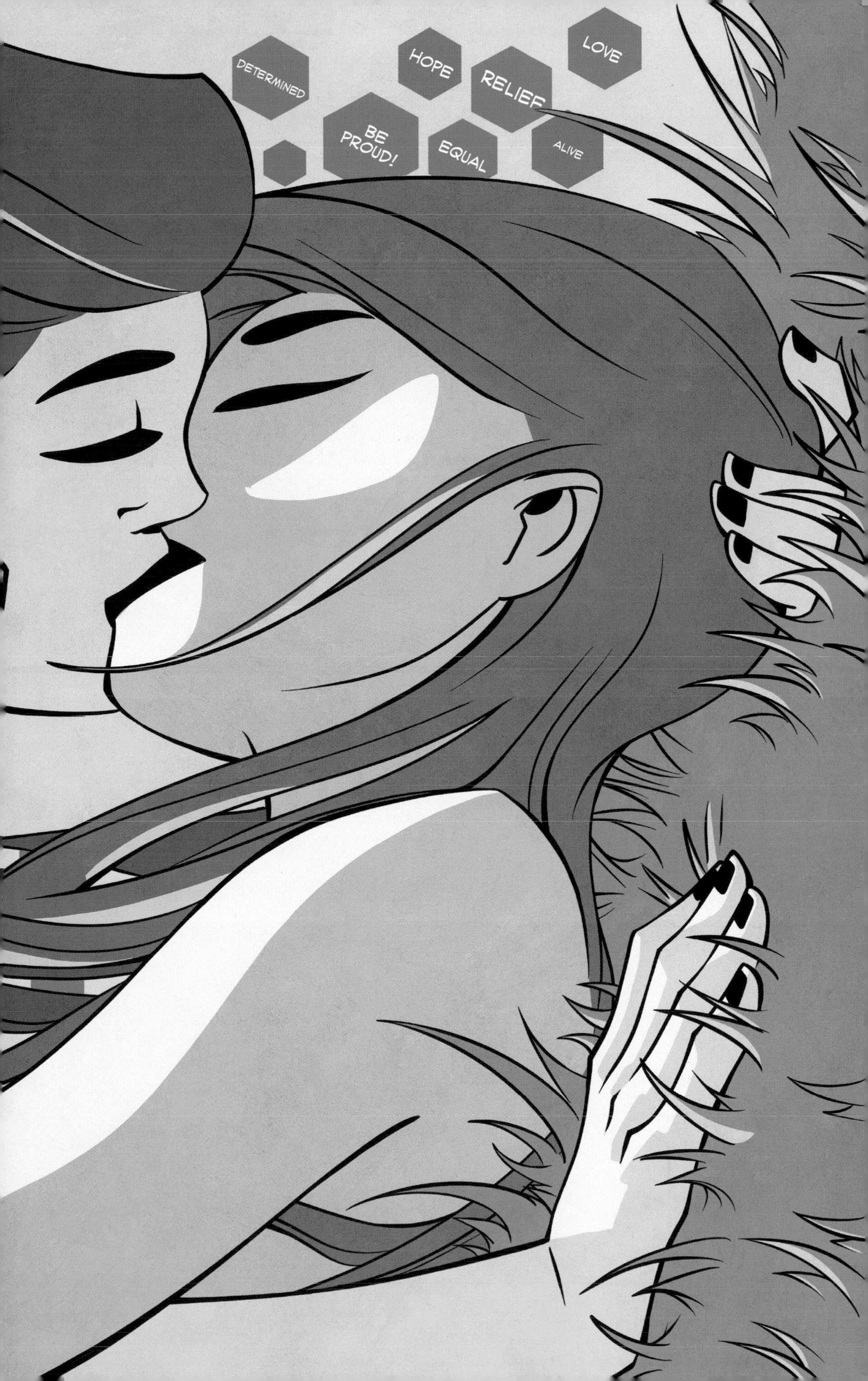
DETERMINED
HOPE
LOVE
RELIEF
BE PROUD!
EQUAL
ALIVE

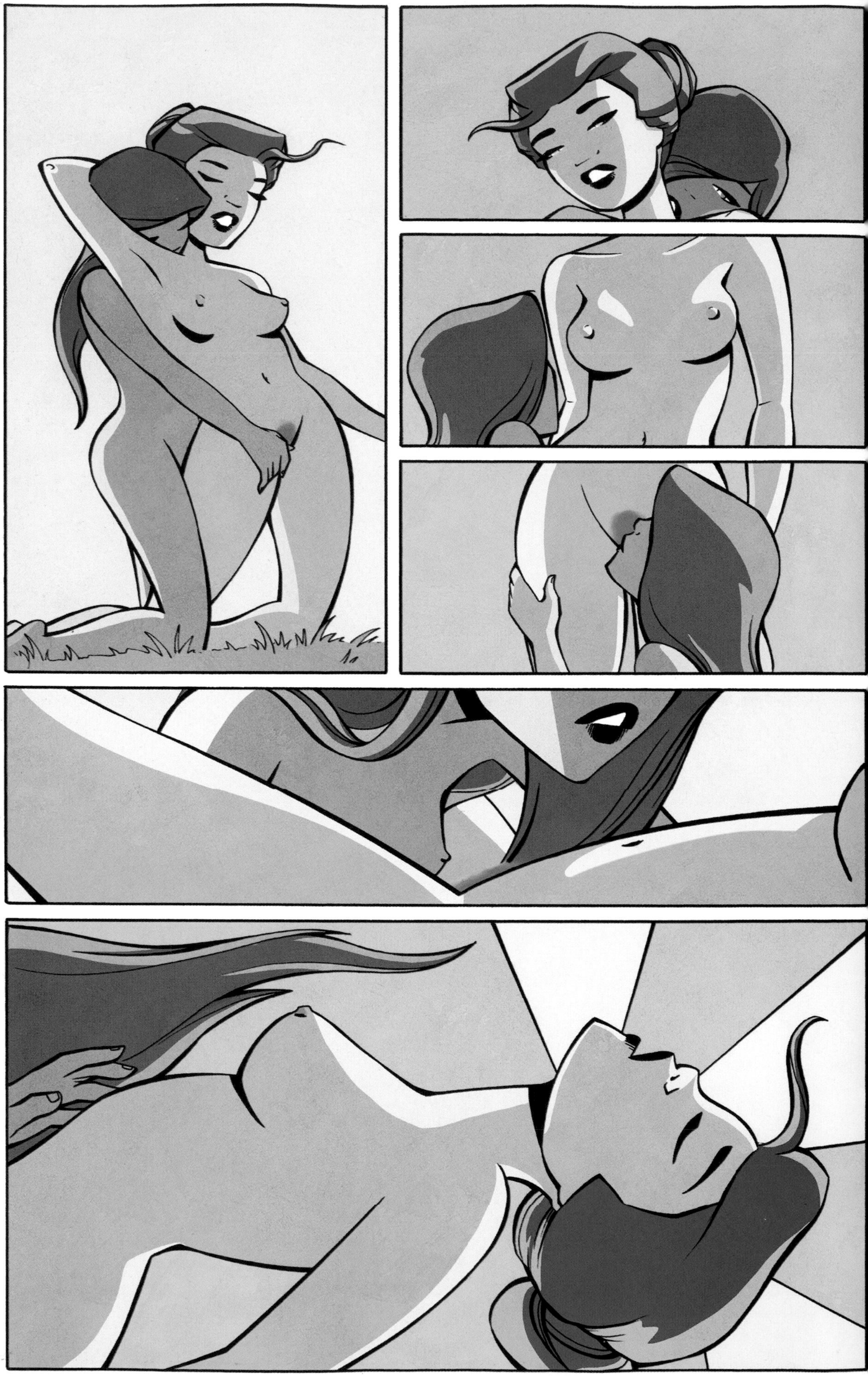

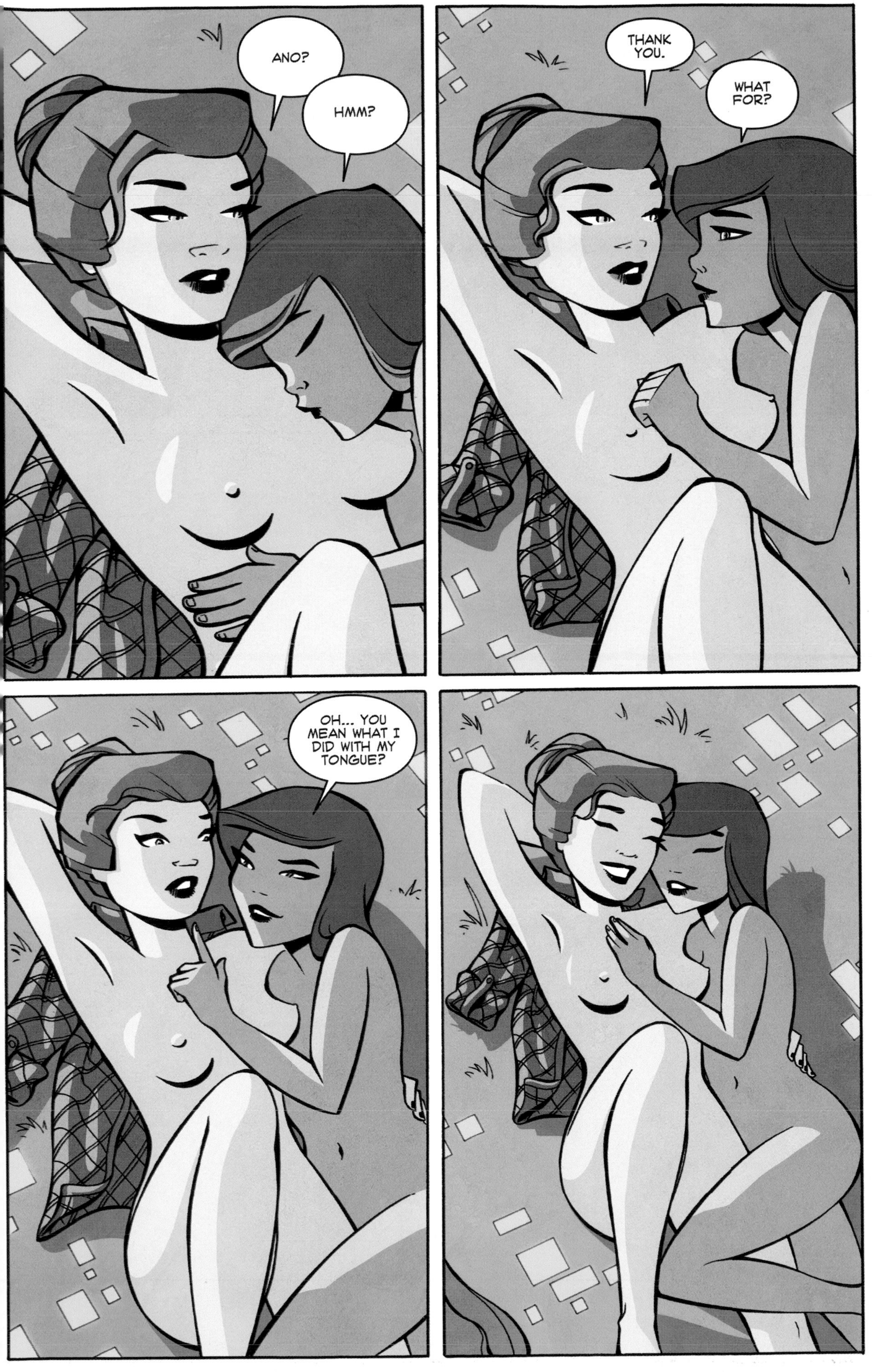
ANO?
HMM?
THANK YOU.
WHAT FOR?
OH... YOU MEAN WHAT I DID WITH MY TONGUE?

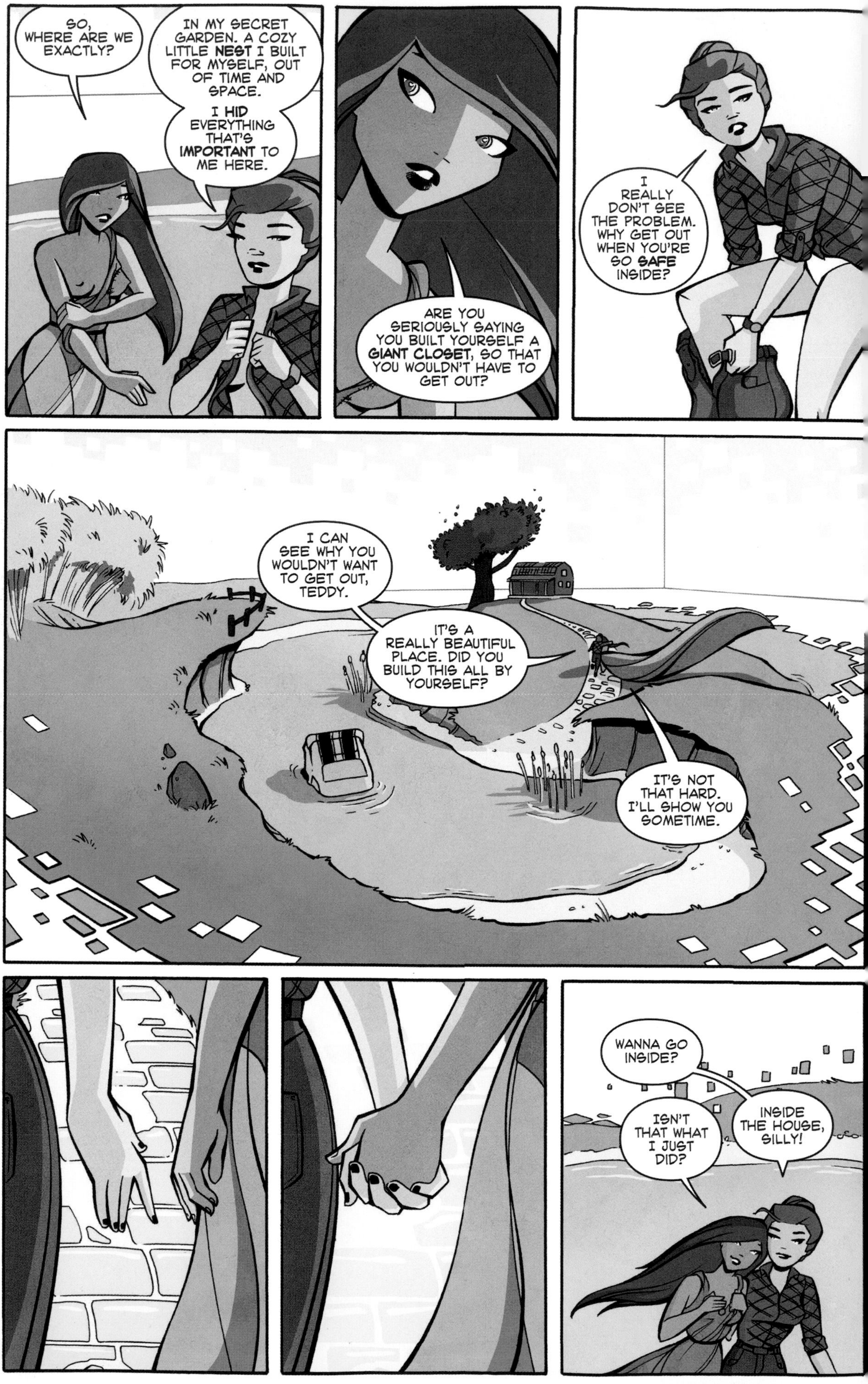

SO, WHERE ARE WE EXACTLY?
IN MY SECRET GARDEN. A COZY LITTLE NEST I BUILT FOR MYSELF, OUT OF TIME AND SPACE.
I HID EVERYTHING THAT'S IMPORTANT TO ME HERE.
ARE YOU SERIOUSLY SAYING YOU BUILT YOURSELF A GIANT CLOSET, SO THAT YOU WOULDN'T HAVE TO GET OUT?
I REALLY DON'T SEE THE PROBLEM. WHY GET OUT WHEN YOU'RE SO SAFE INSIDE?
I CAN SEE WHY YOU WOULDN'T WANT TO GET OUT, TEDDY.
IT'S A REALLY BEAUTIFUL PLACE. DID YOU BUILD THIS ALL BY YOURSELF?
IT'S NOT THAT HARD. I'LL SHOW YOU SOMETIME.
WANNA GO INSIDE?
ISN'T THAT WHAT I JUST DID?
INSIDE THE HOUSE, SILLY!

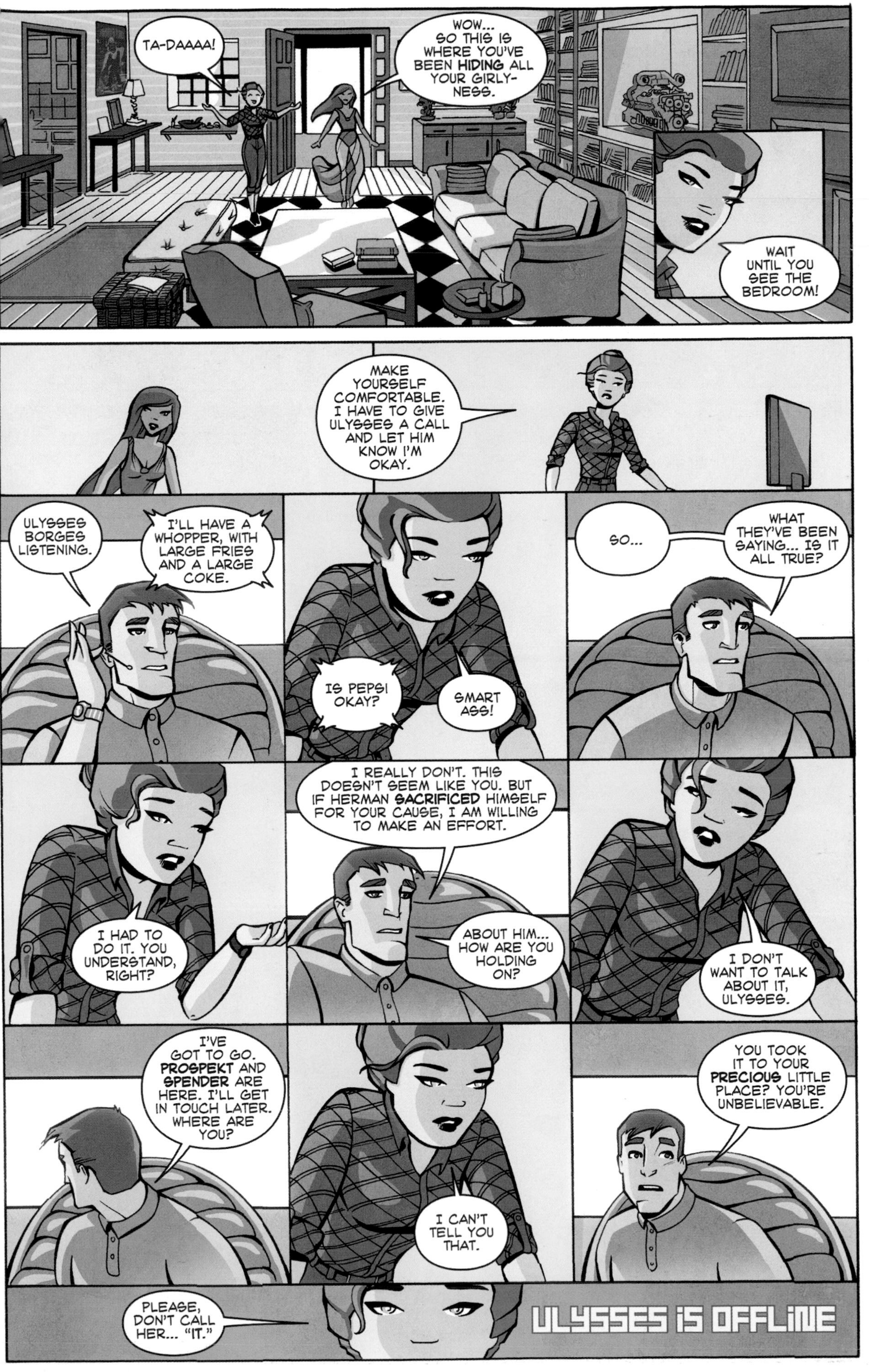
TA-DAAAA!
WOW... SO THIS IS WHERE YOU'VE BEEN HIDING ALL YOUR GIRLY-NESS.
WAIT UNTIL YOU SEE THE BEDROOM!
MAKE YOURSELF COMFORTABLE. I HAVE TO GIVE ULYSSES A CALL AND LET HIM KNOW I'M OKAY.
ULYSSES BORGES LISTENING.
I'LL HAVE A WHOPPER, WITH LARGE FRIES AND A LARGE COKE.
IS PEPSI OKAY?
SMART ASS!
SO...
WHAT THEY'VE BEEN SAYING... IS IT ALL TRUE?
I HAD TO DO IT. YOU UNDERSTAND, RIGHT?
I REALLY DON'T. THIS DOESN'T SEEM LIKE YOU. BUT IF HERMAN SACRIFICED HIMSELF FOR YOUR CAUSE, I AM WILLING TO MAKE AN EFFORT.
ABOUT HIM... HOW ARE YOU HOLDING ON?
I DON'T WANT TO TALK ABOUT IT, ULYSSES.
I'VE GOT TO GO. PROSPEKT AND SPENDER ARE HERE. I'LL GET IN TOUCH LATER. WHERE ARE YOU?
I CAN'T TELL YOU THAT.
YOU TOOK IT TO YOUR PRECIOUS LITTLE PLACE? YOU'RE UNBELIEVABLE.
PLEASE, DON'T CALL HER... "IT."
ULYSSES IS OFFLINE

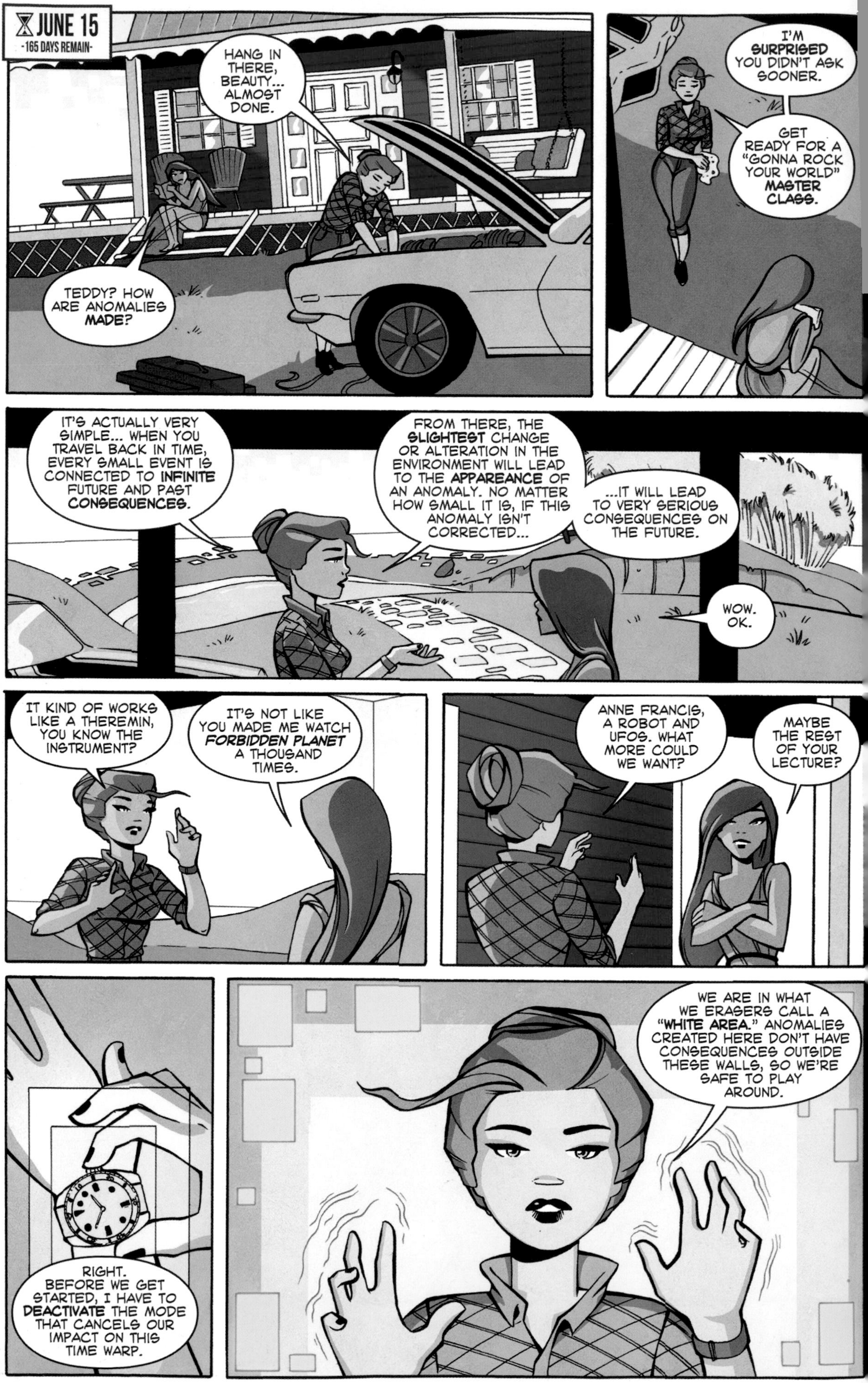
JUNE 15
-165 DAYS REMAIN-
HANG IN THERE, BEAUTY... ALMOST DONE.
TEDDY? HOW ARE ANOMALIES MADE?
I'M SURPRISED YOU DIDN'T ASK SOONER.
GET READY FOR A "GONNA ROCK YOUR WORLD" MASTER CLASS.
IT'S ACTUALLY VERY SIMPLE... WHEN YOU TRAVEL BACK IN TIME, EVERY SMALL EVENT IS CONNECTED TO INFINITE FUTURE AND PAST CONSEQUENCES.
FROM THERE, THE SLIGHTEST CHANGE OR ALTERATION IN THE ENVIRONMENT WILL LEAD TO THE APPAREANCE OF AN ANOMALY. NO MATTER HOW SMALL IT IS, IF THIS ANOMALY ISN'T CORRECTED...
...IT WILL LEAD TO VERY SERIOUS CONSEQUENCES ON THE FUTURE.
WOW. OK.
IT KIND OF WORKS LIKE A THEREMIN, YOU KNOW THE INSTRUMENT?
IT'S NOT LIKE YOU MADE ME WATCH FORBIDDEN PLANET A THOUSAND TIMES.
ANNE FRANCIS, A ROBOT AND UFOS. WHAT MORE COULD WE WANT?
MAYBE THE REST OF YOUR LECTURE?
RIGHT. BEFORE WE GET STARTED, I HAVE TO DEACTIVATE THE MODE THAT CANCELS OUR IMPACT ON THIS TIME WARP.
WE ARE IN WHAT WE ERASERS CALL A "WHITE AREA." ANOMALIES CREATED HERE DON'T HAVE CONSEQUENCES OUTSIDE THESE WALLS, SO WE'RE SAFE TO PLAY AROUND.

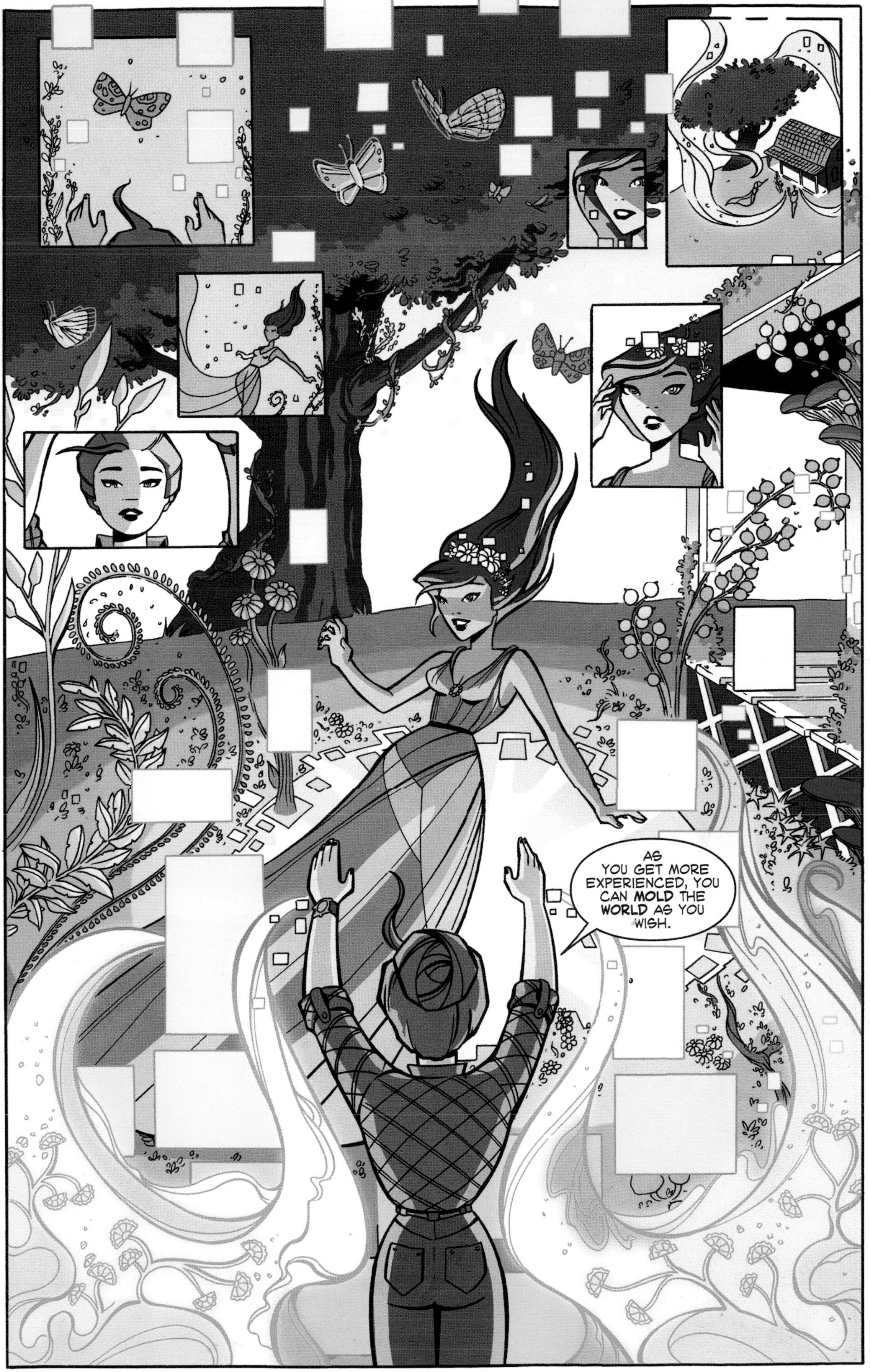
AS YOU GET MORE EXPERIENCED, YOU CAN MOLD THE WORLD AS YOU WISH.

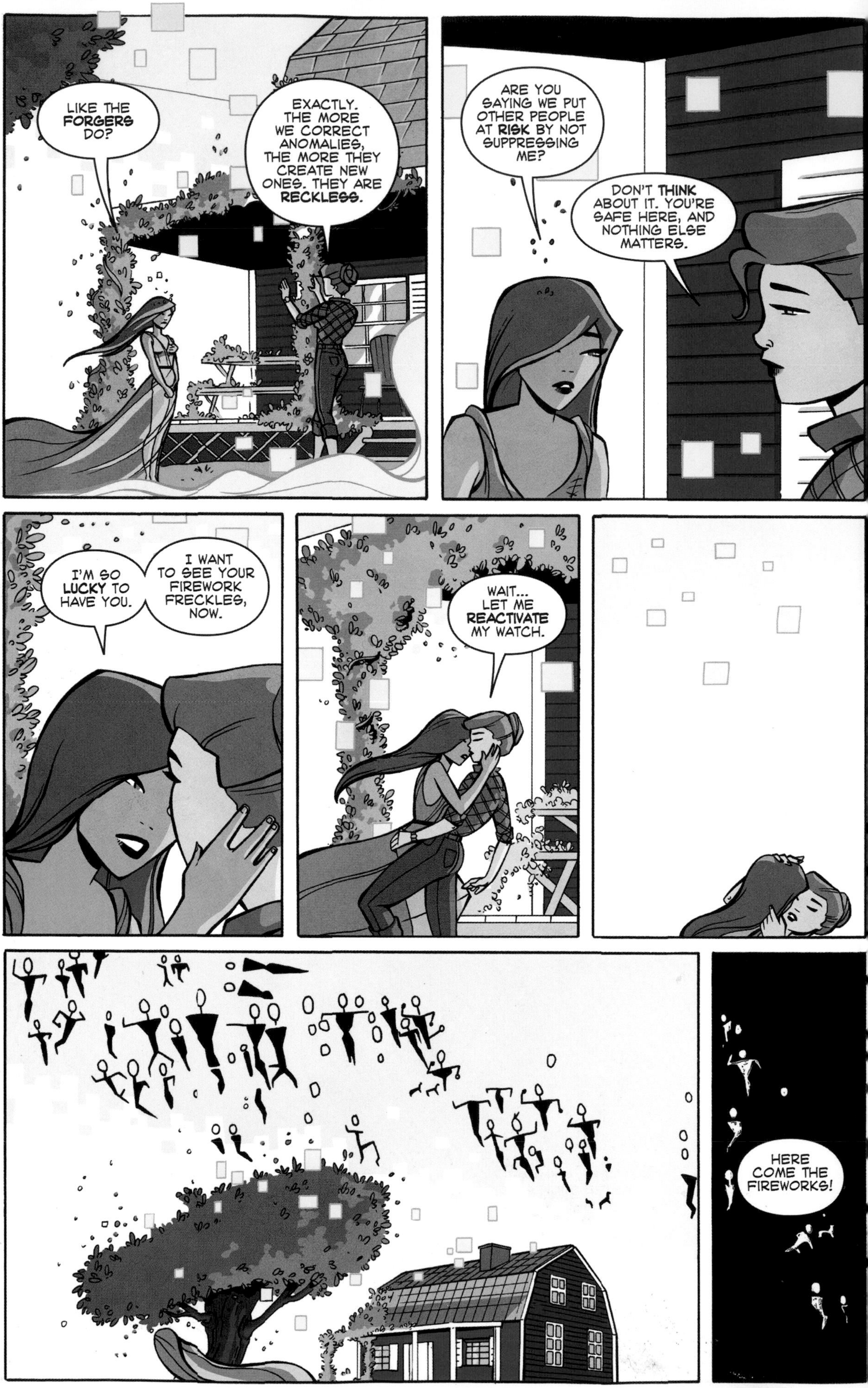
LIKE THE FORGERS DO?
EXACTLY. THE MORE WE CORRECT ANOMALIES, THE MORE THEY CREATE NEW ONES. THEY ARE RECKLESS.
ARE YOU SAYING WE PUT OTHER PEOPLE AT RISK BY NOT SUPPRESSING ME?
DON'T THINK ABOUT IT. YOU'RE SAFE HERE, AND NOTHING ELSE MATTERS.
I'M SO LUCKY TO HAVE YOU.
I WANT TO SEE YOUR FIREWORK FRECKLES, NOW.
WAIT... LET ME REACTIVATE MY WATCH.
HERE COME THE FIREWORKS!

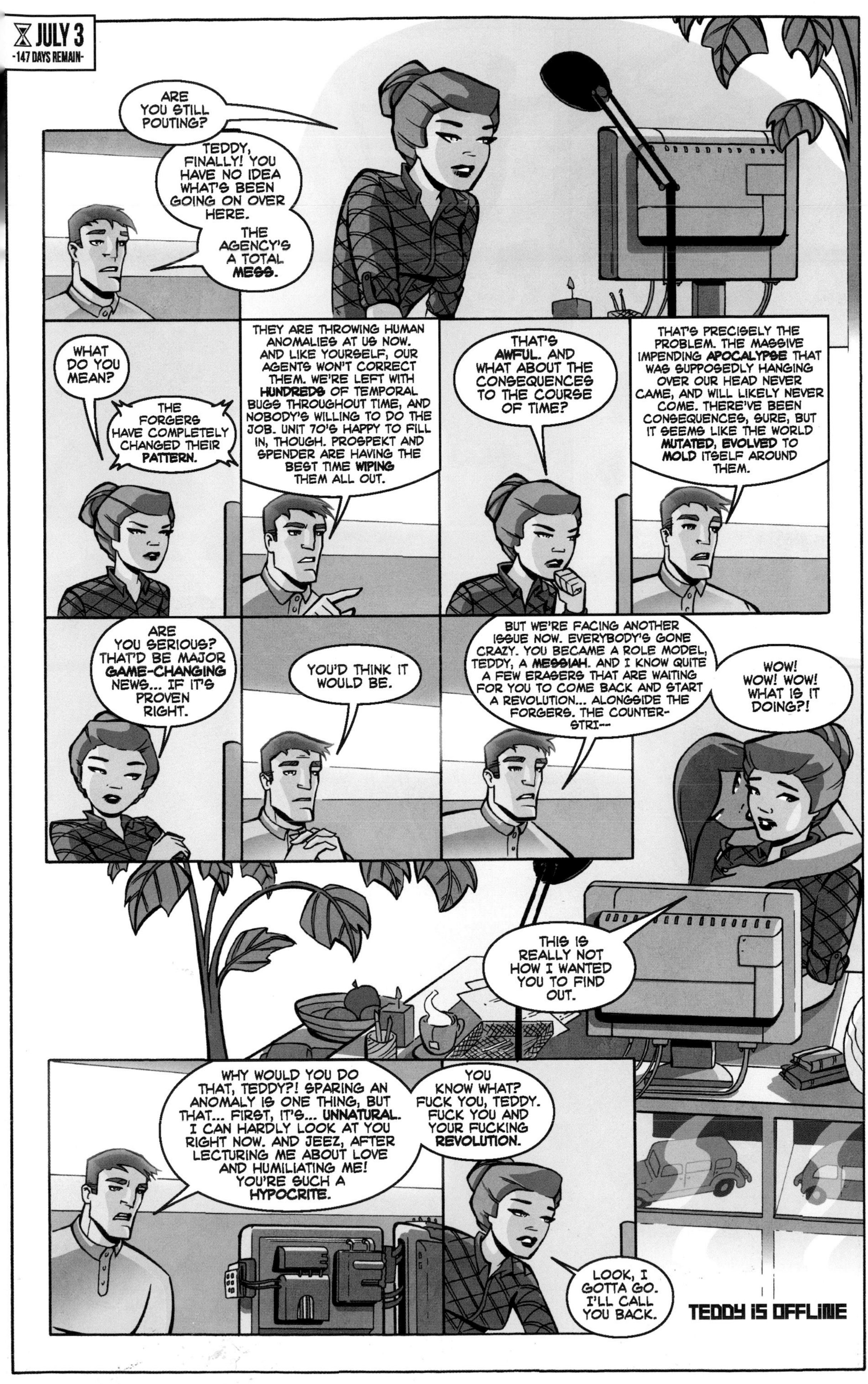
JULY 3
-147 DAYS REMAIN-
ARE YOU STILL POUTING?
TEDDY, FINALLY! YOU HAVE NO IDEA WHAT'S BEEN GOING ON OVER HERE.
THE AGENCY'S A TOTAL MESS.
WHAT DO YOU MEAN?
THE FORGERS HAVE COMPLETELY CHANGED THEIR PATTERN.
THEY ARE THROWING HUMAN ANOMALIES AT US NOW. AND LIKE YOURSELF, OUR AGENTS WON'T CORRECT THEM. WE'RE LEFT WITH HUNDREDS OF TEMPORAL BUGS THROUGHOUT TIME, AND NOBODY'S WILLING TO DO THE JOB. UNIT 70'S HAPPY TO FILL IN, THOUGH. PROSPEKT AND SPENDER ARE HAVING THE BEST TIME WIPING THEM ALL OUT.
THAT'S AWFUL. AND WHAT ABOUT THE CONSEQUENCES TO THE COURSE OF TIME?
THAT'S PRECISELY THE PROBLEM. THE MASSIVE IMPENDING APOCALYPSE THAT WAS SUPPOSEDLY HANGING OVER OUR HEAD NEVER CAME, AND WILL LIKELY NEVER COME. THERE'VE BEEN CONSEQUENCES, SURE, BUT IT SEEMS LIKE THE WORLD MUTATED, EVOLVED TO MOLD ITSELF AROUND THEM.
ARE YOU SERIOUS? THAT'D BE MAJOR GAME-CHANGING NEWS... IF IT'S PROVEN RIGHT.
YOU'D THINK IT WOULD BE.
BUT WE'RE FACING ANOTHER ISSUE NOW. EVERYBODY'S GONE CRAZY. YOU BECAME A ROLE MODEL, TEDDY, A MESSIAH. AND I KNOW QUITE A FEW ERASERS THAT ARE WAITING FOR YOU TO COME BACK AND START A REVOLUTION... ALONGSIDE THE FORGERS. THE COUNTER-STRI--
WOW! WOW! WOW! WHAT IS IT DOING?!
THIS IS REALLY NOT HOW I WANTED YOU TO FIND OUT.
WHY WOULD YOU DO THAT, TEDDY?! SPARING AN ANOMALY IS ONE THING, BUT THAT... FIRST, IT'S... UNNATURAL. I CAN HARDLY LOOK AT YOU RIGHT NOW. AND JEEZ, AFTER LECTURING ME ABOUT LOVE AND HUMILIATING ME! YOU'RE SUCH A HYPOCRITE.
YOU KNOW WHAT? FUCK YOU, TEDDY. FUCK YOU AND YOUR FUCKING REVOLUTION.
LOOK, I GOTTA GO. I'LL CALL YOU BACK.
TEDDY IS OFFLINE

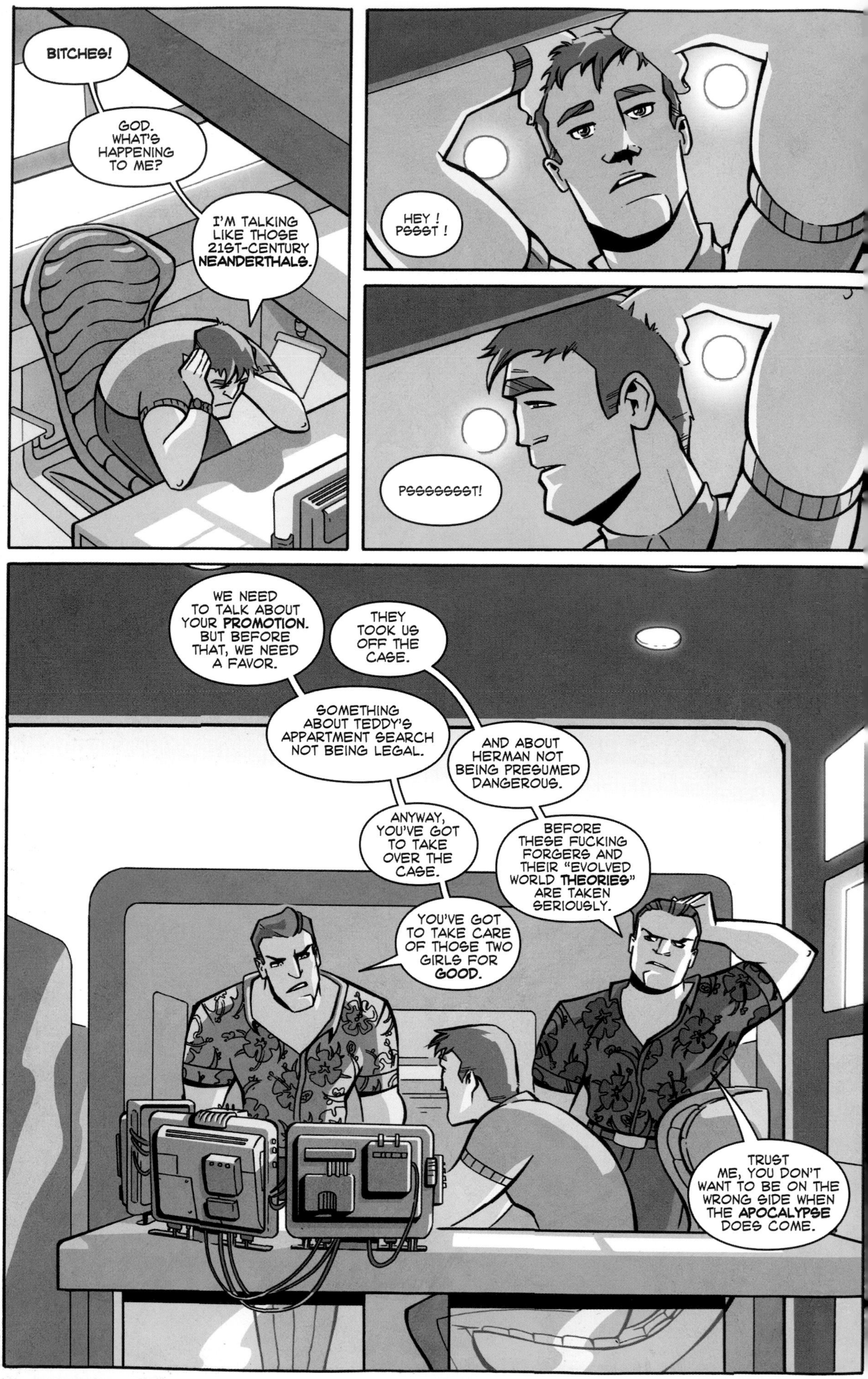
BITCHES!
GOD. WHAT'S HAPPENING TO ME?
I'M TALKING LIKE THOSE 21ST-CENTURY **NEANDERTHALS.**
HEY ! PSSST !
PSSSSSSST!
WE NEED TO TALK ABOUT YOUR **PROMOTION**. BUT BEFORE THAT, WE NEED A FAVOR.
THEY TOOK US OFF THE CASE.
SOMETHING ABOUT TEDDY'S APPARTMENT SEARCH NOT BEING LEGAL.
AND ABOUT HERMAN NOT BEING PRESUMED DANGEROUS.
ANYWAY, YOU'VE GOT TO TAKE OVER THE CASE.
BEFORE THESE FUCKING FORGERS AND THEIR "EVOLVED WORLD **THEORIES**" ARE TAKEN SERIOUSLY.
YOU'VE GOT TO TAKE CARE OF THOSE TWO GIRLS FOR **GOOD.**
TRUST ME, YOU DON'T WANT TO BE ON THE WRONG SIDE WHEN THE **APOCALYPSE** DOES COME.

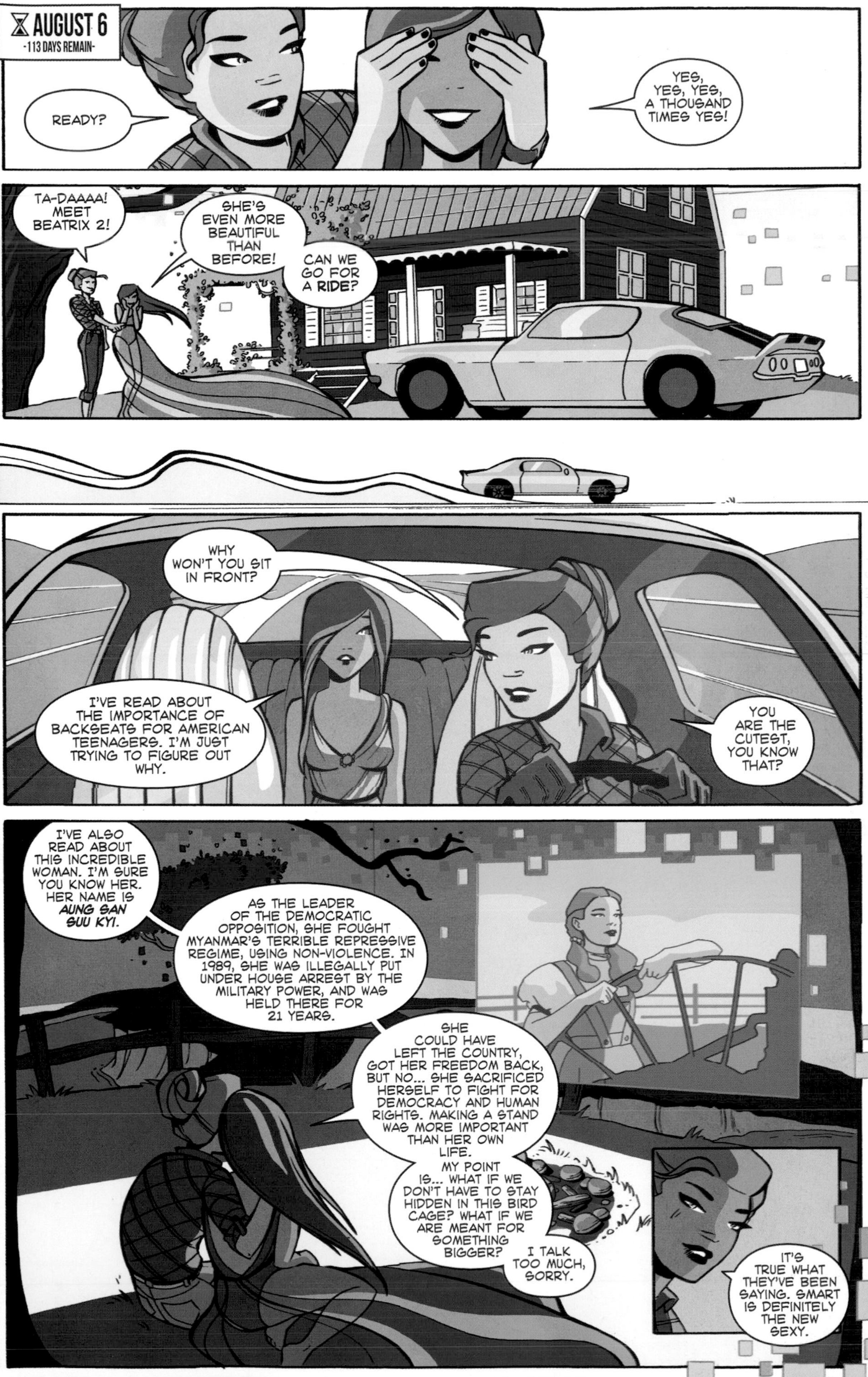
AUGUST 6
-113 DAYS REMAIN-
READY?
YES, YES, YES, A THOUSAND TIMES YES!
TA-DAAAA! MEET BEATRIX 2!
SHE'S EVEN MORE BEAUTIFUL THAN BEFORE!
CAN WE GO FOR A **RIDE**?
WHY WON'T YOU SIT IN FRONT?
I'VE READ ABOUT THE IMPORTANCE OF BACKSEATS FOR AMERICAN TEENAGERS. I'M JUST TRYING TO FIGURE OUT WHY.
YOU ARE THE CUTEST, YOU KNOW THAT?
I'VE ALSO READ ABOUT THIS INCREDIBLE WOMAN. I'M SURE YOU KNOW HER. HER NAME IS ***AUNG SAN SUU KYI***.
AS THE LEADER OF THE DEMOCRATIC OPPOSITION, SHE FOUGHT MYANMAR'S TERRIBLE REPRESSIVE REGIME, USING NON-VIOLENCE. IN 1989, SHE WAS ILLEGALLY PUT UNDER HOUSE ARREST BY THE MILITARY POWER, AND WAS HELD THERE FOR 21 YEARS.
SHE COULD HAVE LEFT THE COUNTRY, GOT HER FREEDOM BACK, BUT NO... SHE SACRIFICED HERSELF TO FIGHT FOR DEMOCRACY AND HUMAN RIGHTS. MAKING A STAND WAS MORE IMPORTANT THAN HER OWN LIFE.
MY POINT IS... WHAT IF WE DON'T HAVE TO STAY HIDDEN IN THIS BIRD CAGE? WHAT IF WE ARE MEANT FOR SOMETHING BIGGER?
I TALK TOO MUCH, SORRY.
IT'S TRUE WHAT THEY'VE BEEN SAYING. SMART IS DEFINITELY THE NEW SEXY.

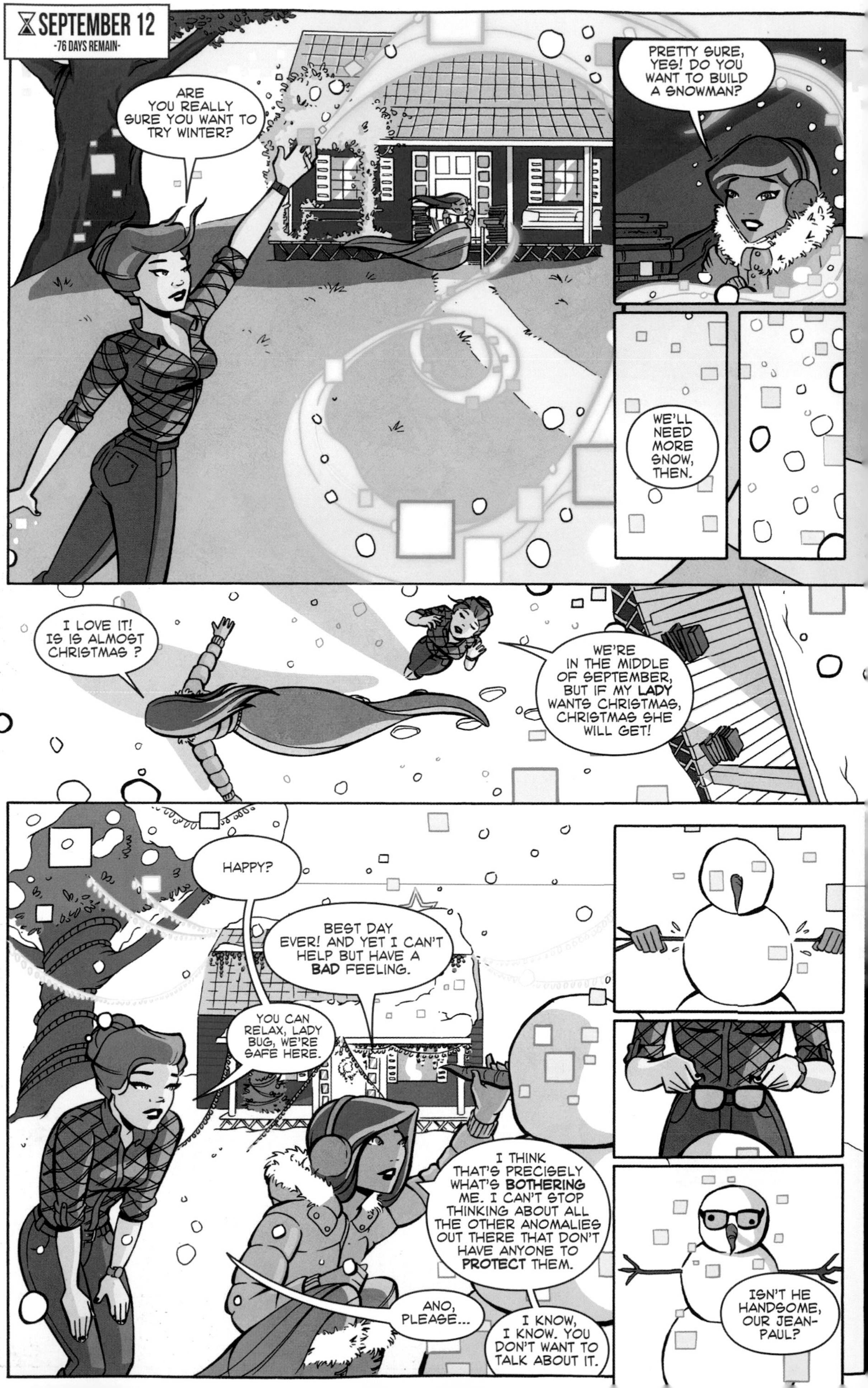
SEPTEMBER 12
-76 DAYS REMAIN-
ARE YOU REALLY SURE YOU WANT TO TRY WINTER?
PRETTY SURE, YES! DO YOU WANT TO BUILD A SNOWMAN?
WE'LL NEED MORE SNOW, THEN.
I LOVE IT! IS IS ALMOST CHRISTMAS ?
WE'RE IN THE MIDDLE OF SEPTEMBER, BUT IF MY LADY WANTS CHRISTMAS, CHRISTMAS SHE WILL GET!
HAPPY?
BEST DAY EVER! AND YET I CAN'T HELP BUT HAVE A BAD FEELING.
YOU CAN RELAX, LADY BUG, WE'RE SAFE HERE.
I THINK THAT'S PRECISELY WHAT'S BOTHERING ME. I CAN'T STOP THINKING ABOUT ALL THE OTHER ANOMALIES OUT THERE THAT DON'T HAVE ANYONE TO PROTECT THEM.
ANO, PLEASE...
I KNOW, I KNOW. YOU DON'T WANT TO TALK ABOUT IT.
ISN'T HE HANDSOME, OUR JEAN-PAUL?

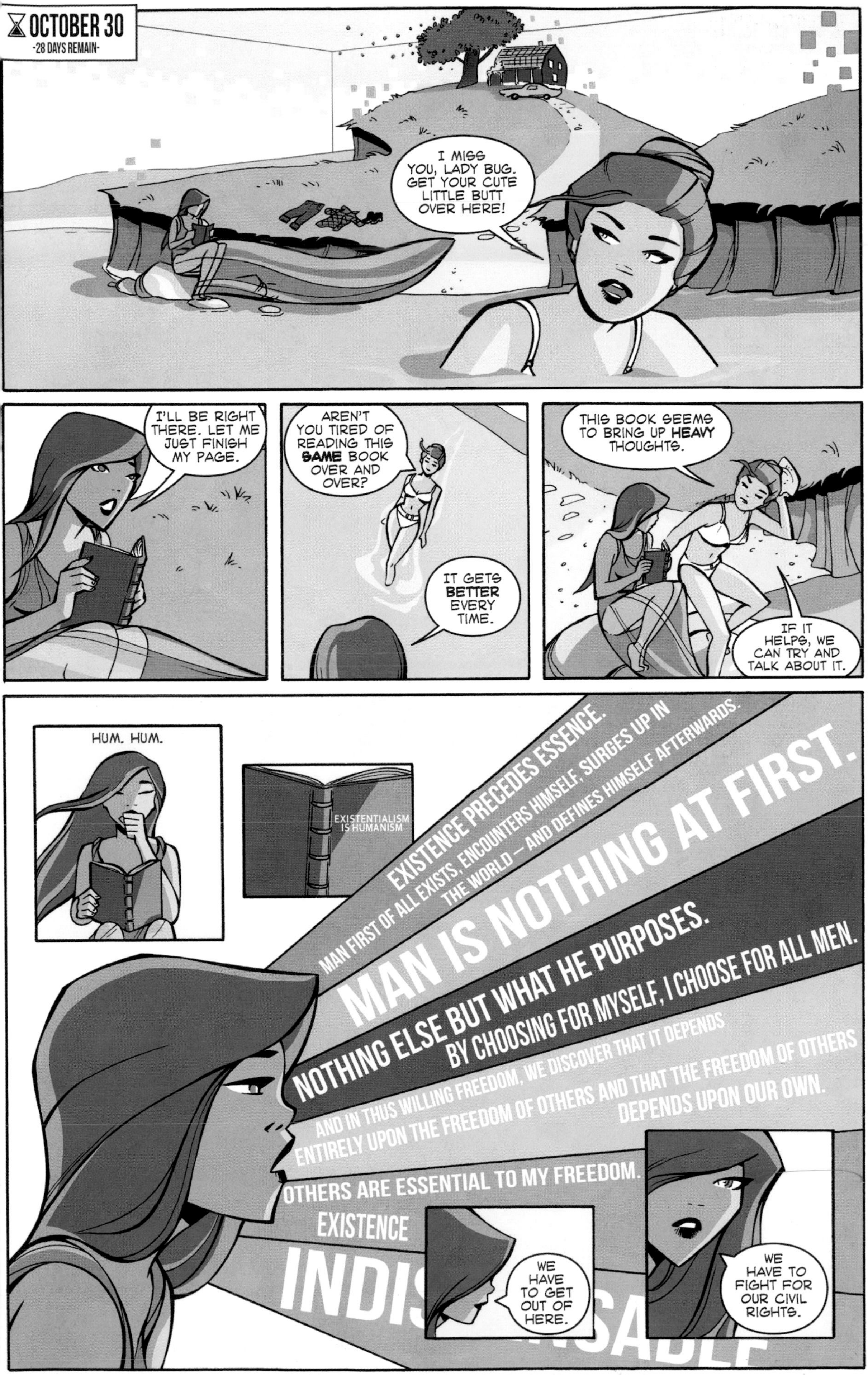
OCTOBER 30
-28 DAYS REMAIN-
I MISS YOU, LADY BUG. GET YOUR CUTE LITTLE BUTT OVER HERE!
I'LL BE RIGHT THERE. LET ME JUST FINISH MY PAGE.
AREN'T YOU TIRED OF READING THIS SAME BOOK OVER AND OVER?
IT GETS BETTER EVERY TIME.
THIS BOOK SEEMS TO BRING UP HEAVY THOUGHTS.
IF IT HELPS, WE CAN TRY AND TALK ABOUT IT.
HUM. HUM.
EXISTENTIALISM IS HUMANISM
EXISTENCE PRECEDES ESSENCE.
MAN FIRST OF ALL EXISTS, ENCOUNTERS HIMSELF, SURGES UP IN THE WORLD – AND DEFINES HIMSELF AFTERWARDS.
MAN IS NOTHING AT FIRST.
NOTHING ELSE BUT WHAT HE PURPOSES.
BY CHOOSING FOR MYSELF, I CHOOSE FOR ALL MEN.
AND IN THUS WILLING FREEDOM, WE DISCOVER THAT IT DEPENDS ENTIRELY UPON THE FREEDOM OF OTHERS AND THAT THE FREEDOM OF OTHERS DEPENDS UPON OUR OWN.
OTHERS ARE ESSENTIAL TO MY FREEDOM.
EXISTENCE
WE HAVE TO GET OUT OF HERE.
WE HAVE TO FIGHT FOR OUR CIVIL RIGHTS.

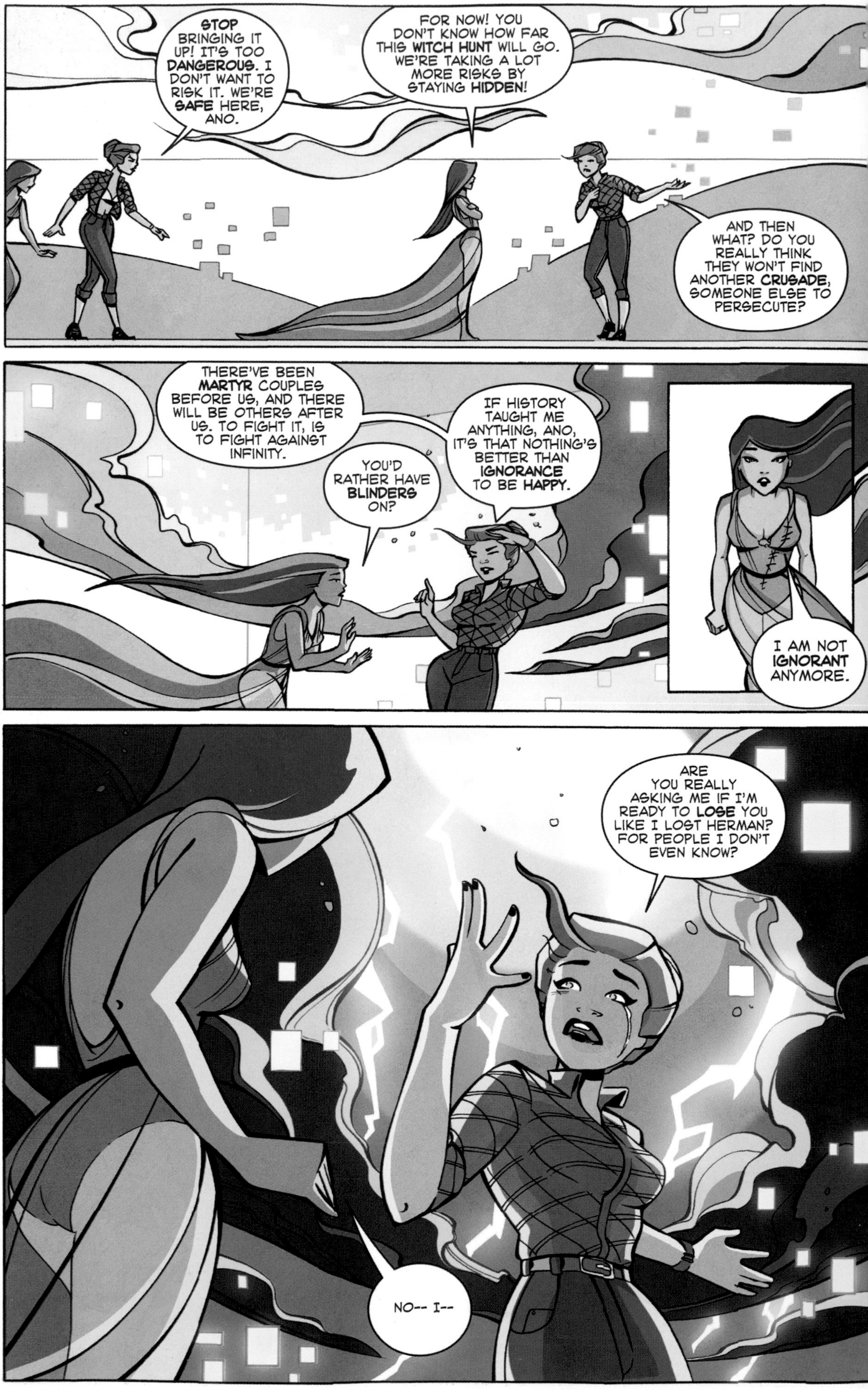
STOP BRINGING IT UP! IT'S TOO DANGEROUS. I DON'T WANT TO RISK IT. WE'RE SAFE HERE, ANO.
FOR NOW! YOU DON'T KNOW HOW FAR THIS WITCH HUNT WILL GO. WE'RE TAKING A LOT MORE RISKS BY STAYING HIDDEN!
AND THEN WHAT? DO YOU REALLY THINK THEY WON'T FIND ANOTHER CRUSADE, SOMEONE ELSE TO PERSECUTE?
THERE'VE BEEN MARTYR COUPLES BEFORE US, AND THERE WILL BE OTHERS AFTER US. TO FIGHT IT, IS TO FIGHT AGAINST INFINITY.
IF HISTORY TAUGHT ME ANYTHING, ANO, IT'S THAT NOTHING'S BETTER THAN IGNORANCE TO BE HAPPY.
YOU'D RATHER HAVE BLINDERS ON?
I AM NOT IGNORANT ANYMORE.
ARE YOU REALLY ASKING ME IF I'M READY TO LOSE YOU LIKE I LOST HERMAN? FOR PEOPLE I DON'T EVEN KNOW?
NO-- I--

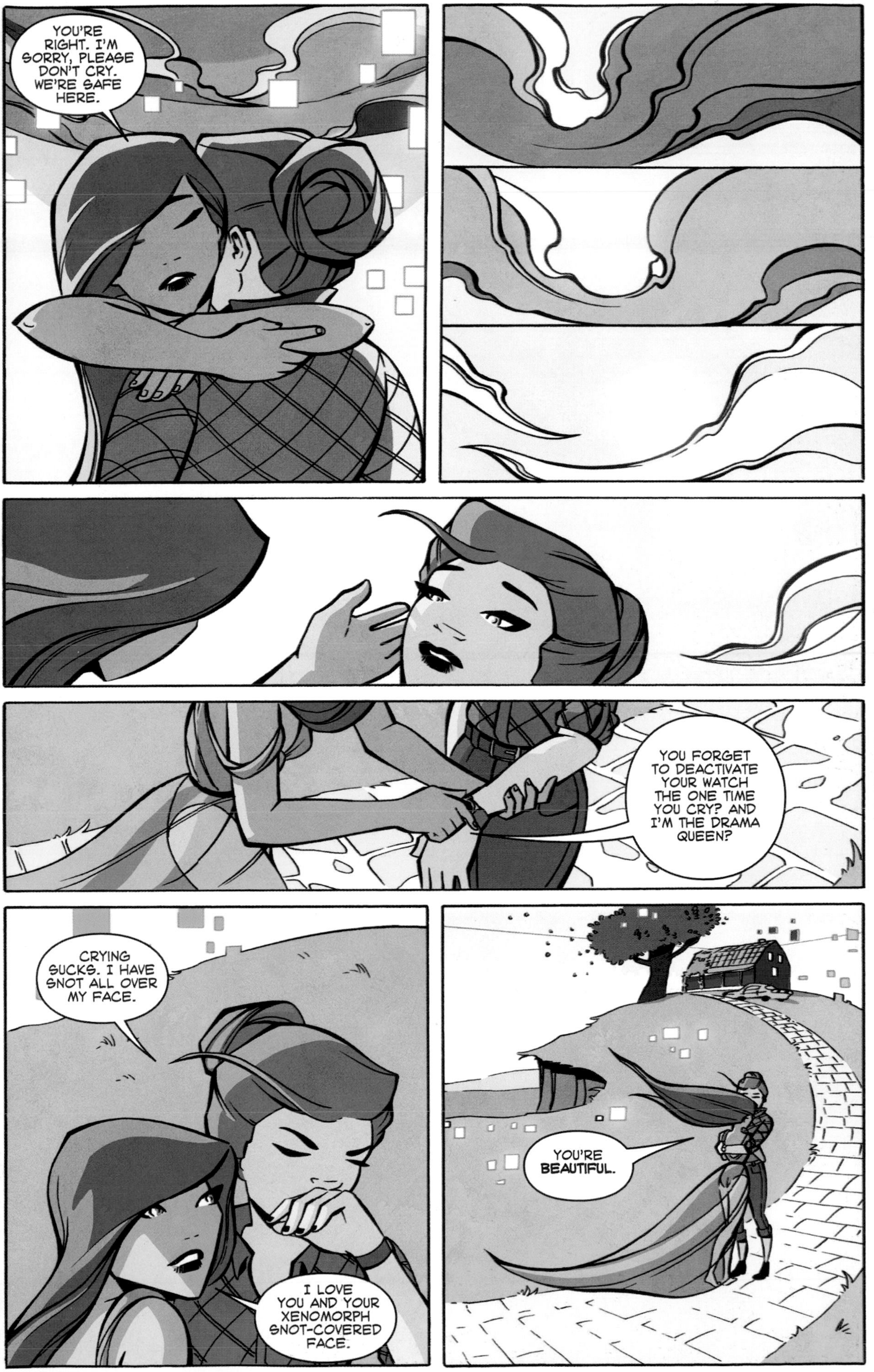
YOU'RE RIGHT. I'M SORRY, PLEASE DON'T CRY. WE'RE SAFE HERE.
YOU FORGET TO DEACTIVATE YOUR WATCH THE ONE TIME YOU CRY? AND I'M THE DRAMA QUEEN?
CRYING SUCKS. I HAVE SNOT ALL OVER MY FACE.
I LOVE YOU AND YOUR XENOMORPH SNOT-COVERED FACE.
YOU'RE BEAUTIFUL.

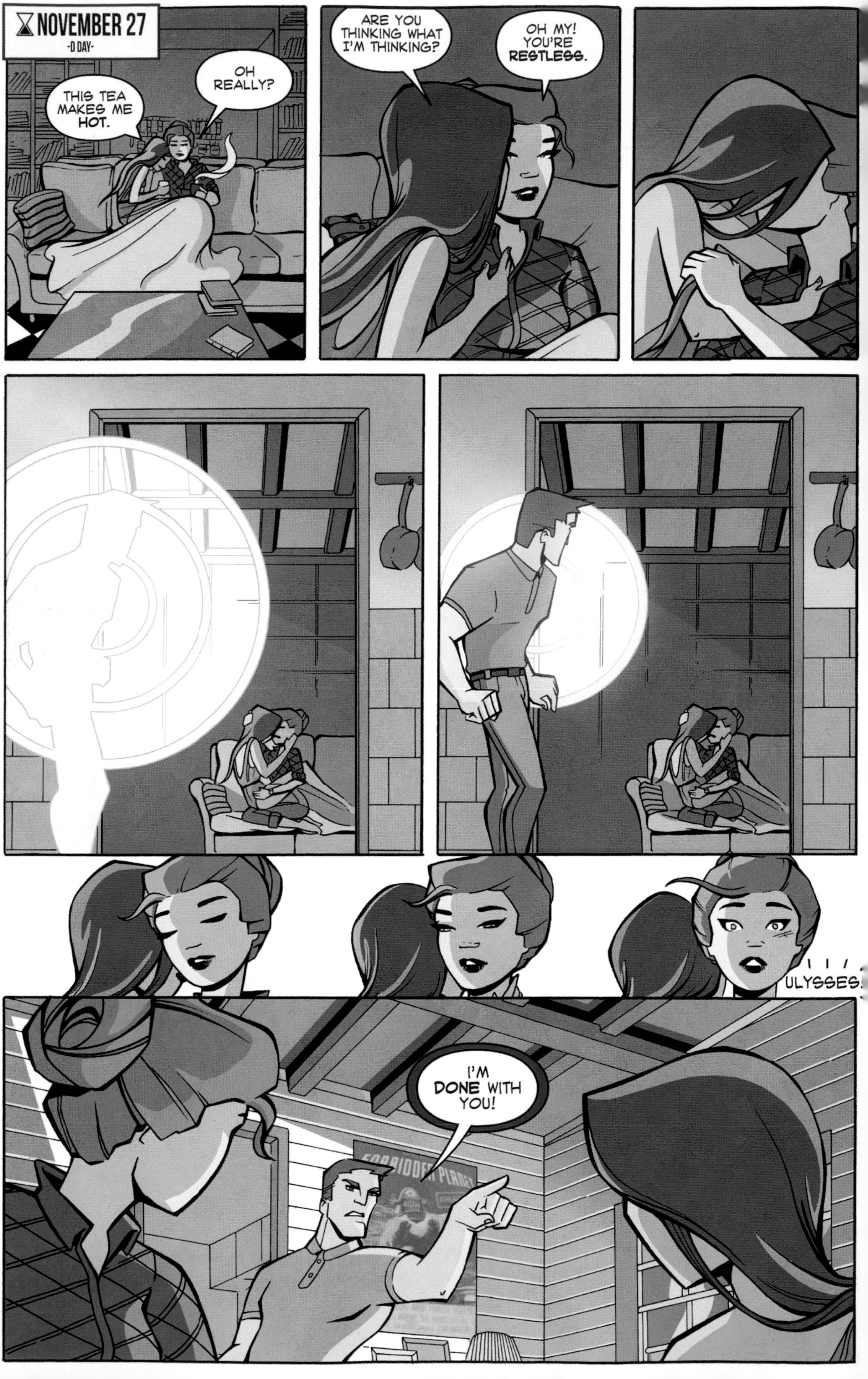
NOVEMBER 27
-D DAY-
THIS TEA MAKES ME HOT.
OH REALLY?
ARE YOU THINKING WHAT I'M THINKING?
OH MY! YOU'RE RESTLESS.
ULYSSES!
I'M DONE WITH YOU!
FORBIDDEN PLANET

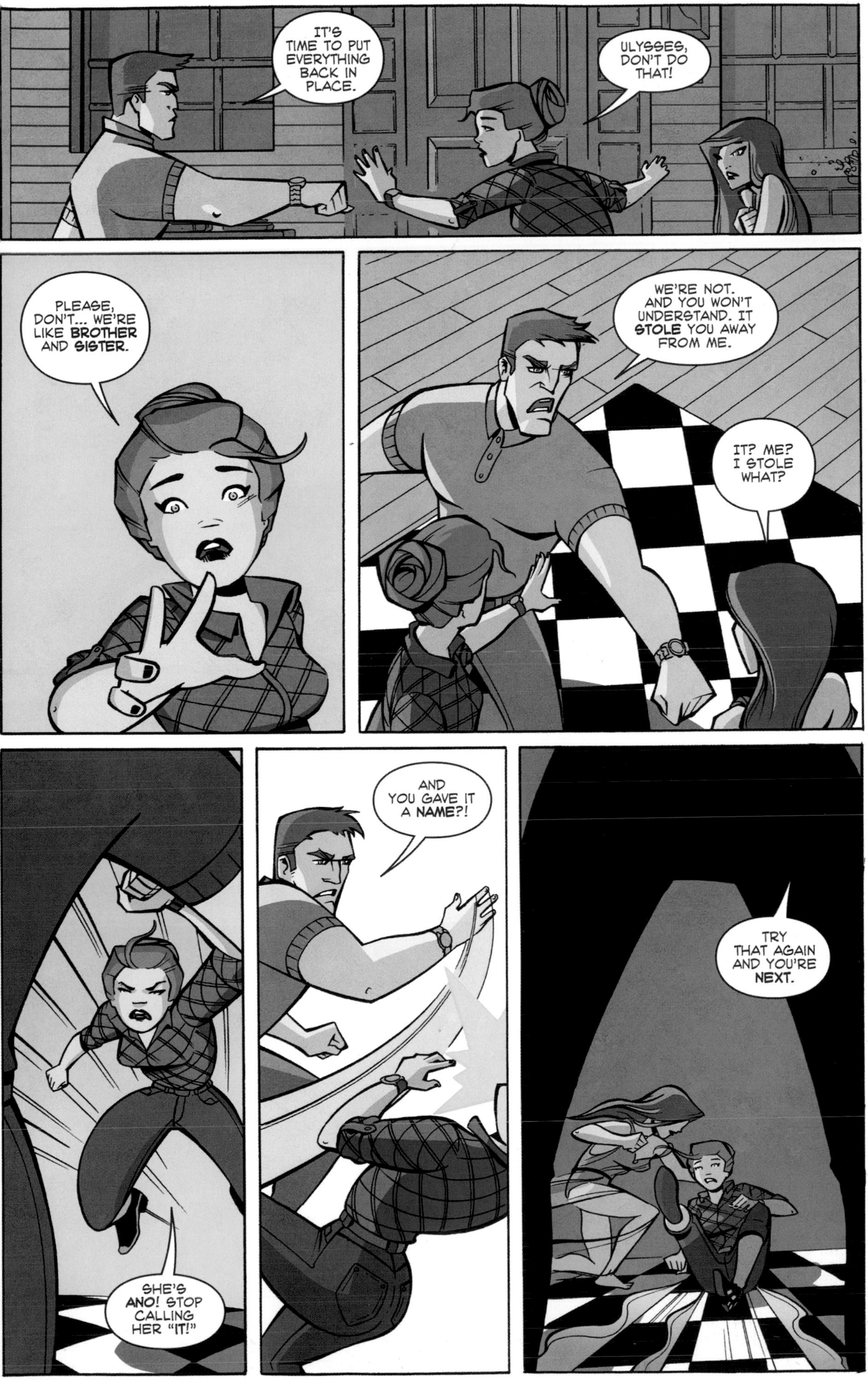
IT'S TIME TO PUT EVERYTHING BACK IN PLACE.
ULYSSES, DON'T DO THAT!
PLEASE, DON'T... WE'RE LIKE BROTHER AND SISTER.
WE'RE NOT. AND YOU WON'T UNDERSTAND. IT STOLE YOU AWAY FROM ME.
IT? ME? I STOLE WHAT?
SHE'S ANO! STOP CALLING HER "IT!"
AND YOU GAVE IT A NAME?!
TRY THAT AGAIN AND YOU'RE NEXT.

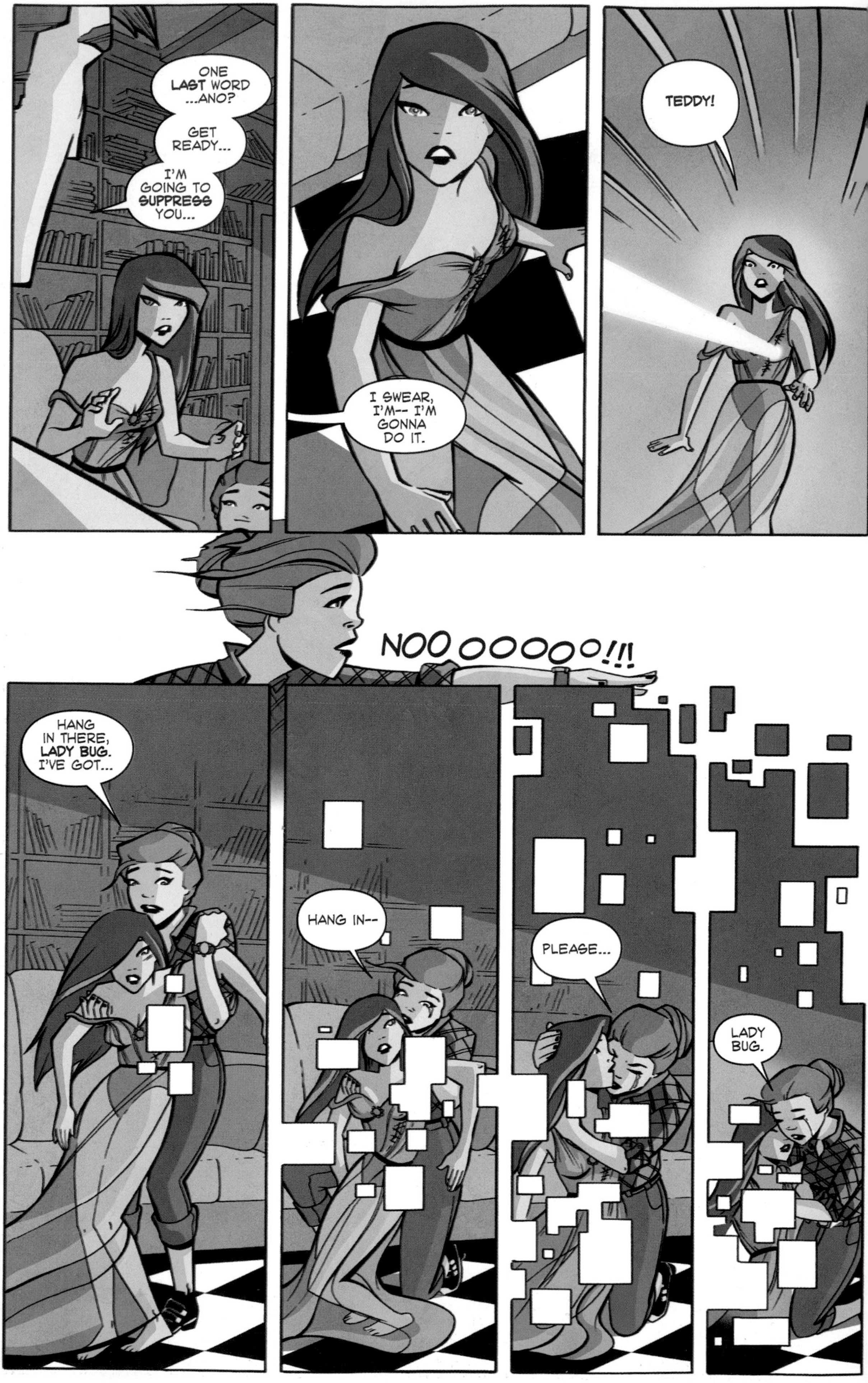
ONE LAST WORD ...ANO?
GET READY...
I'M GOING TO SUPPRESS YOU...
I SWEAR, I'M-- I'M GONNA DO IT.
TEDDY!
NOO OOOOOO!!!
HANG IN THERE, LADY BUG. I'VE GOT...
HANG IN--
PLEASE...
LADY BUG.

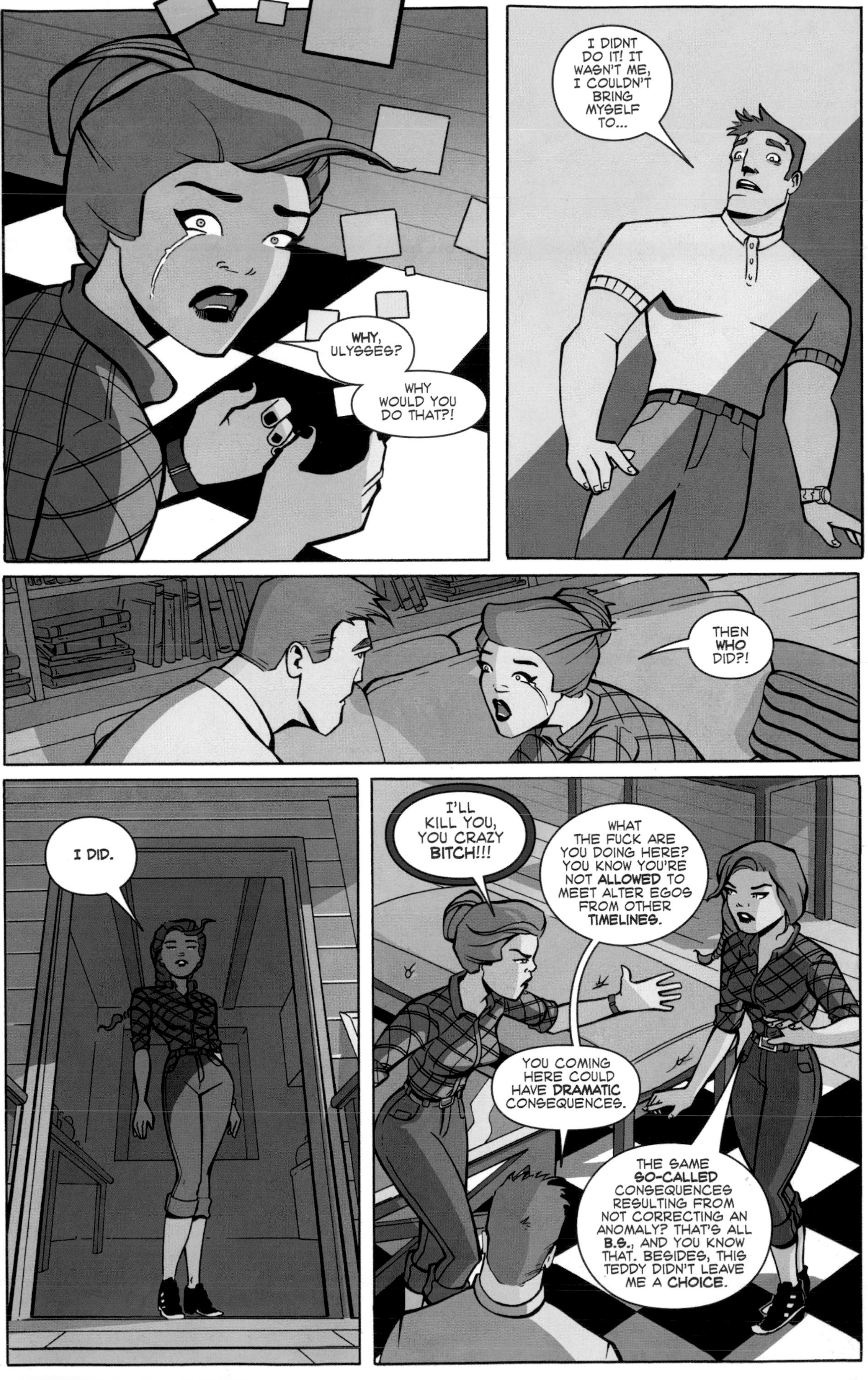
WHY, ULYSSES?
WHY WOULD YOU DO THAT?!
I DIDNT DO IT! IT WASN'T ME, I COULDN'T BRING MYSELF TO...
THEN WHO DID?!
I DID.
I'LL KILL YOU, YOU CRAZY BITCH!!!
WHAT THE FUCK ARE YOU DOING HERE? YOU KNOW YOU'RE NOT ALLOWED TO MEET ALTER EGOS FROM OTHER TIMELINES.
YOU COMING HERE COULD HAVE DRAMATIC CONSEQUENCES.
THE SAME SO-CALLED CONSEQUENCES RESULTING FROM NOT CORRECTING AN ANOMALY? THAT'S ALL B.S., AND YOU KNOW THAT. BESIDES, THIS TEDDY DIDN'T LEAVE ME A CHOICE.

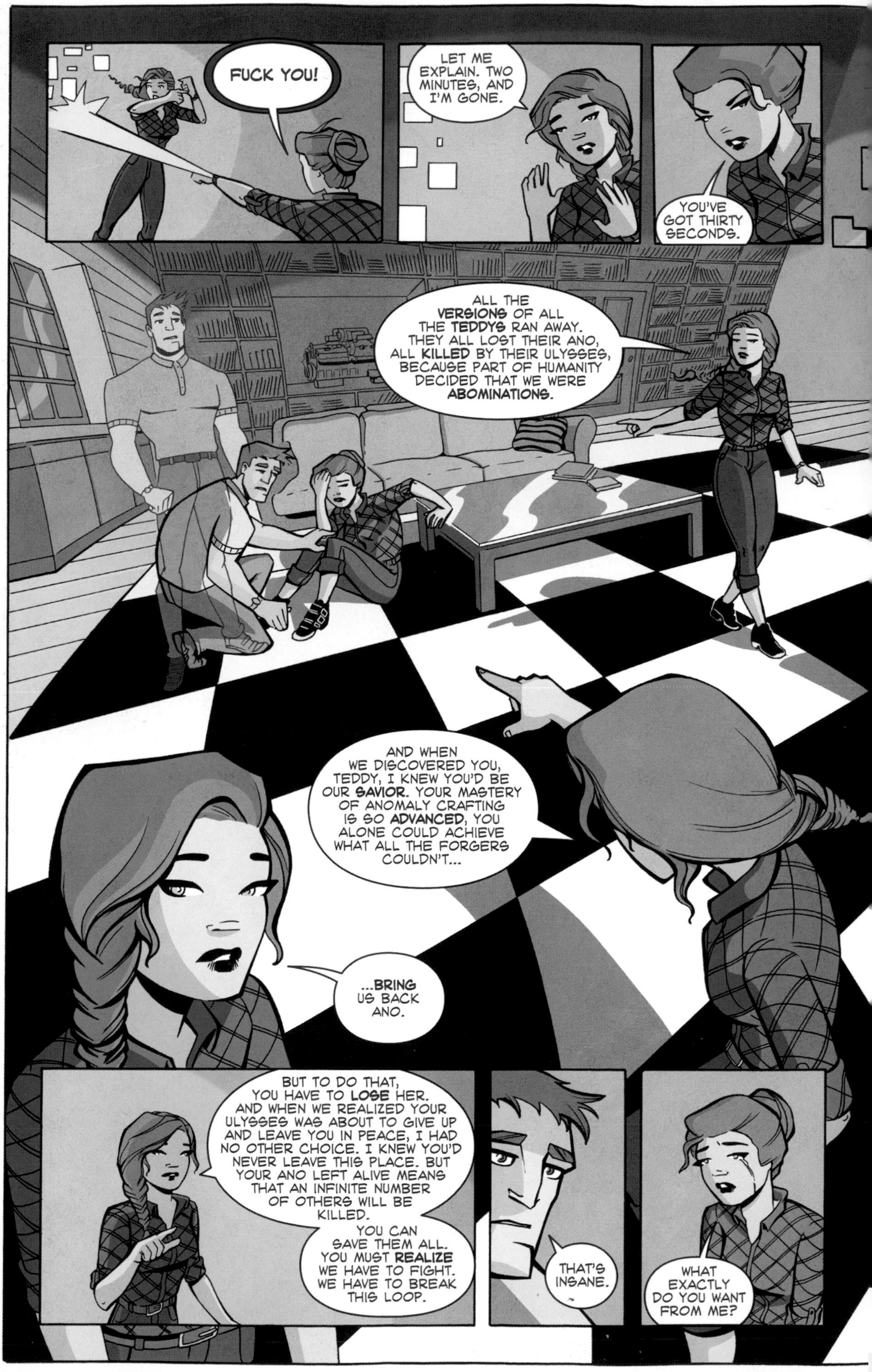
FUCK YOU!
LET ME EXPLAIN. TWO MINUTES, AND I'M GONE.
YOU'VE GOT THIRTY SECONDS.
ALL THE VERSIONS OF ALL THE TEDDYS RAN AWAY. THEY ALL LOST THEIR ANO, ALL KILLED BY THEIR ULYSSES, BECAUSE PART OF HUMANITY DECIDED THAT WE WERE ABOMINATIONS.
AND WHEN WE DISCOVERED YOU, TEDDY, I KNEW YOU'D BE OUR SAVIOR. YOUR MASTERY OF ANOMALY CRAFTING IS SO ADVANCED, YOU ALONE COULD ACHIEVE WHAT ALL THE FORGERS COULDN'T...
...BRING US BACK ANO.
BUT TO DO THAT, YOU HAVE TO LOSE HER. AND WHEN WE REALIZED YOUR ULYSSES WAS ABOUT TO GIVE UP AND LEAVE YOU IN PEACE, I HAD NO OTHER CHOICE. I KNEW YOU'D NEVER LEAVE THIS PLACE. BUT YOUR ANO LEFT ALIVE MEANS THAT AN INFINITE NUMBER OF OTHERS WILL BE KILLED.
YOU CAN SAVE THEM ALL. YOU MUST REALIZE WE HAVE TO FIGHT. WE HAVE TO BREAK THIS LOOP.
THAT'S INSANE.
WHAT EXACTLY DO YOU WANT FROM ME?

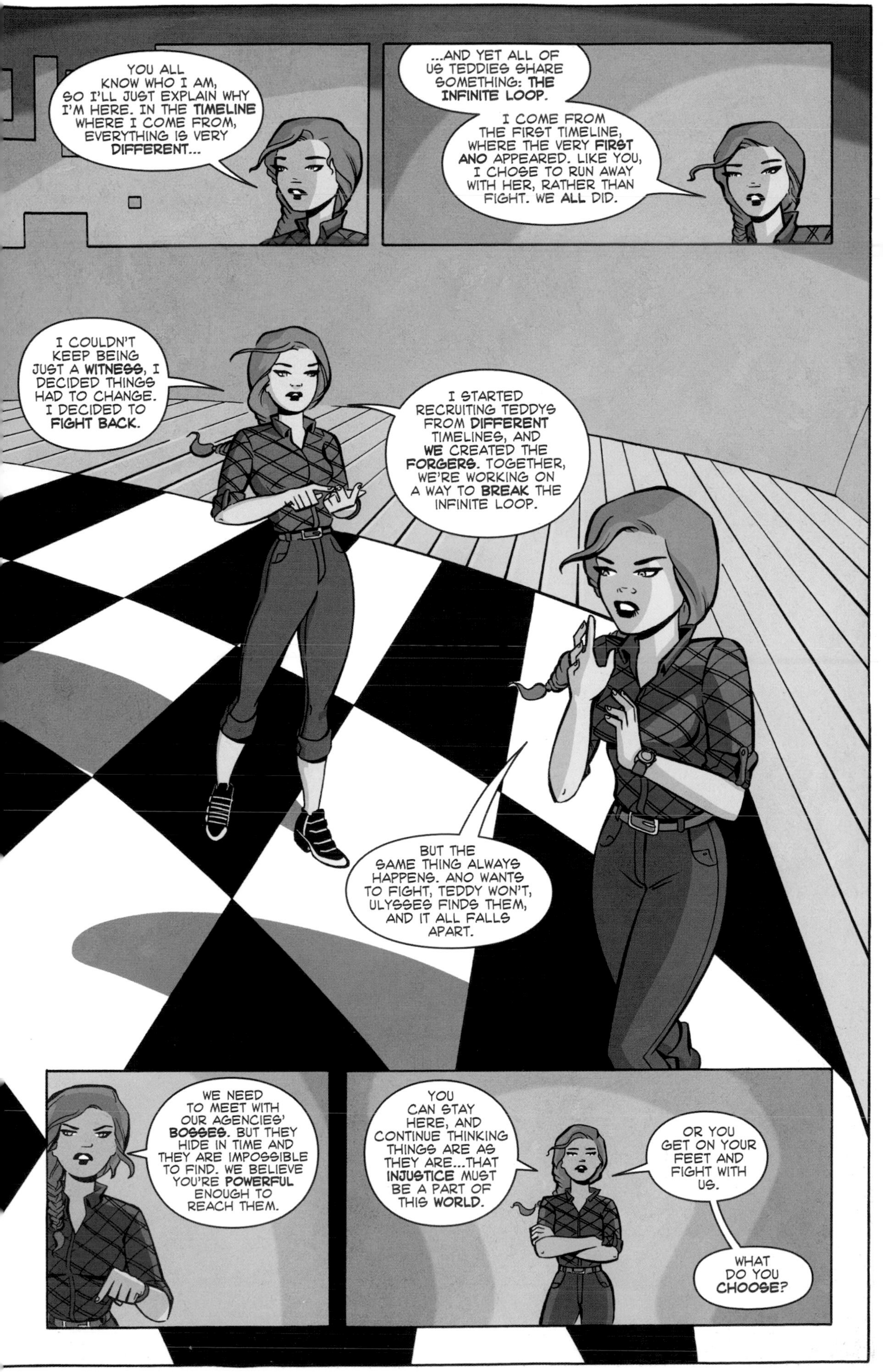
YOU ALL KNOW WHO I AM, SO I'LL JUST EXPLAIN WHY I'M HERE. IN THE **TIMELINE** WHERE I COME FROM, EVERYTHING IS VERY **DIFFERENT**...
...AND YET ALL OF US TEDDIES SHARE SOMETHING: **THE INFINITE LOOP**.
I COME FROM THE FIRST TIMELINE, WHERE THE VERY **FIRST ANO** APPEARED. LIKE YOU, I CHOSE TO RUN AWAY WITH HER, RATHER THAN FIGHT. WE **ALL** DID.
I COULDN'T KEEP BEING JUST A **WITNESS**, I DECIDED THINGS HAD TO CHANGE. I DECIDED TO **FIGHT BACK**.
I STARTED RECRUITING TEDDYS FROM **DIFFERENT** TIMELINES, AND **WE** CREATED THE **FORGERS**. TOGETHER, WE'RE WORKING ON A WAY TO **BREAK** THE INFINITE LOOP.
BUT THE SAME THING ALWAYS HAPPENS. ANO WANTS TO FIGHT, TEDDY WON'T, ULYSSES FINDS THEM, AND IT ALL FALLS APART.
WE NEED TO MEET WITH OUR AGENCIES' **BOSSES**. BUT THEY HIDE IN TIME AND THEY ARE IMPOSSIBLE TO FIND. WE BELIEVE YOU'RE **POWERFUL** ENOUGH TO REACH THEM.
YOU CAN STAY HERE, AND CONTINUE THINKING THINGS ARE AS THEY ARE...THAT **INJUSTICE** MUST BE A PART OF THIS **WORLD**.
OR YOU GET ON YOUR FEET AND FIGHT WITH US.
WHAT DO YOU **CHOOSE?**

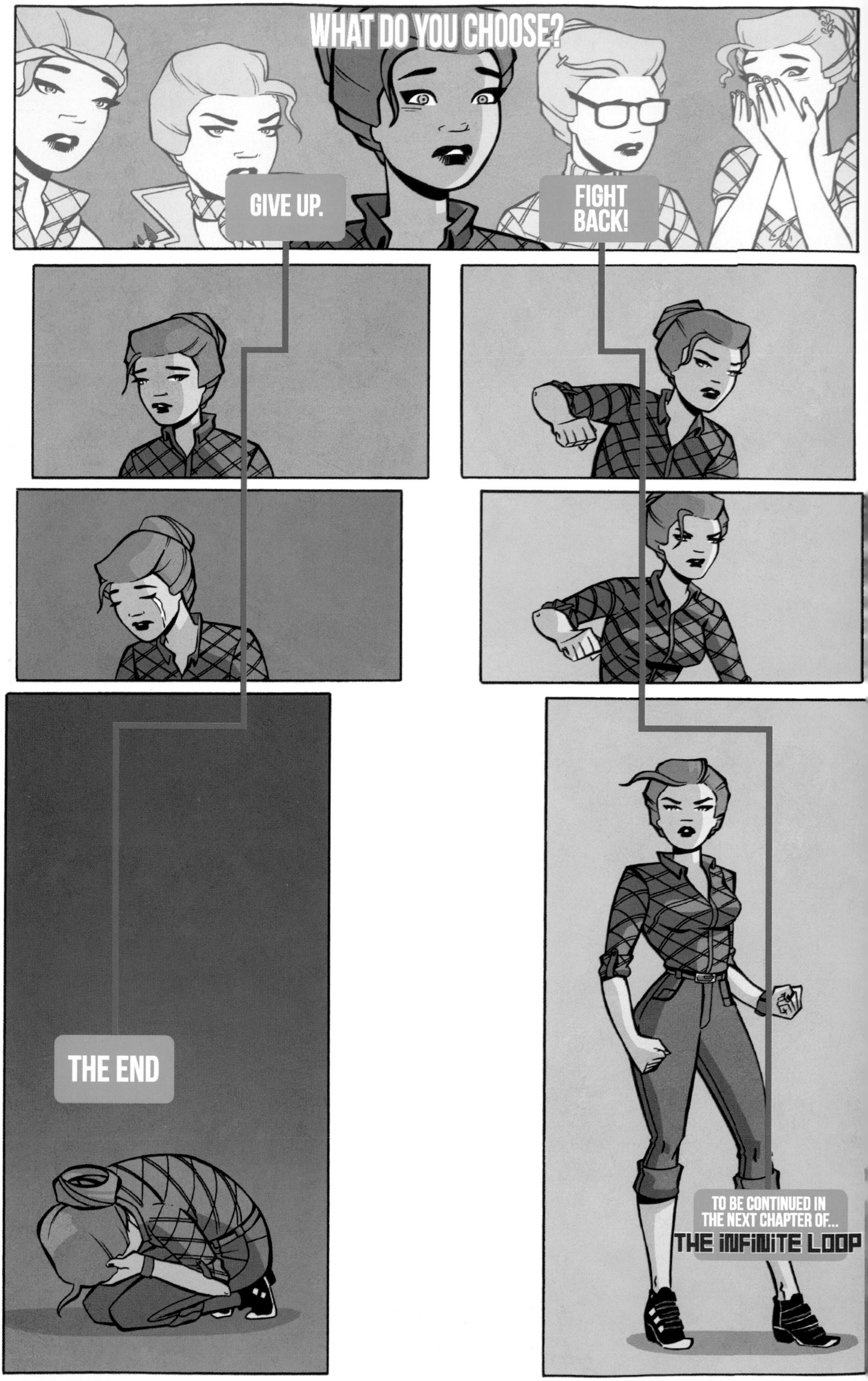
WHAT DO YOU CHOOSE?
GIVE UP.
FIGHT BACK!
THE END
TO BE CONTINUED IN THE NEXT CHAPTER OF...
THE INFINITE LOOP

Art by CHARLIE ADLARD

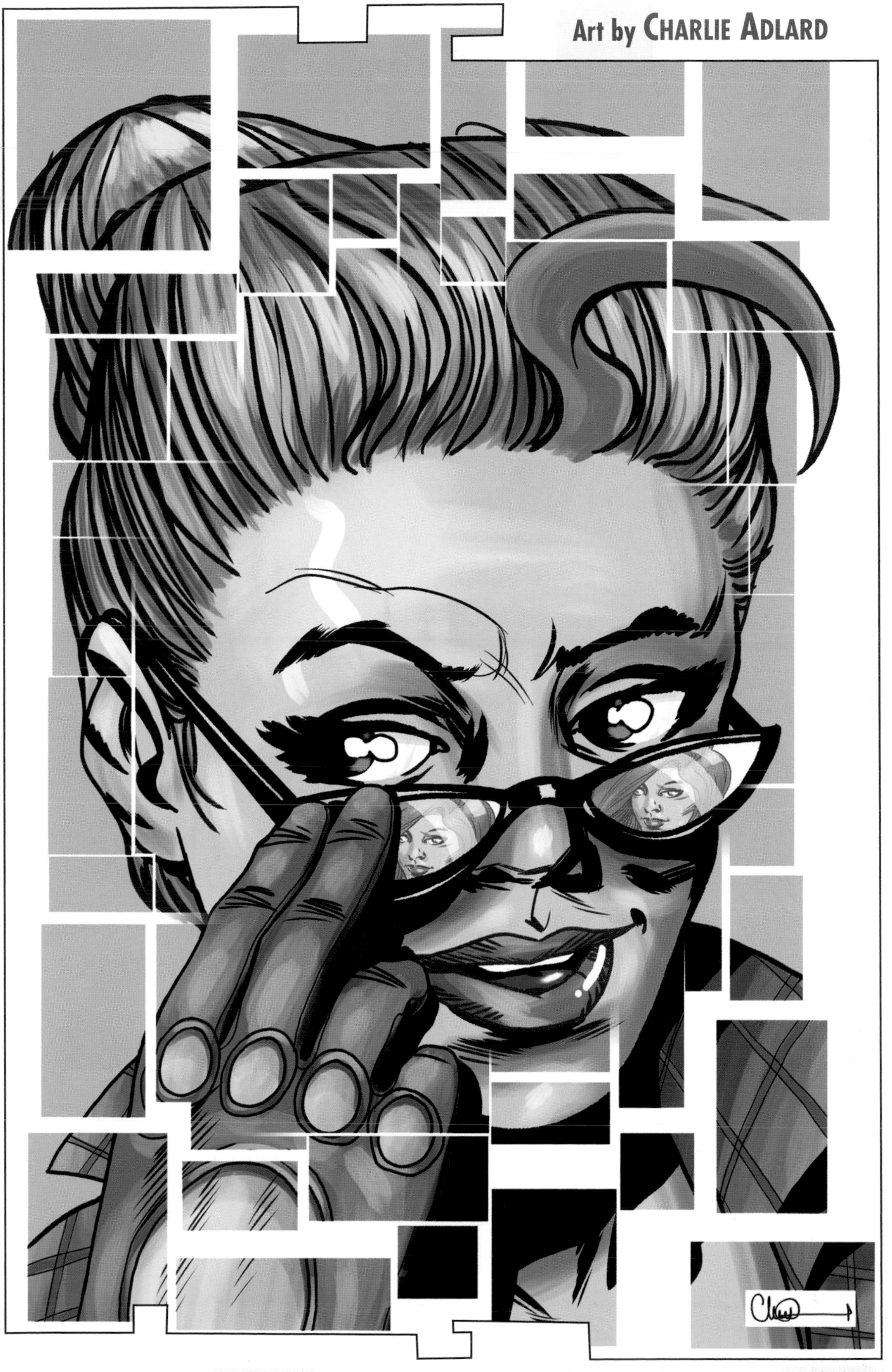

Art by ELSA CHARRETIER

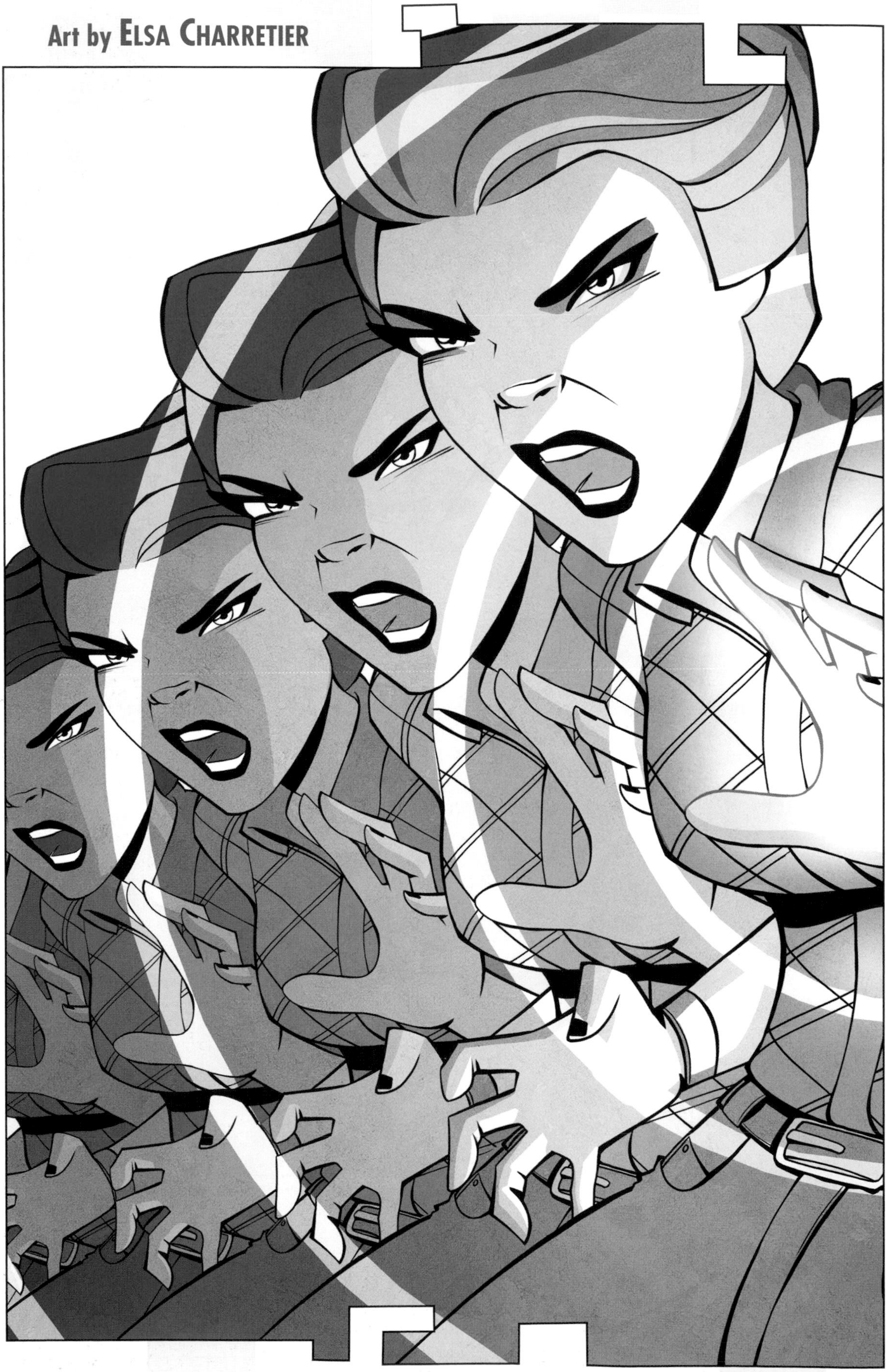

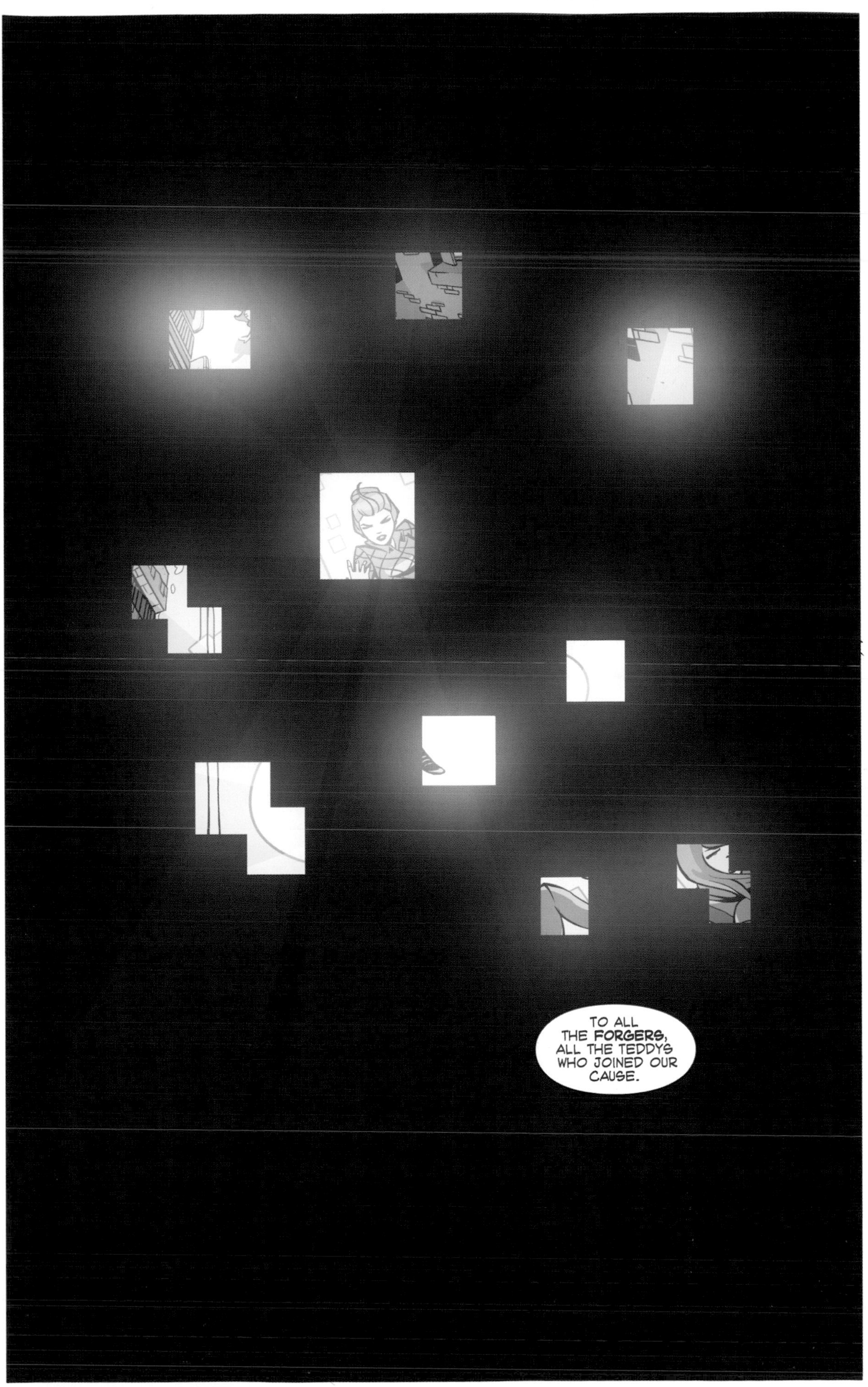
TO ALL THE **FORGERS**, ALL THE TEDDYS WHO JOINED OUR CAUSE.

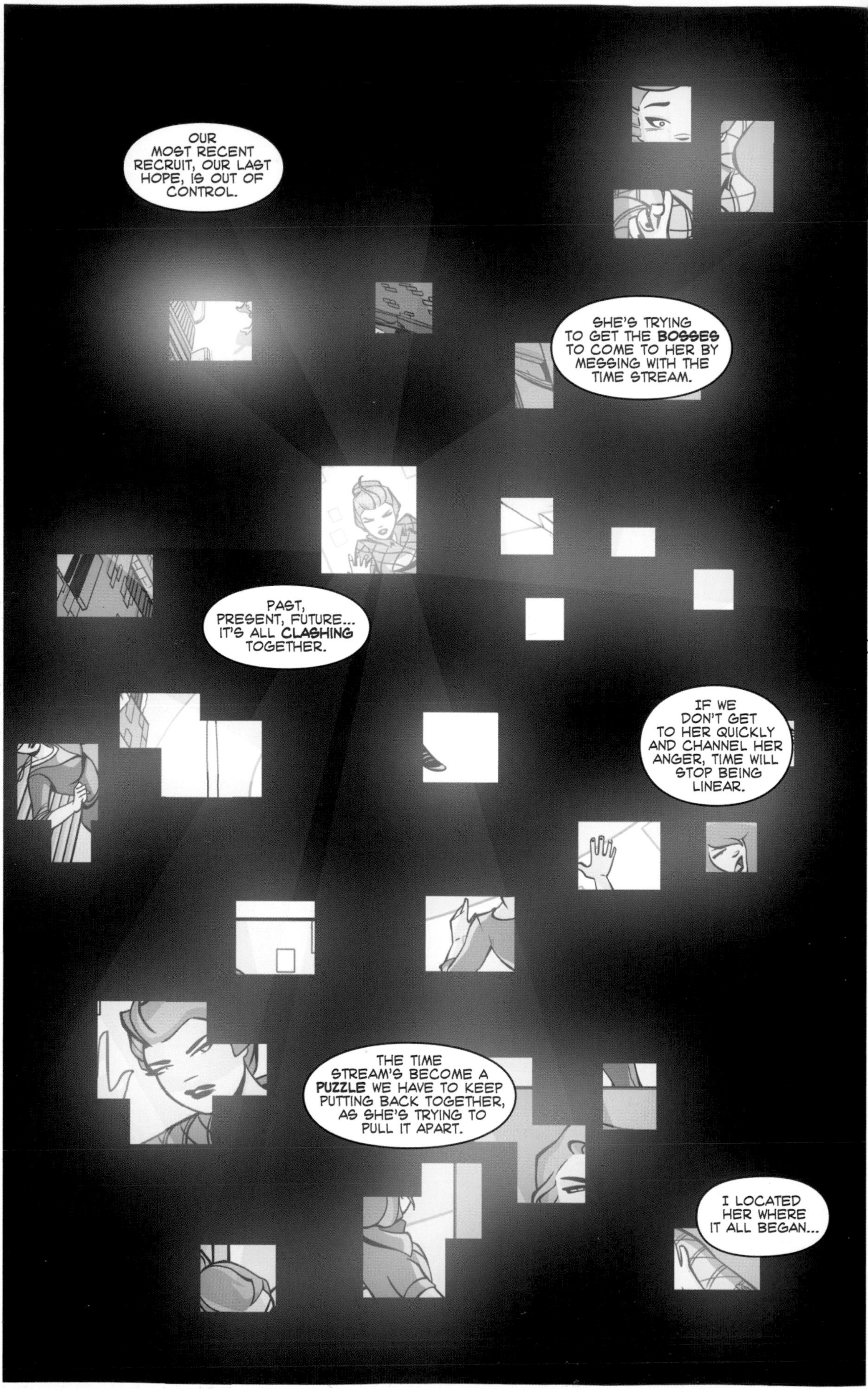
OUR MOST RECENT RECRUIT, OUR LAST HOPE, IS OUT OF CONTROL.
SHE'S TRYING TO GET THE **BOSSES** TO COME TO HER BY MESSING WITH THE TIME STREAM.
PAST, PRESENT, FUTURE... IT'S ALL **CLASHING** TOGETHER.
IF WE DON'T GET TO HER QUICKLY AND CHANNEL HER ANGER, TIME WILL STOP BEING LINEAR.
THE TIME STREAM'S BECOME A **PUZZLE** WE HAVE TO KEEP PUTTING BACK TOGETHER, AS SHE'S TRYING TO PULL IT APART.
I LOCATED HER WHERE IT ALL BEGAN...

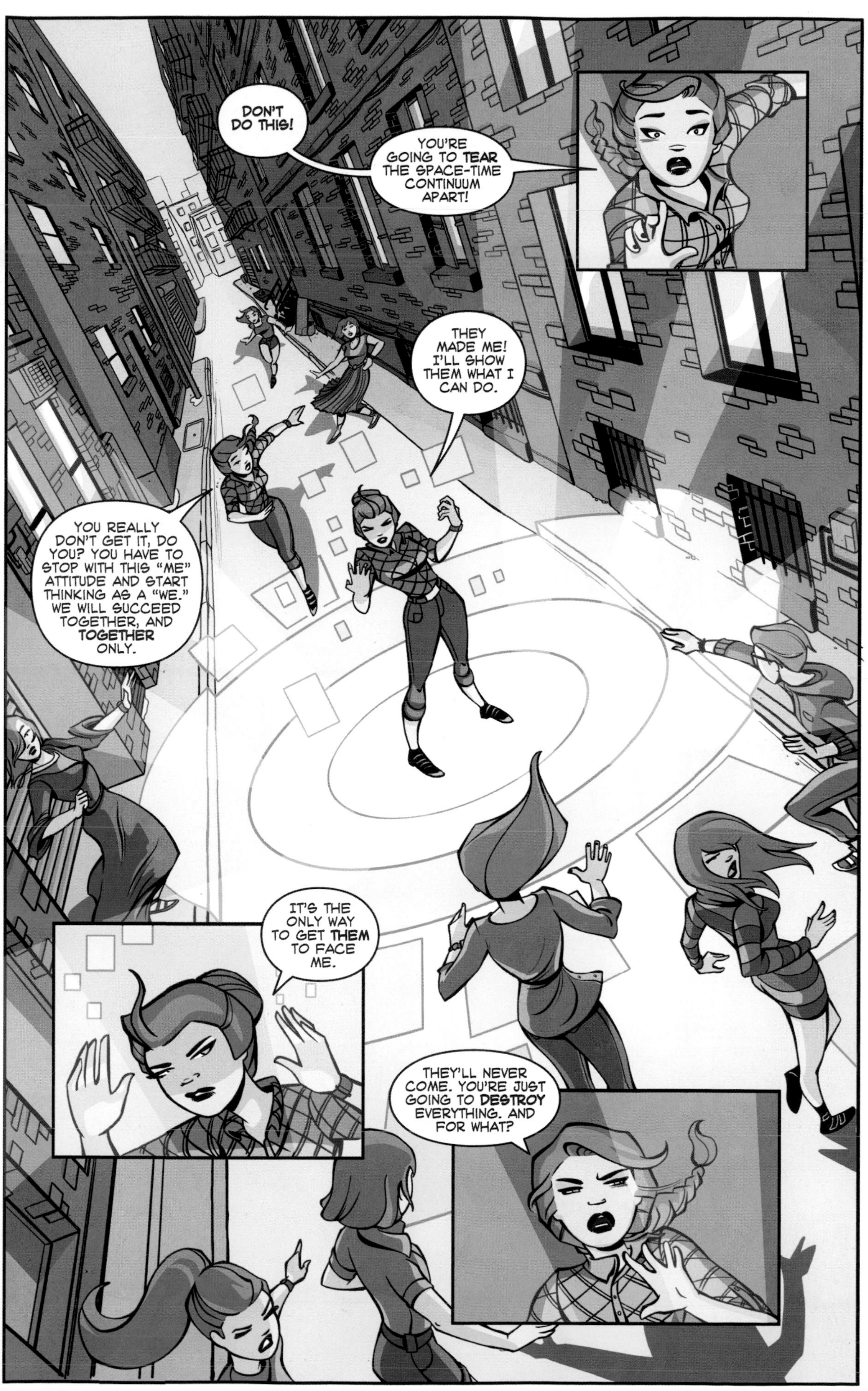

DON'T DO THIS!
YOU'RE GOING TO TEAR THE SPACE-TIME CONTINUUM APART!
THEY MADE ME! I'LL SHOW THEM WHAT I CAN DO.
YOU REALLY DON'T GET IT, DO YOU? YOU HAVE TO STOP WITH THIS "ME" ATTITUDE AND START THINKING AS A "WE." WE WILL SUCCEED TOGETHER, AND TOGETHER ONLY.
IT'S THE ONLY WAY TO GET THEM TO FACE ME.
THEY'LL NEVER COME. YOU'RE JUST GOING TO DESTROY EVERYTHING. AND FOR WHAT?

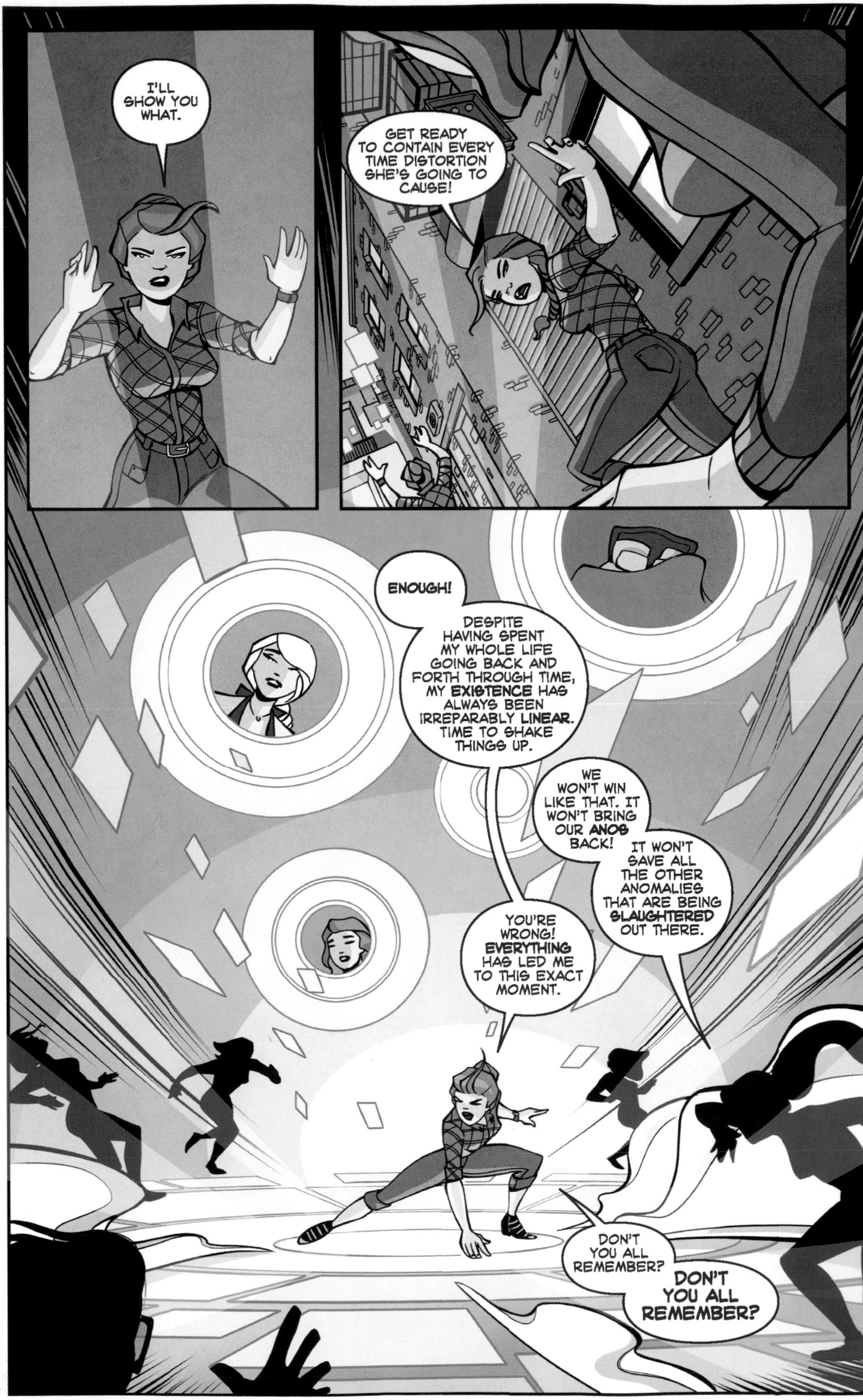
I'LL SHOW YOU WHAT.
GET READY TO CONTAIN EVERY TIME DISTORTION SHE'S GOING TO CAUSE!
ENOUGH!
DESPITE HAVING SPENT MY WHOLE LIFE GOING BACK AND FORTH THROUGH TIME, MY EXISTENCE HAS ALWAYS BEEN IRREPARABLY LINEAR. TIME TO SHAKE THINGS UP.
WE WON'T WIN LIKE THAT. IT WON'T BRING OUR ANOS BACK!
IT WON'T SAVE ALL THE OTHER ANOMALIES THAT ARE BEING SLAUGHTERED OUT THERE.
YOU'RE WRONG! EVERYTHING HAS LED ME TO THIS EXACT MOMENT.
DON'T YOU ALL REMEMBER?
DON'T YOU ALL REMEMBER?

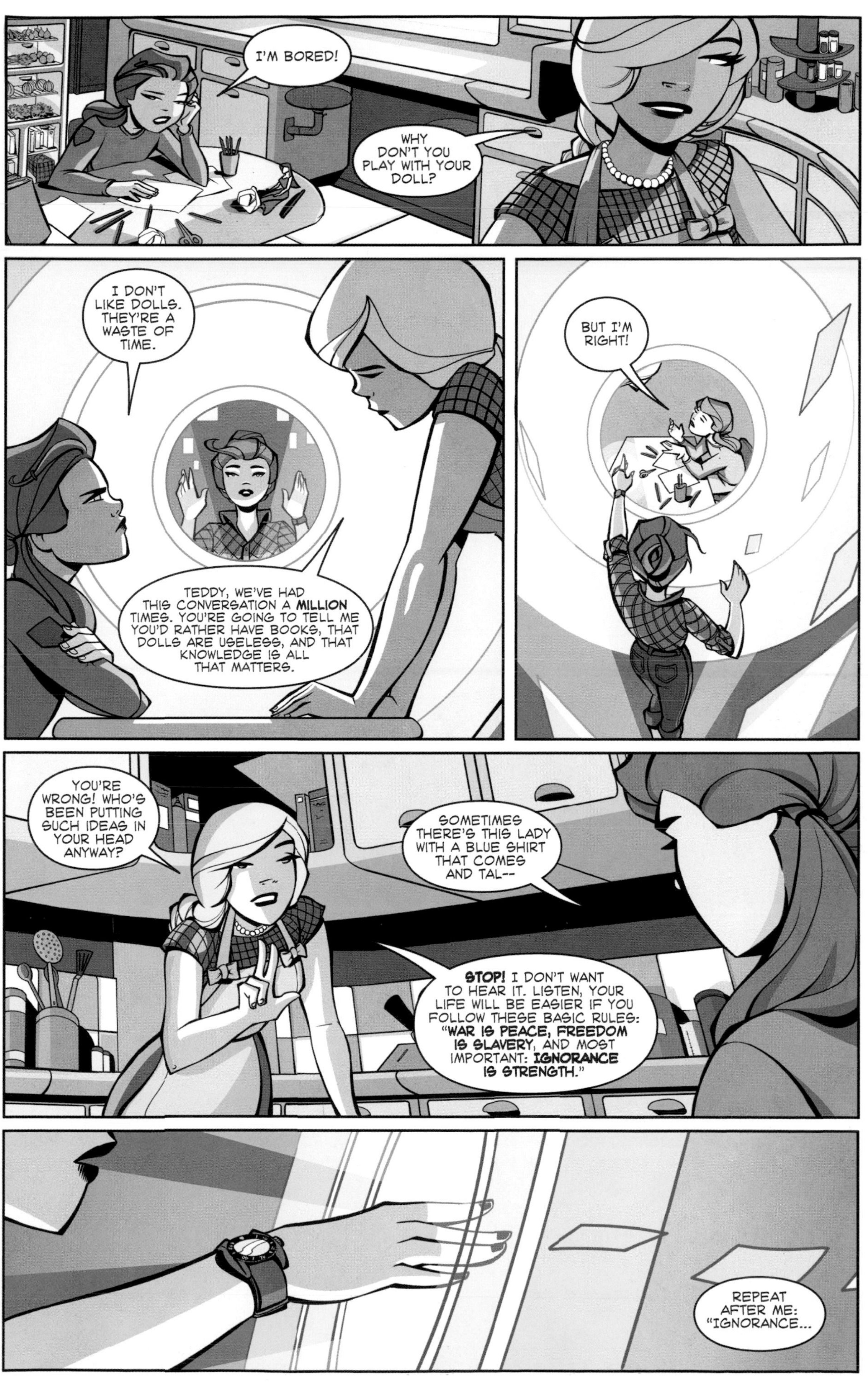
I'M BORED!
WHY DON'T YOU PLAY WITH YOUR DOLL?
I DON'T LIKE DOLLS. THEY'RE A WASTE OF TIME.
TEDDY, WE'VE HAD THIS CONVERSATION A **MILLION** TIMES. YOU'RE GOING TO TELL ME YOU'D RATHER HAVE BOOKS, THAT DOLLS ARE USELESS, AND THAT KNOWLEDGE IS ALL THAT MATTERS.
BUT I'M RIGHT!
YOU'RE WRONG! WHO'S BEEN PUTTING SUCH IDEAS IN YOUR HEAD ANYWAY?
SOMETIMES THERE'S THIS LADY WITH A BLUE SHIRT THAT COMES AND TAL--
STOP! I DON'T WANT TO HEAR IT. LISTEN, YOUR LIFE WILL BE EASIER IF YOU FOLLOW THESE BASIC RULES: "**WAR IS PEACE, FREEDOM IS SLAVERY**, AND MOST IMPORTANT: **IGNORANCE IS STRENGTH**."
REPEAT AFTER ME: "IGNORANCE...

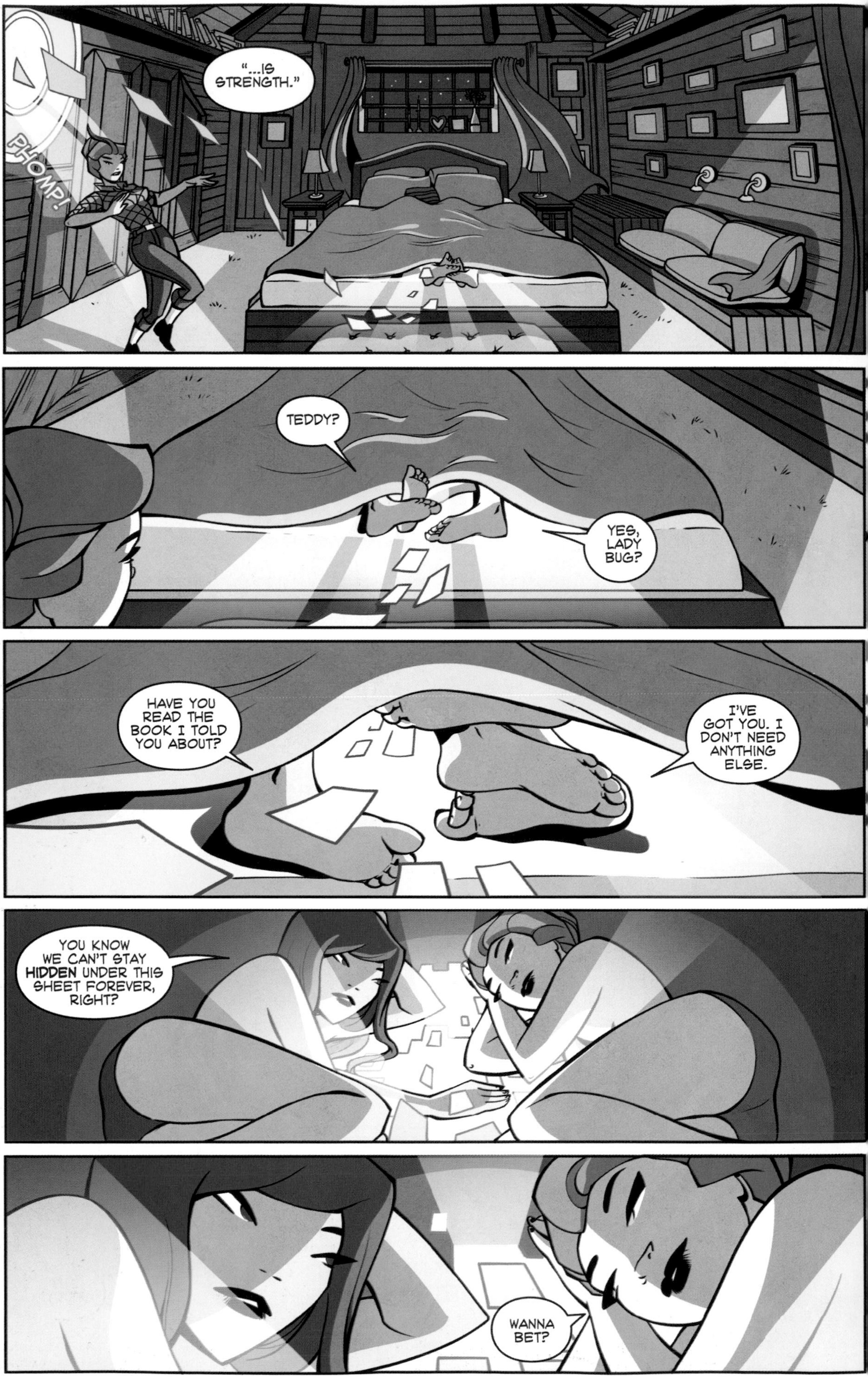
"...IS STRENGTH."
PHOMP!
TEDDY?
YES, LADY BUG?
HAVE YOU READ THE BOOK I TOLD YOU ABOUT?
I'VE GOT YOU. I DON'T NEED ANYTHING ELSE.
YOU KNOW WE CAN'T STAY **HIDDEN** UNDER THIS SHEET FOREVER, RIGHT?
WANNA BET?

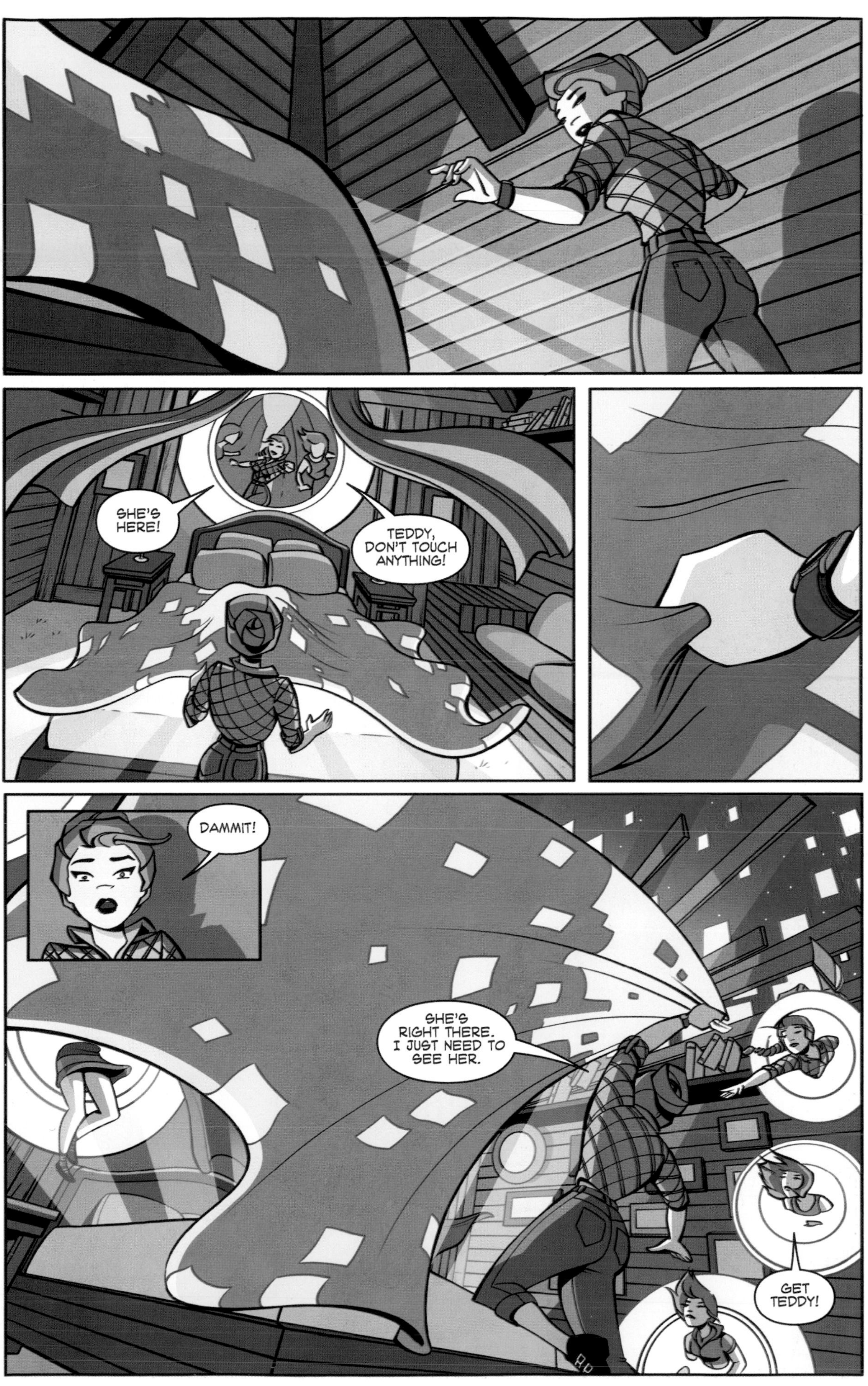
SHE'S HERE!
TEDDY, DON'T TOUCH ANYTHING!
DAMMIT!
SHE'S RIGHT THERE. I JUST NEED TO SEE HER.
GET TEDDY!

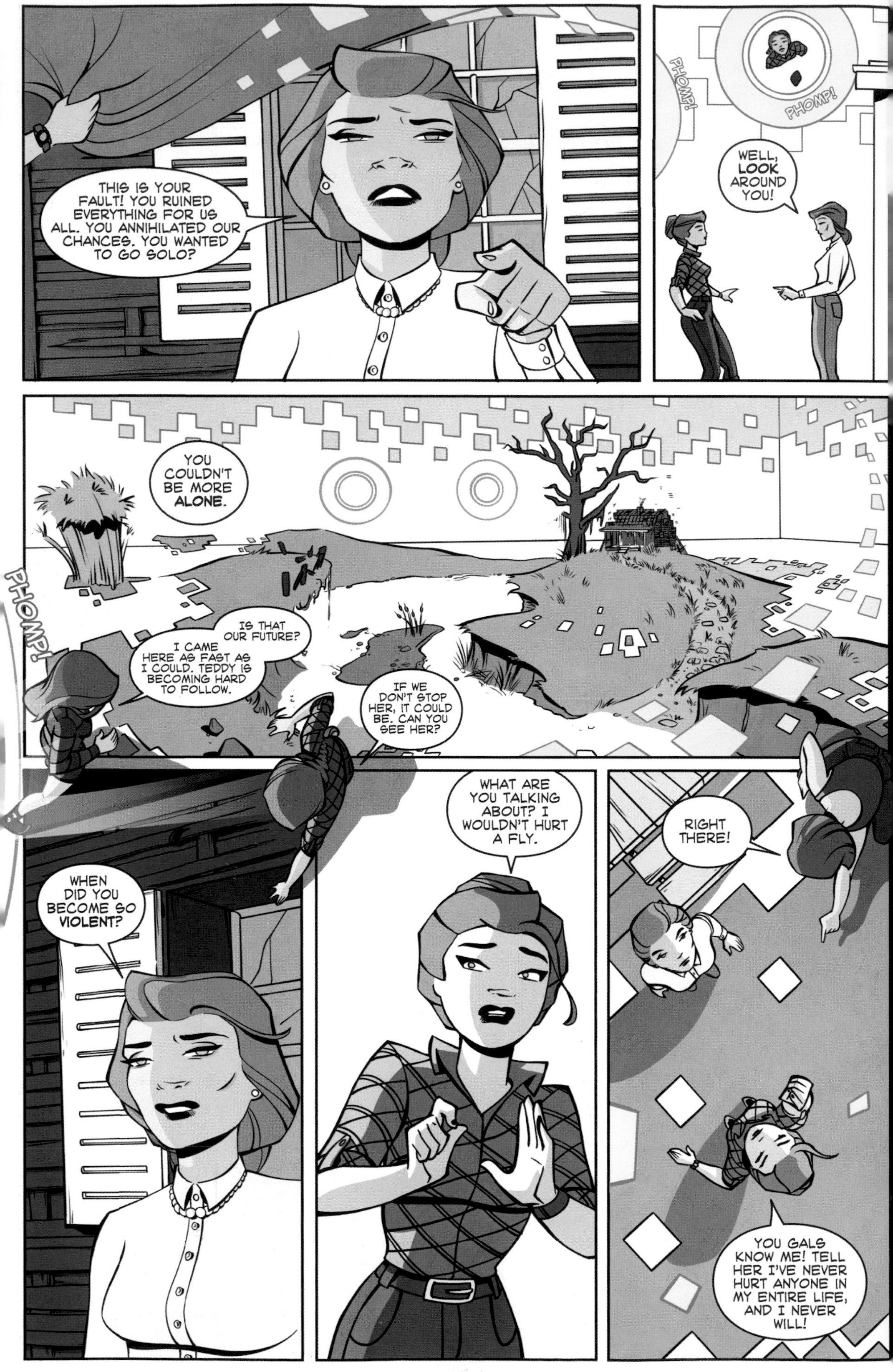
THIS IS YOUR FAULT! YOU RUINED EVERYTHING FOR US ALL. YOU ANNIHILATED OUR CHANCES. YOU WANTED TO GO SOLO?
PHOMP!
PHOMP!
WELL, LOOK AROUND YOU!
YOU COULDN'T BE MORE ALONE.
PHOMP!
IS THAT OUR FUTURE?
I CAME HERE AS FAST AS I COULD. TEDDY IS BECOMING HARD TO FOLLOW.
IF WE DON'T STOP HER, IT COULD BE. CAN YOU SEE HER?
WHEN DID YOU BECOME SO VIOLENT?
WHAT ARE YOU TALKING ABOUT? I WOULDN'T HURT A FLY.
RIGHT THERE!
YOU GALS KNOW ME! TELL HER I'VE NEVER HURT ANYONE IN MY ENTIRE LIFE, AND I NEVER WILL!

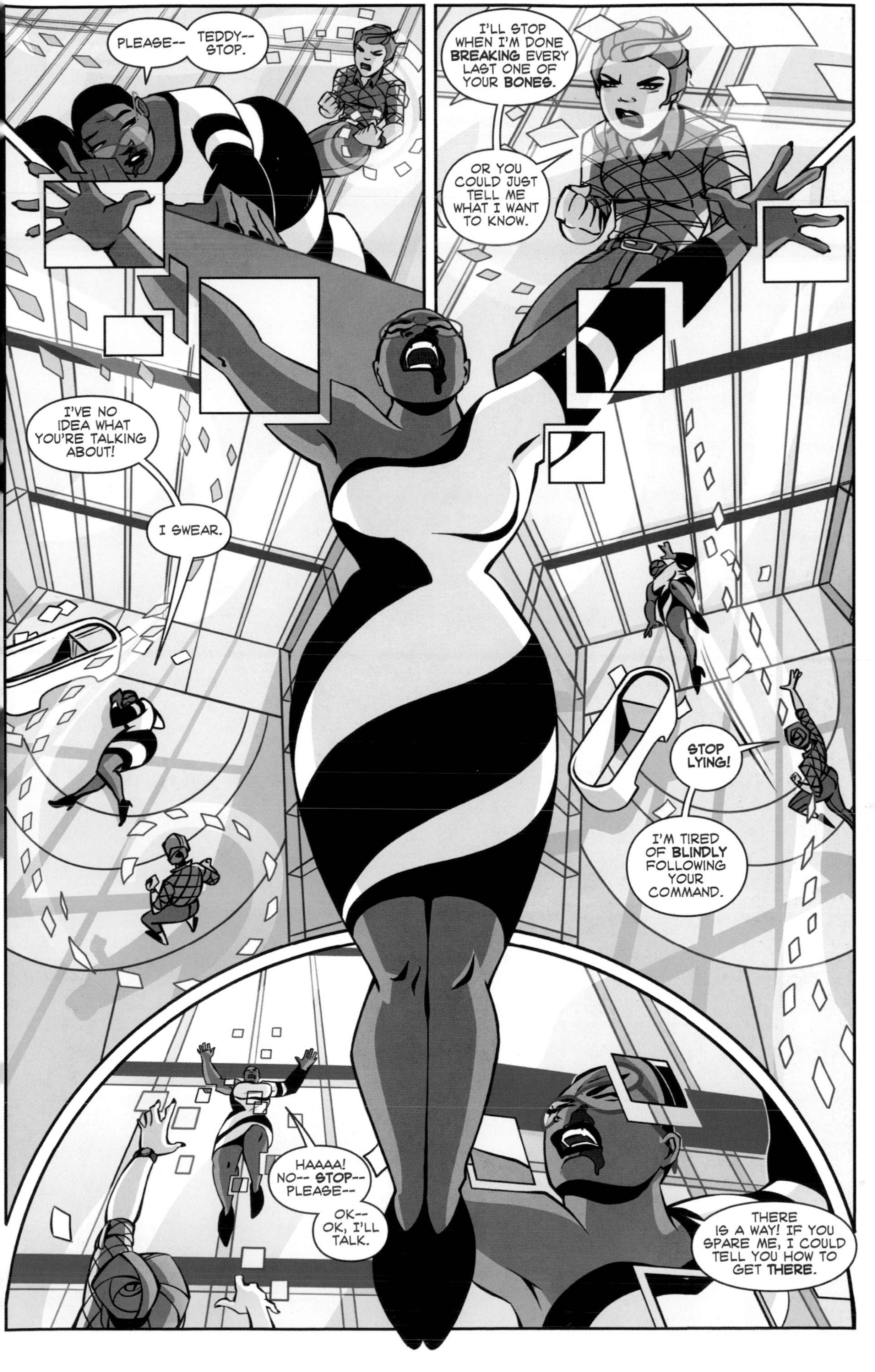
PLEASE--
TEDDY-- STOP.
I'LL STOP WHEN I'M DONE BREAKING EVERY LAST ONE OF YOUR BONES.
OR YOU COULD JUST TELL ME WHAT I WANT TO KNOW.
I'VE NO IDEA WHAT YOU'RE TALKING ABOUT!
I SWEAR.
STOP LYING!
I'M TIRED OF BLINDLY FOLLOWING YOUR COMMAND.
HAAAA! NO-- STOP-- PLEASE--
OK-- OK, I'LL TALK.
THERE IS A WAY! IF YOU SPARE ME, I COULD TELL YOU HOW TO GET THERE.

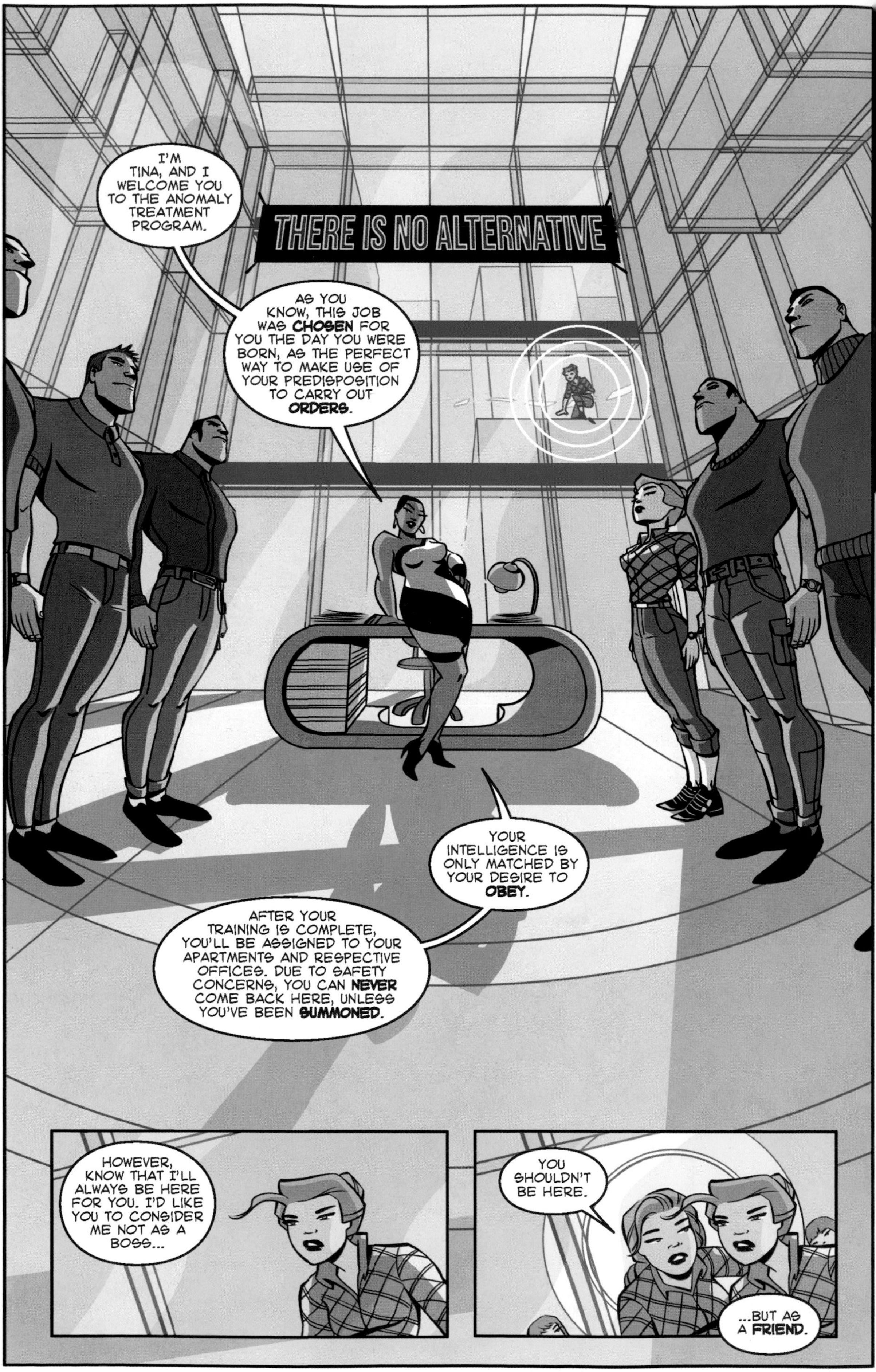
THERE IS NO ALTERNATIVE
I'M TINA, AND I WELCOME YOU TO THE ANOMALY TREATMENT PROGRAM.
AS YOU KNOW, THIS JOB WAS CHOSEN FOR YOU THE DAY YOU WERE BORN, AS THE PERFECT WAY TO MAKE USE OF YOUR PREDISPOSITION TO CARRY OUT ORDERS.
YOUR INTELLIGENCE IS ONLY MATCHED BY YOUR DESIRE TO OBEY.
AFTER YOUR TRAINING IS COMPLETE, YOU'LL BE ASSIGNED TO YOUR APARTMENTS AND RESPECTIVE OFFICES. DUE TO SAFETY CONCERNS, YOU CAN NEVER COME BACK HERE, UNLESS YOU'VE BEEN SUMMONED.
HOWEVER, KNOW THAT I'LL ALWAYS BE HERE FOR YOU. I'D LIKE YOU TO CONSIDER ME NOT AS A BOSS...
YOU SHOULDN'T BE HERE.
...BUT AS A FRIEND.

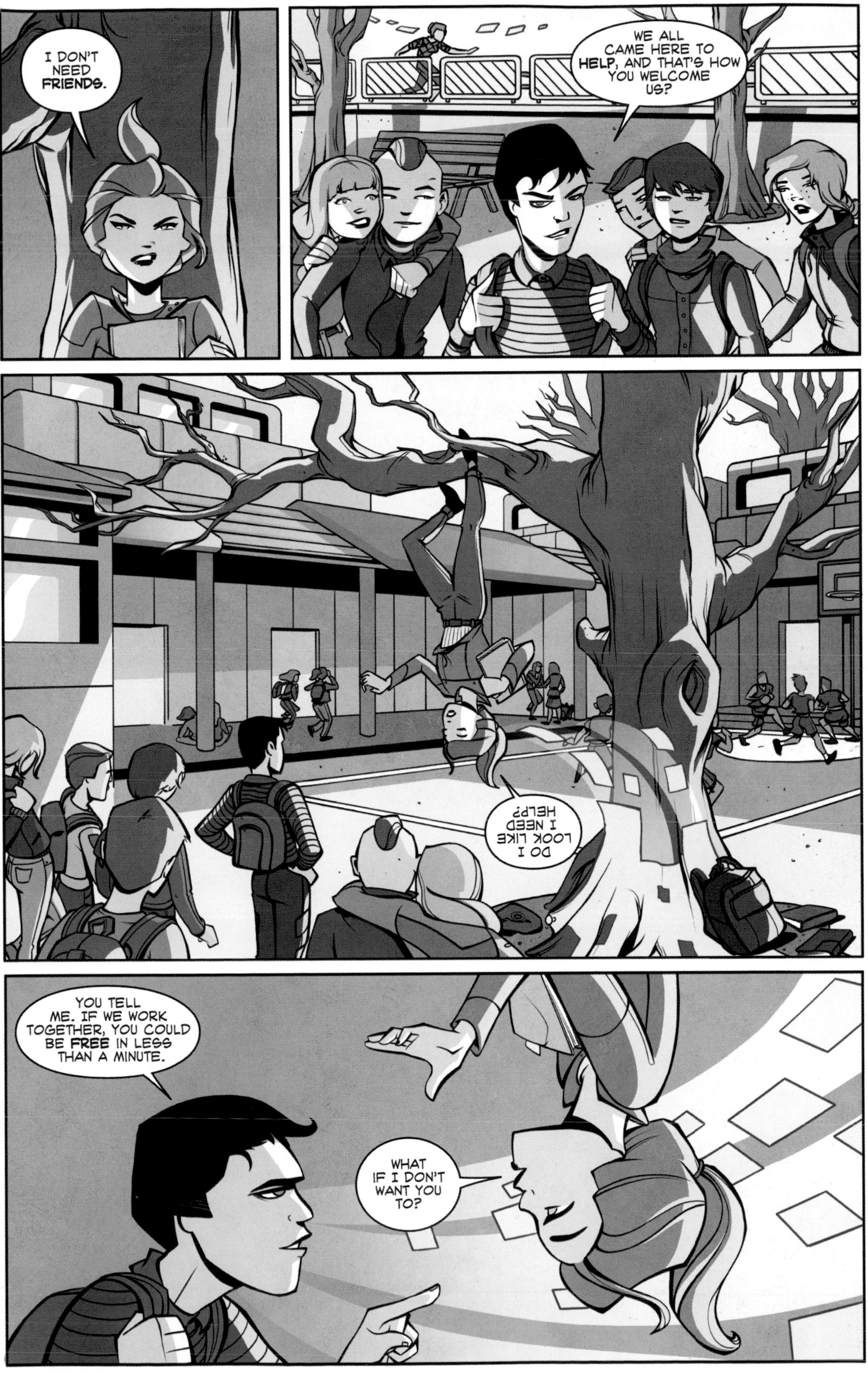

I DON'T NEED FRIENDS.
WE ALL CAME HERE TO HELP, AND THAT'S HOW YOU WELCOME US?
DO I LOOK LIKE I NEED HELP?
YOU TELL ME. IF WE WORK TOGETHER, YOU COULD BE FREE IN LESS THAN A MINUTE.
WHAT IF I DON'T WANT YOU TO?

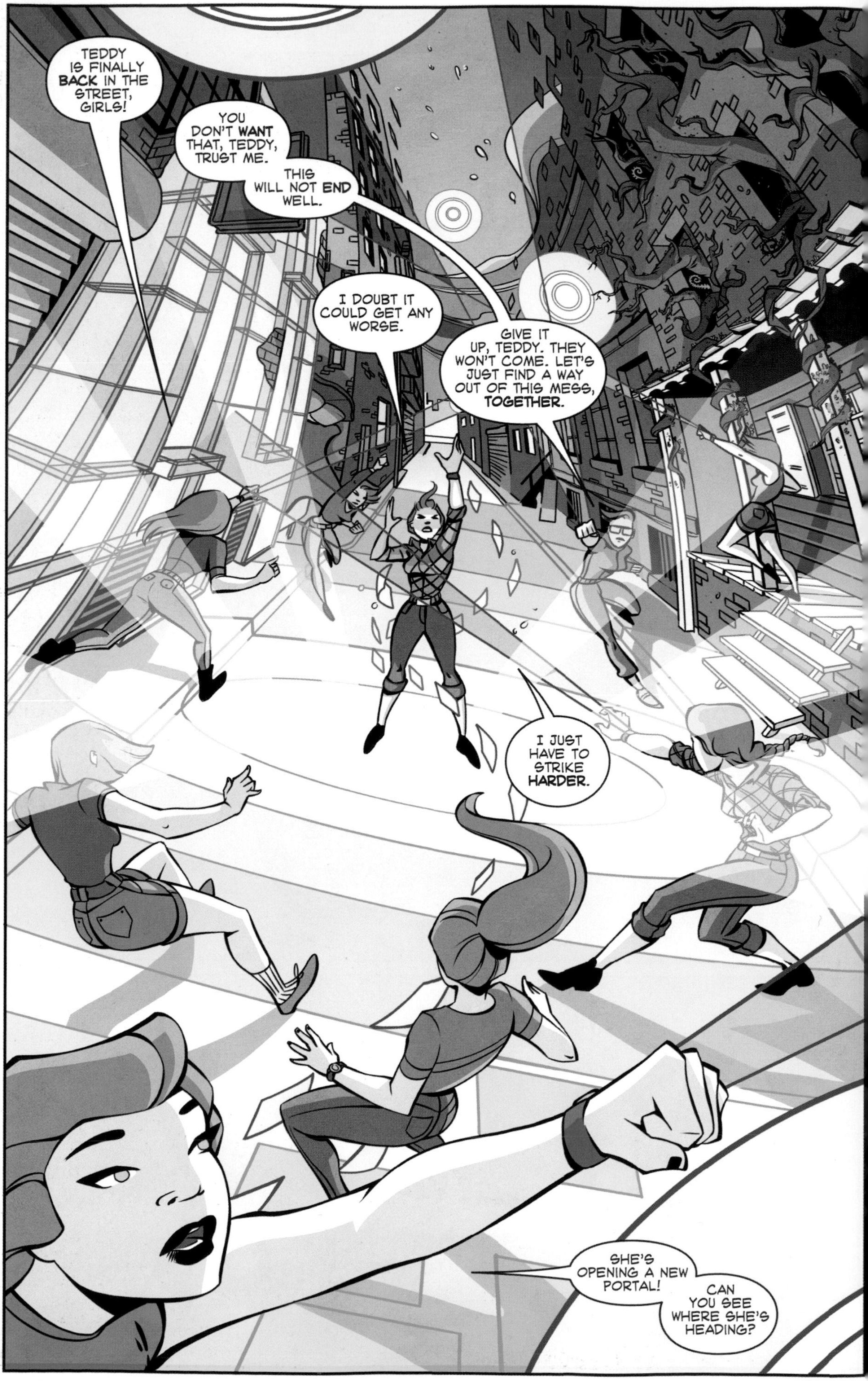
TEDDY IS FINALLY BACK IN THE STREET, GIRLS!
YOU DON'T WANT THAT, TEDDY, TRUST ME.
THIS WILL NOT END WELL.
I DOUBT IT COULD GET ANY WORSE.
GIVE IT UP, TEDDY. THEY WON'T COME. LET'S JUST FIND A WAY OUT OF THIS MESS, TOGETHER.
I JUST HAVE TO STRIKE HARDER.
SHE'S OPENING A NEW PORTAL!
CAN YOU SEE WHERE SHE'S HEADING?

PLEASE TELL ME SHE'S NOT BACK TO THE TIME WARP!

SINCE YOU WANT TO TRY EVERYTHING SO BADLY, YOU CAN'T MISS A FIRST GLASS OF WINE.

YOU KNOW YOU DON'T HAVE TO GET ME DRUNK TO GET ME IN YOUR BED, RIGHT?

OH, COME ON, ANO! I STILL HAVE WRIST CRAMPS.

HERE.

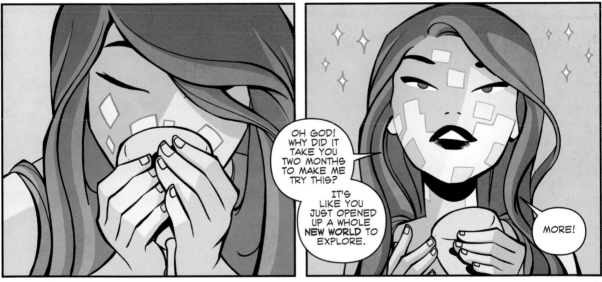

OH GOD! WHY DID IT TAKE YOU TWO MONTHS TO MAKE ME TRY THIS?

IT'S LIKE YOU JUST OPENED UP A WHOLE NEW WORLD TO EXPLORE.

MORE!

IT LOOKS LIKE YOU'RE GOING TO HAVE YOUR FIRST HANGOVER AS WELL!

OH YEAH? WHAT IS IT LIKE? GOOD?

GOOD? NOPE. USEFUL? SOMETIMES.

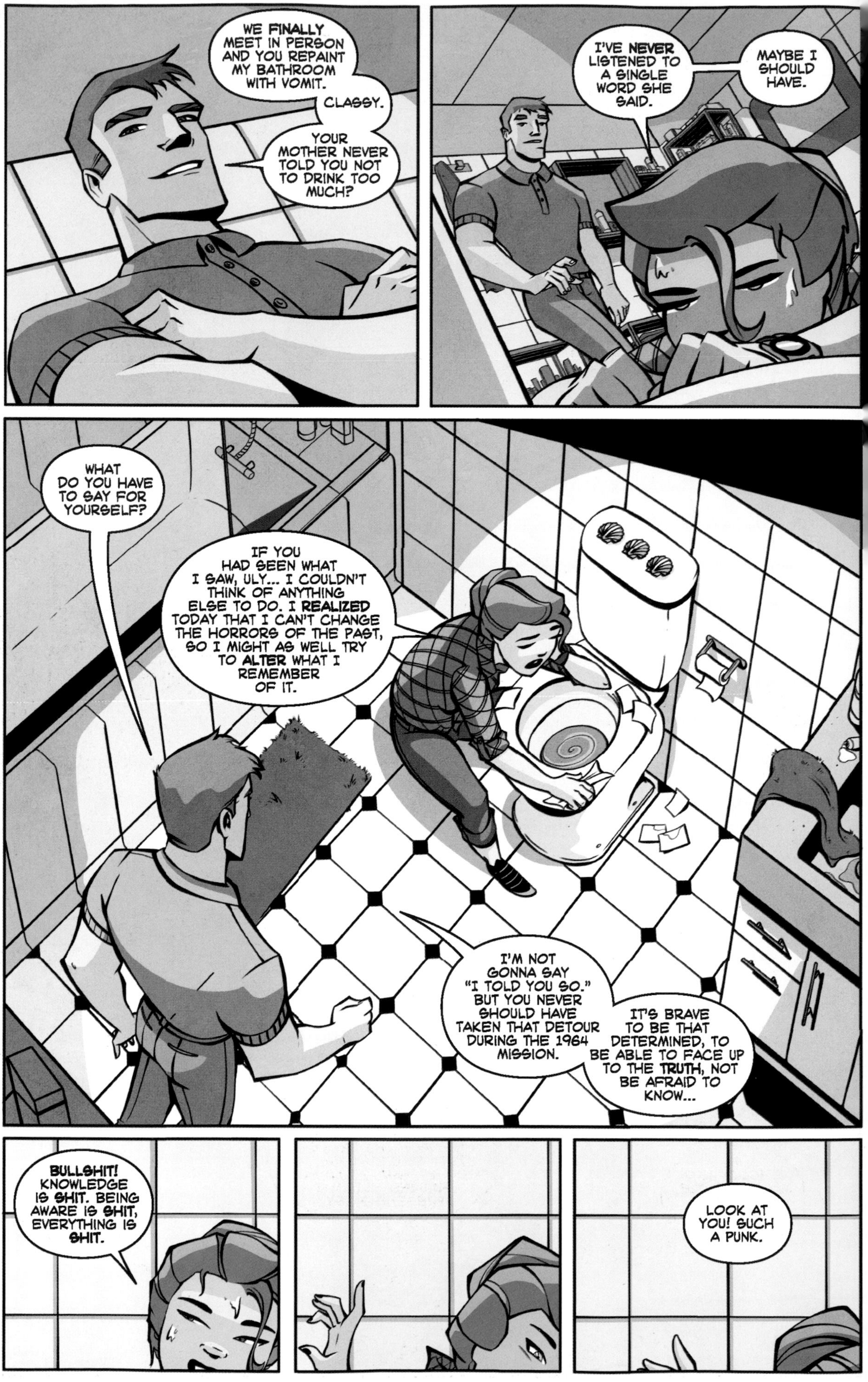
WE FINALLY MEET IN PERSON AND YOU REPAINT MY BATHROOM WITH VOMIT.
CLASSY.
YOUR MOTHER NEVER TOLD YOU NOT TO DRINK TOO MUCH?
I'VE NEVER LISTENED TO A SINGLE WORD SHE SAID.
MAYBE I SHOULD HAVE.
WHAT DO YOU HAVE TO SAY FOR YOURSELF?
IF YOU HAD SEEN WHAT I SAW, ULY... I COULDN'T THINK OF ANYTHING ELSE TO DO. I REALIZED TODAY THAT I CAN'T CHANGE THE HORRORS OF THE PAST, SO I MIGHT AS WELL TRY TO ALTER WHAT I REMEMBER OF IT.
I'M NOT GONNA SAY "I TOLD YOU SO." BUT YOU NEVER SHOULD HAVE TAKEN THAT DETOUR DURING THE 1964 MISSION.
IT'S BRAVE TO BE THAT DETERMINED, TO BE ABLE TO FACE UP TO THE TRUTH, NOT BE AFRAID TO KNOW...
BULLSHIT! KNOWLEDGE IS SHIT. BEING AWARE IS SHIT, EVERYTHING IS SHIT.
LOOK AT YOU! SUCH A PUNK.

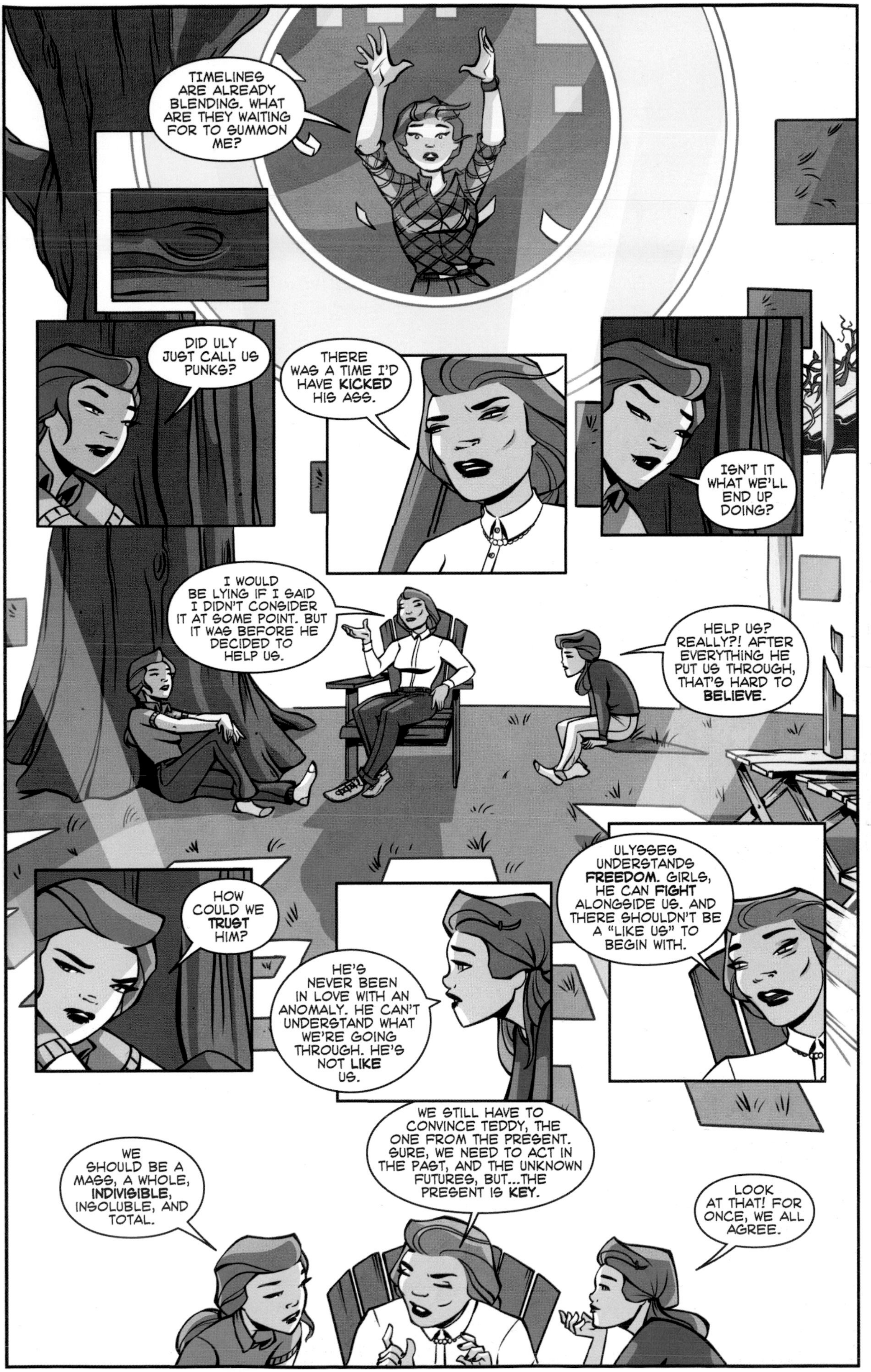
TIMELINES ARE ALREADY BLENDING. WHAT ARE THEY WAITING FOR TO SUMMON ME?
DID ULY JUST CALL US PUNKS?
THERE WAS A TIME I'D HAVE KICKED HIS ASS.
ISN'T IT WHAT WE'LL END UP DOING?
I WOULD BE LYING IF I SAID I DIDN'T CONSIDER IT AT SOME POINT. BUT IT WAS BEFORE HE DECIDED TO HELP US.
HELP US? REALLY?! AFTER EVERYTHING HE PUT US THROUGH, THAT'S HARD TO BELIEVE.
HOW COULD WE TRUST HIM?
HE'S NEVER BEEN IN LOVE WITH AN ANOMALY. HE CAN'T UNDERSTAND WHAT WE'RE GOING THROUGH. HE'S NOT LIKE US.
ULYSSES UNDERSTANDS FREEDOM. GIRLS, HE CAN FIGHT ALONGSIDE US. AND THERE SHOULDN'T BE A "LIKE US" TO BEGIN WITH.
WE SHOULD BE A MASS, A WHOLE, INDIVISIBLE, INSOLUBLE, AND TOTAL.
WE STILL HAVE TO CONVINCE TEDDY, THE ONE FROM THE PRESENT. SURE, WE NEED TO ACT IN THE PAST, AND THE UNKNOWN FUTURES, BUT...THE PRESENT IS KEY.
LOOK AT THAT! FOR ONCE, WE ALL AGREE.

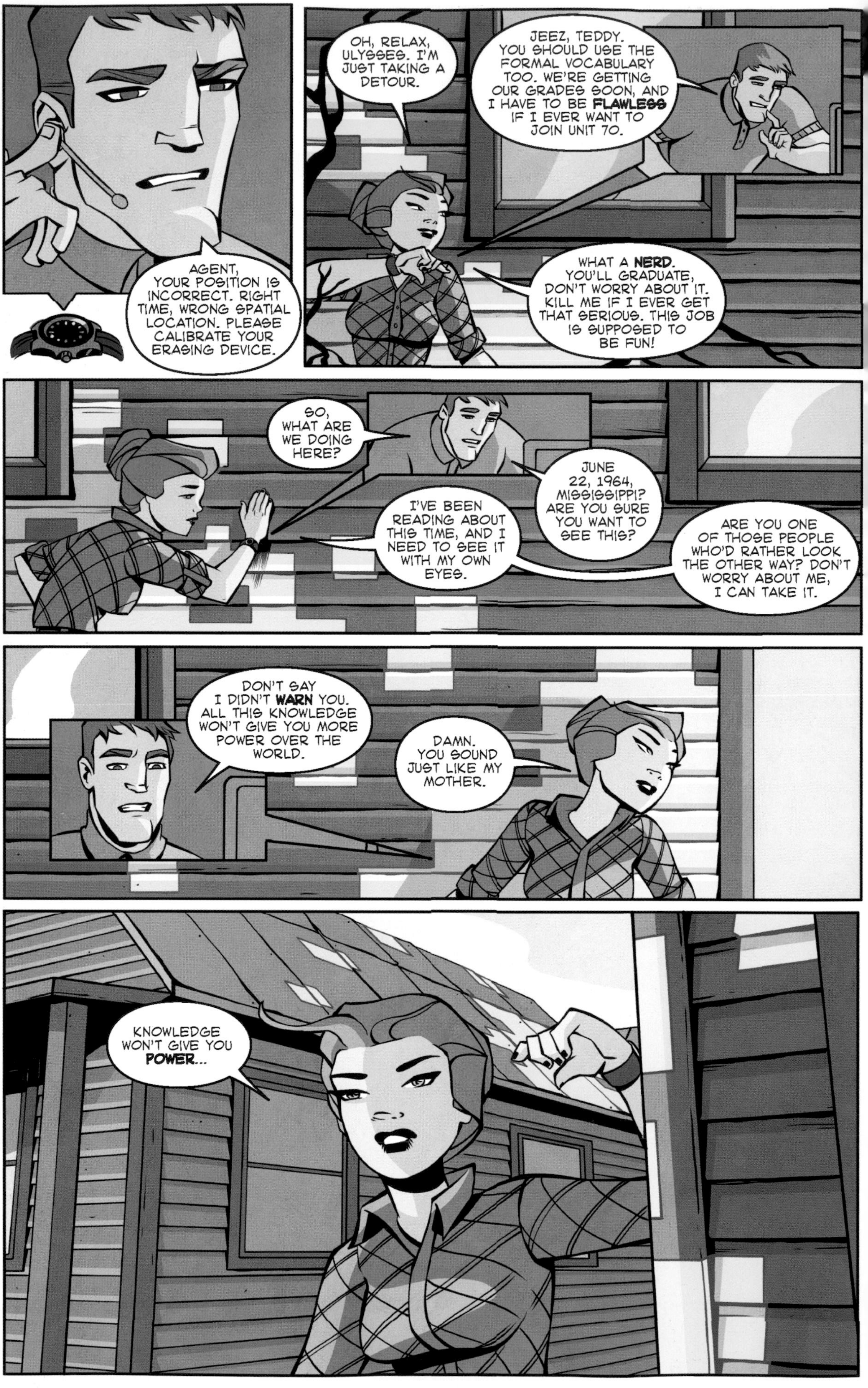
AGENT, YOUR POSITION IS INCORRECT. RIGHT TIME, WRONG SPATIAL LOCATION. PLEASE CALIBRATE YOUR ERASING DEVICE.
OH, RELAX, ULYSSES. I'M JUST TAKING A DETOUR.
JEEZ, TEDDY. YOU SHOULD USE THE FORMAL VOCABULARY TOO. WE'RE GETTING OUR GRADES SOON, AND I HAVE TO BE **FLAWLESS** IF I EVER WANT TO JOIN UNIT 70.
WHAT A **NERD**. YOU'LL GRADUATE, DON'T WORRY ABOUT IT. KILL ME IF I EVER GET THAT SERIOUS. THIS JOB IS SUPPOSED TO BE FUN!
SO, WHAT ARE WE DOING HERE?
I'VE BEEN READING ABOUT THIS TIME, AND I NEED TO SEE IT WITH MY OWN EYES.
JUNE 22, 1964, MISSISSIPPI? ARE YOU SURE YOU WANT TO SEE THIS?
ARE YOU ONE OF THOSE PEOPLE WHO'D RATHER LOOK THE OTHER WAY? DON'T WORRY ABOUT ME, I CAN TAKE IT.
DON'T SAY I DIDN'T **WARN** YOU. ALL THIS KNOWLEDGE WON'T GIVE YOU MORE POWER OVER THE WORLD.
DAMN. YOU SOUND JUST LIKE MY MOTHER.
KNOWLEDGE WON'T GIVE YOU **POWER**...

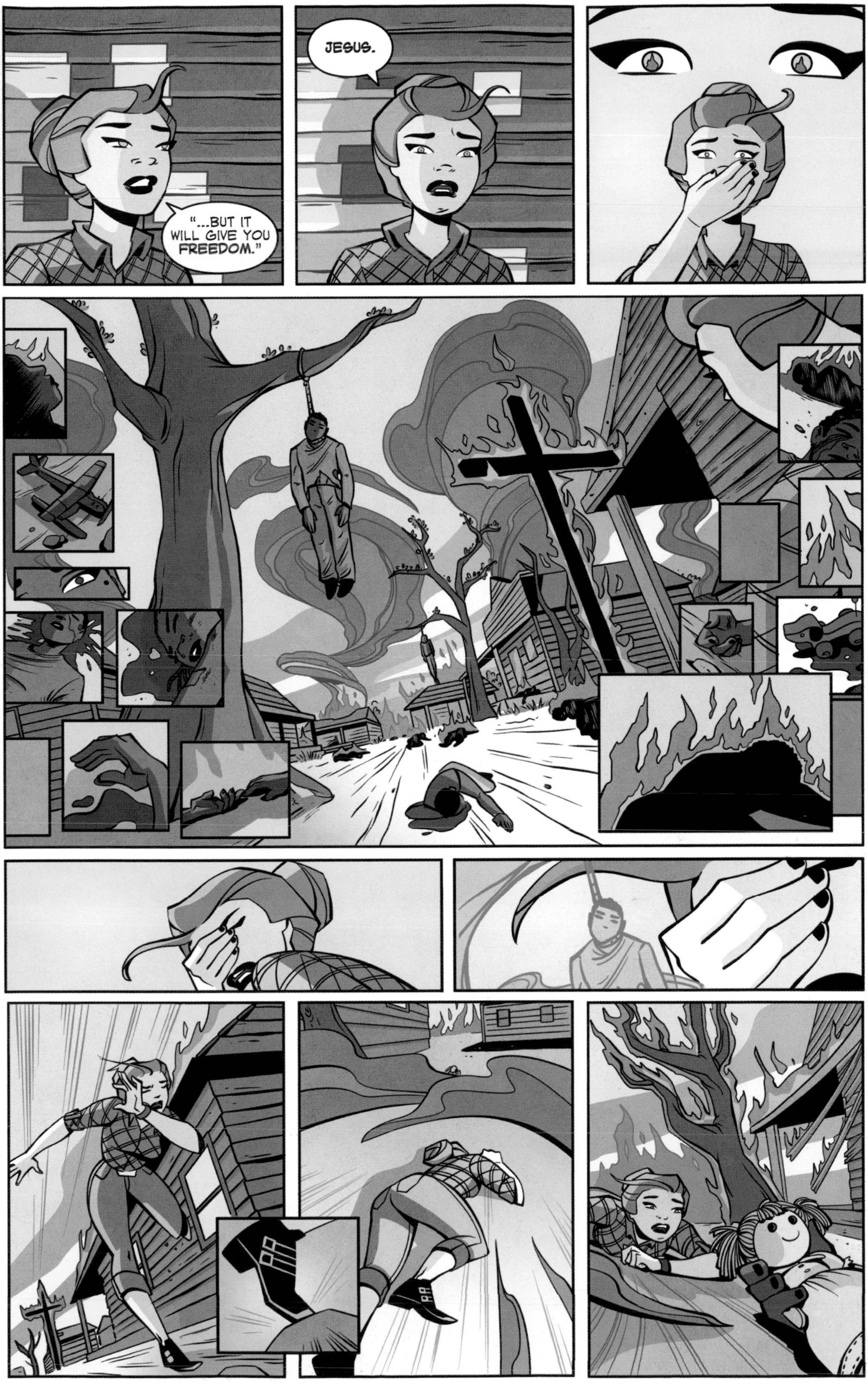
"...BUT IT WILL GIVE YOU FREEDOM."
JESUS.

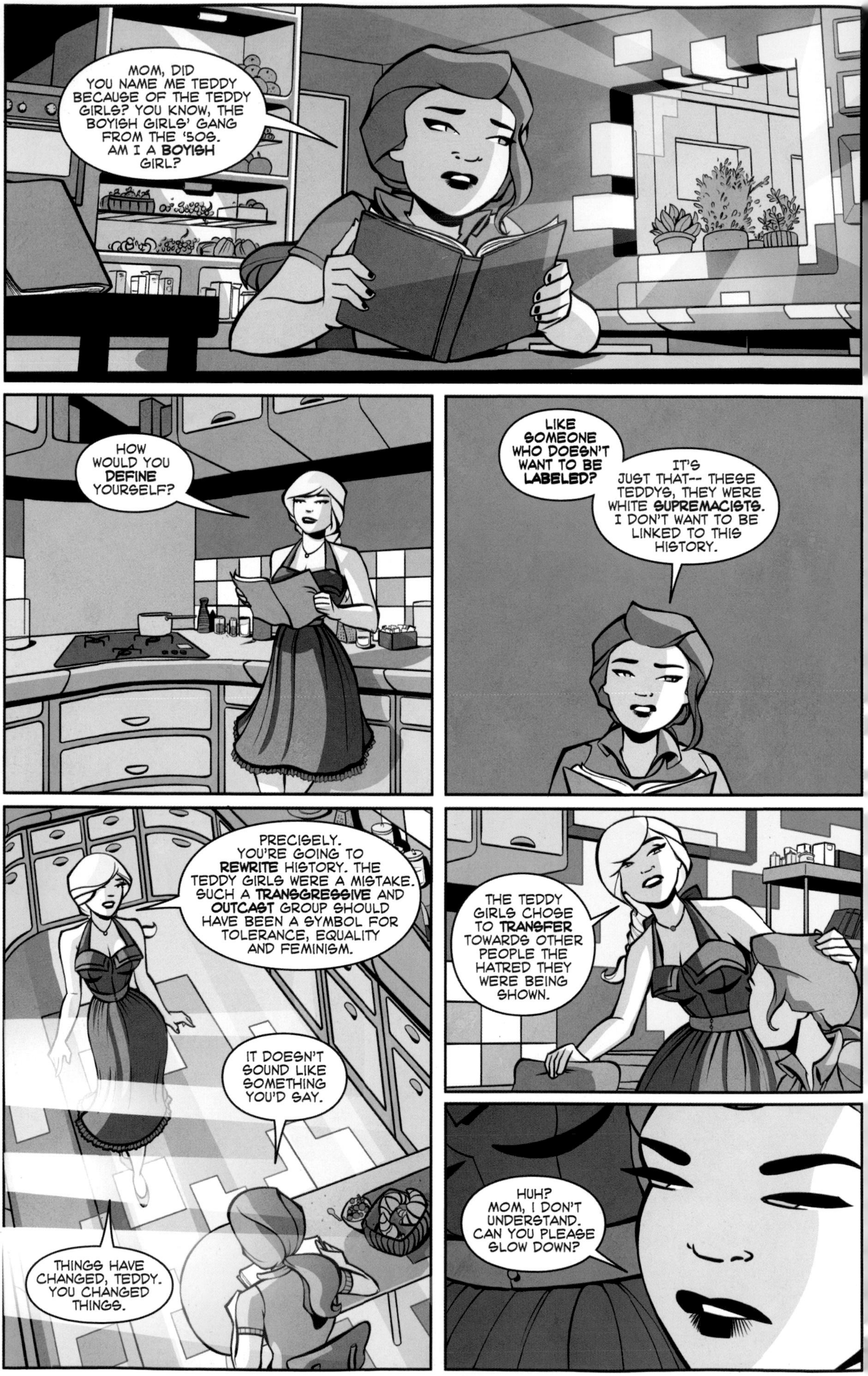

MOM, DID YOU NAME ME TEDDY BECAUSE OF THE TEDDY GIRLS? YOU KNOW, THE BOYISH GIRLS' GANG FROM THE '50S. AM I A **BOYISH** GIRL?
HOW WOULD YOU **DEFINE** YOURSELF?
LIKE **SOMEONE WHO DOESN'T WANT TO BE LABELED?**
IT'S JUST THAT-- THESE TEDDYS, THEY WERE WHITE **SUPREMACISTS.** I DON'T WANT TO BE LINKED TO THIS HISTORY.
PRECISELY. YOU'RE GOING TO **REWRITE** HISTORY. THE TEDDY GIRLS WERE A MISTAKE. SUCH A **TRANSGRESSIVE** AND **OUTCAST** GROUP SHOULD HAVE BEEN A SYMBOL FOR TOLERANCE, EQUALITY AND FEMINISM.
IT DOESN'T SOUND LIKE SOMETHING YOU'D SAY.
THINGS HAVE CHANGED, TEDDY. YOU CHANGED THINGS.
THE TEDDY GIRLS CHOSE TO **TRANSFER** TOWARDS OTHER PEOPLE THE HATRED THEY WERE BEING SHOWN.
HUH? MOM, I DON'T UNDERSTAND. CAN YOU PLEASE SLOW DOWN?

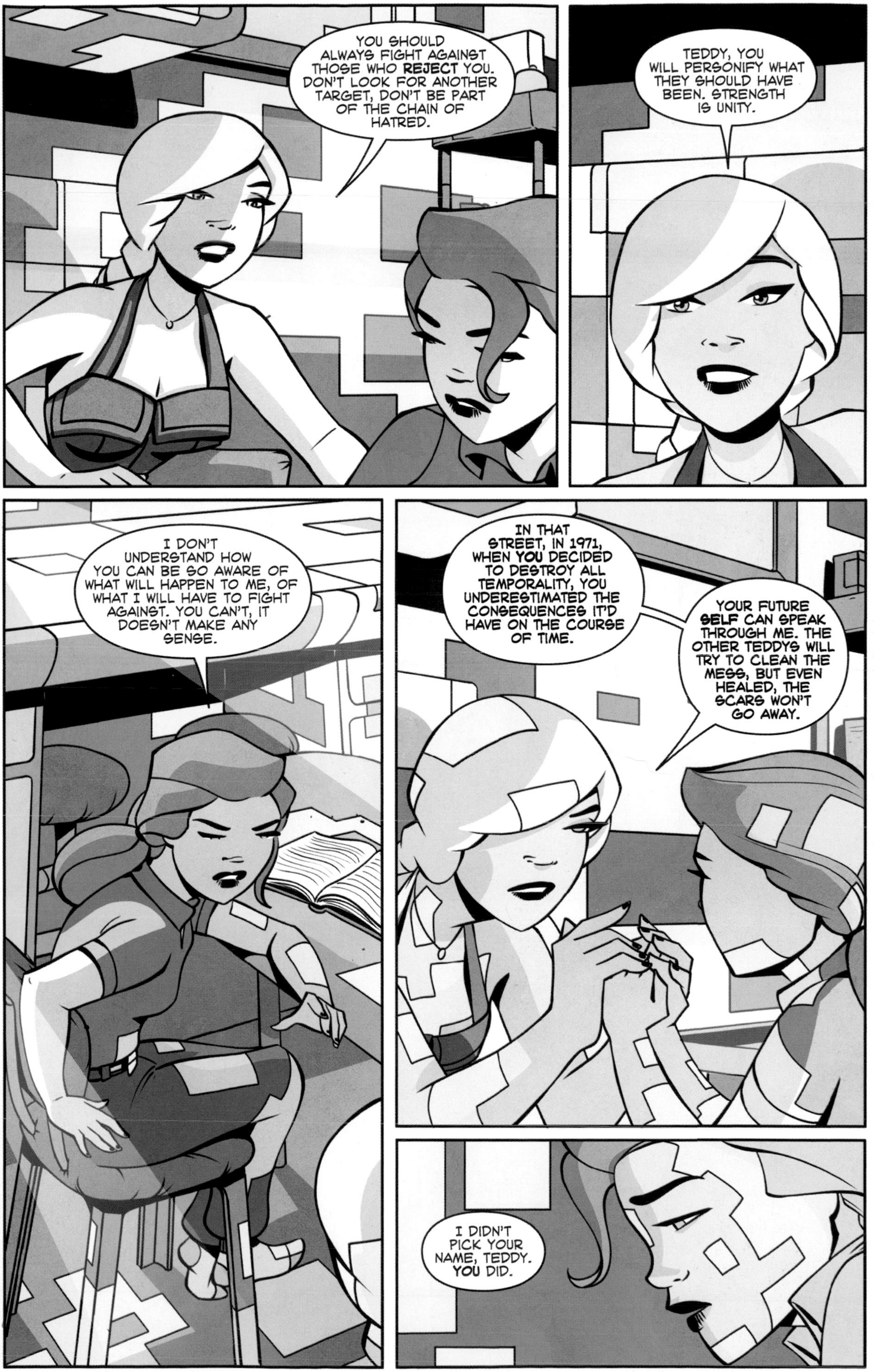
YOU SHOULD ALWAYS FIGHT AGAINST THOSE WHO **REJECT** YOU. DON'T LOOK FOR ANOTHER TARGET, DON'T BE PART OF THE CHAIN OF HATRED.
TEDDY, YOU WILL PERSONIFY WHAT THEY SHOULD HAVE BEEN. STRENGTH IS UNITY.
I DON'T UNDERSTAND HOW YOU CAN BE SO AWARE OF WHAT WILL HAPPEN TO ME, OF WHAT I WILL HAVE TO FIGHT AGAINST. YOU CAN'T, IT DOESN'T MAKE ANY SENSE.
IN THAT STREET, IN 1971, WHEN **YOU** DECIDED TO DESTROY ALL TEMPORALITY, YOU UNDERESTIMATED THE CONSEQUENCES IT'D HAVE ON THE COURSE OF TIME.
YOUR FUTURE **SELF** CAN SPEAK THROUGH ME. THE OTHER TEDDYS WILL TRY TO CLEAN THE MESS, BUT EVEN HEALED, THE SCARS WON'T GO AWAY.
I DIDN'T PICK YOUR NAME, TEDDY. **YOU** DID.

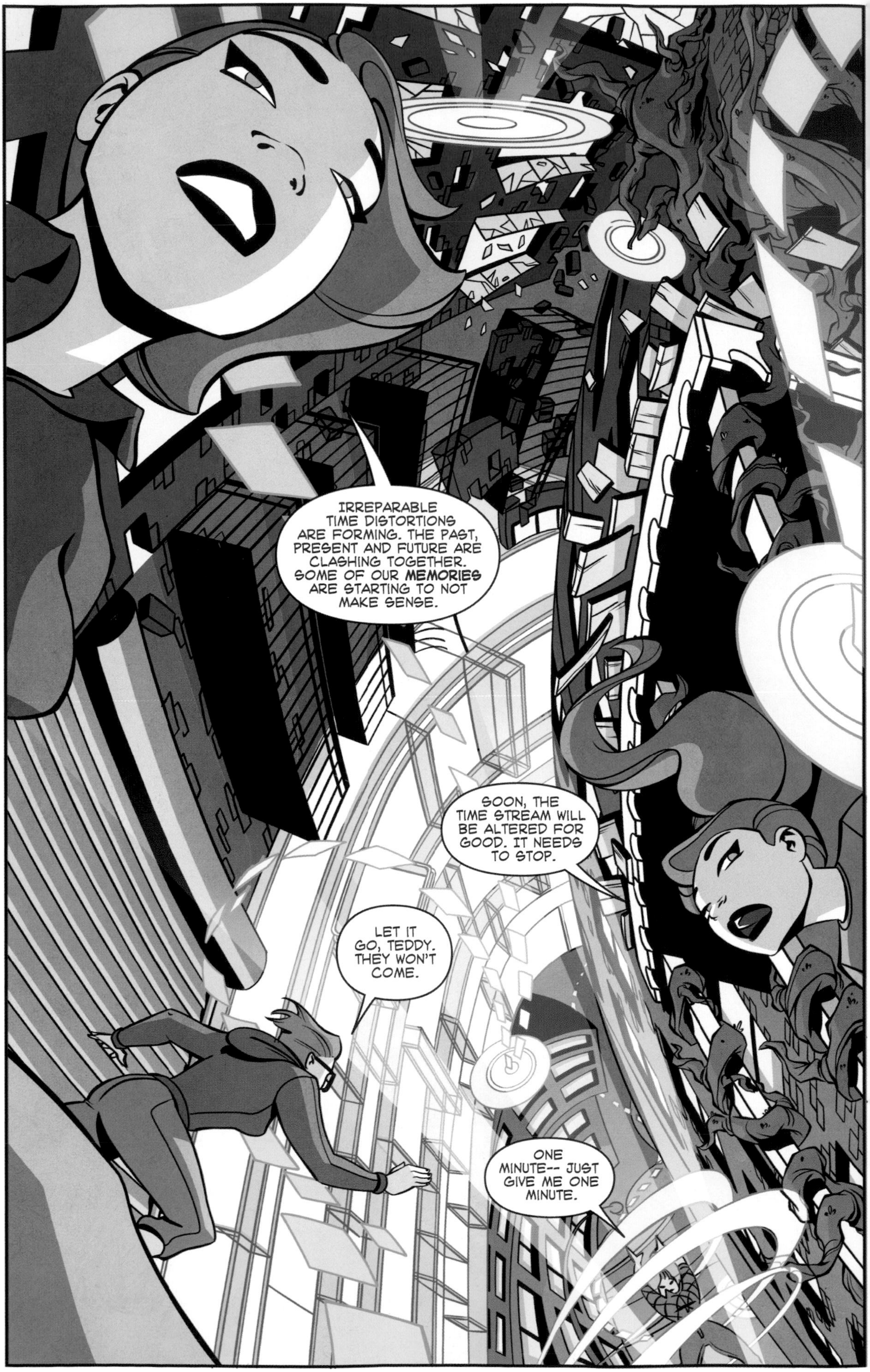
IRREPARABLE TIME DISTORTIONS ARE FORMING. THE PAST, PRESENT AND FUTURE ARE CLASHING TOGETHER. SOME OF OUR **MEMORIES** ARE STARTING TO NOT MAKE SENSE.
SOON, THE TIME STREAM WILL BE ALTERED FOR GOOD. IT NEEDS TO STOP.
LET IT GO, TEDDY. THEY WON'T COME.
ONE MINUTE-- JUST GIVE ME ONE MINUTE.

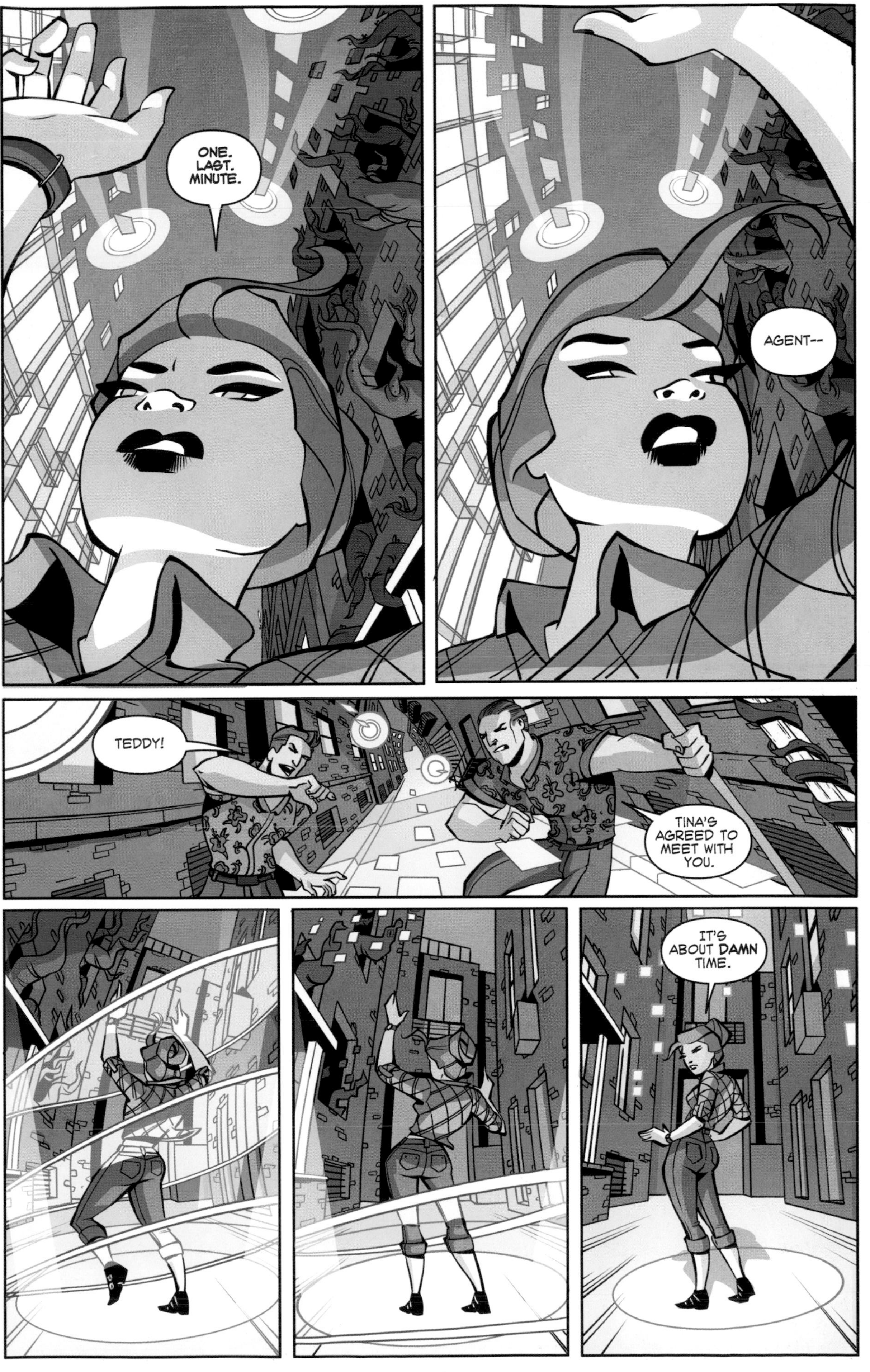
ONE. LAST. MINUTE.
AGENT--
TEDDY!
TINA'S AGREED TO MEET WITH YOU.
IT'S ABOUT DAMN TIME.

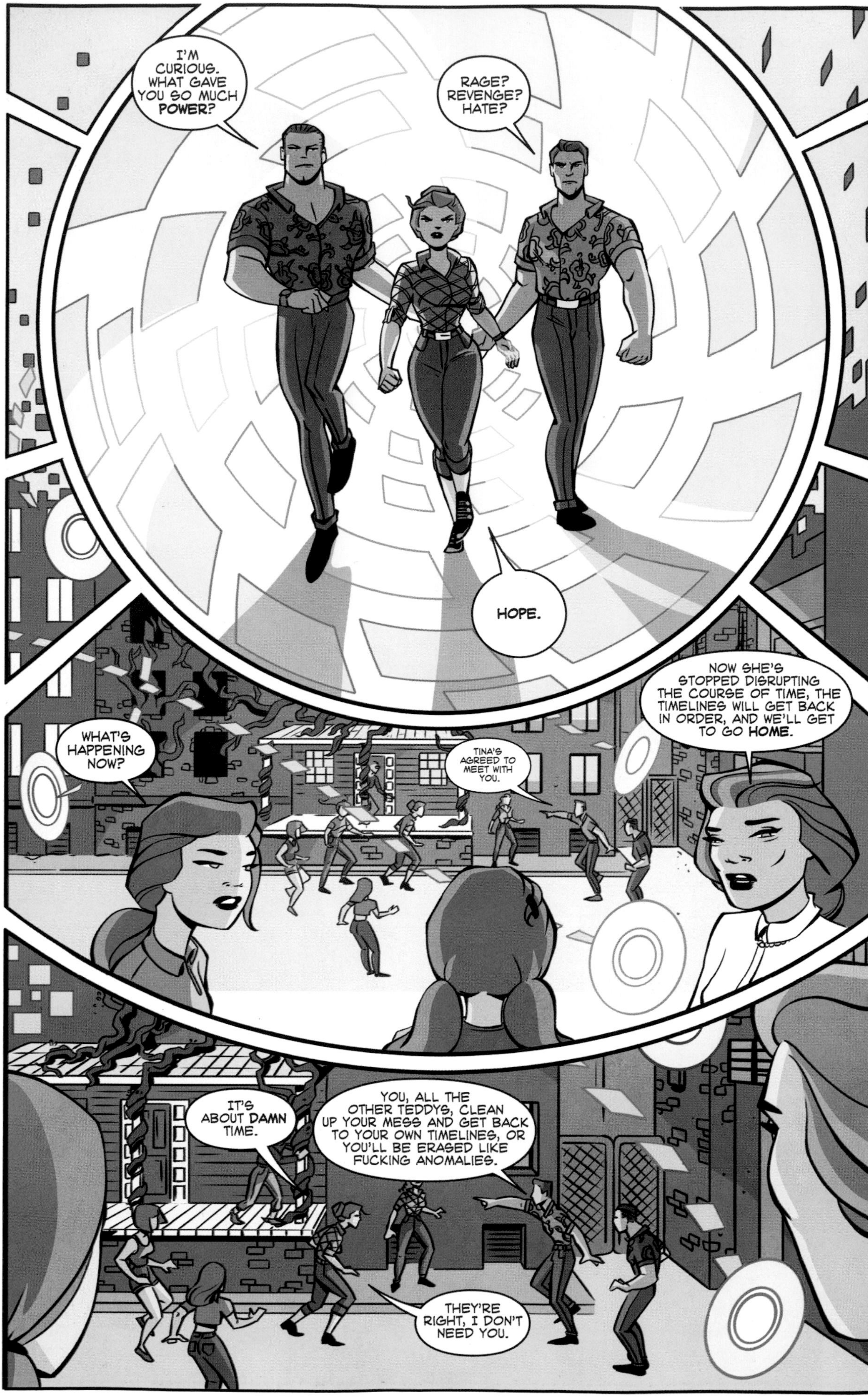
I'M CURIOUS. WHAT GAVE YOU SO MUCH POWER?
RAGE? REVENGE? HATE?
HOPE.
WHAT'S HAPPENING NOW?
TINA'S AGREED TO MEET WITH YOU.
NOW SHE'S STOPPED DISRUPTING THE COURSE OF TIME, THE TIMELINES WILL GET BACK IN ORDER, AND WE'LL GET TO GO HOME.
IT'S ABOUT DAMN TIME.
YOU, ALL THE OTHER TEDDYS, CLEAN UP YOUR MESS AND GET BACK TO YOUR OWN TIMELINES, OR YOU'LL BE ERASED LIKE FUCKING ANOMALIES.
THEY'RE RIGHT, I DON'T NEED YOU.

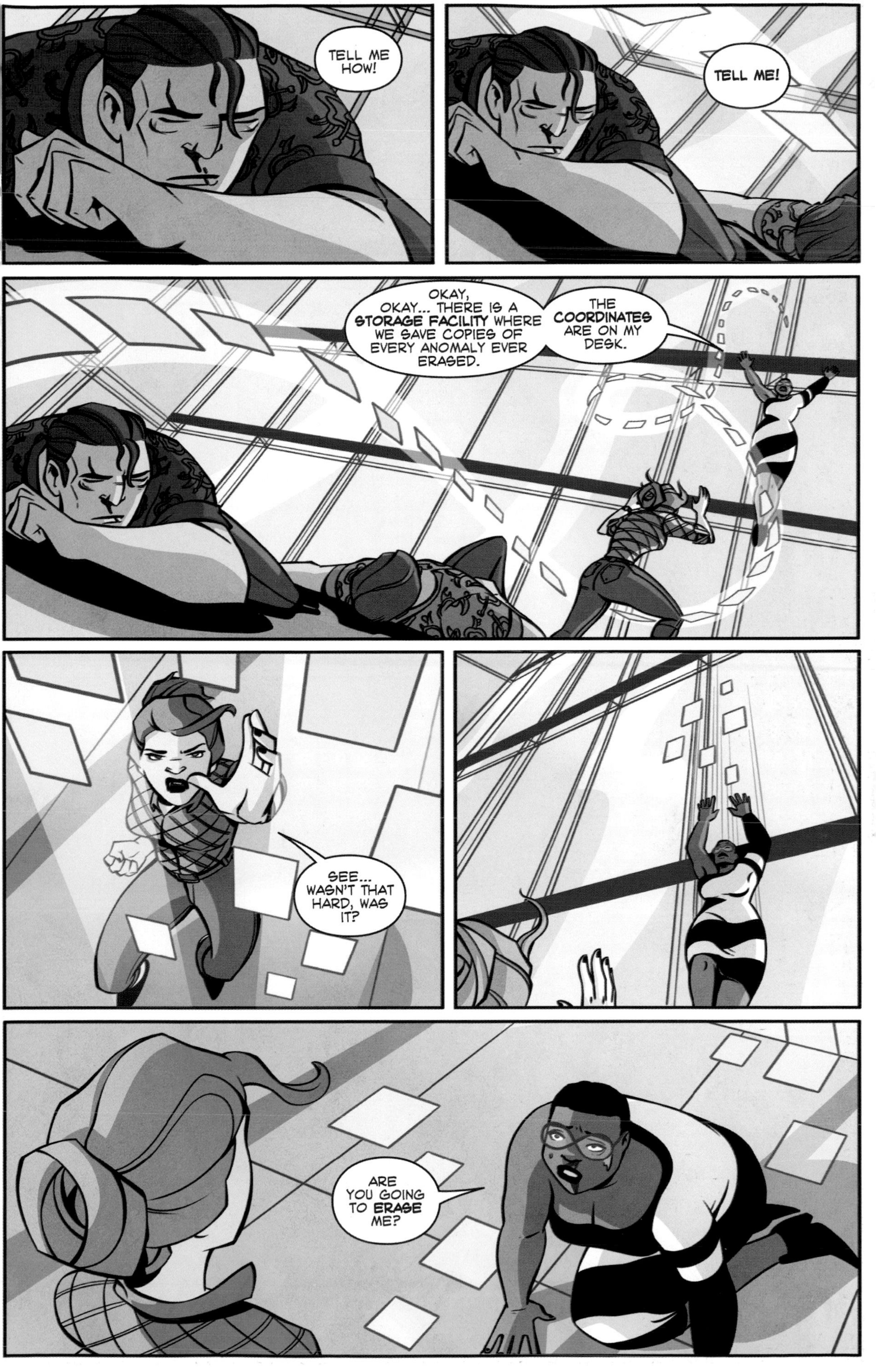
TELL ME HOW!
TELL ME!
OKAY, OKAY... THERE IS A STORAGE FACILITY WHERE WE SAVE COPIES OF EVERY ANOMALY EVER ERASED.
THE COORDINATES ARE ON MY DESK.
SEE... WASN'T THAT HARD, WAS IT?
ARE YOU GOING TO ERASE ME?

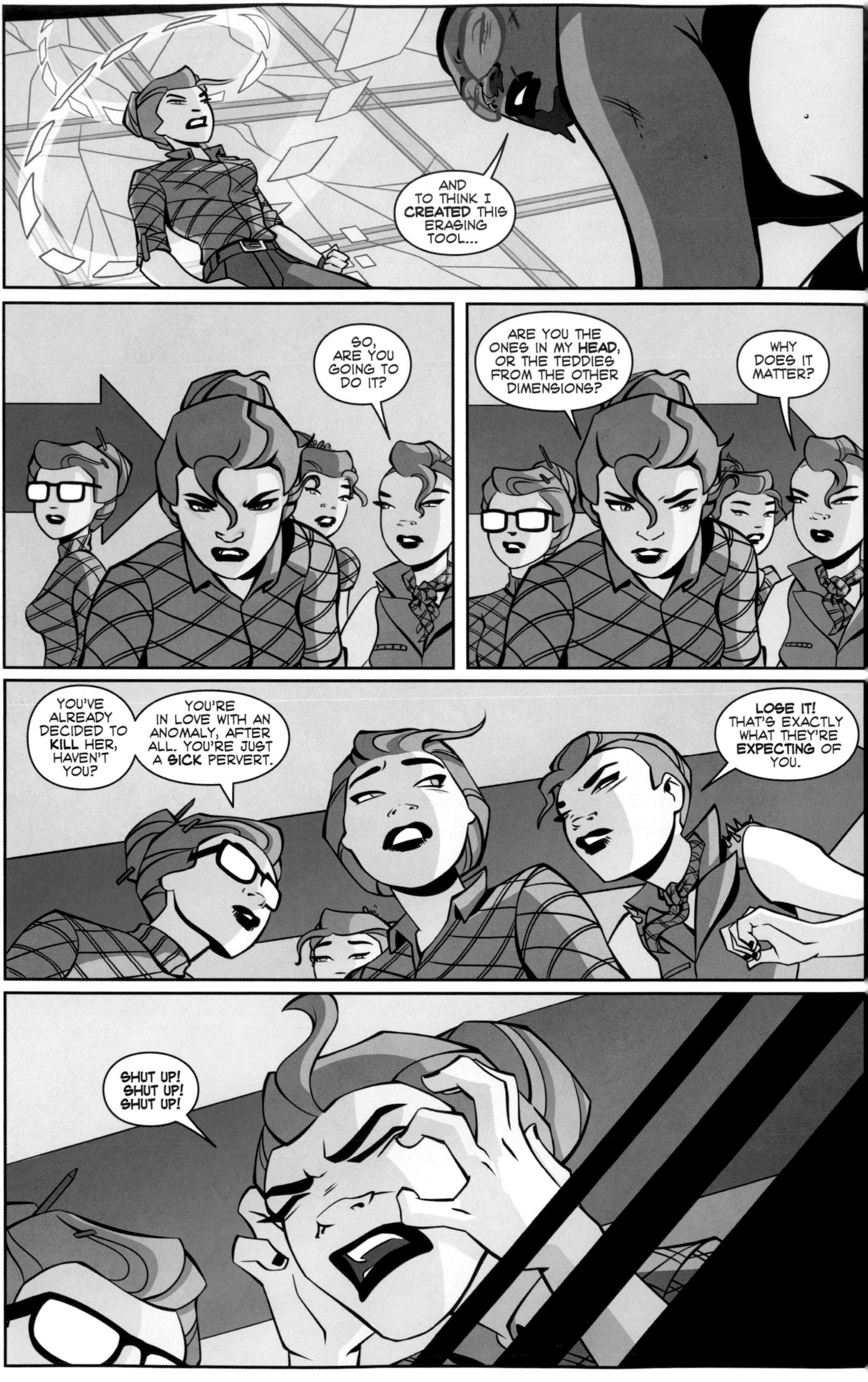
AND TO THINK I **CREATED** THIS ERASING TOOL...
SO, ARE YOU GOING TO DO IT?
ARE YOU THE ONES IN MY **HEAD**, OR THE TEDDIES FROM THE OTHER DIMENSIONS?
WHY DOES IT MATTER?
YOU'VE ALREADY DECIDED TO **KILL** HER, HAVEN'T YOU?
YOU'RE IN LOVE WITH AN ANOMALY, AFTER ALL. YOU'RE JUST A **SICK** PERVERT.
LOSE IT! THAT'S EXACTLY WHAT THEY'RE **EXPECTING** OF YOU.
SHUT UP! SHUT UP! SHUT UP!

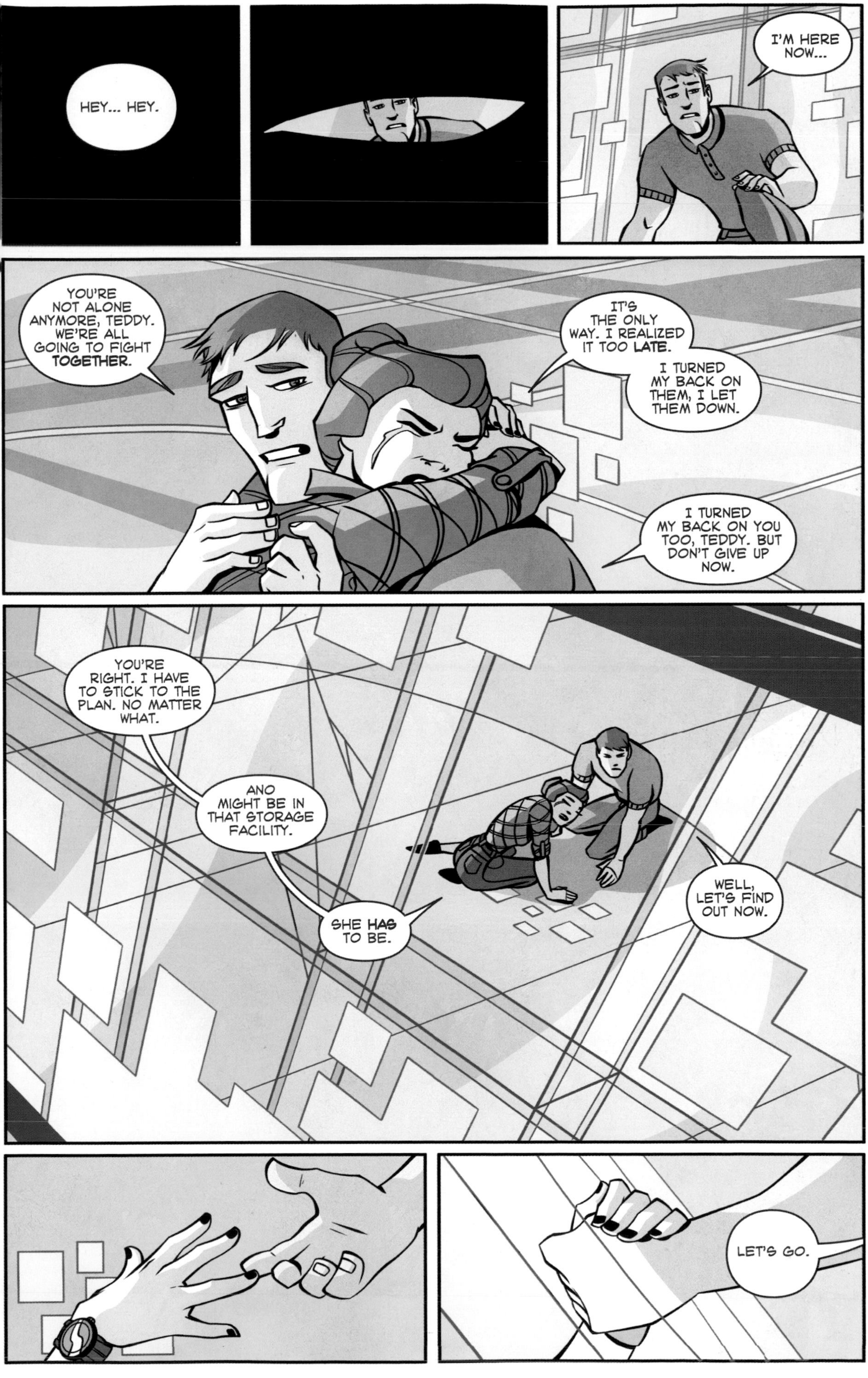
HEY... HEY.
I'M HERE NOW...
YOU'RE NOT ALONE ANYMORE, TEDDY. WE'RE ALL GOING TO FIGHT **TOGETHER**.
IT'S THE ONLY WAY. I REALIZED IT TOO **LATE**.
I TURNED MY BACK ON THEM, I LET THEM DOWN.
I TURNED MY BACK ON YOU TOO, TEDDY. BUT DON'T GIVE UP NOW.
YOU'RE RIGHT. I HAVE TO STICK TO THE PLAN. NO MATTER WHAT.
ANO MIGHT BE IN THAT STORAGE FACILITY.
SHE **HAS** TO BE.
WELL, LET'S FIND OUT NOW.
LET'S GO.

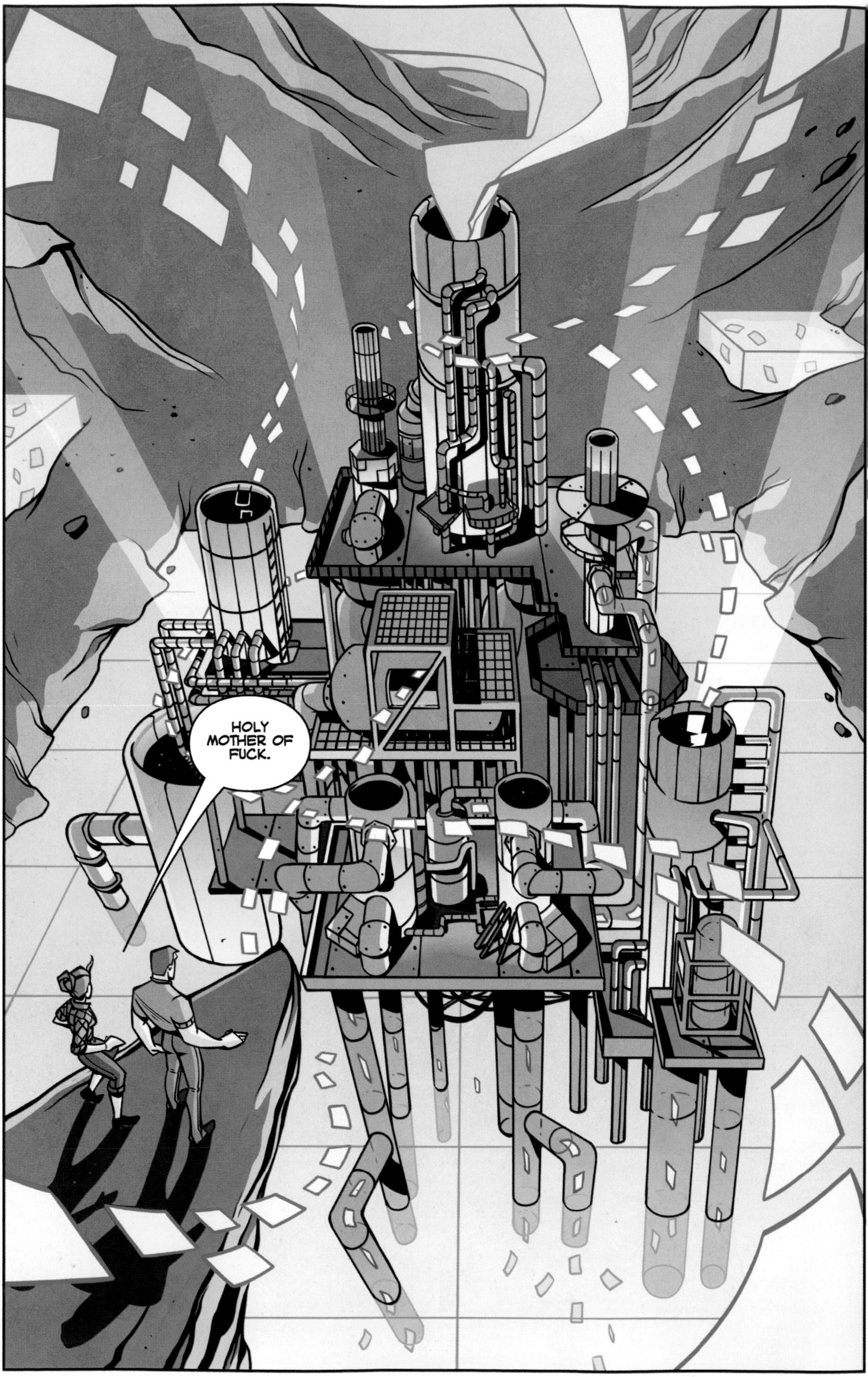
HOLY MOTHER OF FUCK.

Art by **GERALD PAREL**

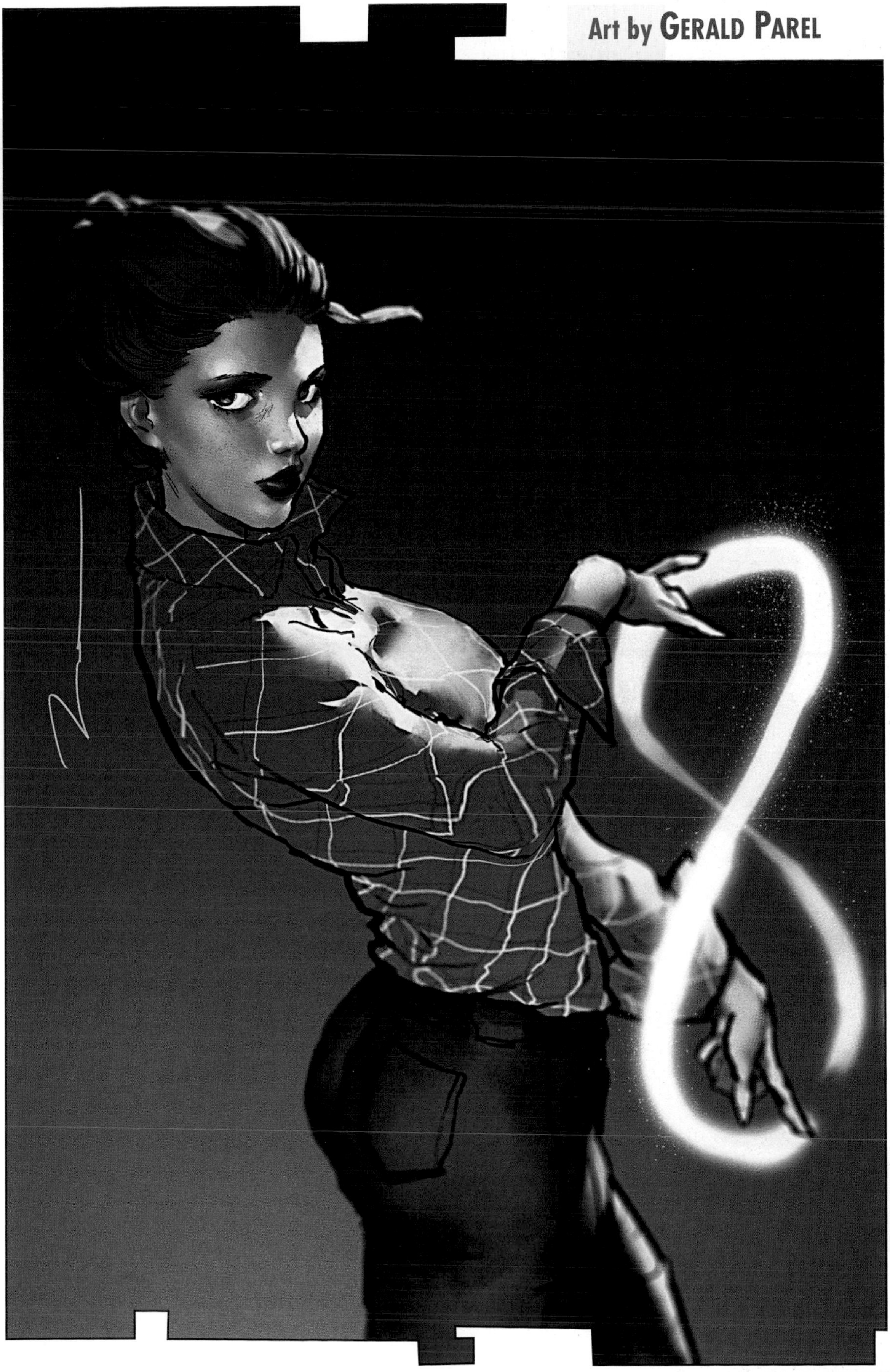

Art by Elsa Charretier

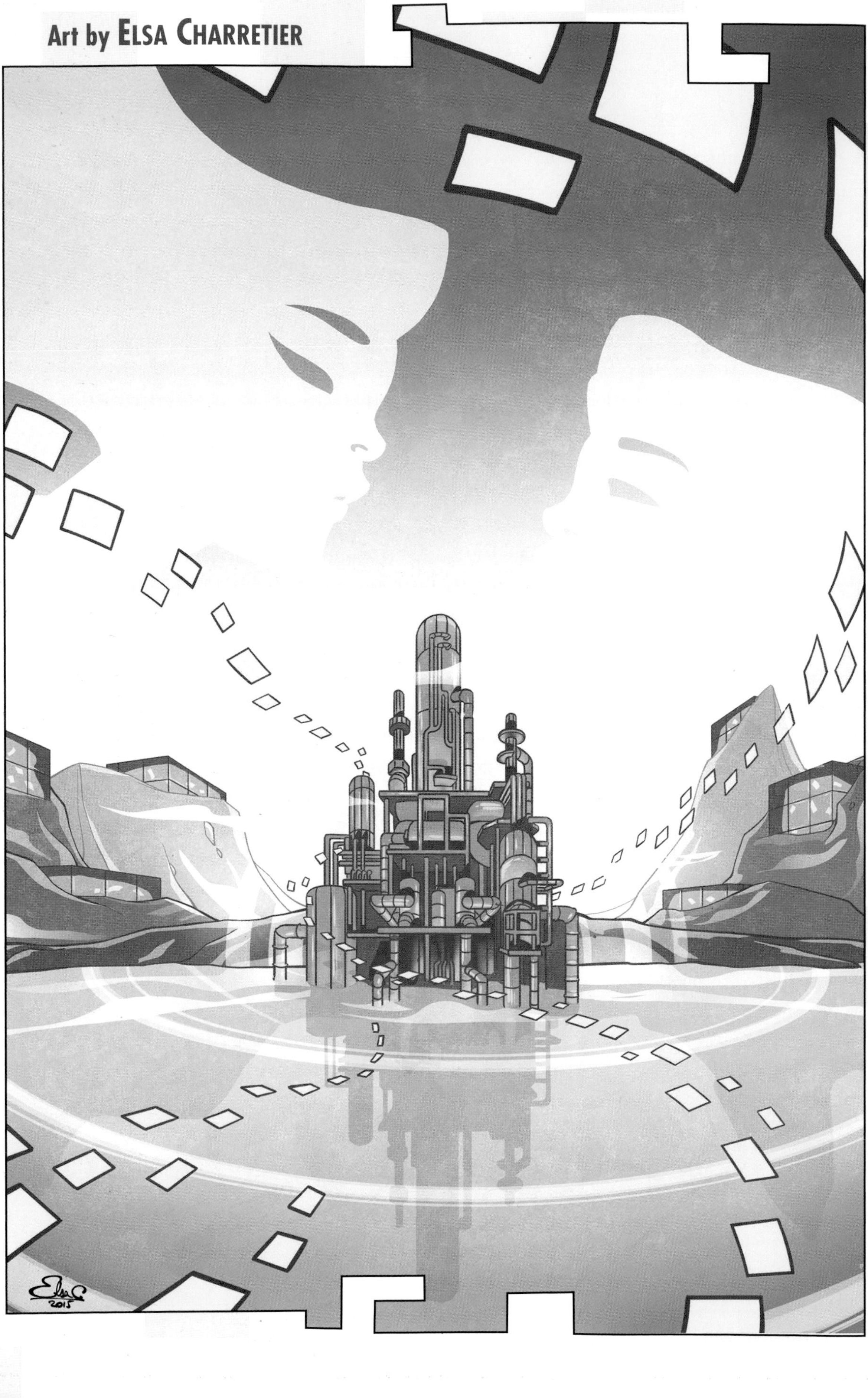
Elsa C
2015

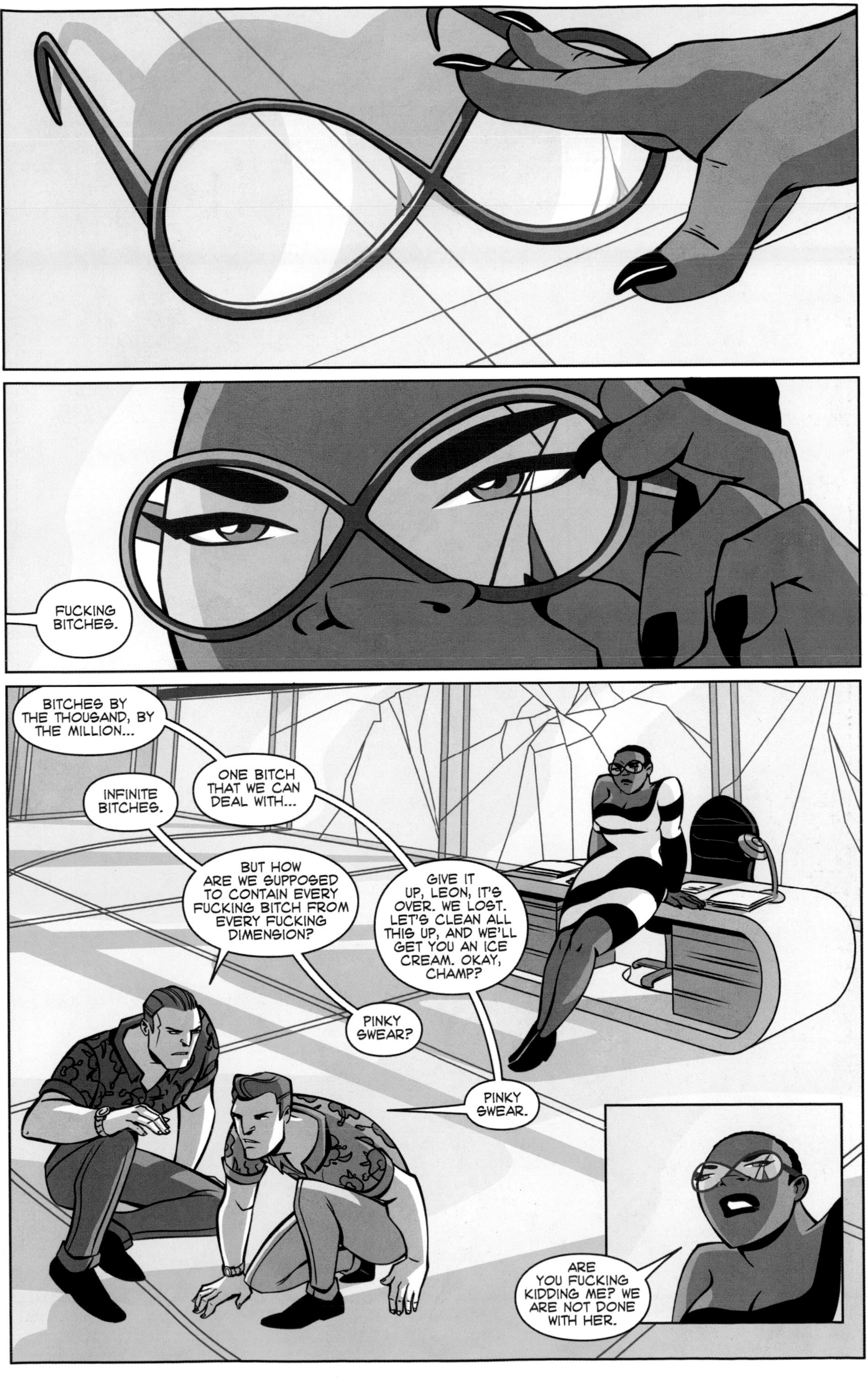
FUCKING BITCHES.
BITCHES BY THE THOUSAND, BY THE MILLION...
ONE BITCH THAT WE CAN DEAL WITH...
INFINITE BITCHES.
BUT HOW ARE WE SUPPOSED TO CONTAIN EVERY FUCKING BITCH FROM EVERY FUCKING DIMENSION?
GIVE IT UP, LEON, IT'S OVER. WE LOST. LET'S CLEAN ALL THIS UP, AND WE'LL GET YOU AN ICE CREAM. OKAY, CHAMP?
PINKY SWEAR?
PINKY SWEAR.
ARE YOU FUCKING KIDDING ME? WE ARE NOT DONE WITH HER.

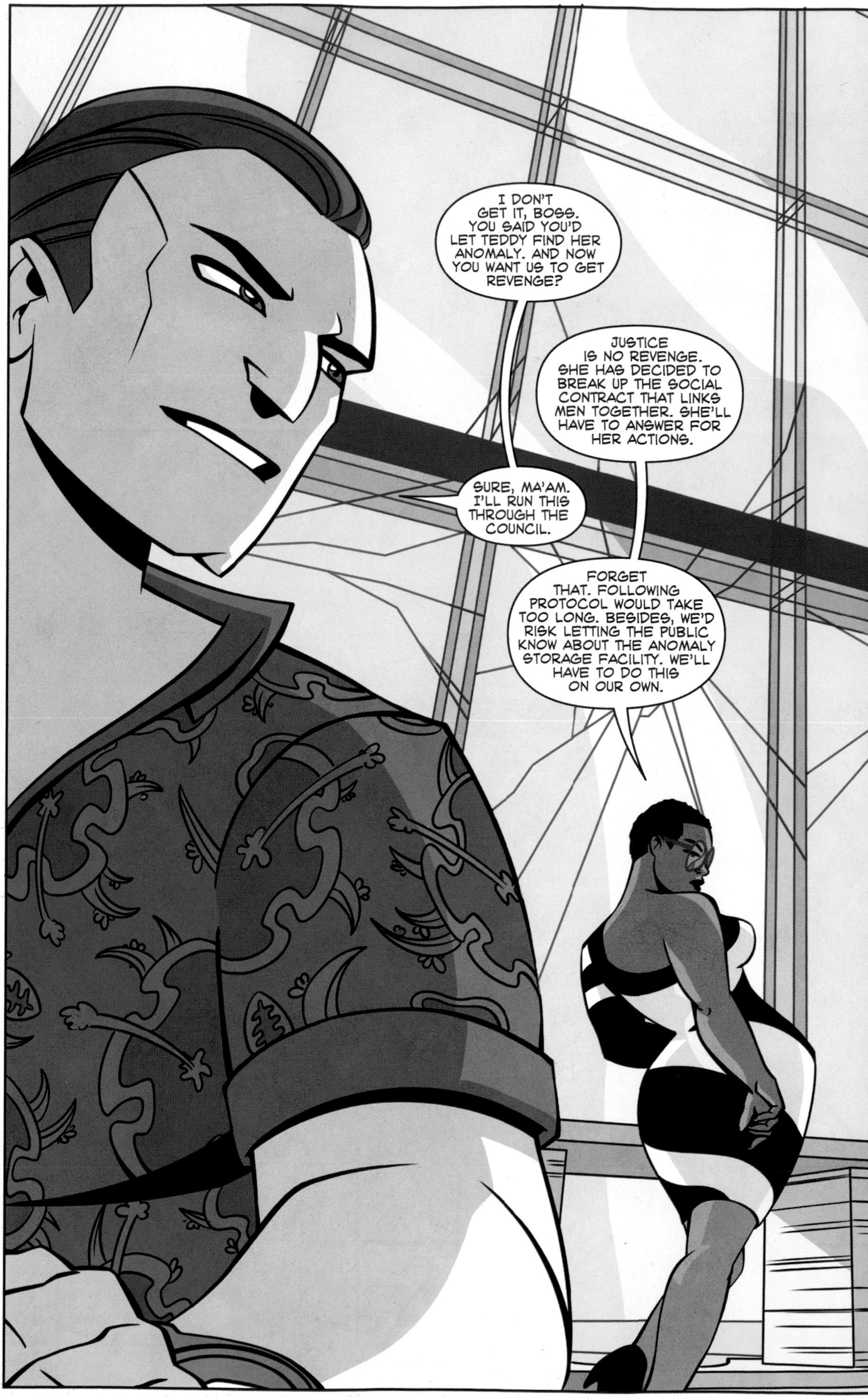
I DON'T GET IT, BOSS. YOU SAID YOU'D LET TEDDY FIND HER ANOMALY. AND NOW YOU WANT US TO GET REVENGE?
JUSTICE IS NO REVENGE. SHE HAS DECIDED TO BREAK UP THE SOCIAL CONTRACT THAT LINKS MEN TOGETHER. SHE'LL HAVE TO ANSWER FOR HER ACTIONS.
SURE, MA'AM. I'LL RUN THIS THROUGH THE COUNCIL.
FORGET THAT. FOLLOWING PROTOCOL WOULD TAKE TOO LONG. BESIDES, WE'D RISK LETTING THE PUBLIC KNOW ABOUT THE ANOMALY STORAGE FACILITY. WE'LL HAVE TO DO THIS ON OUR OWN.

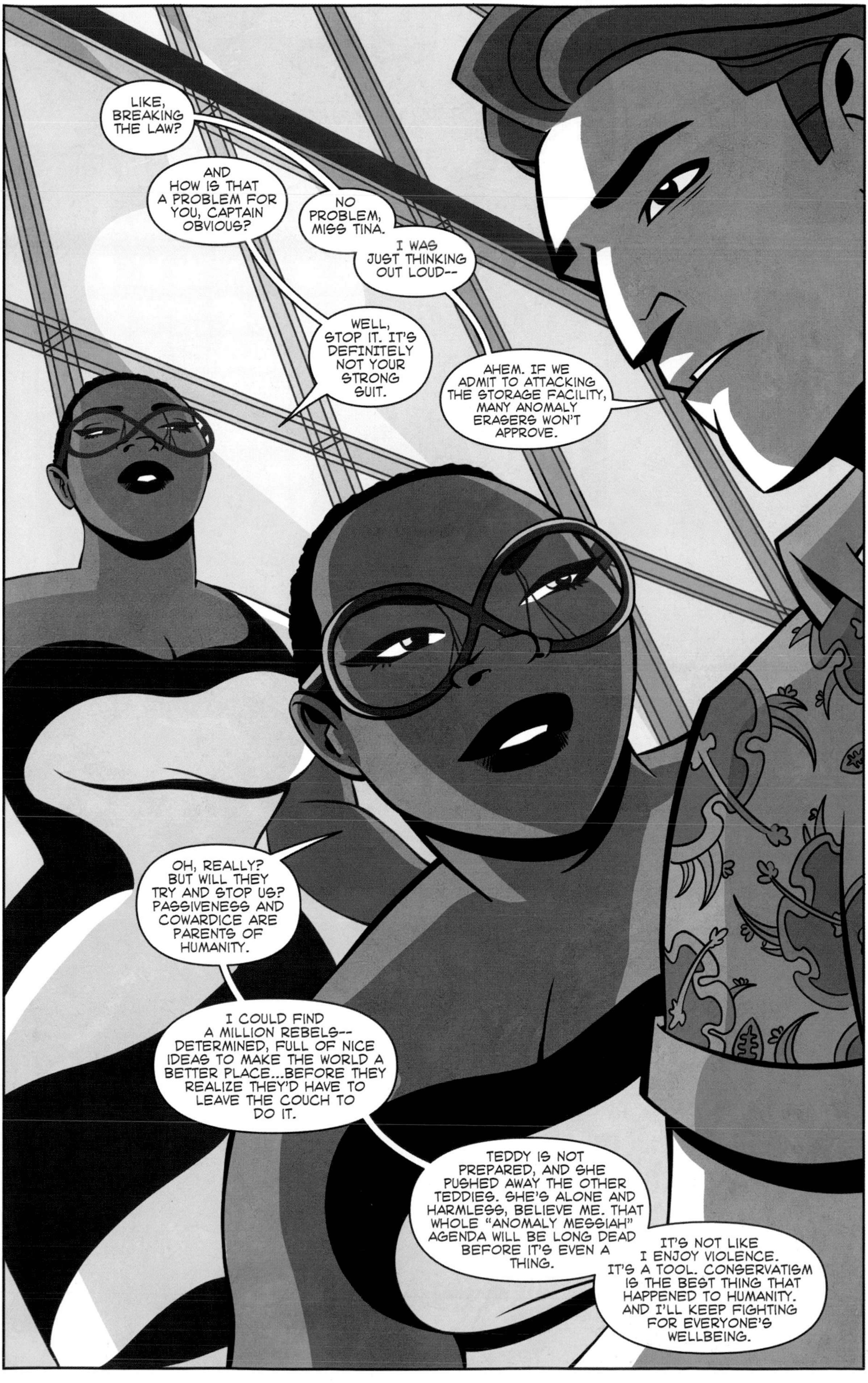
LIKE, BREAKING THE LAW?
AND HOW IS THAT A PROBLEM FOR YOU, CAPTAIN OBVIOUS?
NO PROBLEM, MISS TINA.
I WAS JUST THINKING OUT LOUD--
WELL, STOP IT. IT'S DEFINITELY NOT YOUR STRONG SUIT.
AHEM. IF WE ADMIT TO ATTACKING THE STORAGE FACILITY, MANY ANOMALY ERASERS WON'T APPROVE.
OH, REALLY? BUT WILL THEY TRY AND STOP US? PASSIVENESS AND COWARDICE ARE PARENTS OF HUMANITY.
I COULD FIND A MILLION REBELS--DETERMINED, FULL OF NICE IDEAS TO MAKE THE WORLD A BETTER PLACE...BEFORE THEY REALIZE THEY'D HAVE TO LEAVE THE COUCH TO DO IT.
TEDDY IS NOT PREPARED, AND SHE PUSHED AWAY THE OTHER TEDDIES. SHE'S ALONE AND HARMLESS, BELIEVE ME. THAT WHOLE "ANOMALY MESSIAH" AGENDA WILL BE LONG DEAD BEFORE IT'S EVEN A THING.
IT'S NOT LIKE I ENJOY VIOLENCE. IT'S A TOOL. CONSERVATISM IS THE BEST THING THAT HAPPENED TO HUMANITY. AND I'LL KEEP FIGHTING FOR EVERYONE'S WELLBEING.

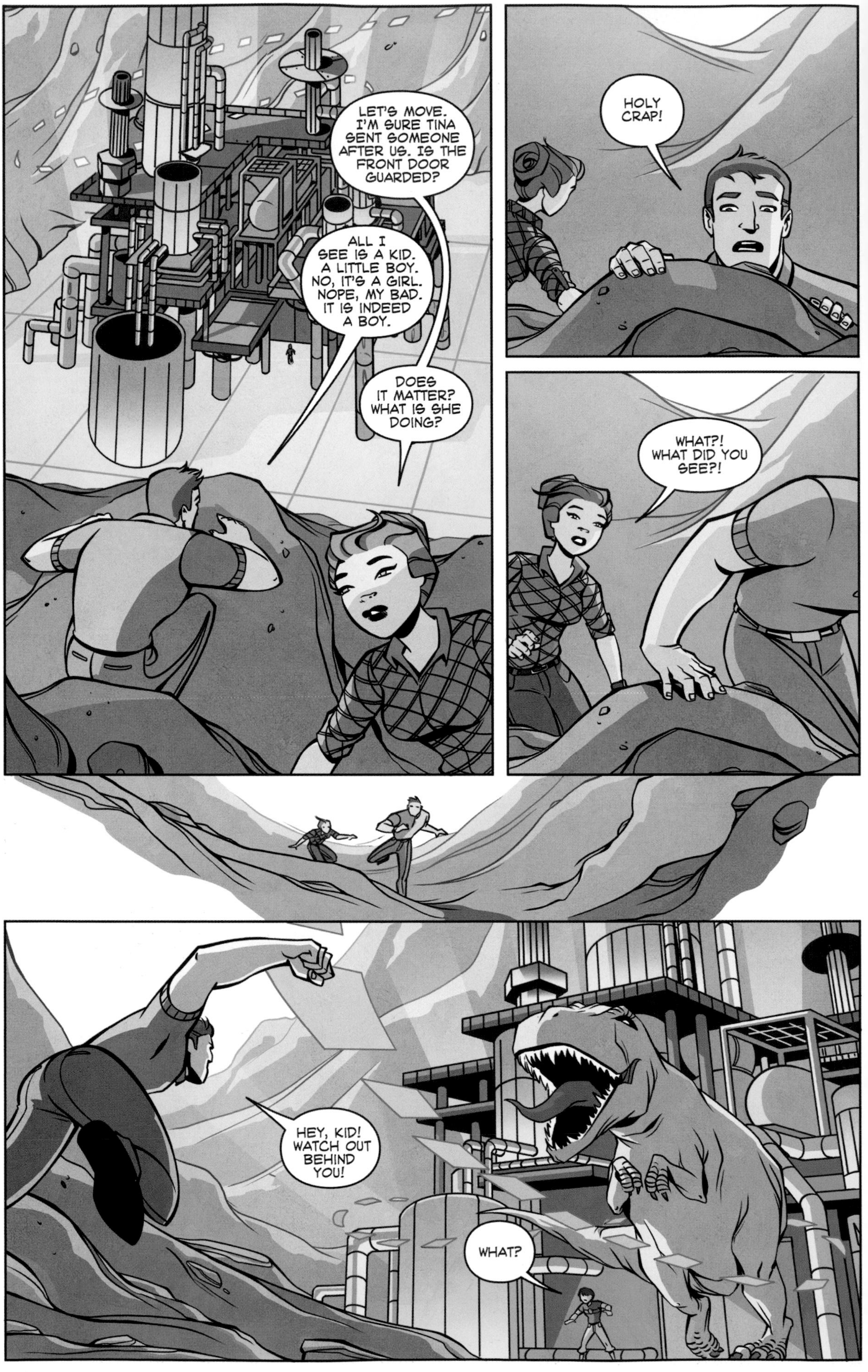

LET'S MOVE. I'M SURE TINA SENT SOMEONE AFTER US. IS THE FRONT DOOR GUARDED?
ALL I SEE IS A KID. A LITTLE BOY. NO, IT'S A GIRL. NOPE, MY BAD. IT IS INDEED A BOY.
DOES IT MATTER? WHAT IS SHE DOING?
HOLY CRAP!
WHAT?! WHAT DID YOU SEE?!
HEY, KID! WATCH OUT BEHIND YOU!
WHAT?

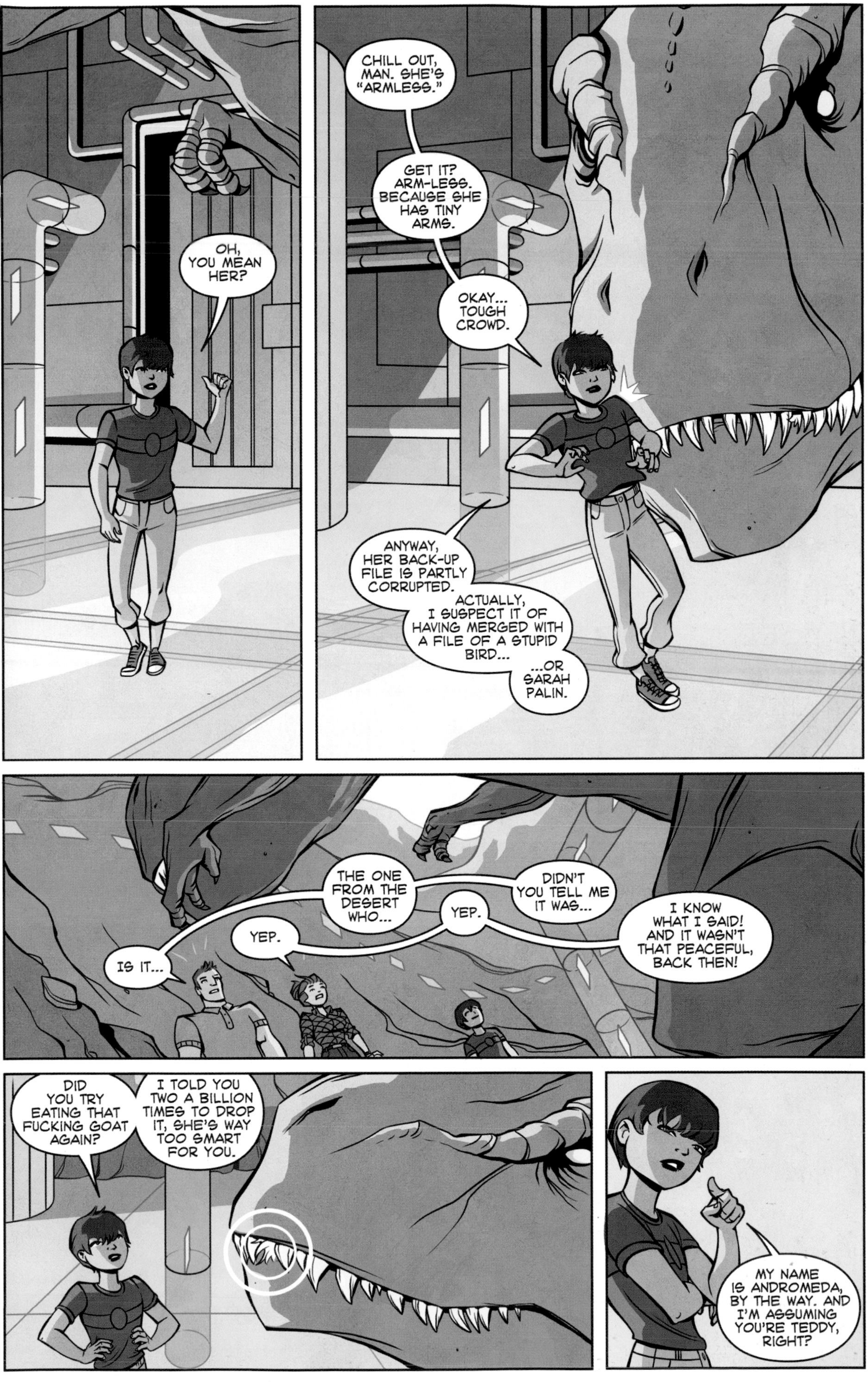

OH, YOU MEAN HER?
CHILL OUT, MAN. SHE'S "ARMLESS."
GET IT? ARM-LESS. BECAUSE SHE HAS TINY ARMS.
OKAY... TOUGH CROWD.
ANYWAY, HER BACK-UP FILE IS PARTLY CORRUPTED.
ACTUALLY, I SUSPECT IT OF HAVING MERGED WITH A FILE OF A STUPID BIRD...
...OR SARAH PALIN.
IS IT...
YEP.
THE ONE FROM THE DESERT WHO...
YEP.
DIDN'T YOU TELL ME IT WAS...
I KNOW WHAT I SAID! AND IT WASN'T THAT PEACEFUL, BACK THEN!
DID YOU TRY EATING THAT FUCKING GOAT AGAIN?
I TOLD YOU TWO A BILLION TIMES TO DROP IT, SHE'S WAY TOO SMART FOR YOU.
MY NAME IS ANDROMEDA, BY THE WAY. AND I'M ASSUMING YOU'RE TEDDY, RIGHT?

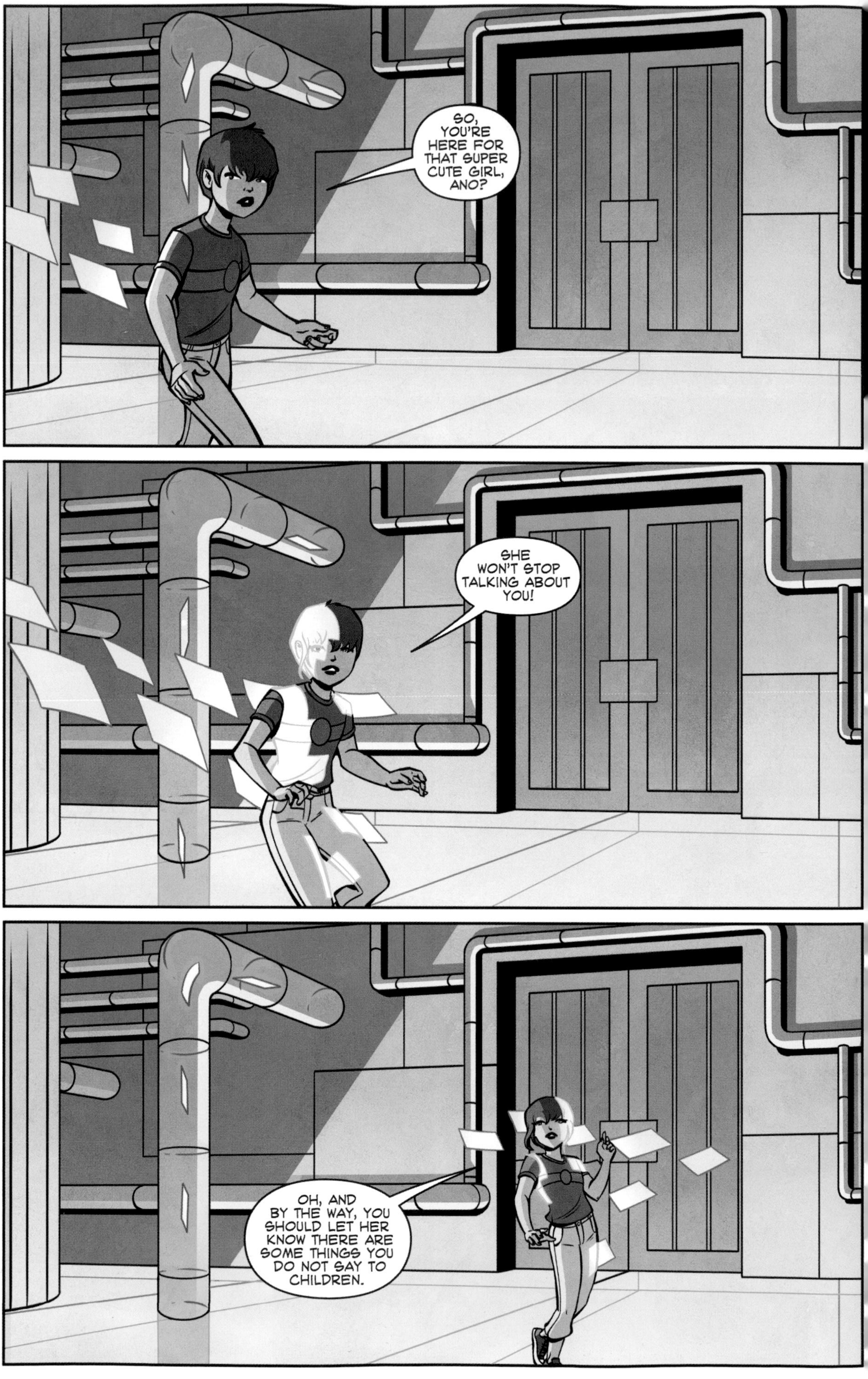
SO, YOU'RE HERE FOR THAT SUPER CUTE GIRL, ANO?
SHE WON'T STOP TALKING ABOUT YOU!
OH, AND BY THE WAY, YOU SHOULD LET HER KNOW THERE ARE SOME THINGS YOU DO NOT SAY TO CHILDREN.

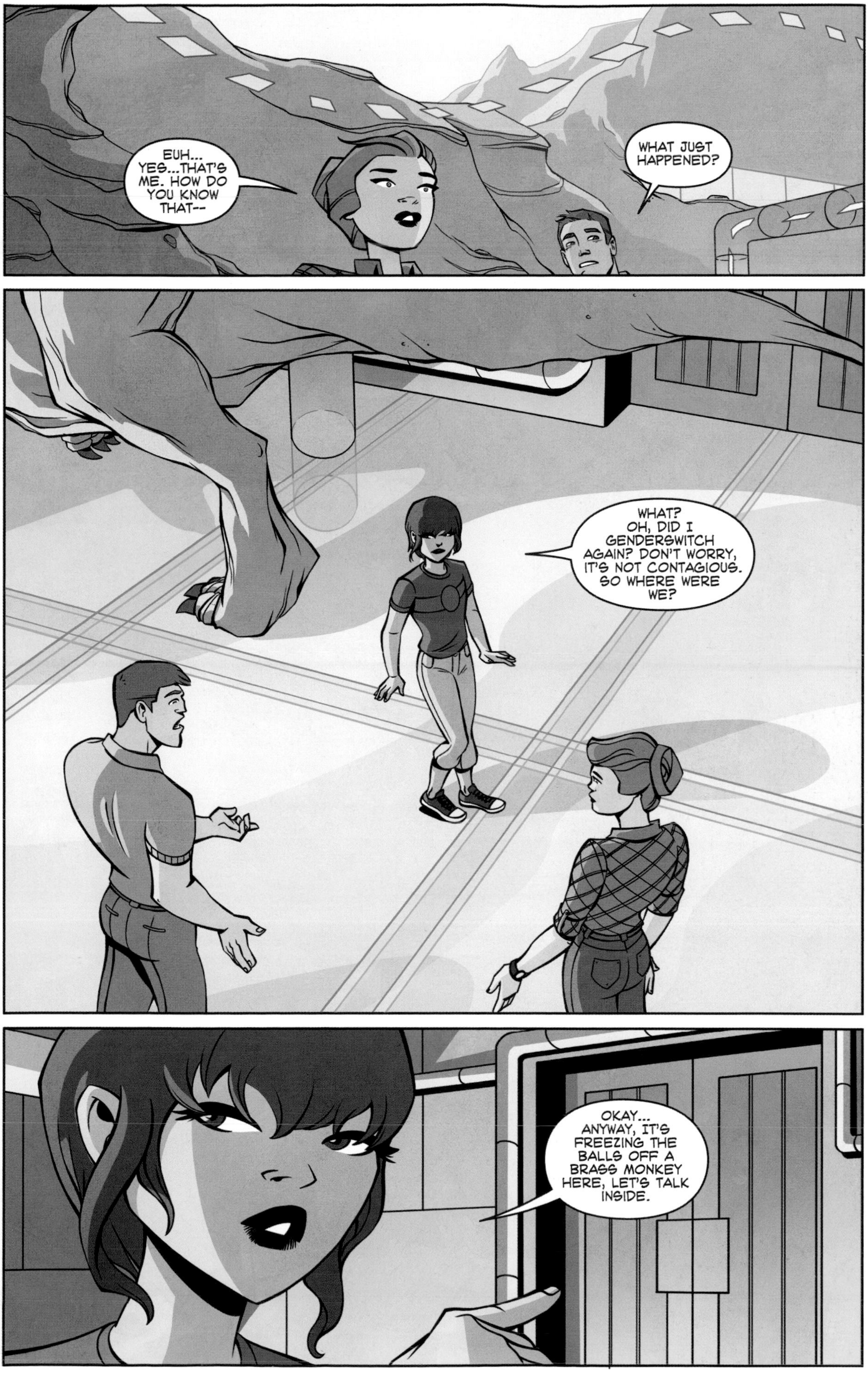
EUH... YES...THAT'S ME. HOW DO YOU KNOW THAT--
WHAT JUST HAPPENED?
WHAT? OH, DID I GENDERSWITCH AGAIN? DON'T WORRY, IT'S NOT CONTAGIOUS. SO WHERE WERE WE?
OKAY... ANYWAY, IT'S FREEZING THE BALLS OFF A BRASS MONKEY HERE, LET'S TALK INSIDE.

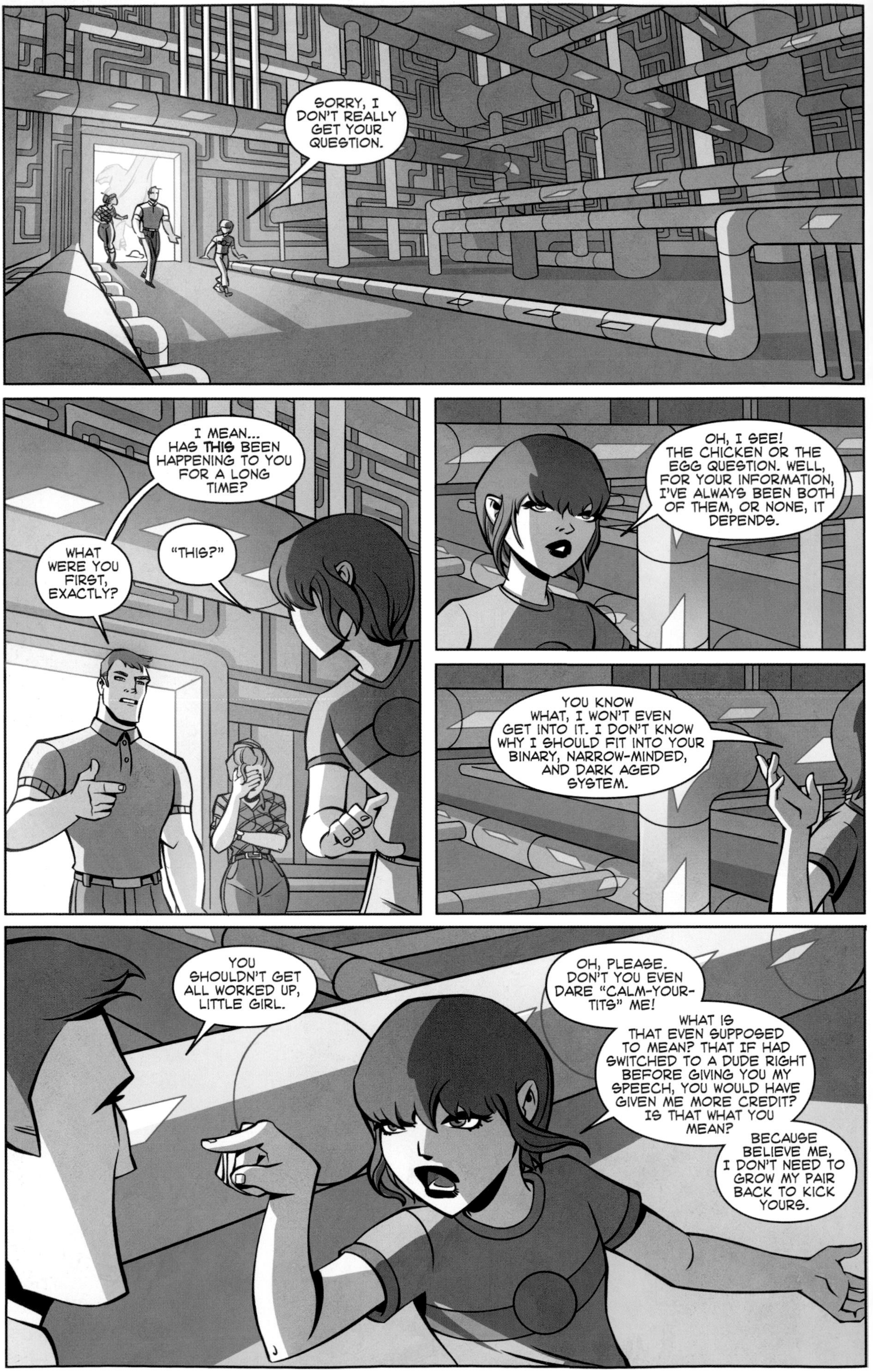
SORRY, I DON'T REALLY GET YOUR QUESTION.
I MEAN... HAS THIS BEEN HAPPENING TO YOU FOR A LONG TIME?
WHAT WERE YOU FIRST, EXACTLY?
"THIS?"
OH, I SEE! THE CHICKEN OR THE EGG QUESTION. WELL, FOR YOUR INFORMATION, I'VE ALWAYS BEEN BOTH OF THEM, OR NONE, IT DEPENDS.
YOU KNOW WHAT, I WON'T EVEN GET INTO IT. I DON'T KNOW WHY I SHOULD FIT INTO YOUR BINARY, NARROW-MINDED, AND DARK AGED SYSTEM.
YOU SHOULDN'T GET ALL WORKED UP, LITTLE GIRL.
OH, PLEASE. DON'T YOU EVEN DARE "CALM-YOUR-TITS" ME!
WHAT IS THAT EVEN SUPPOSED TO MEAN? THAT IF HAD SWITCHED TO A DUDE RIGHT BEFORE GIVING YOU MY SPEECH, YOU WOULD HAVE GIVEN ME MORE CREDIT? IS THAT WHAT YOU MEAN?
BECAUSE BELIEVE ME, I DON'T NEED TO GROW MY PAIR BACK TO KICK YOURS.

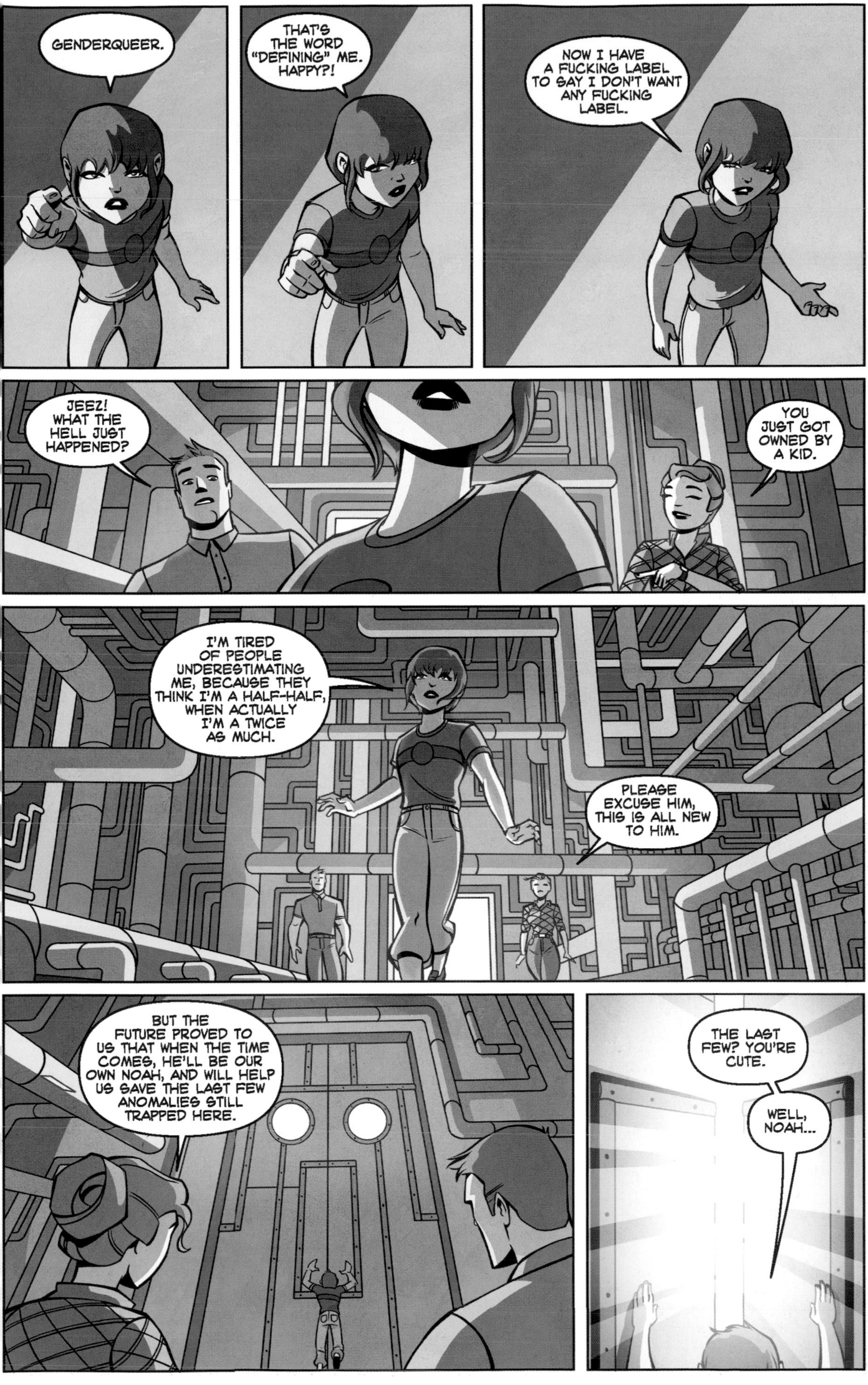
GENDERQUEER.
THAT'S THE WORD "DEFINING" ME. HAPPY?!
NOW I HAVE A FUCKING LABEL TO SAY I DON'T WANT ANY FUCKING LABEL.
JEEZ! WHAT THE HELL JUST HAPPENED?
YOU JUST GOT OWNED BY A KID.
I'M TIRED OF PEOPLE UNDERESTIMATING ME, BECAUSE THEY THINK I'M A HALF-HALF, WHEN ACTUALLY I'M A TWICE AS MUCH.
PLEASE EXCUSE HIM, THIS IS ALL NEW TO HIM.
BUT THE FUTURE PROVED TO US THAT WHEN THE TIME COMES, HE'LL BE OUR OWN NOAH, AND WILL HELP US SAVE THE LAST FEW ANOMALIES STILL TRAPPED HERE.
THE LAST FEW? YOU'RE CUTE.
WELL, NOAH...

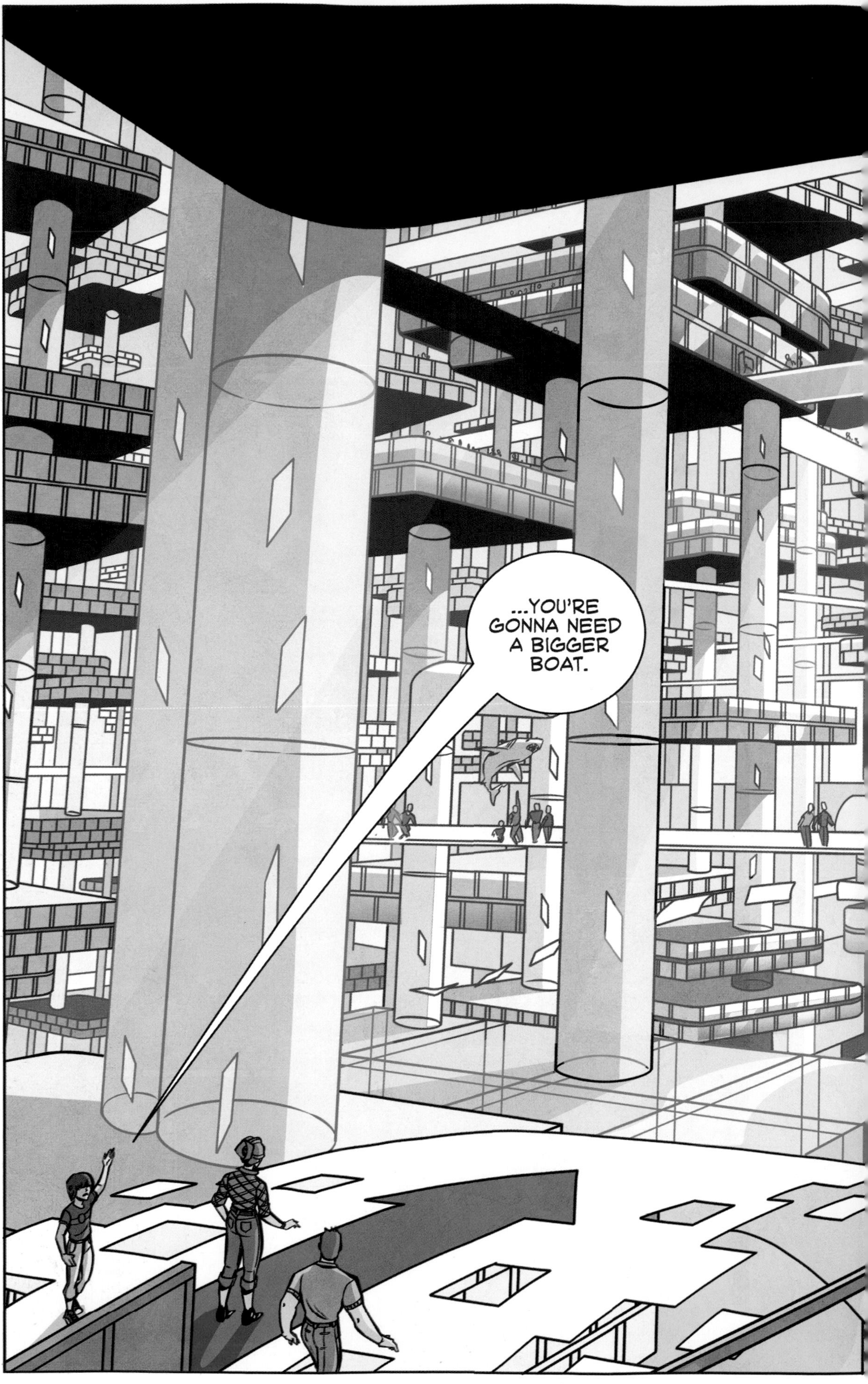
...YOU'RE GONNA NEED A BIGGER BOAT.

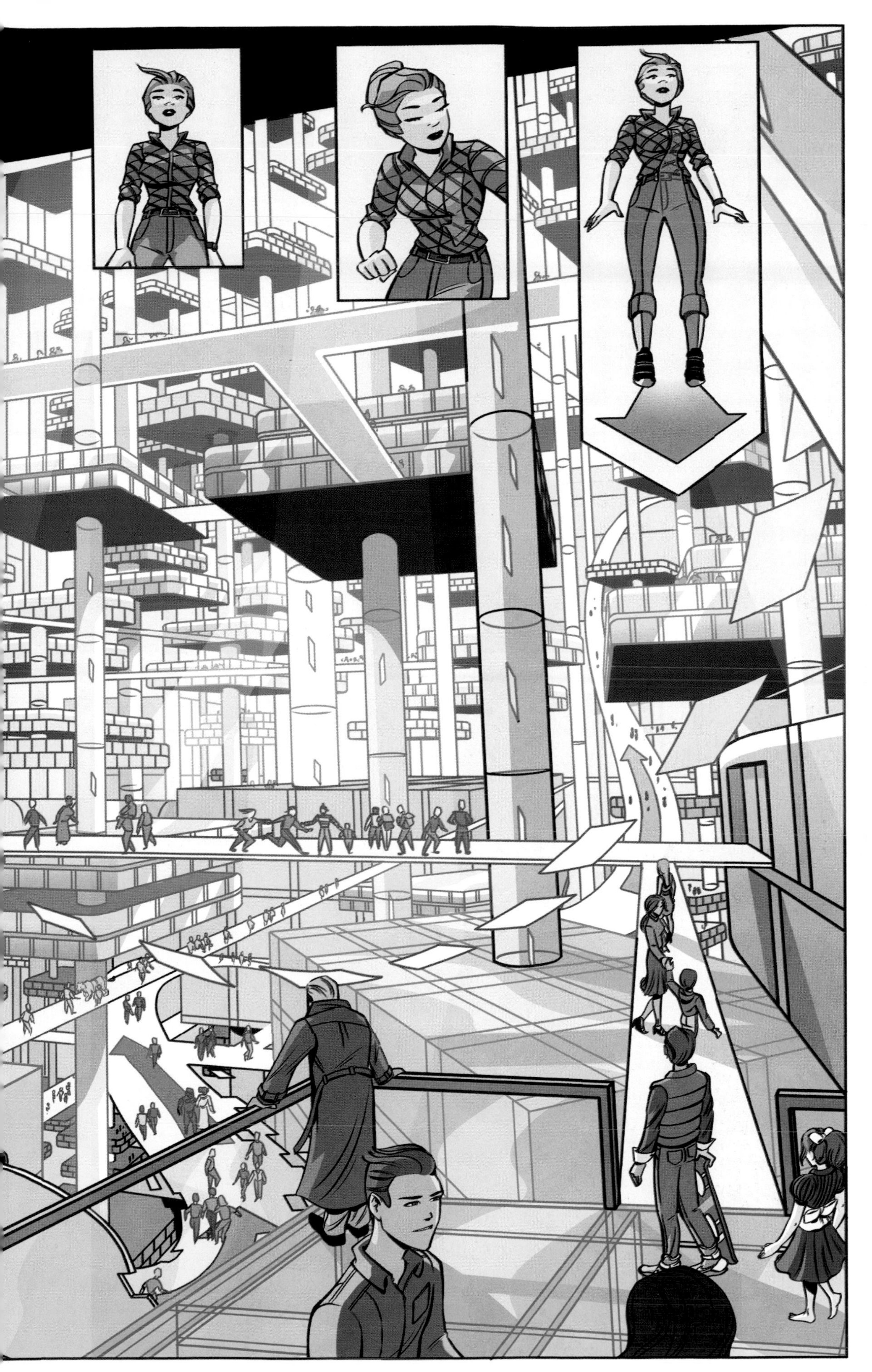

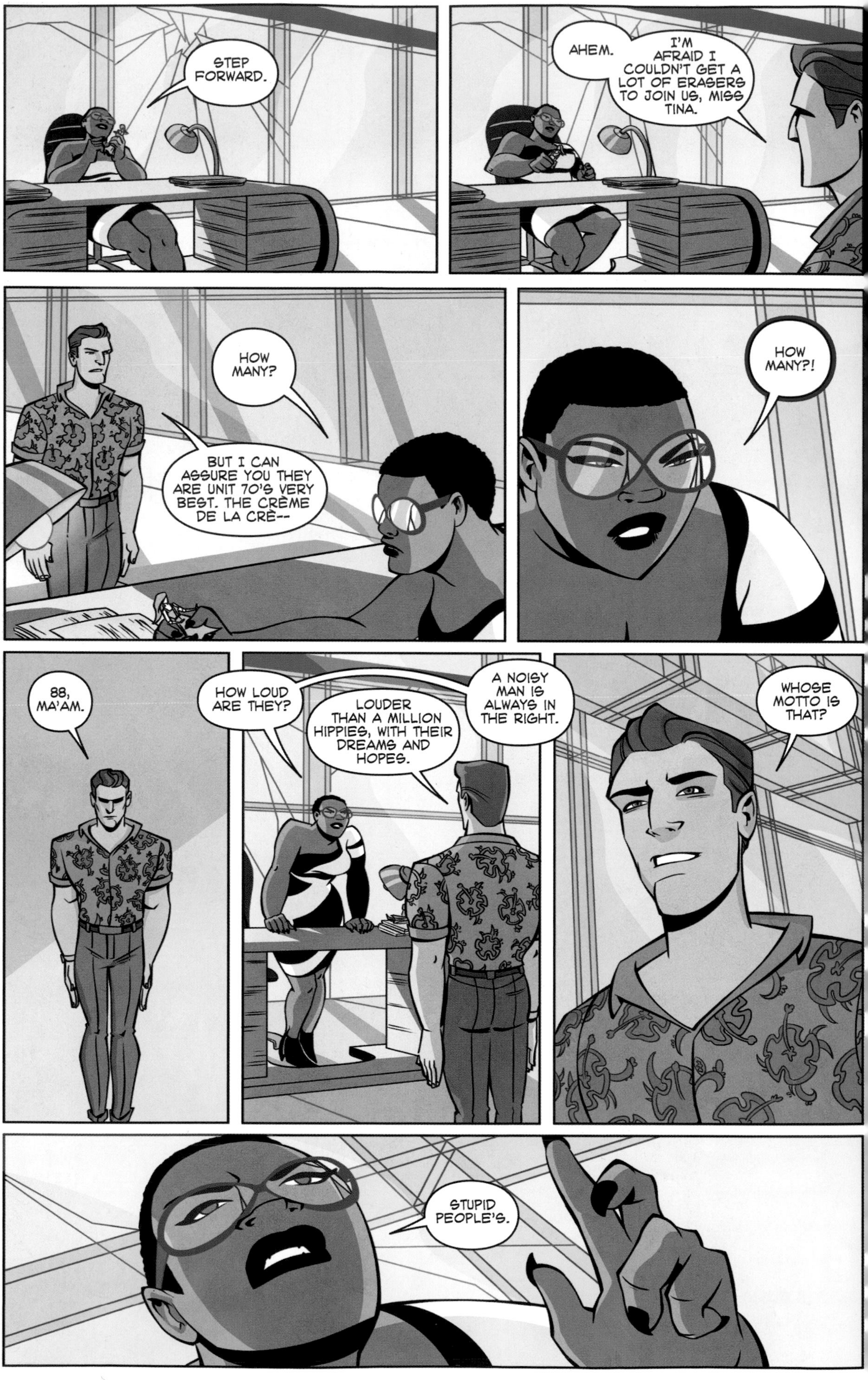
STEP FORWARD.
AHEM.
I'M AFRAID I COULDN'T GET A LOT OF ERASERS TO JOIN US, MISS TINA.
HOW MANY?
BUT I CAN ASSURE YOU THEY ARE UNIT 70'S VERY BEST. THE CRÈME DE LA CRÈ--
HOW MANY?!
88, MA'AM.
HOW LOUD ARE THEY?
LOUDER THAN A MILLION HIPPIES, WITH THEIR DREAMS AND HOPES.
A NOISY MAN IS ALWAYS IN THE RIGHT.
WHOSE MOTTO IS THAT?
STUPID PEOPLE'S.

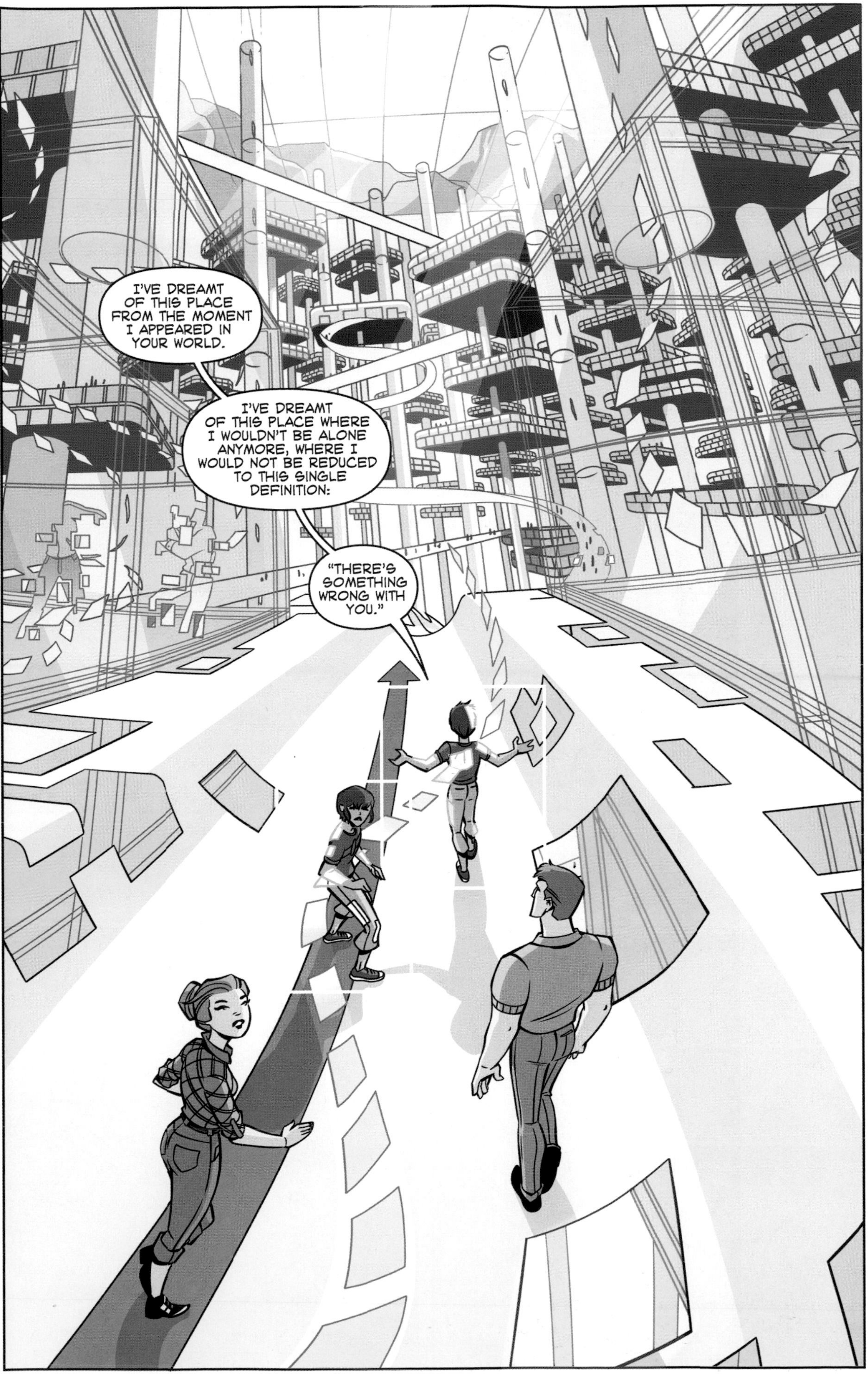
I'VE DREAMT OF THIS PLACE FROM THE MOMENT I APPEARED IN YOUR WORLD.
I'VE DREAMT OF THIS PLACE WHERE I WOULDN'T BE ALONE ANYMORE, WHERE I WOULD NOT BE REDUCED TO THIS SINGLE DEFINITION:
"THERE'S SOMETHING WRONG WITH YOU."

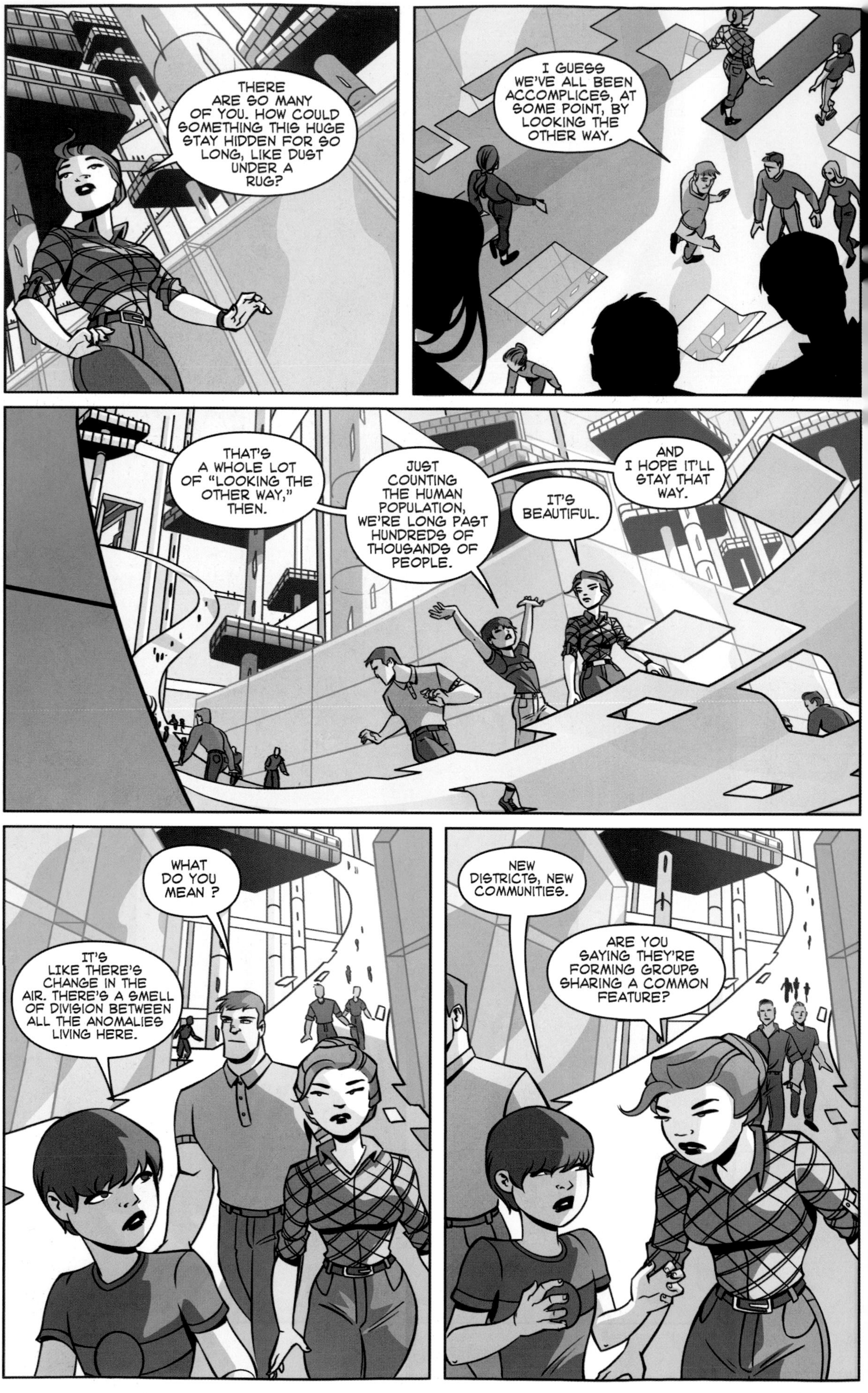
THERE ARE SO MANY OF YOU. HOW COULD SOMETHING THIS HUGE STAY HIDDEN FOR SO LONG, LIKE DUST UNDER A RUG?
I GUESS WE'VE ALL BEEN ACCOMPLICES, AT SOME POINT, BY LOOKING THE OTHER WAY.
THAT'S A WHOLE LOT OF "LOOKING THE OTHER WAY," THEN.
JUST COUNTING THE HUMAN POPULATION, WE'RE LONG PAST HUNDREDS OF THOUSANDS OF PEOPLE.
AND I HOPE IT'LL STAY THAT WAY.
IT'S BEAUTIFUL.
WHAT DO YOU MEAN ?
IT'S LIKE THERE'S CHANGE IN THE AIR. THERE'S A SMELL OF DIVISION BETWEEN ALL THE ANOMALIES LIVING HERE.
NEW DISTRICTS, NEW COMMUNITIES.
ARE YOU SAYING THEY'RE FORMING GROUPS SHARING A COMMON FEATURE?

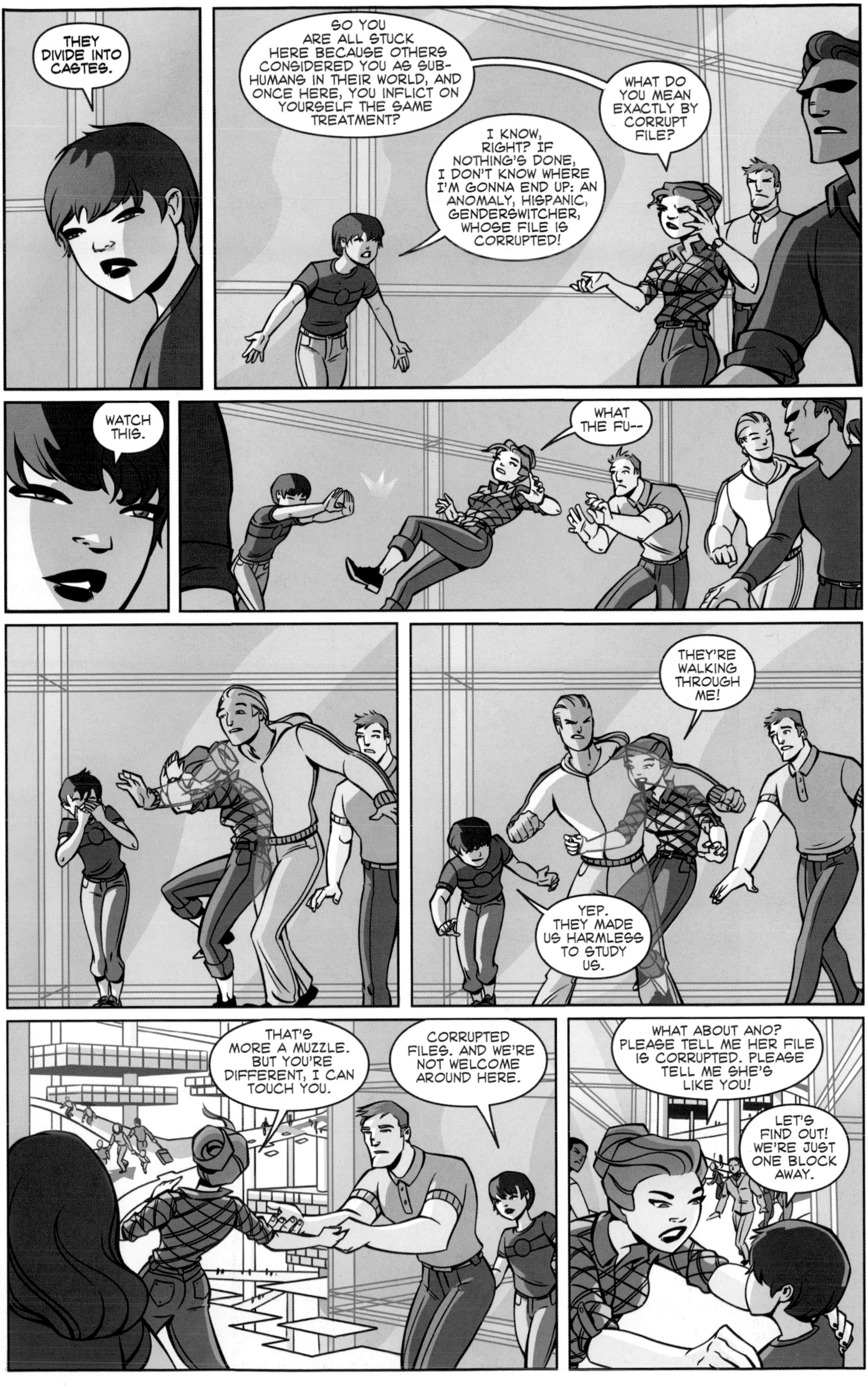
THEY DIVIDE INTO CASTES.
SO YOU ARE ALL STUCK HERE BECAUSE OTHERS CONSIDERED YOU AS SUB-HUMANS IN THEIR WORLD, AND ONCE HERE, YOU INFLICT ON YOURSELF THE SAME TREATMENT?
WHAT DO YOU MEAN EXACTLY BY CORRUPT FILE?
I KNOW, RIGHT? IF NOTHING'S DONE, I DON'T KNOW WHERE I'M GONNA END UP: AN ANOMALY, HISPANIC, GENDERSWITCHER, WHOSE FILE IS CORRUPTED!
WATCH THIS.
WHAT THE FU--
THEY'RE WALKING THROUGH ME!
YEP. THEY MADE US HARMLESS TO STUDY US.
THAT'S MORE A MUZZLE. BUT YOU'RE DIFFERENT, I CAN TOUCH YOU.
CORRUPTED FILES. AND WE'RE NOT WELCOME AROUND HERE.
WHAT ABOUT ANO? PLEASE TELL ME HER FILE IS CORRUPTED. PLEASE TELL ME SHE'S LIKE YOU!
LET'S FIND OUT! WE'RE JUST ONE BLOCK AWAY.

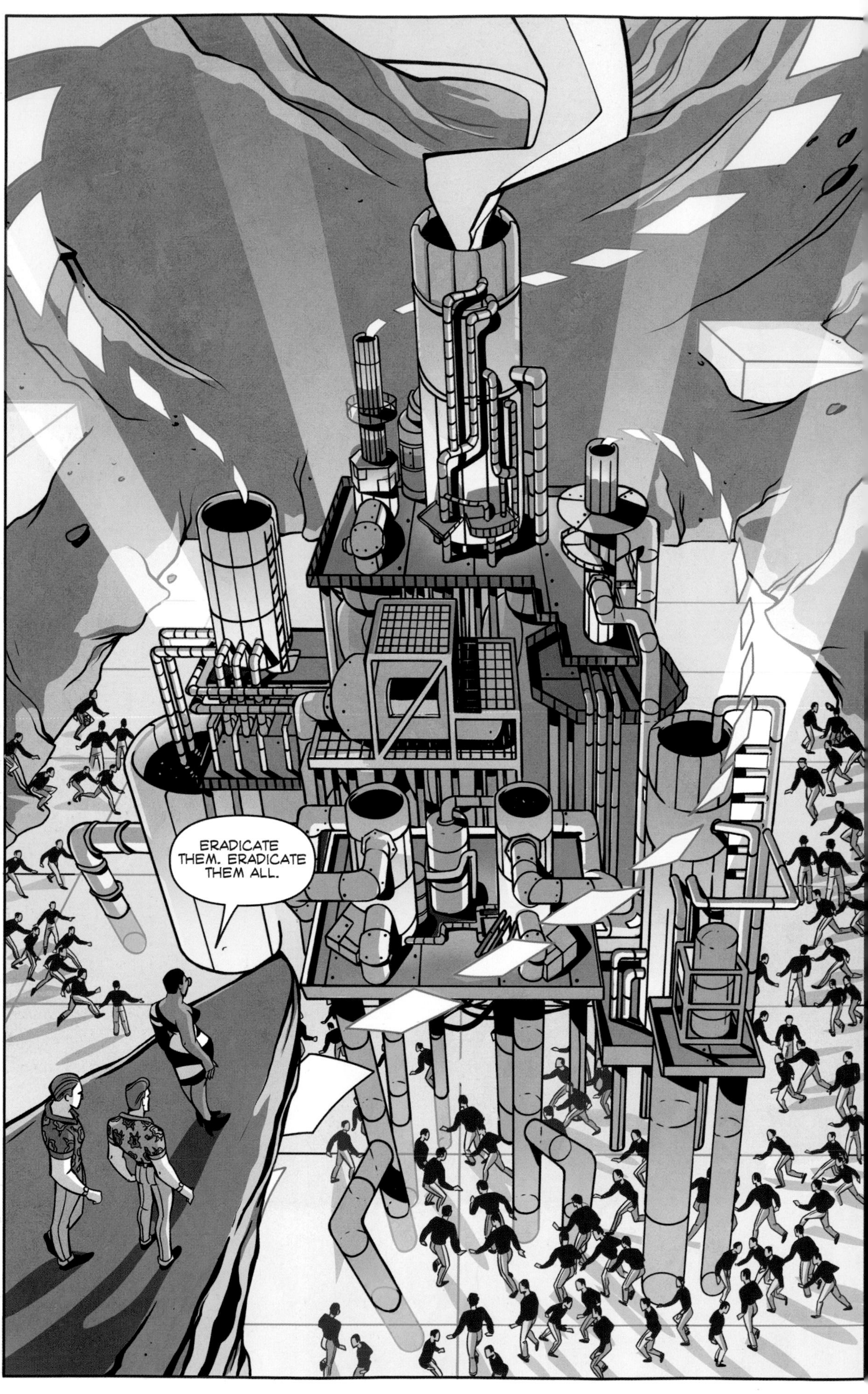
ERADICATE THEM. ERADICATE THEM ALL.

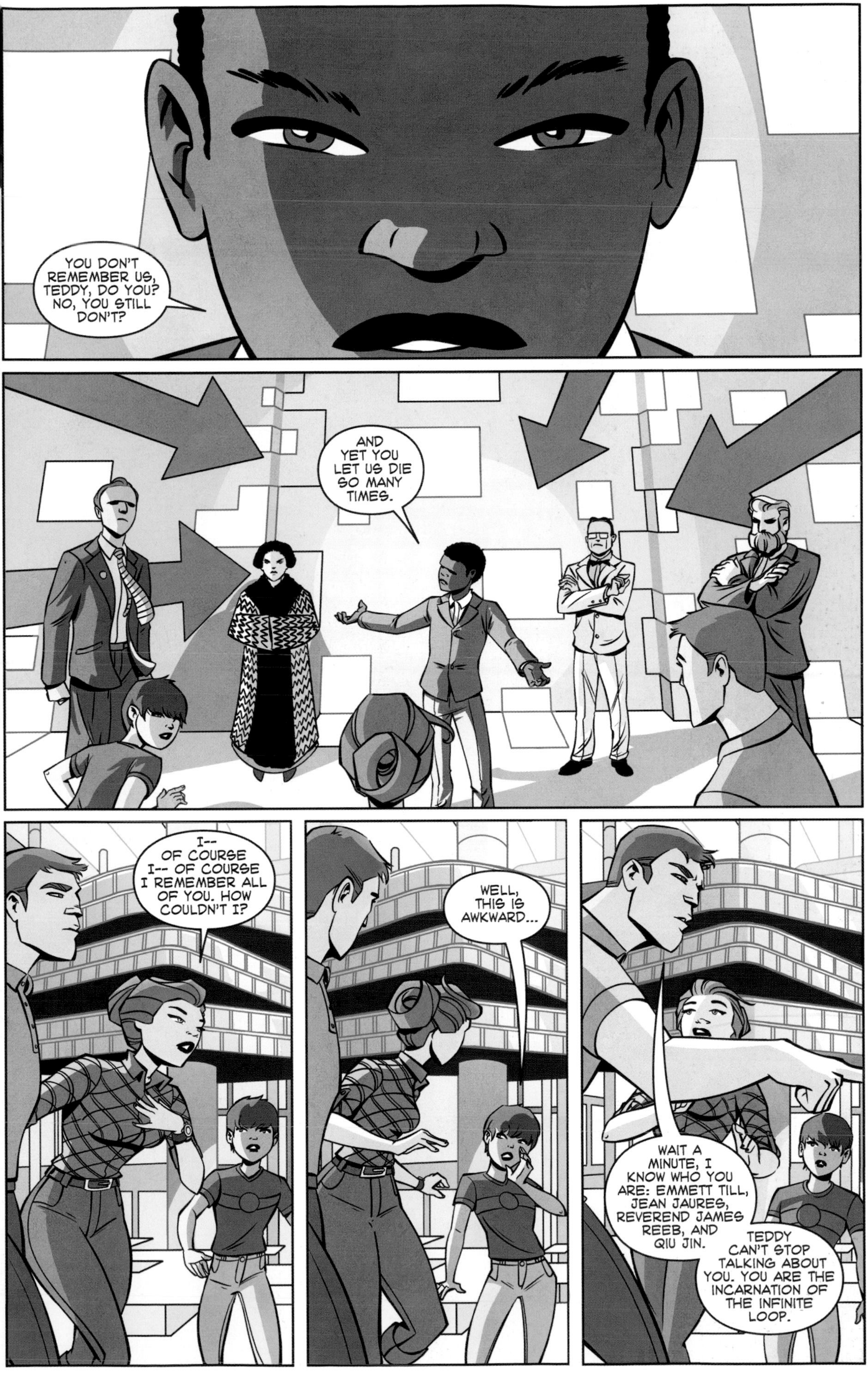
YOU DON'T REMEMBER US, TEDDY, DO YOU? NO, YOU STILL DON'T?
AND YET YOU LET US DIE SO MANY TIMES.
I-- OF COURSE I-- OF COURSE I REMEMBER ALL OF YOU. HOW COULDN'T I?
WELL, THIS IS AWKWARD...
WAIT A MINUTE, I KNOW WHO YOU ARE: EMMETT TILL, JEAN JAURES, REVEREND JAMES REEB, AND QIU JIN.
TEDDY CAN'T STOP TALKING ABOUT YOU. YOU ARE THE INCARNATION OF THE INFINITE LOOP.

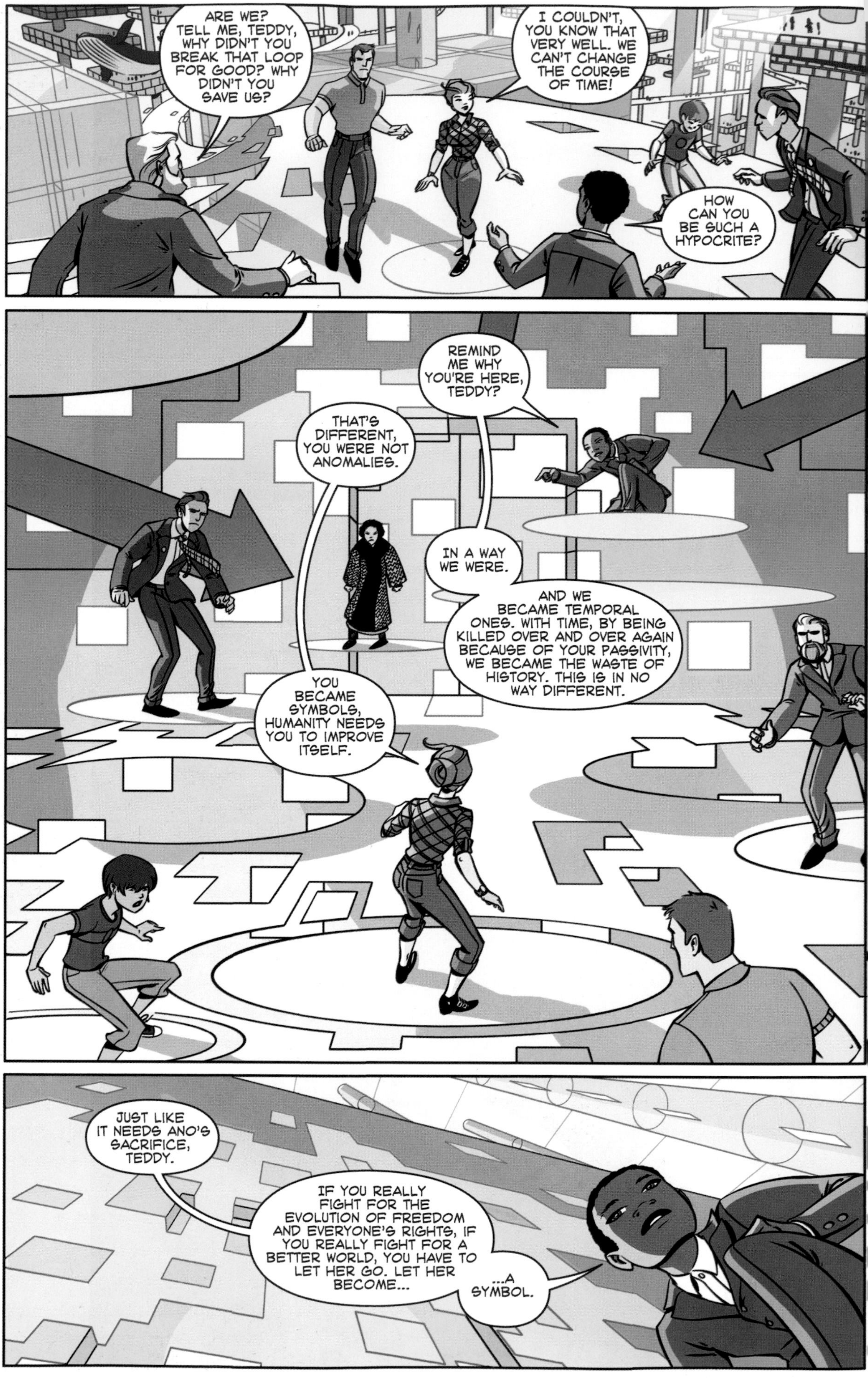
ARE WE? TELL ME, TEDDY, WHY DIDN'T YOU BREAK THAT LOOP FOR GOOD? WHY DIDN'T YOU SAVE US?
I COULDN'T, YOU KNOW THAT VERY WELL. WE CAN'T CHANGE THE COURSE OF TIME!
HOW CAN YOU BE SUCH A HYPOCRITE?
REMIND ME WHY YOU'RE HERE, TEDDY?
THAT'S DIFFERENT, YOU WERE NOT ANOMALIES.
IN A WAY WE WERE.
AND WE BECAME TEMPORAL ONES. WITH TIME, BY BEING KILLED OVER AND OVER AGAIN BECAUSE OF YOUR PASSIVITY, WE BECAME THE WASTE OF HISTORY. THIS IS IN NO WAY DIFFERENT.
YOU BECAME SYMBOLS, HUMANITY NEEDS YOU TO IMPROVE ITSELF.
JUST LIKE IT NEEDS ANO'S SACRIFICE, TEDDY.
IF YOU REALLY FIGHT FOR THE EVOLUTION OF FREEDOM AND EVERYONE'S RIGHTS, IF YOU REALLY FIGHT FOR A BETTER WORLD, YOU HAVE TO LET HER GO. LET HER BECOME...
...A SYMBOL.

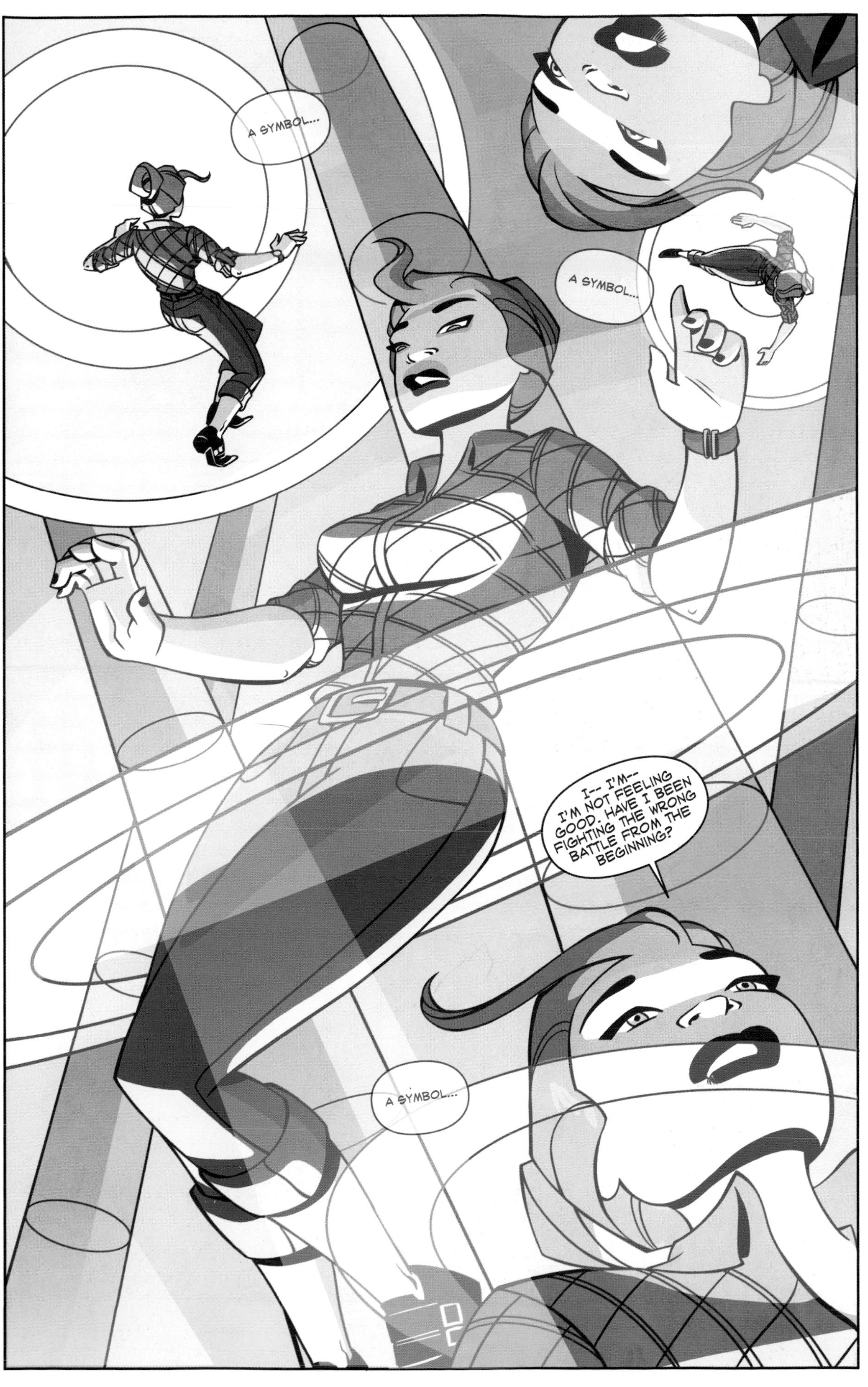
A SYMBOL...
A SYMBOL...
I-- I'M-- I'M NOT FEELING GOOD. HAVE I BEEN FIGHTING THE WRONG BATTLE FROM THE BEGINNING?
A SYMBOL...

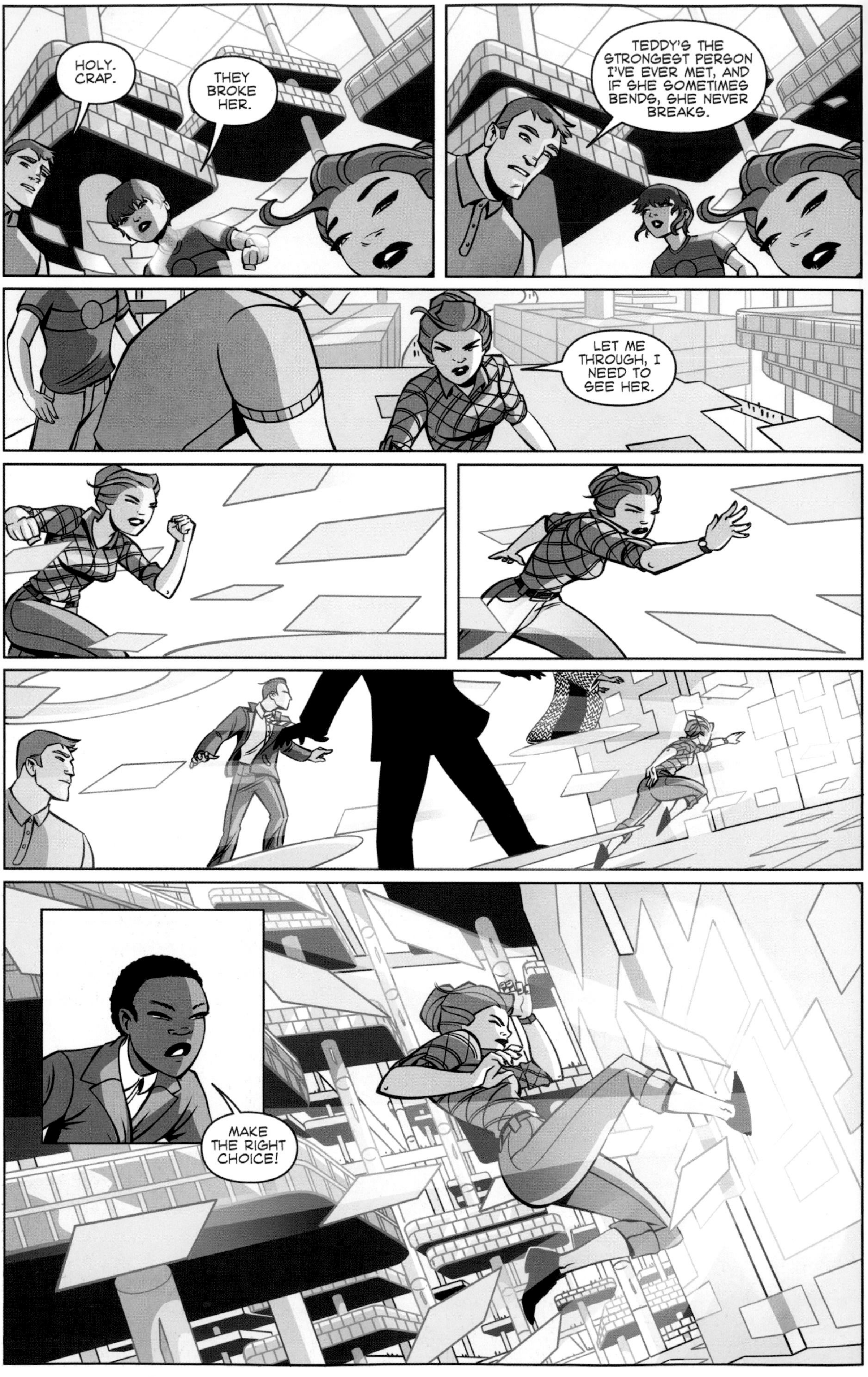
HOLY. CRAP.
THEY BROKE HER.
TEDDY'S THE STRONGEST PERSON I'VE EVER MET, AND IF SHE SOMETIMES BENDS, SHE NEVER BREAKS.
LET ME THROUGH, I NEED TO SEE HER.
MAKE THE RIGHT CHOICE!

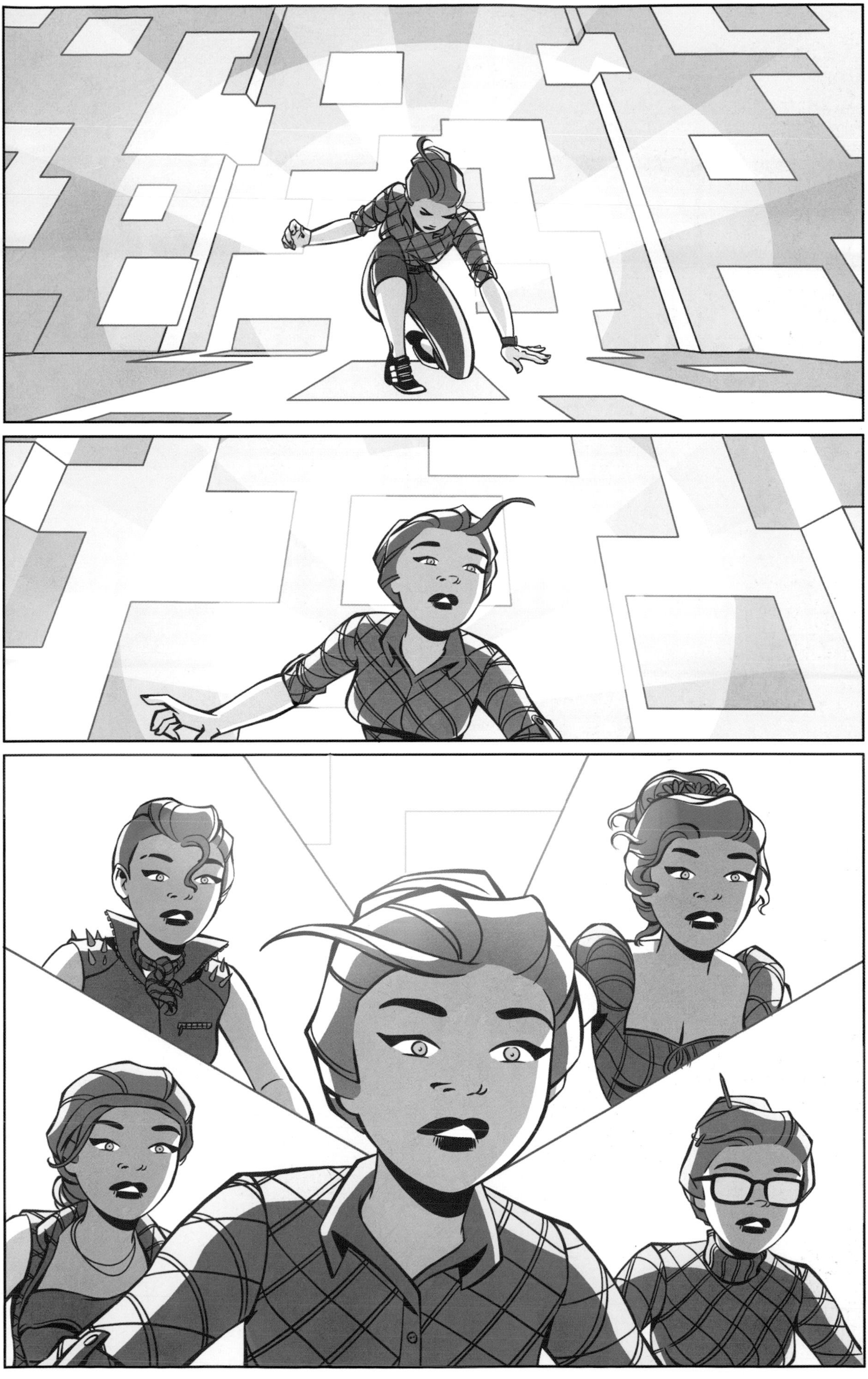

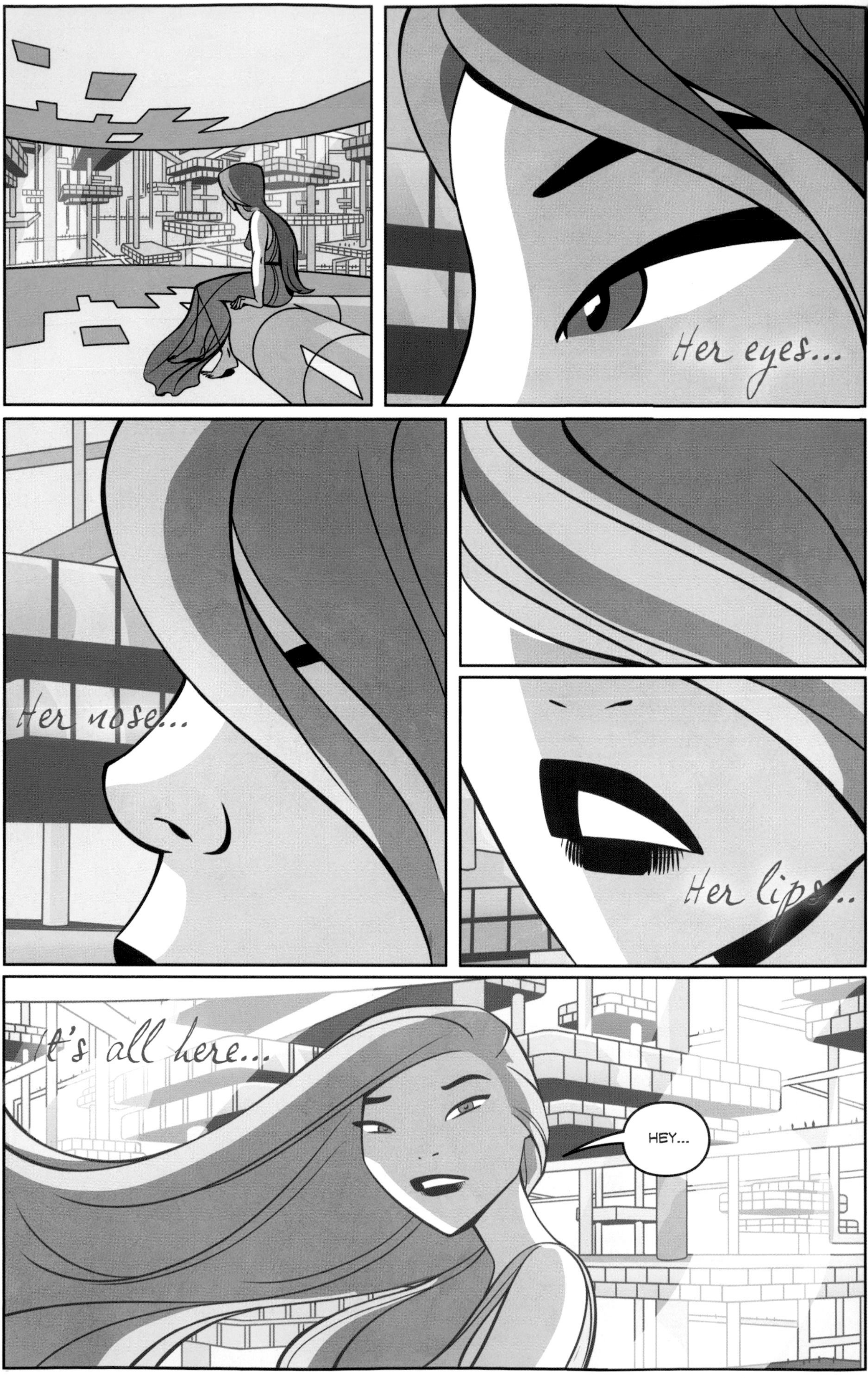
Her eyes...
Her nose...
Her lips...
It's all here...
HEY...

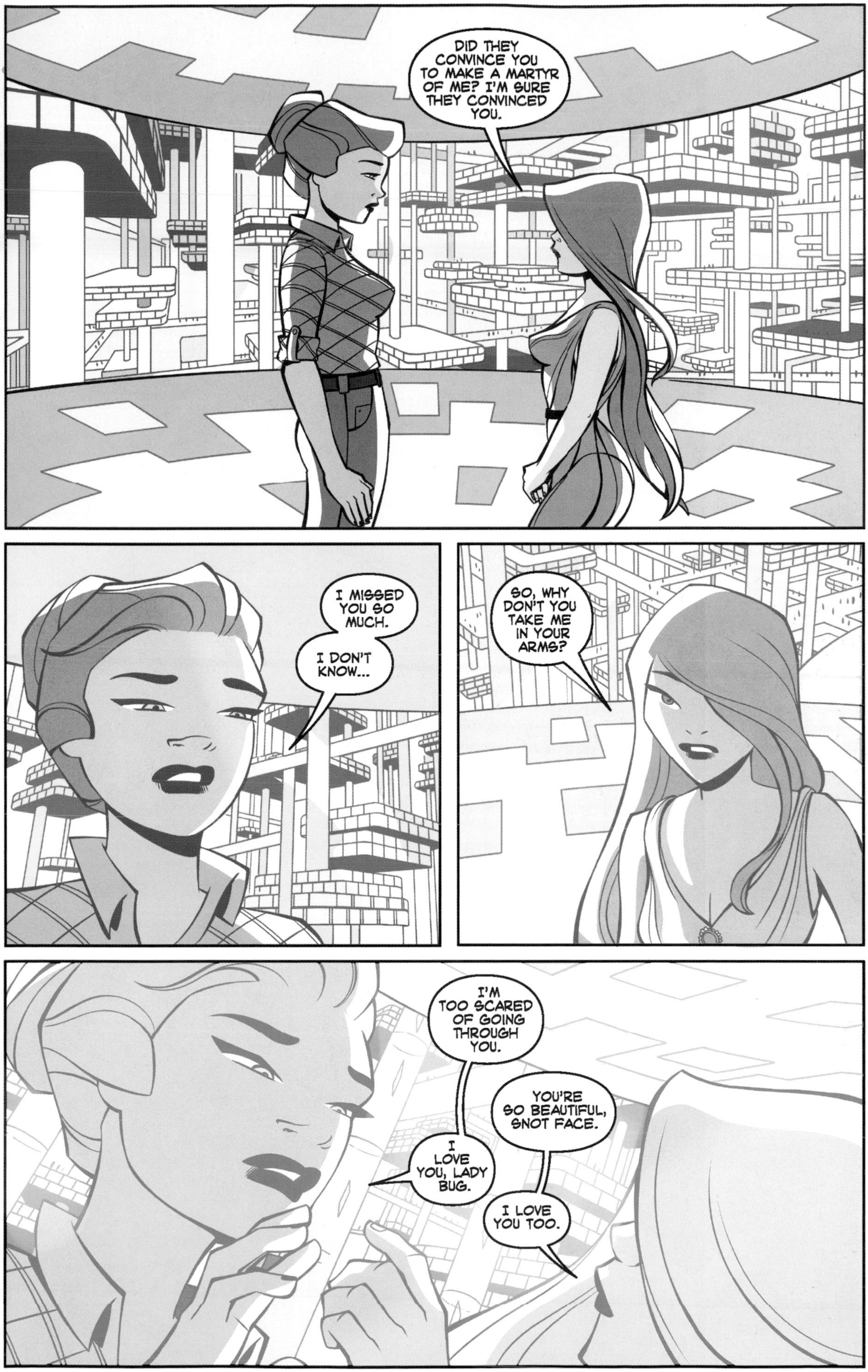
DID THEY CONVINCE YOU TO MAKE A MARTYR OF ME? I'M SURE THEY CONVINCED YOU.
I MISSED YOU SO MUCH.
I DON'T KNOW...
SO, WHY DON'T YOU TAKE ME IN YOUR ARMS?
I'M TOO SCARED OF GOING THROUGH YOU.
YOU'RE SO BEAUTIFUL, SNOT FACE.
I LOVE YOU, LADY BUG.
I LOVE YOU TOO.

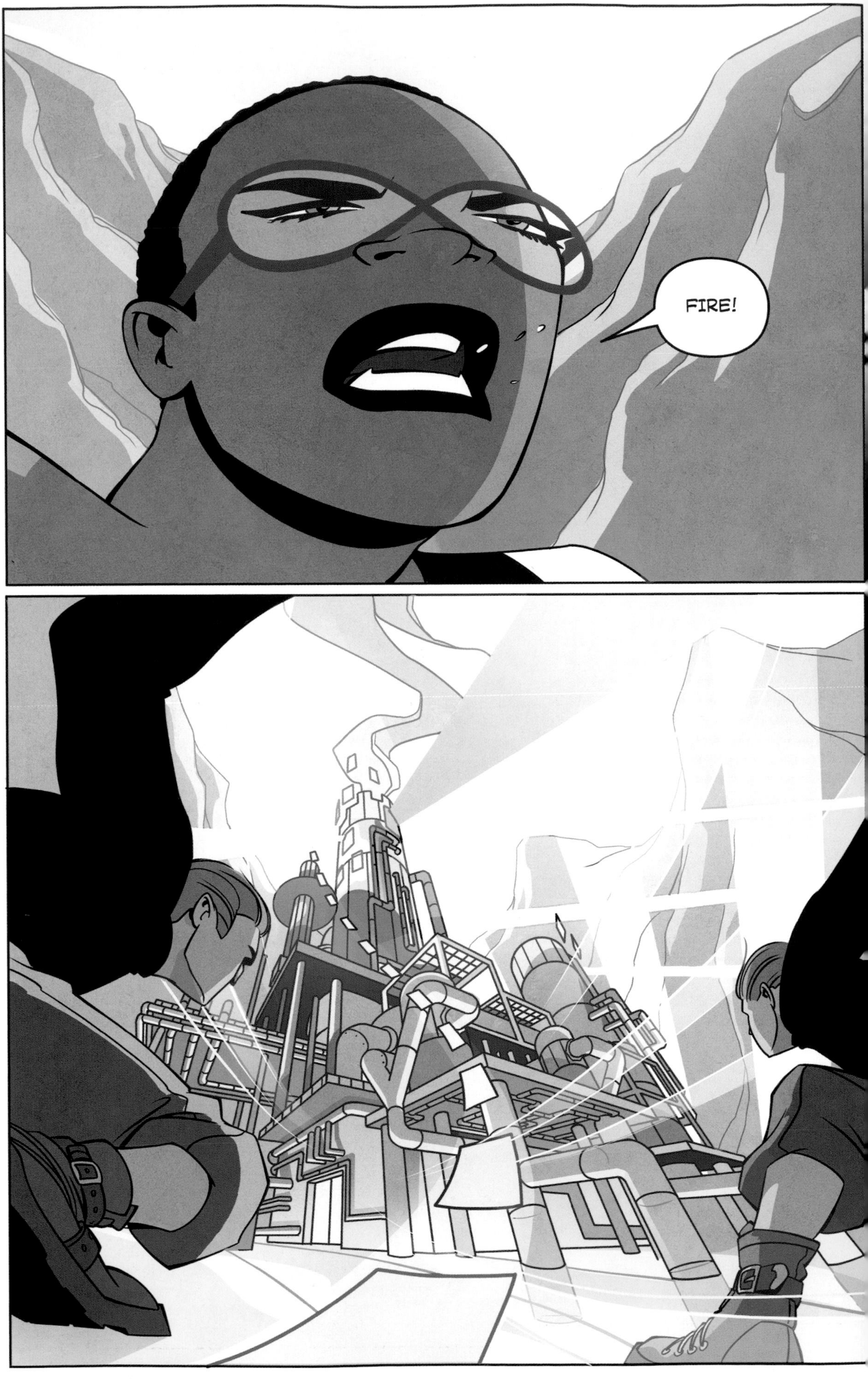
FIRE!

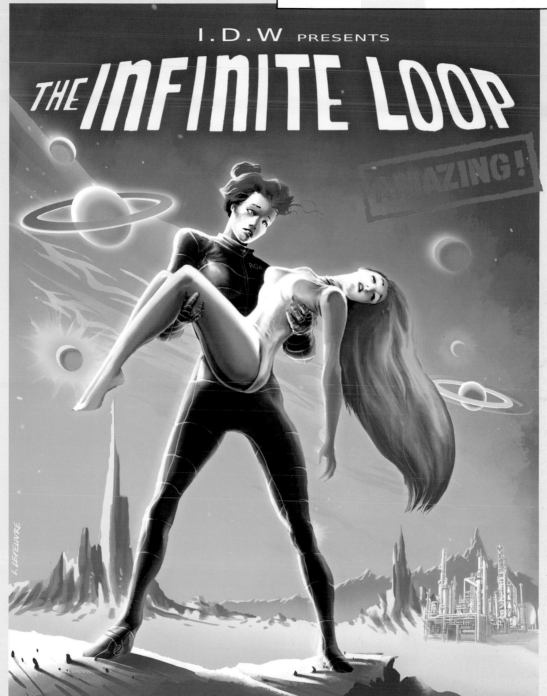

Art by LAURENT LEFEUVRE

I.D.W PRESENTS

THE INFINITE LOOP

AMAZING!

STARRING PIERRICK COLINET · ELSA CHARRETIER   SUB COVER LAURENT LEFEUVRE

EDITOR SARAH GAYDOS   AND INTRODUCING ANDROMEDA   EDITOR-IN-CHIEF CHRIS RYALL

PRESIDENT GREG GOLDSTEIN   PUBLISHER TED ADAMS IN CINEMASCOPE AND COLOR $3.99 ISSUE #5

AN IDEA AND DESIGN WORKS COMIC BOOK

Art by Elsa Charretier

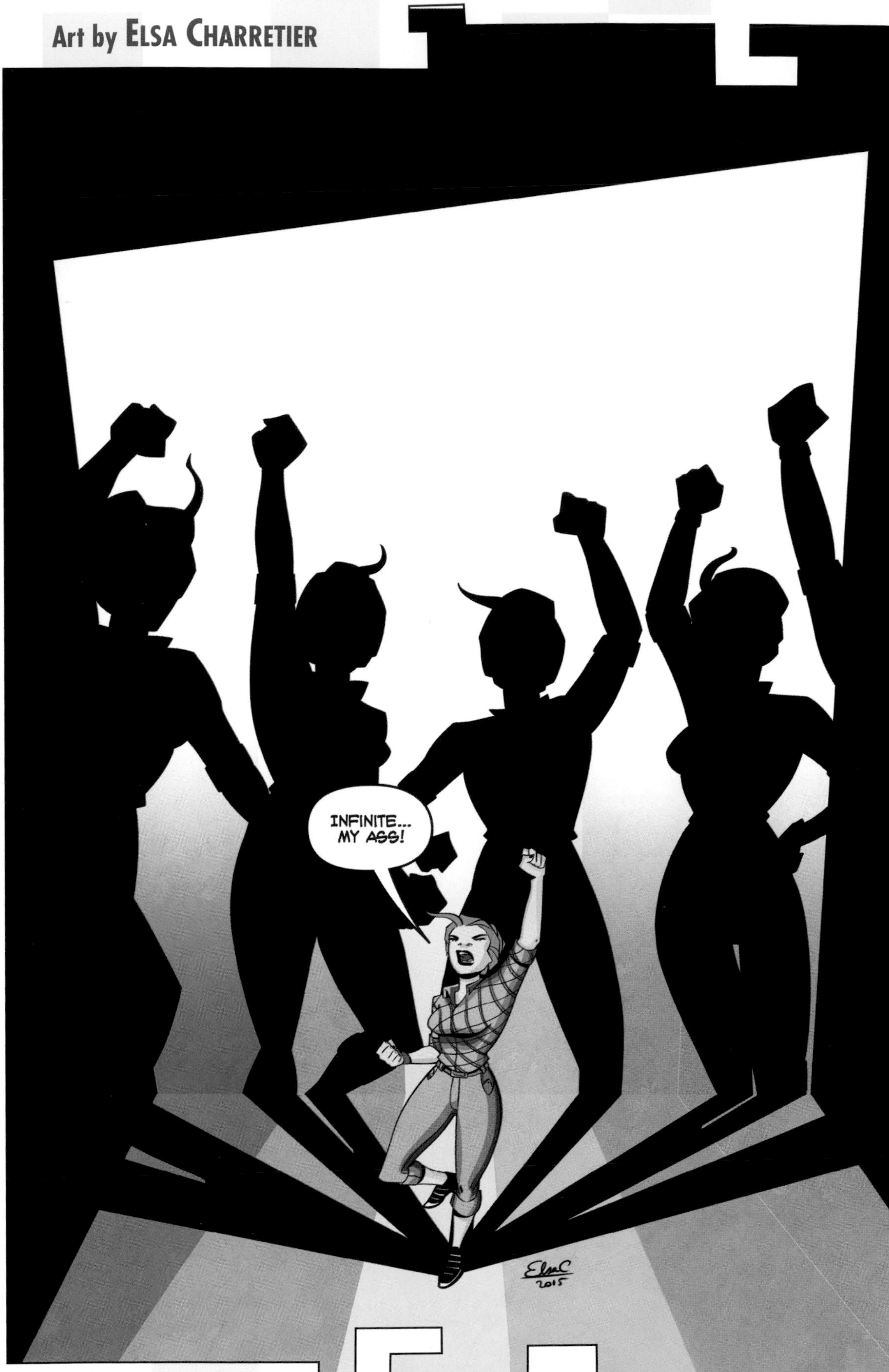
INFINITE... MY ASS!
ElsaC 2015

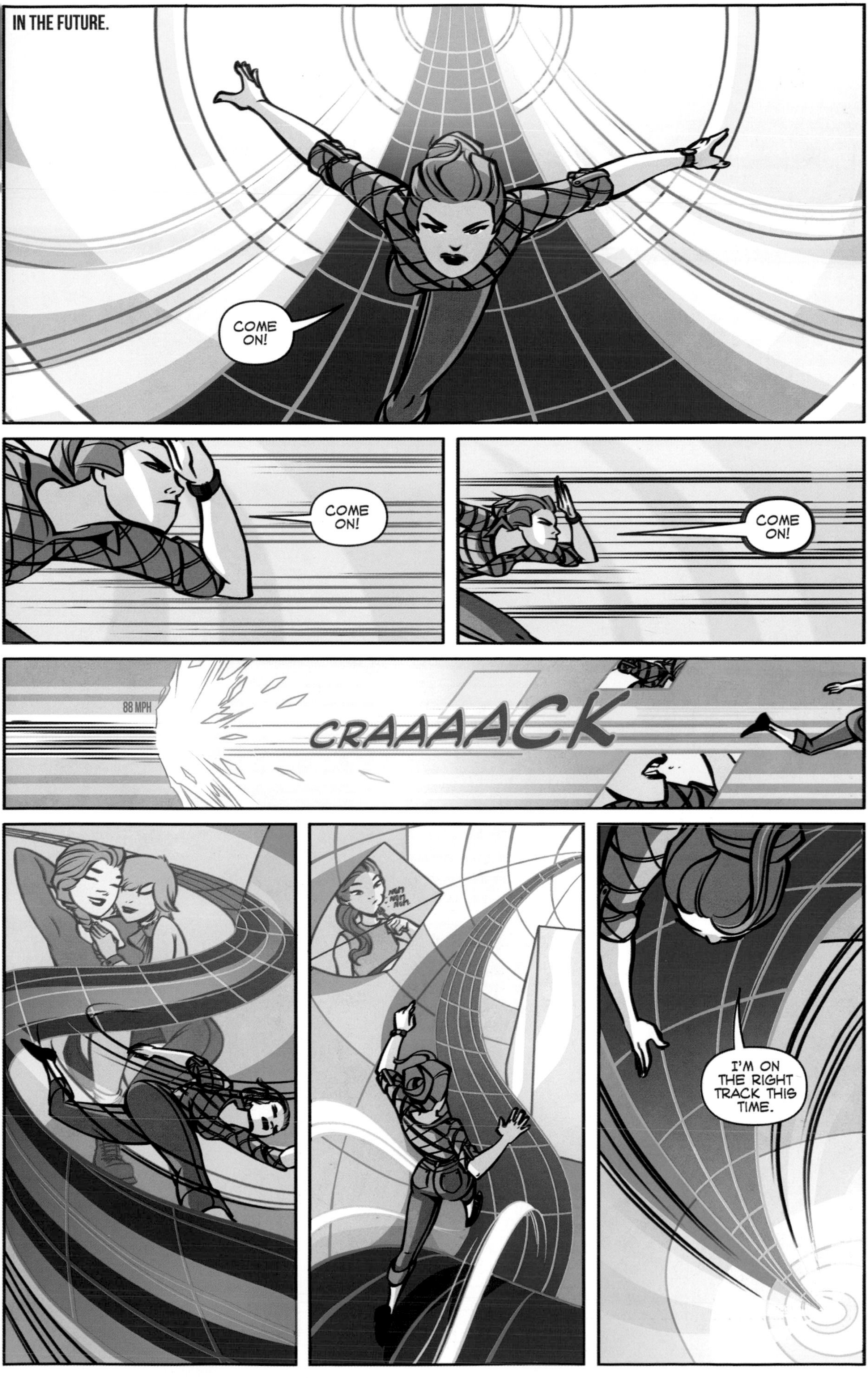

IN THE FUTURE.
COME ON!
COME ON!
COME ON!
88 MPH
CRAAAACK
I'M ON THE RIGHT TRACK THIS TIME.

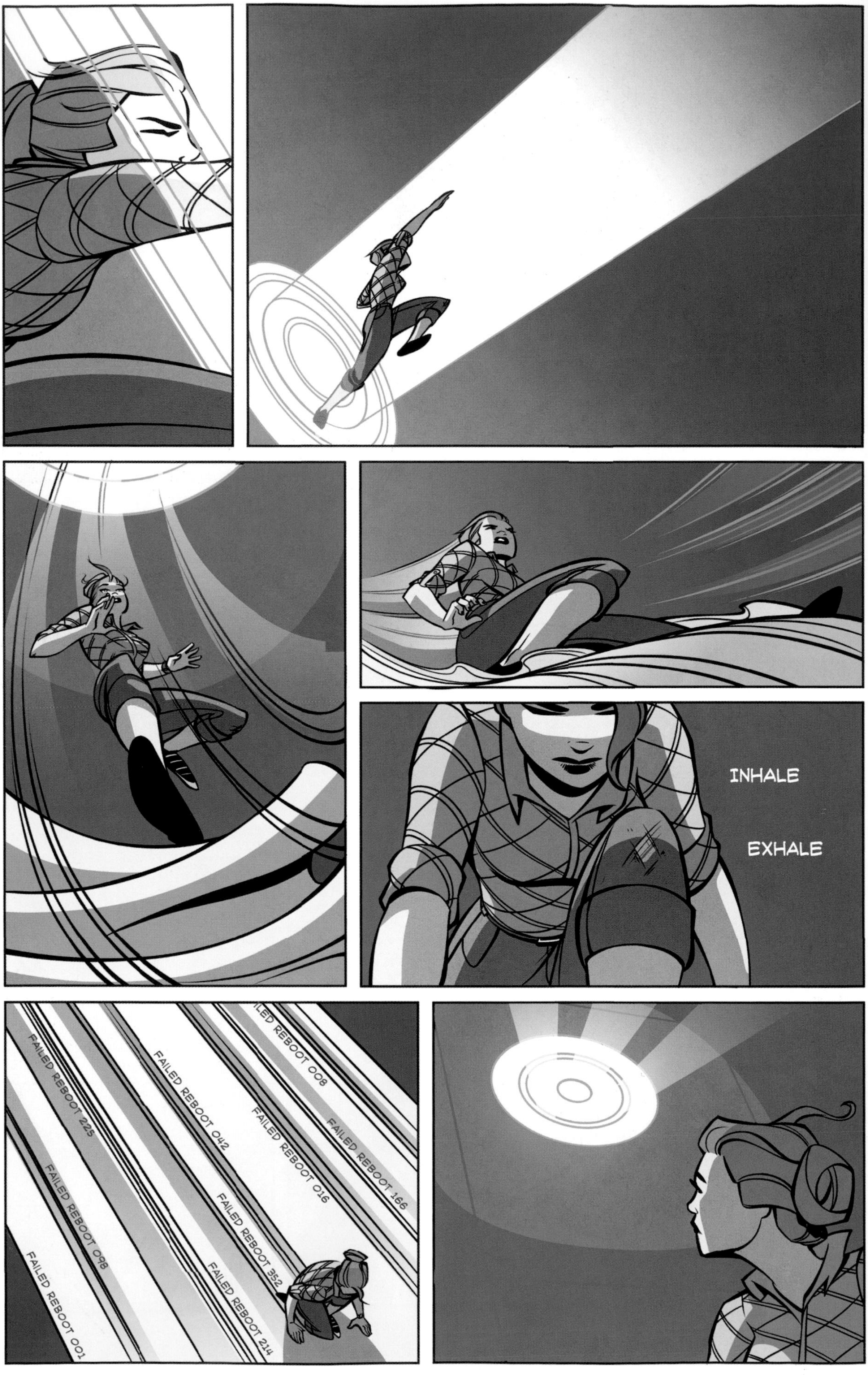
INHALE
EXHALE
FAILED REBOOT 008
FAILED REBOOT 166
FAILED REBOOT 016
FAILED REBOOT 042
FAILED REBOOT 225
FAILED REBOOT 098
FAILED REBOOT 352
FAILED REBOOT 214
FAILED REBOOT 001

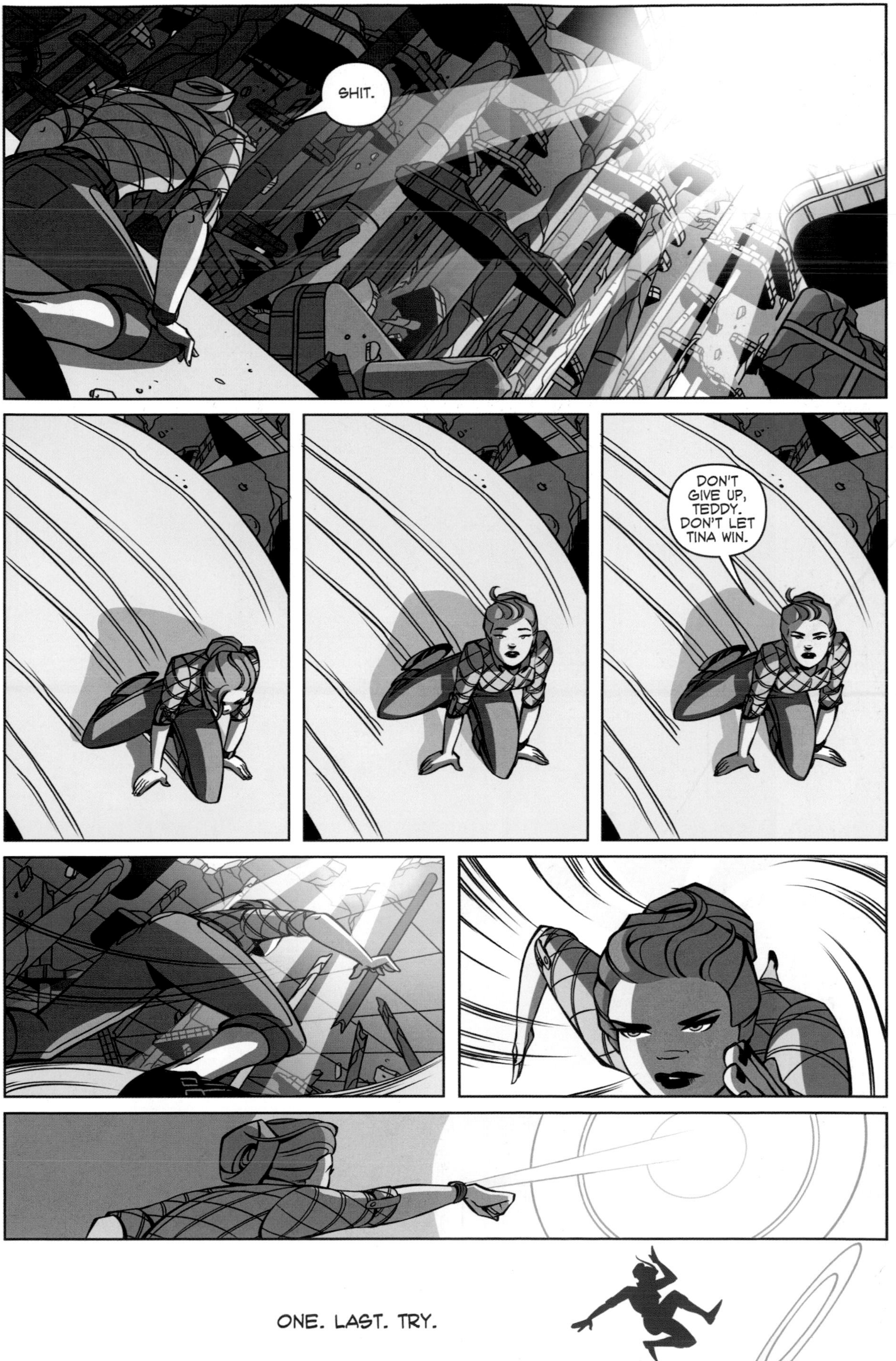
SHIT.
DON'T GIVE UP, TEDDY. DON'T LET TINA WIN.
ONE. LAST. TRY.

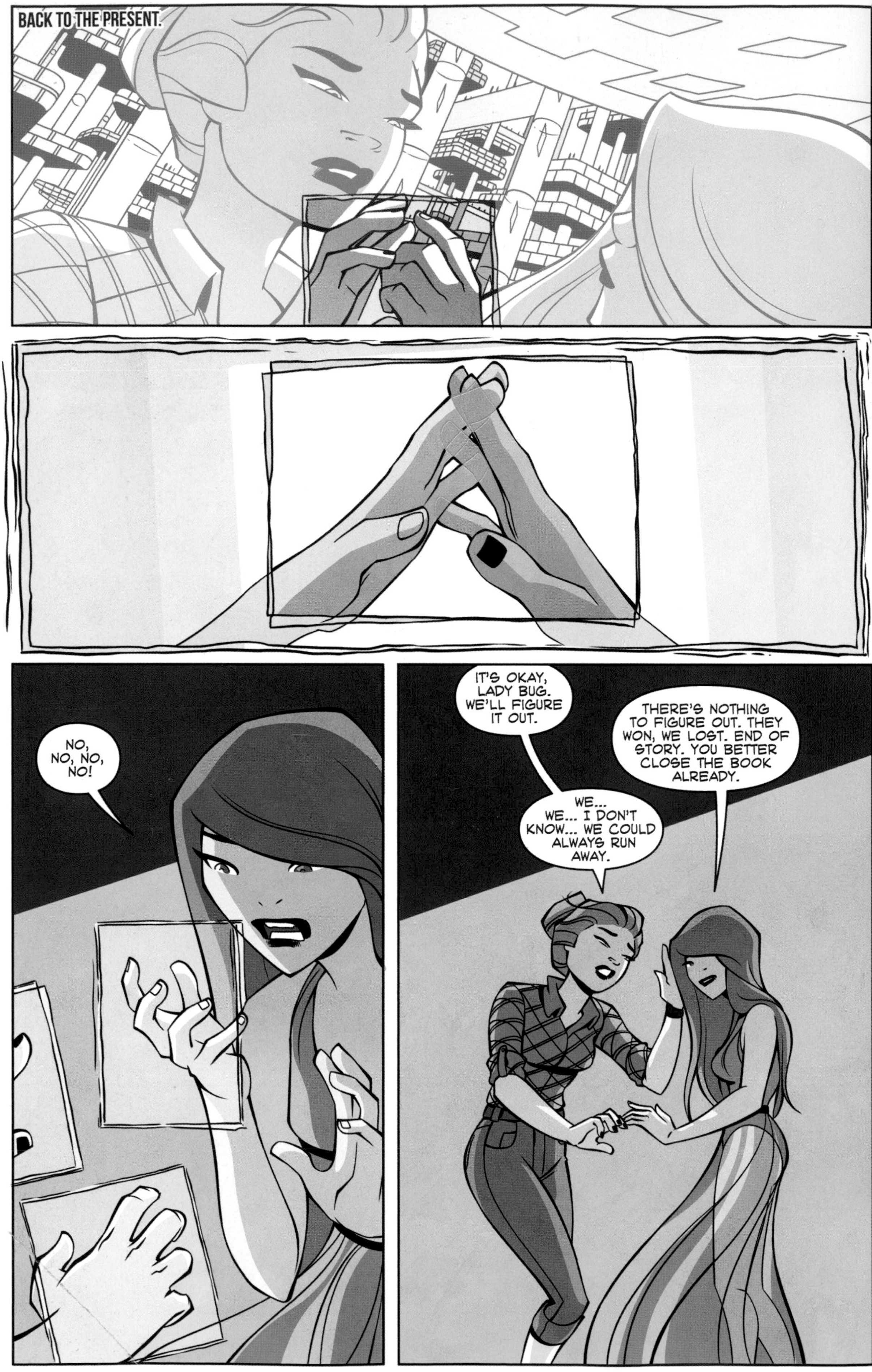
BACK TO THE PRESENT.
NO, NO, NO, NO!
IT'S OKAY, LADY BUG. WE'LL FIGURE IT OUT.
THERE'S NOTHING TO FIGURE OUT. THEY WON, WE LOST. END OF STORY. YOU BETTER CLOSE THE BOOK ALREADY.
WE... WE... I DON'T KNOW... WE COULD ALWAYS RUN AWAY.

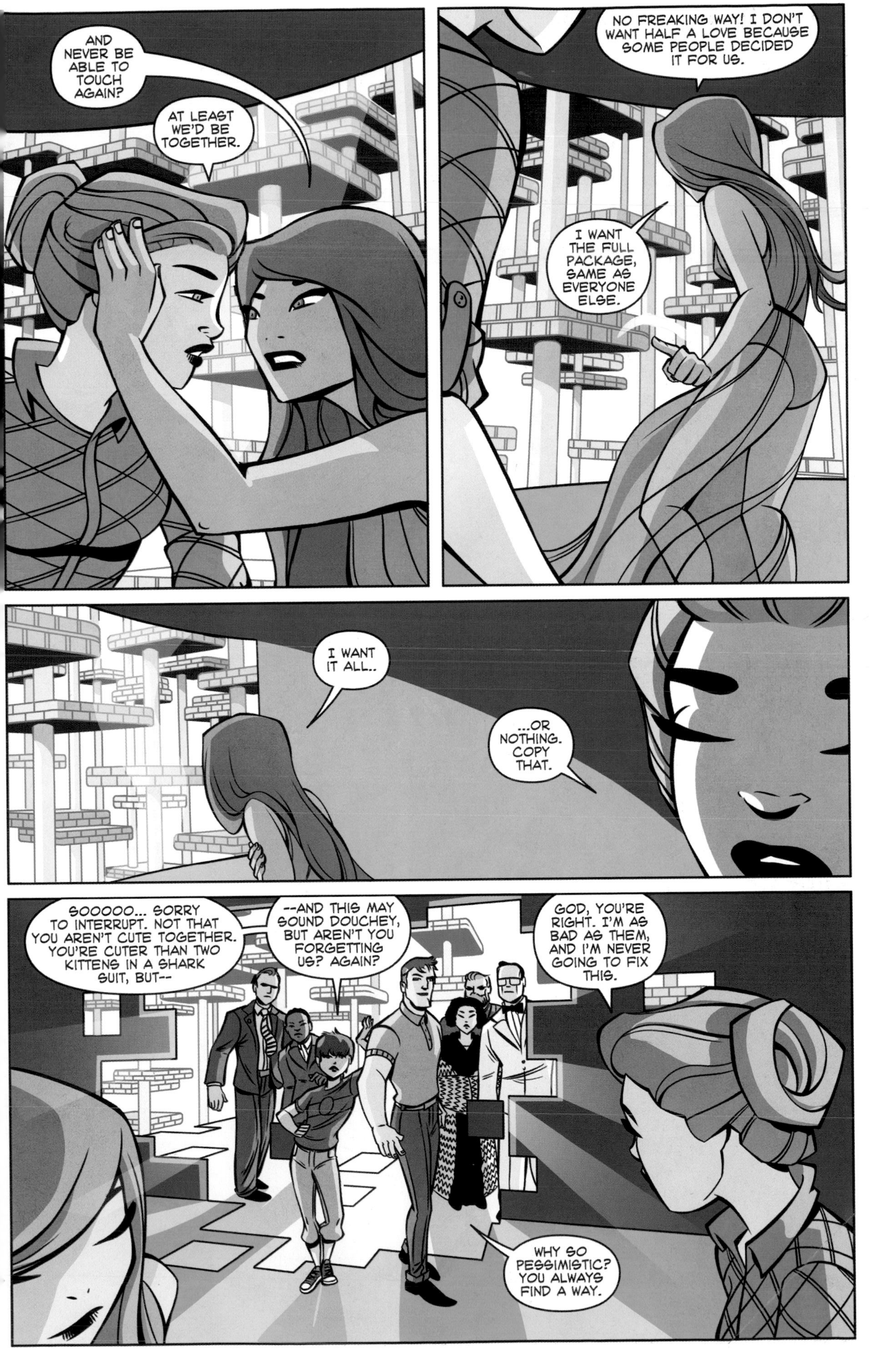
AND NEVER BE ABLE TO TOUCH AGAIN?
AT LEAST WE'D BE TOGETHER.
NO FREAKING WAY! I DON'T WANT HALF A LOVE BECAUSE SOME PEOPLE DECIDED IT FOR US.
I WANT THE FULL PACKAGE, SAME AS EVERYONE ELSE.
I WANT IT ALL..
...OR NOTHING. COPY THAT.
SOOOOO... SORRY TO INTERRUPT. NOT THAT YOU AREN'T CUTE TOGETHER. YOU'RE CUTER THAN TWO KITTENS IN A SHARK SUIT, BUT--
--AND THIS MAY SOUND DOUCHEY, BUT AREN'T YOU FORGETTING US? AGAIN?
GOD, YOU'RE RIGHT. I'M AS BAD AS THEM, AND I'M NEVER GOING TO FIX THIS.
WHY SO PESSIMISTIC? YOU ALWAYS FIND A WAY.

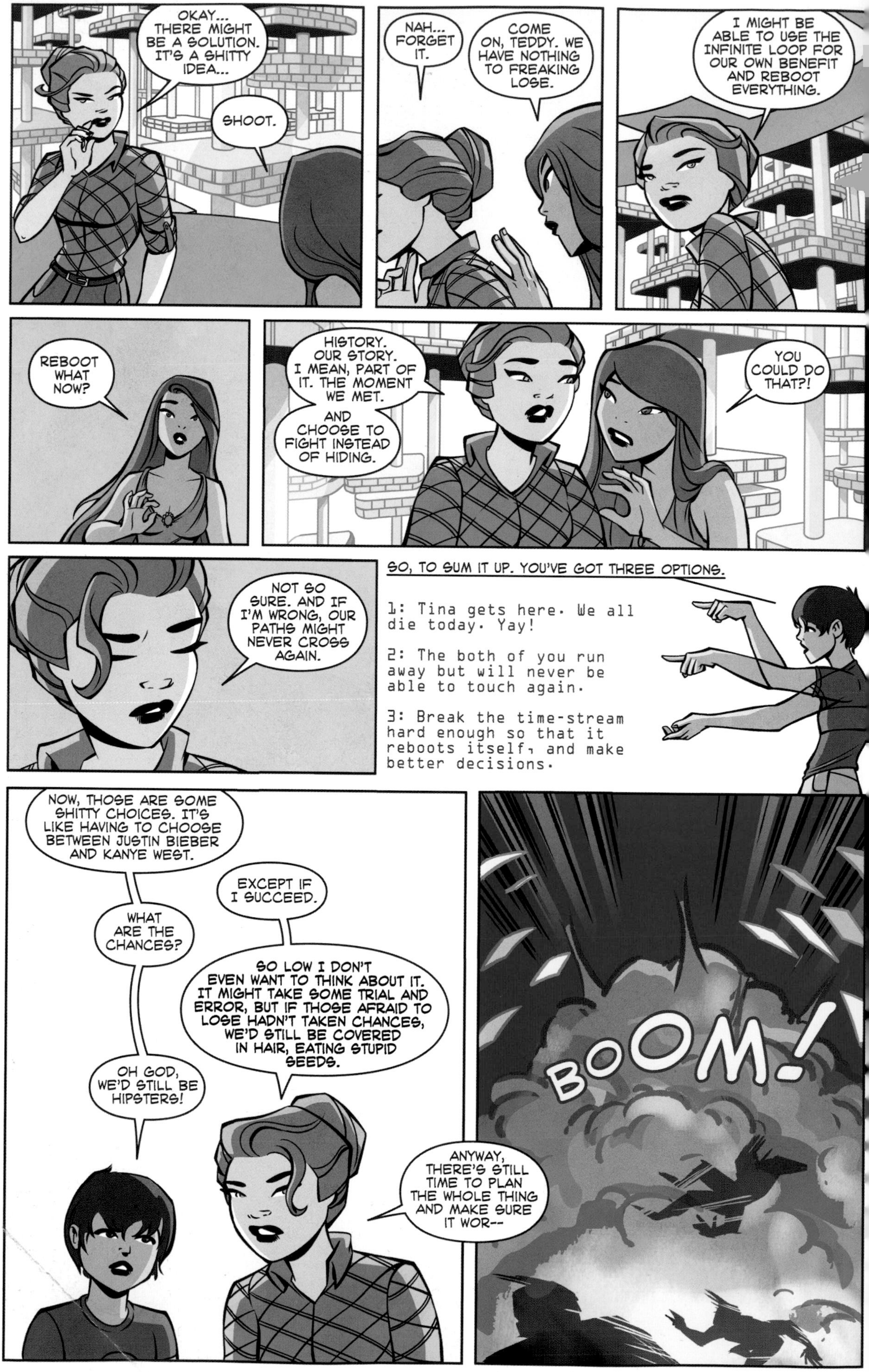
OKAY... THERE MIGHT BE A SOLUTION. IT'S A SHITTY IDEA...
SHOOT.
NAH... FORGET IT.
COME ON, TEDDY. WE HAVE NOTHING TO FREAKING LOSE.
I MIGHT BE ABLE TO USE THE INFINITE LOOP FOR OUR OWN BENEFIT AND REBOOT EVERYTHING.
REBOOT WHAT NOW?
HISTORY. OUR STORY. I MEAN, PART OF IT. THE MOMENT WE MET.
AND CHOOSE TO FIGHT INSTEAD OF HIDING.
YOU COULD DO THAT?!
NOT SO SURE. AND IF I'M WRONG, OUR PATHS MIGHT NEVER CROSS AGAIN.
SO, TO SUM IT UP. YOU'VE GOT THREE OPTIONS.
1: Tina gets here. We all die today. Yay!
2: The both of you run away but will never be able to touch again.
3: Break the time-stream hard enough so that it reboots itself, and make better decisions.
NOW, THOSE ARE SOME SHITTY CHOICES. IT'S LIKE HAVING TO CHOOSE BETWEEN JUSTIN BIEBER AND KANYE WEST.
EXCEPT IF I SUCCEED.
WHAT ARE THE CHANCES?
SO LOW I DON'T EVEN WANT TO THINK ABOUT IT. IT MIGHT TAKE SOME TRIAL AND ERROR, BUT IF THOSE AFRAID TO LOSE HADN'T TAKEN CHANCES, WE'D STILL BE COVERED IN HAIR, EATING STUPID SEEDS.
OH GOD, WE'D STILL BE HIPSTERS!
ANYWAY, THERE'S STILL TIME TO PLAN THE WHOLE THING AND MAKE SURE IT WOR--
BOOM!

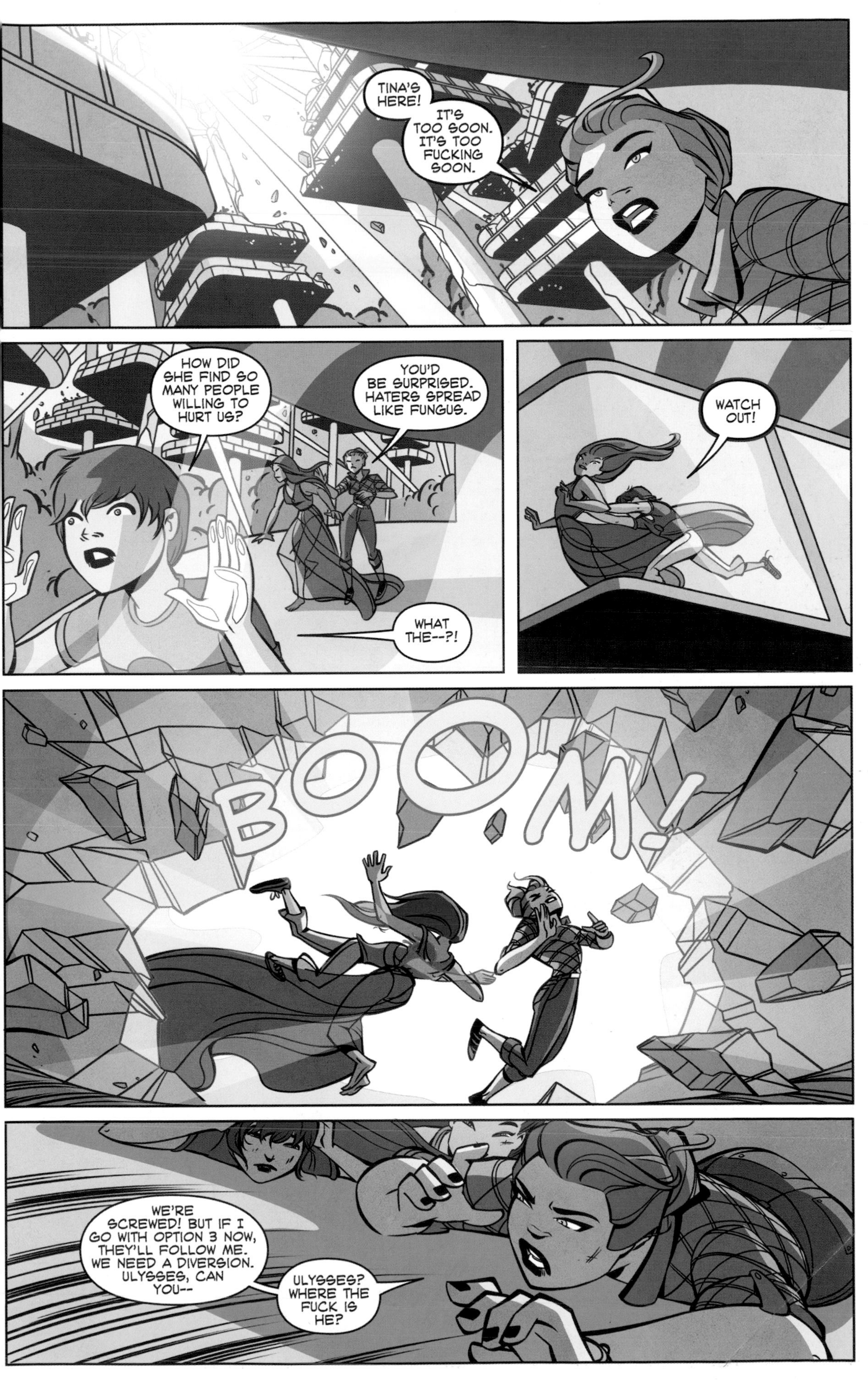
TINA'S HERE!
IT'S TOO SOON. IT'S TOO FUCKING SOON.
HOW DID SHE FIND SO MANY PEOPLE WILLING TO HURT US?
YOU'D BE SURPRISED. HATERS SPREAD LIKE FUNGUS.
WHAT THE--?!
WATCH OUT!
BOOM!
WE'RE SCREWED! BUT IF I GO WITH OPTION 3 NOW, THEY'LL FOLLOW ME. WE NEED A DIVERSION. ULYSSES, CAN YOU--
ULYSSES? WHERE THE FUCK IS HE?

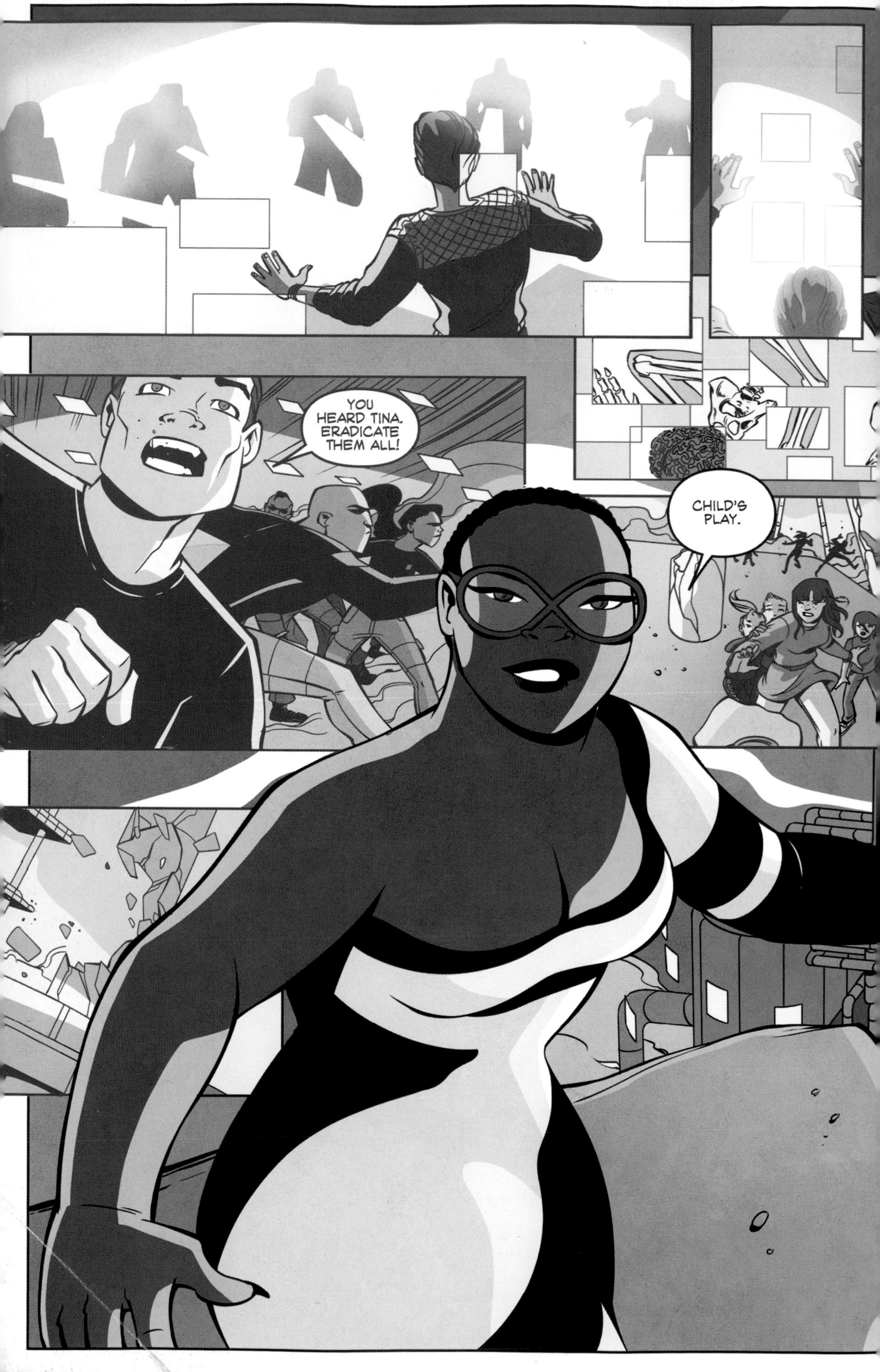
YOU HEARD TINA. ERADICATE THEM ALL!
CHILD'S PLAY.

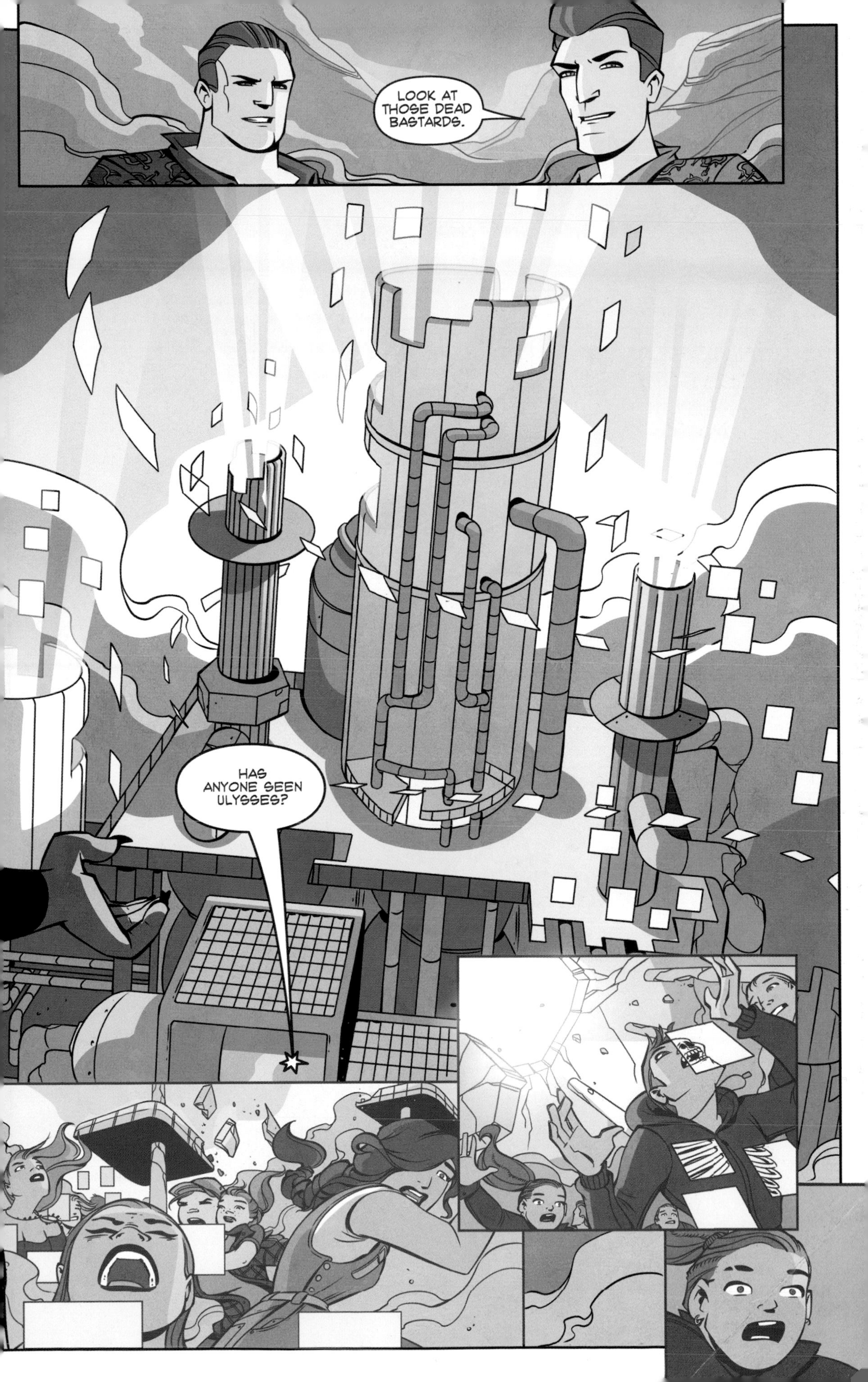
LOOK AT THOSE DEAD BASTARDS.
HAS ANYONE SEEN ULYSSES?

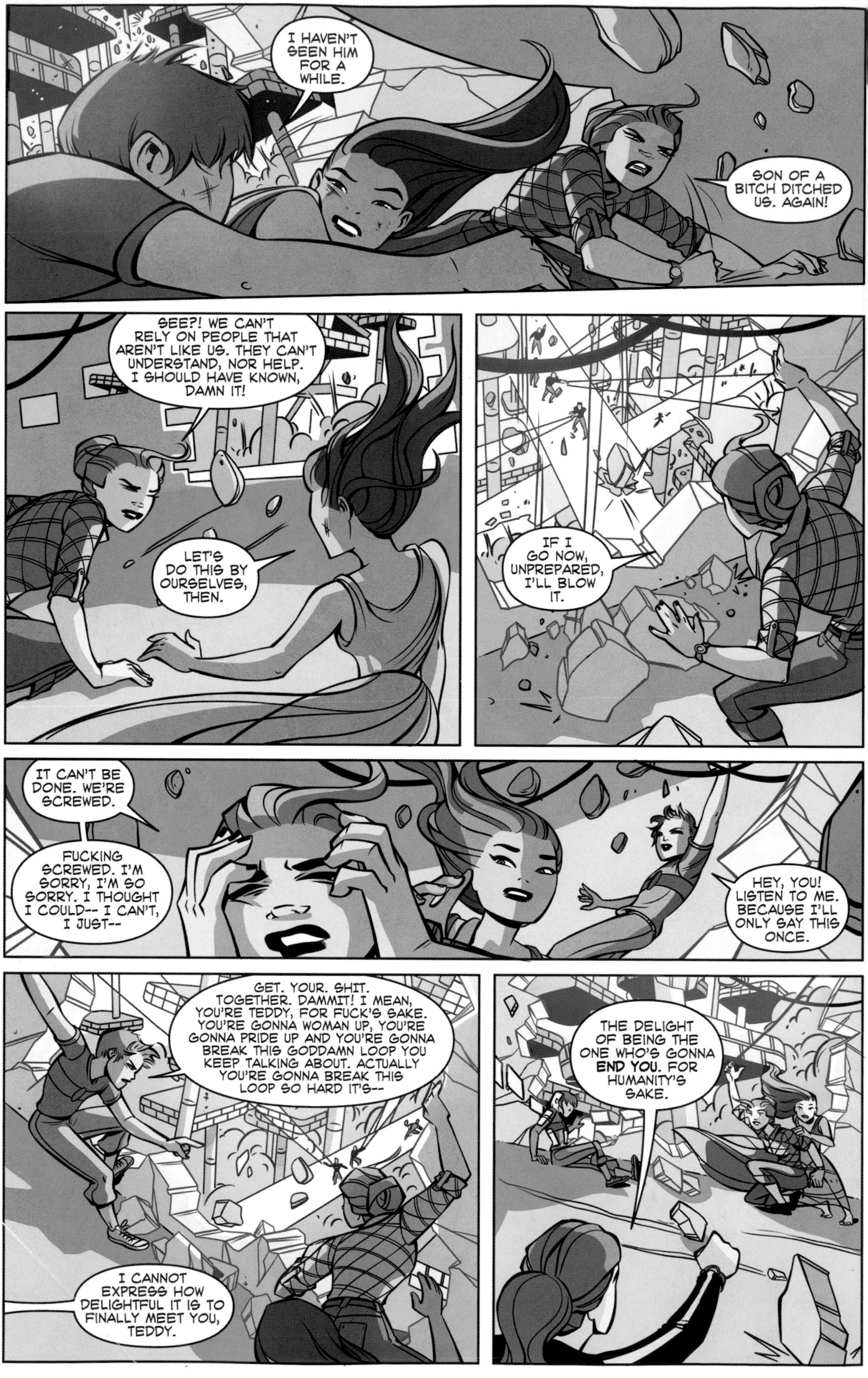
I HAVEN'T SEEN HIM FOR A WHILE.
SON OF A BITCH DITCHED US. AGAIN!
SEE?! WE CAN'T RELY ON PEOPLE THAT AREN'T LIKE US. THEY CAN'T UNDERSTAND, NOR HELP. I SHOULD HAVE KNOWN, DAMN IT!
LET'S DO THIS BY OURSELVES, THEN.
IF I GO NOW, UNPREPARED, I'LL BLOW IT.
IT CAN'T BE DONE. WE'RE SCREWED.
FUCKING SCREWED. I'M SORRY, I'M SO SORRY. I THOUGHT I COULD-- I CAN'T, I JUST--
HEY, YOU! LISTEN TO ME. BECAUSE I'LL ONLY SAY THIS ONCE.
GET. YOUR. SHIT. TOGETHER. DAMMIT! I MEAN, YOU'RE TEDDY, FOR FUCK'S SAKE. YOU'RE GONNA WOMAN UP, YOU'RE GONNA PRIDE UP AND YOU'RE GONNA BREAK THIS GODDAMN LOOP YOU KEEP TALKING ABOUT. ACTUALLY YOU'RE GONNA BREAK THIS LOOP SO HARD IT'S--
I CANNOT EXPRESS HOW DELIGHTFUL IT IS TO FINALLY MEET YOU, TEDDY.
THE DELIGHT OF BEING THE ONE WHO'S GONNA **END YOU.** FOR HUMANITY'S SAKE.

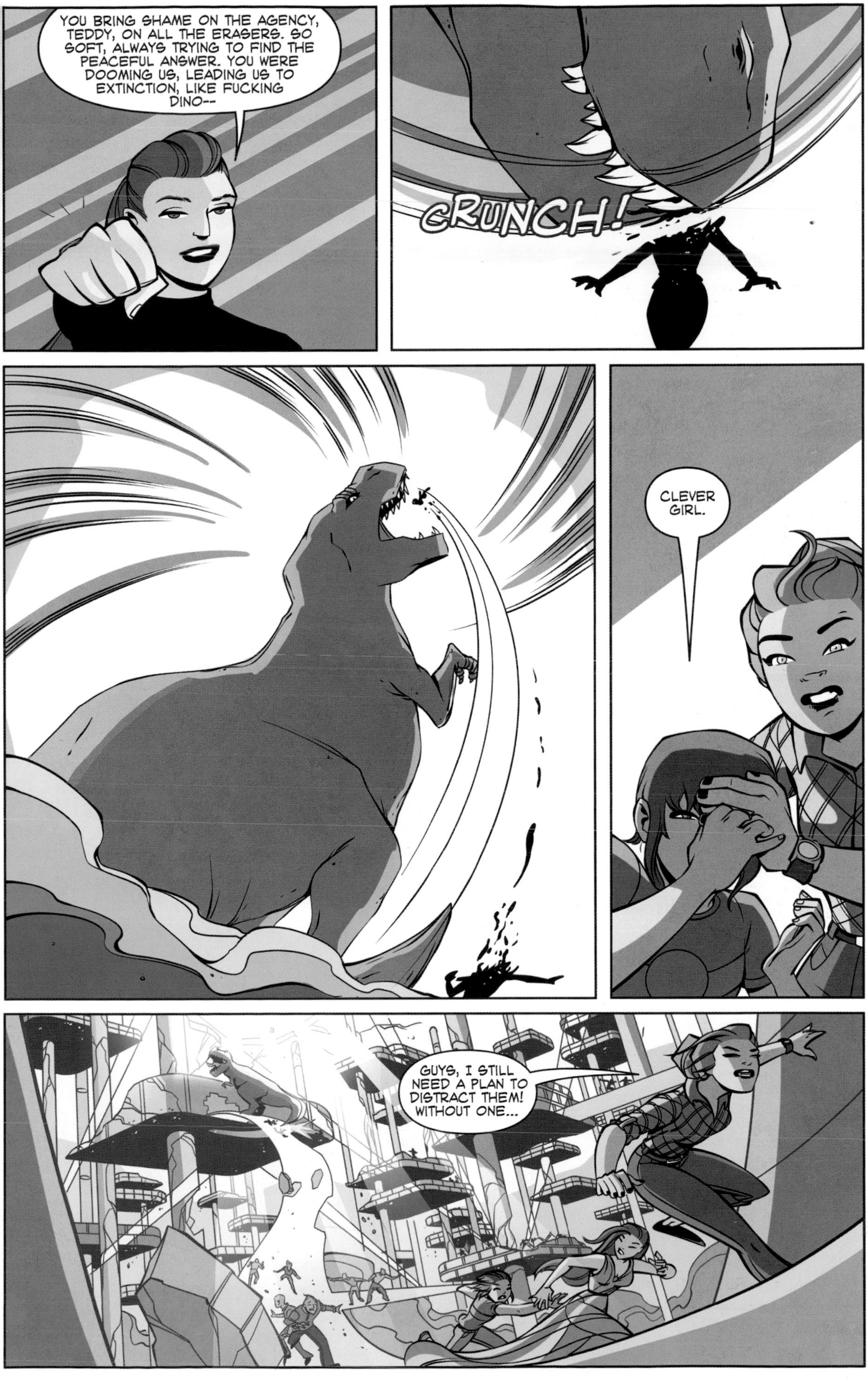
YOU BRING SHAME ON THE AGENCY, TEDDY, ON ALL THE ERASERS. SO SOFT, ALWAYS TRYING TO FIND THE PEACEFUL ANSWER. YOU WERE DOOMING US, LEADING US TO EXTINCTION, LIKE FUCKING DINO--
CRUNCH!
CLEVER GIRL.
GUYS, I STILL NEED A PLAN TO DISTRACT THEM! WITHOUT ONE...

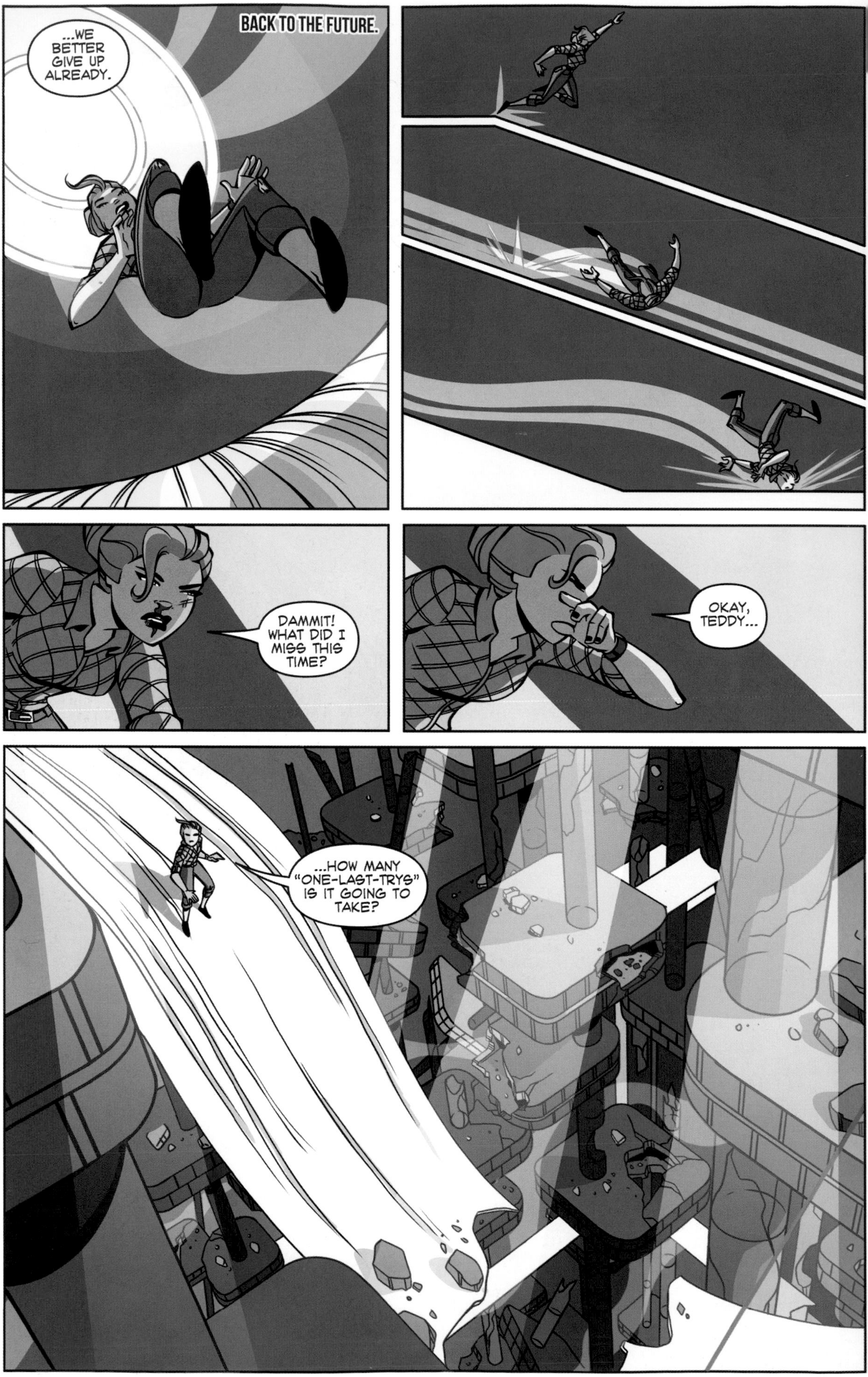
BACK TO THE FUTURE.
...WE BETTER GIVE UP ALREADY.
DAMMIT! WHAT DID I MISS THIS TIME?
OKAY, TEDDY...
...HOW MANY "ONE-LAST-TRYS" IS IT GOING TO TAKE?

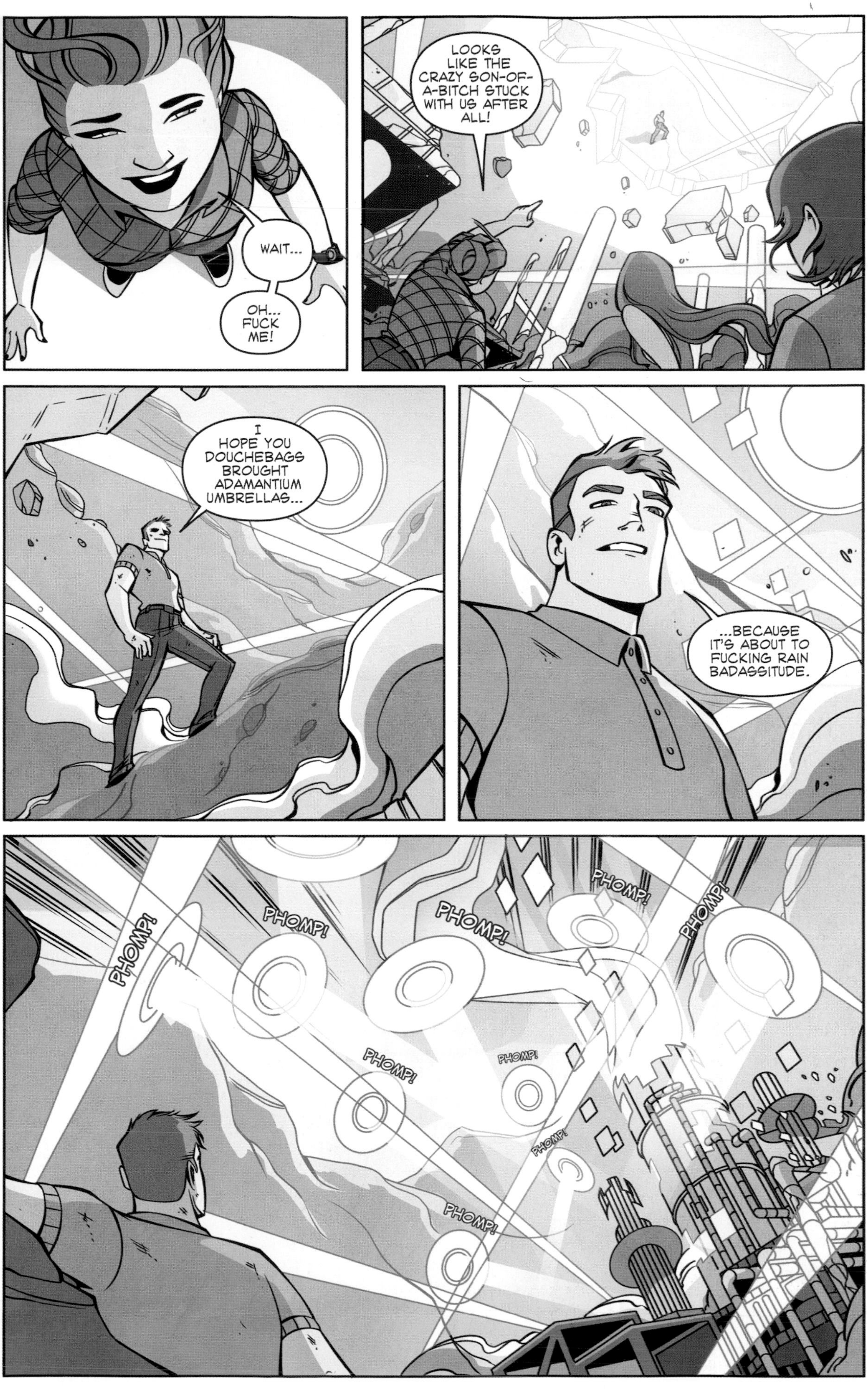
WAIT...
OH... FUCK ME!
LOOKS LIKE THE CRAZY SON-OF-A-BITCH STUCK WITH US AFTER ALL!
I HOPE YOU DOUCHEBAGS BROUGHT ADAMANTIUM UMBRELLAS...
...BECAUSE IT'S ABOUT TO FUCKING RAIN BADASSITUDE.
PHOMP!
PHOMP!
PHOMP!
PHOMP!
PHOMP!
PHOMP!
PHOMP!
PHOMP!
PHOMP!

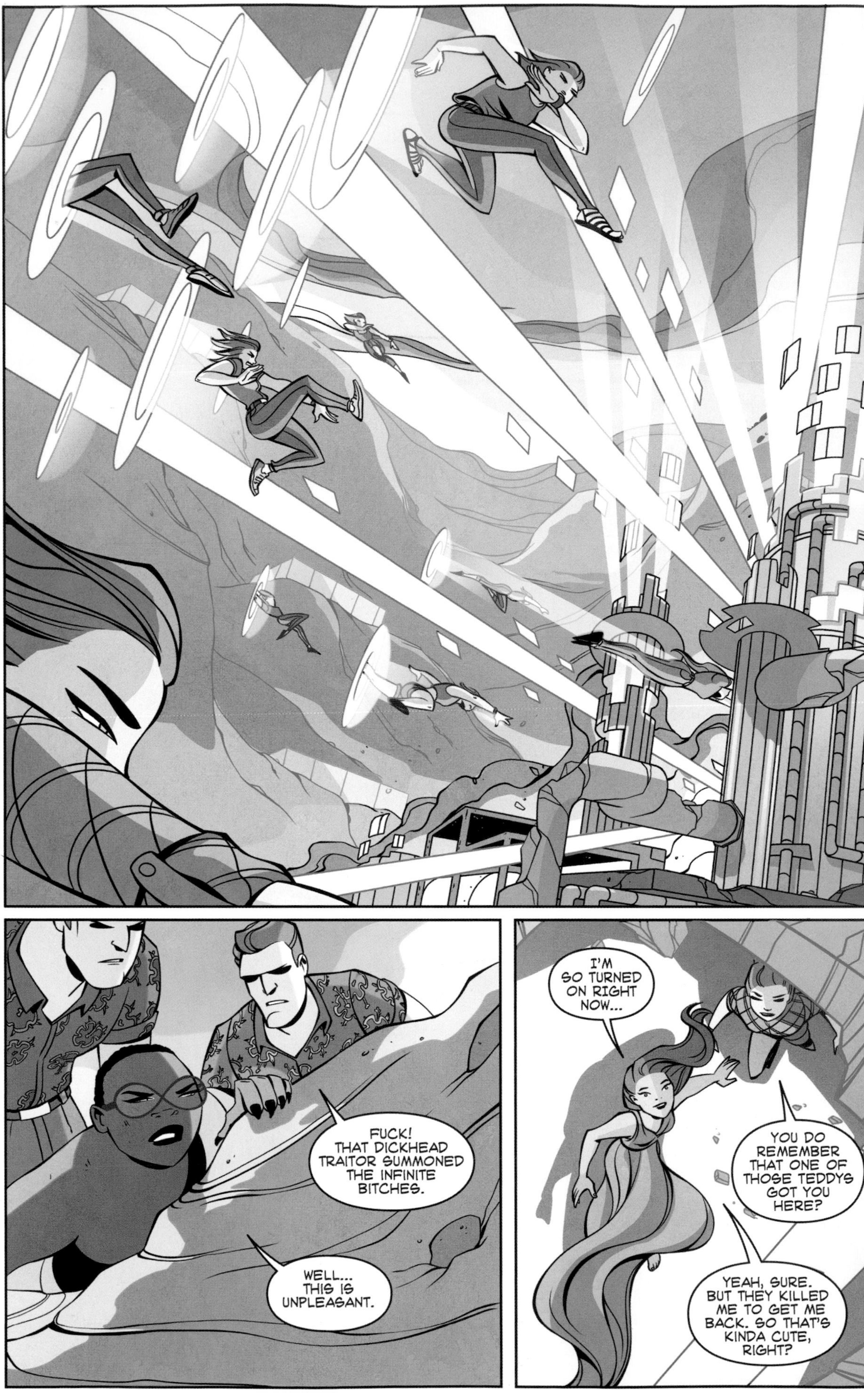
FUCK! THAT DICKHEAD TRAITOR SUMMONED THE INFINITE BITCHES.
WELL... THIS IS UNPLEASANT.
I'M SO TURNED ON RIGHT NOW...
YOU DO REMEMBER THAT ONE OF THOSE TEDDYS GOT YOU HERE?
YEAH, SURE. BUT THEY KILLED ME TO GET ME BACK. SO THAT'S KINDA CUTE, RIGHT?

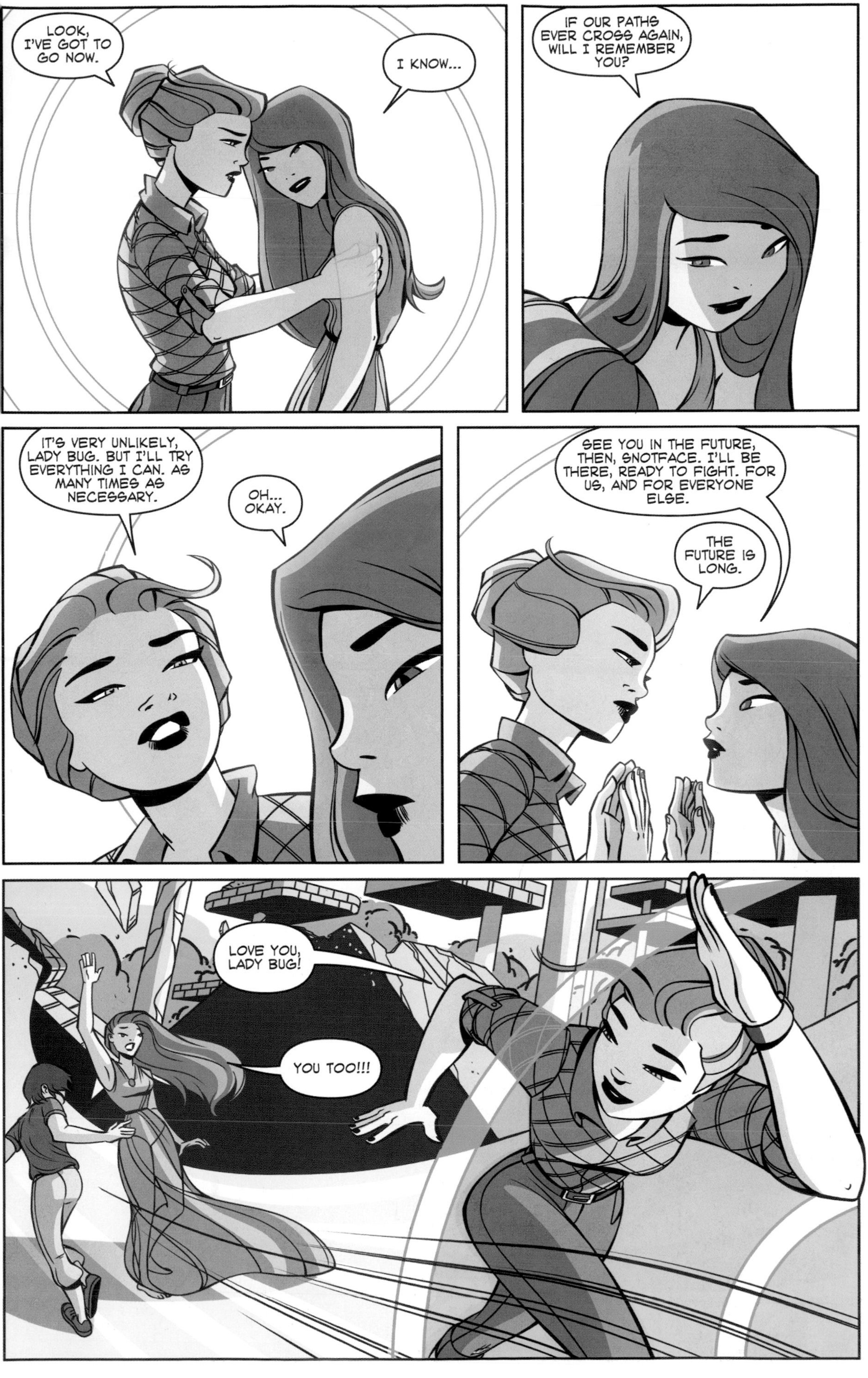
LOOK, I'VE GOT TO GO NOW.
I KNOW...
IF OUR PATHS EVER CROSS AGAIN, WILL I REMEMBER YOU?
IT'S VERY UNLIKELY, LADY BUG. BUT I'LL TRY EVERYTHING I CAN. AS MANY TIMES AS NECESSARY.
OH... OKAY.
SEE YOU IN THE FUTURE, THEN, SNOTFACE. I'LL BE THERE, READY TO FIGHT. FOR US, AND FOR EVERYONE ELSE.
THE FUTURE IS LONG.
LOVE YOU, LADY BUG!
YOU TOO!!!

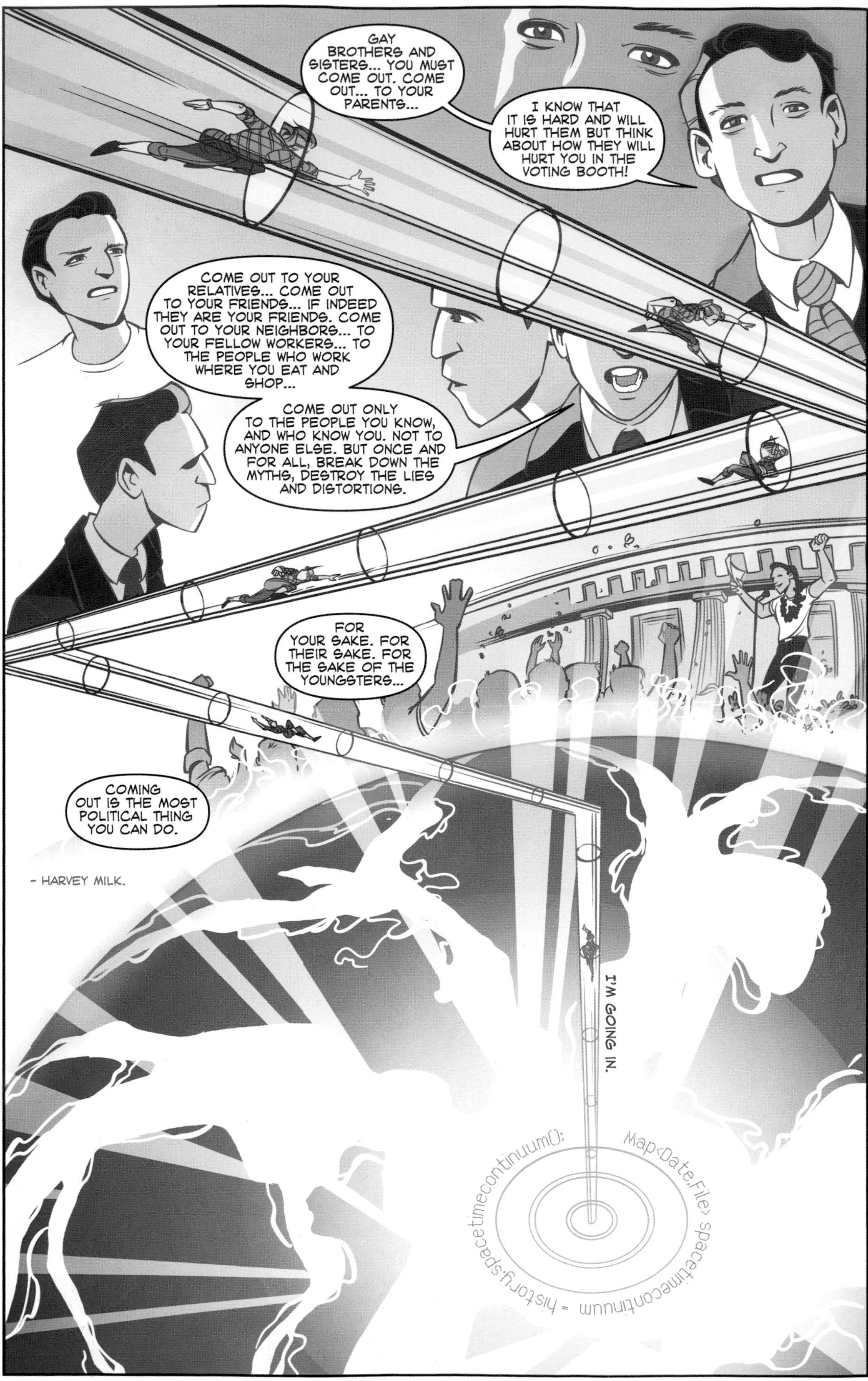

GAY BROTHERS AND SISTERS... YOU MUST COME OUT. COME OUT... TO YOUR PARENTS...
I KNOW THAT IT IS HARD AND WILL HURT THEM BUT THINK ABOUT HOW THEY WILL HURT YOU IN THE VOTING BOOTH!
COME OUT TO YOUR RELATIVES... COME OUT TO YOUR FRIENDS... IF INDEED THEY ARE YOUR FRIENDS. COME OUT TO YOUR NEIGHBORS... TO YOUR FELLOW WORKERS... TO THE PEOPLE WHO WORK WHERE YOU EAT AND SHOP...
COME OUT ONLY TO THE PEOPLE YOU KNOW, AND WHO KNOW YOU. NOT TO ANYONE ELSE. BUT ONCE AND FOR ALL, BREAK DOWN THE MYTHS, DESTROY THE LIES AND DISTORTIONS.
FOR YOUR SAKE. FOR THEIR SAKE. FOR THE SAKE OF THE YOUNGSTERS...
COMING OUT IS THE MOST POLITICAL THING YOU CAN DO.
- HARVEY MILK.
I'M GOING IN.
Map<Date,File> spacetimecontinuum = history.spacetimecontinuum();

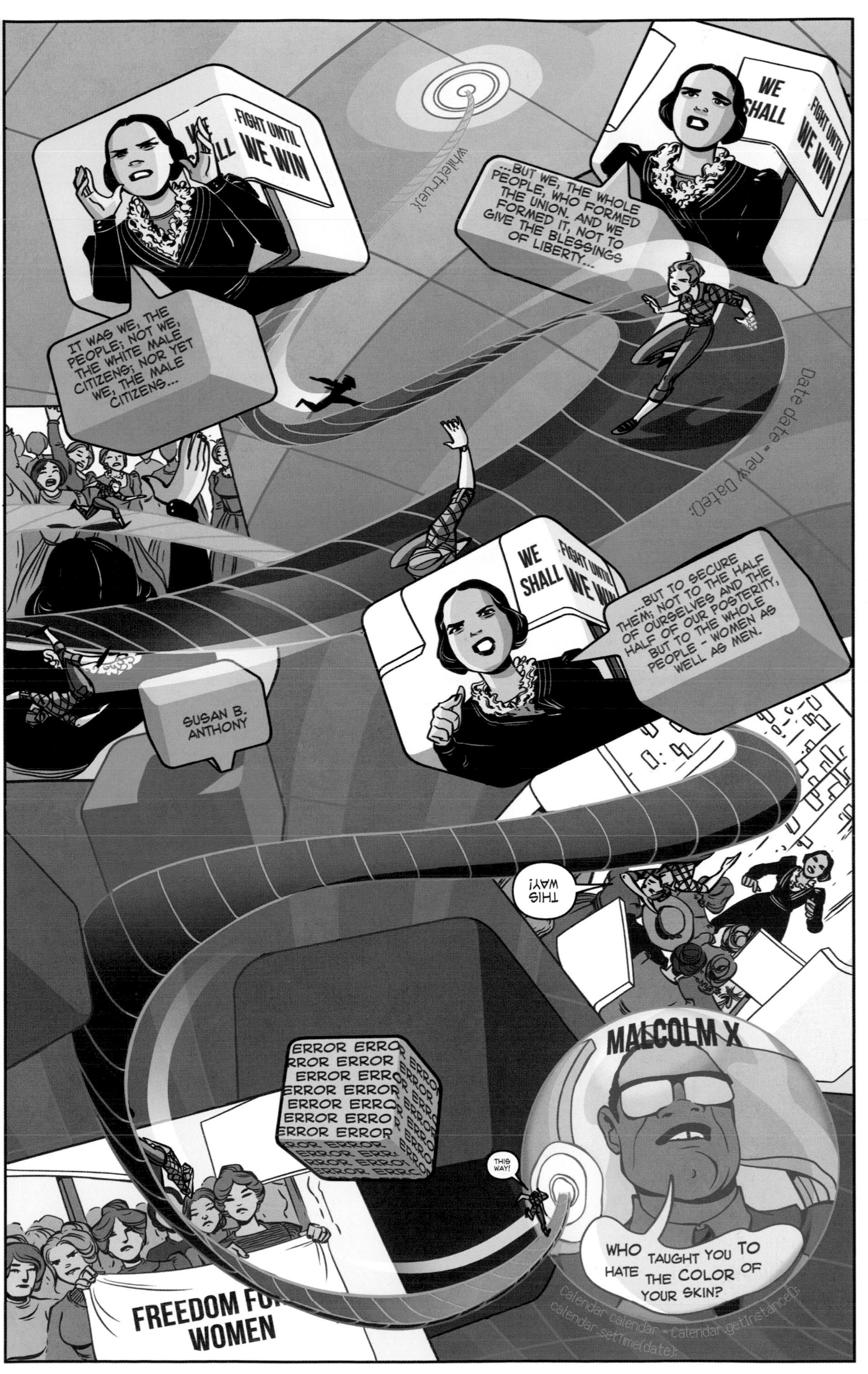
WE SHALL FIGHT UNTIL WE WIN
IT WAS WE, THE PEOPLE; NOT WE, THE WHITE MALE CITIZENS; NOR YET WE, THE MALE CITIZENS...
while(true){
WE SHALL FIGHT UNTIL WE WIN
...BUT WE, THE WHOLE PEOPLE, WHO FORMED THE UNION. AND WE FORMED IT, NOT TO GIVE THE BLESSINGS OF LIBERTY...
Date date = new Date();
WE SHALL FIGHT UNTIL WE WIN
...BUT TO SECURE THEM; NOT TO THE HALF OF OURSELVES AND THE HALF OF OUR POSTERITY, BUT TO THE WHOLE PEOPLE - WOMEN AS WELL AS MEN.
SUSAN B. ANTHONY
THIS WAY!
ERROR ERROR ERROR ERROR ERROR ERROR ERROR ERROR ERROR ERROR ERROR ERROR
MALCOLM X
THIS WAY!
WHO TAUGHT YOU TO HATE THE COLOR OF YOUR SKIN?
FREEDOM FOR WOMEN
Calendar calendar = Calendar.getInstance();
calendar.setTime(date);

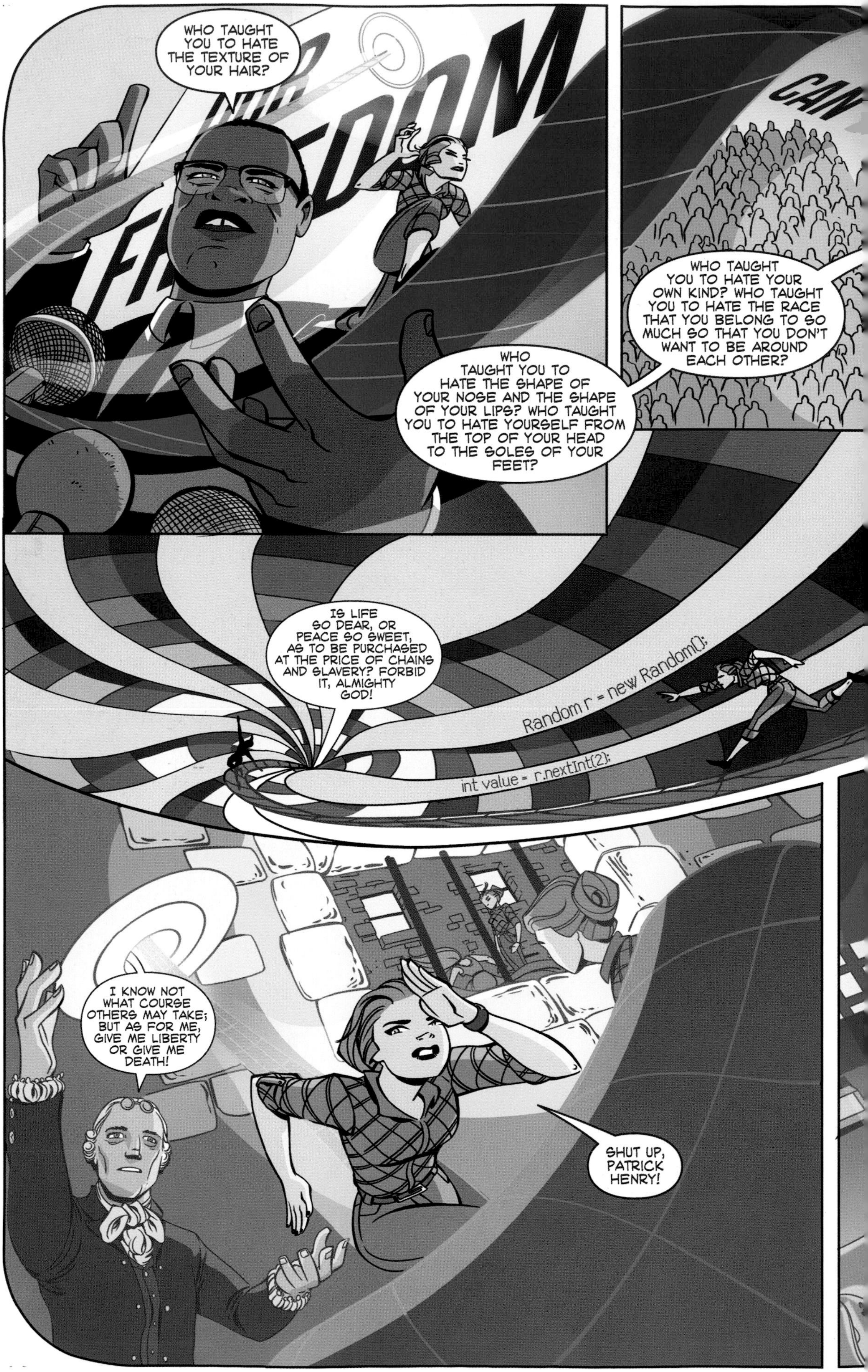
WHO TAUGHT YOU TO HATE THE TEXTURE OF YOUR HAIR?
FREEDOM
WHO TAUGHT YOU TO HATE THE SHAPE OF YOUR NOSE AND THE SHAPE OF YOUR LIPS? WHO TAUGHT YOU TO HATE YOURSELF FROM THE TOP OF YOUR HEAD TO THE SOLES OF YOUR FEET?
CAN
WHO TAUGHT YOU TO HATE YOUR OWN KIND? WHO TAUGHT YOU TO HATE THE RACE THAT YOU BELONG TO SO MUCH SO THAT YOU DON'T WANT TO BE AROUND EACH OTHER?
IS LIFE SO DEAR, OR PEACE SO SWEET, AS TO BE PURCHASED AT THE PRICE OF CHAINS AND SLAVERY? FORBID IT, ALMIGHTY GOD!
Random r = new Random();
int value = r.nextInt(2);
I KNOW NOT WHAT COURSE OTHERS MAY TAKE; BUT AS FOR ME, GIVE ME LIBERTY OR GIVE ME DEATH!
SHUT UP, PATRICK HENRY!

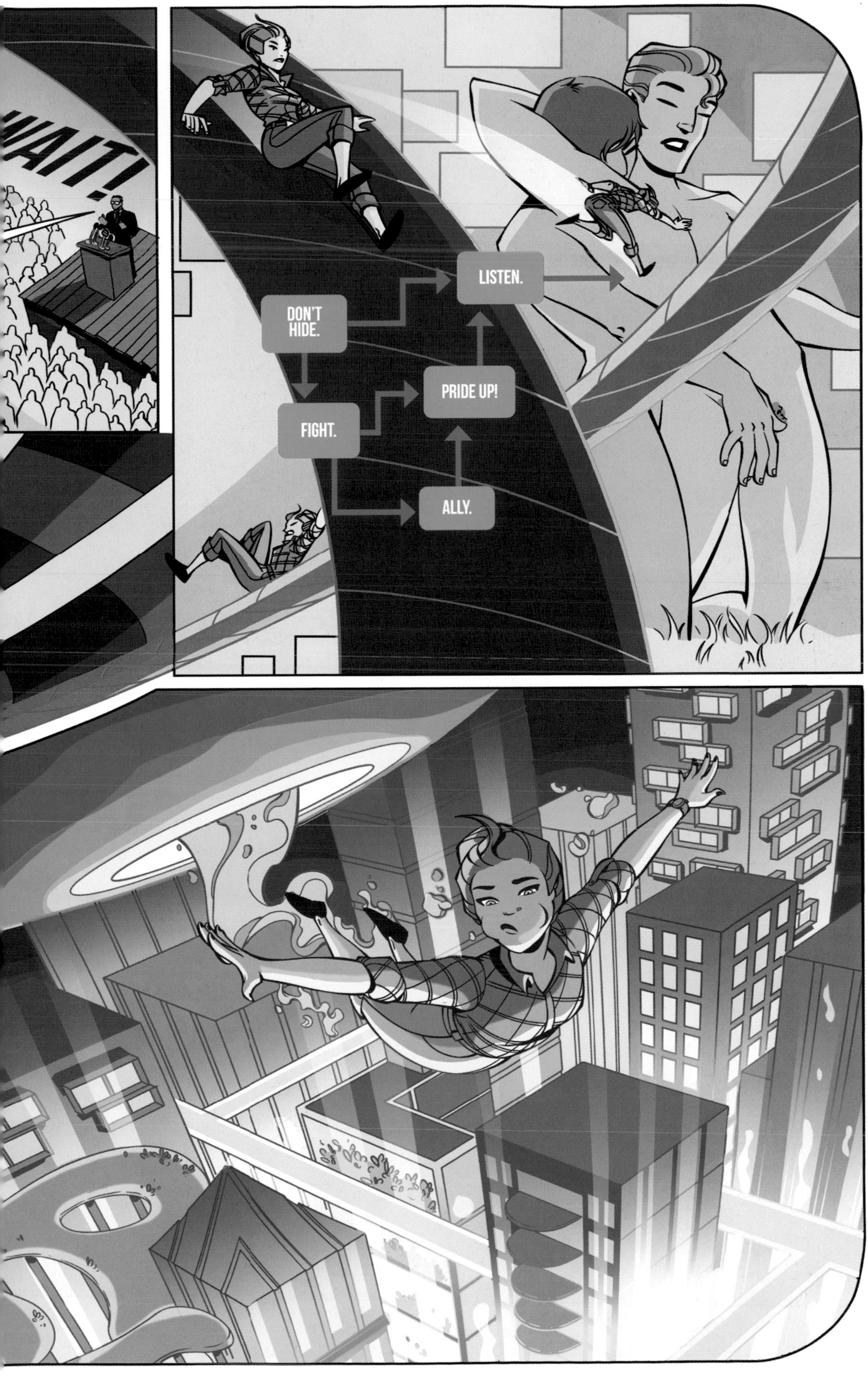
WAIT!
DON'T HIDE.
FIGHT.
ALLY.
PRIDE UP!
LISTEN.

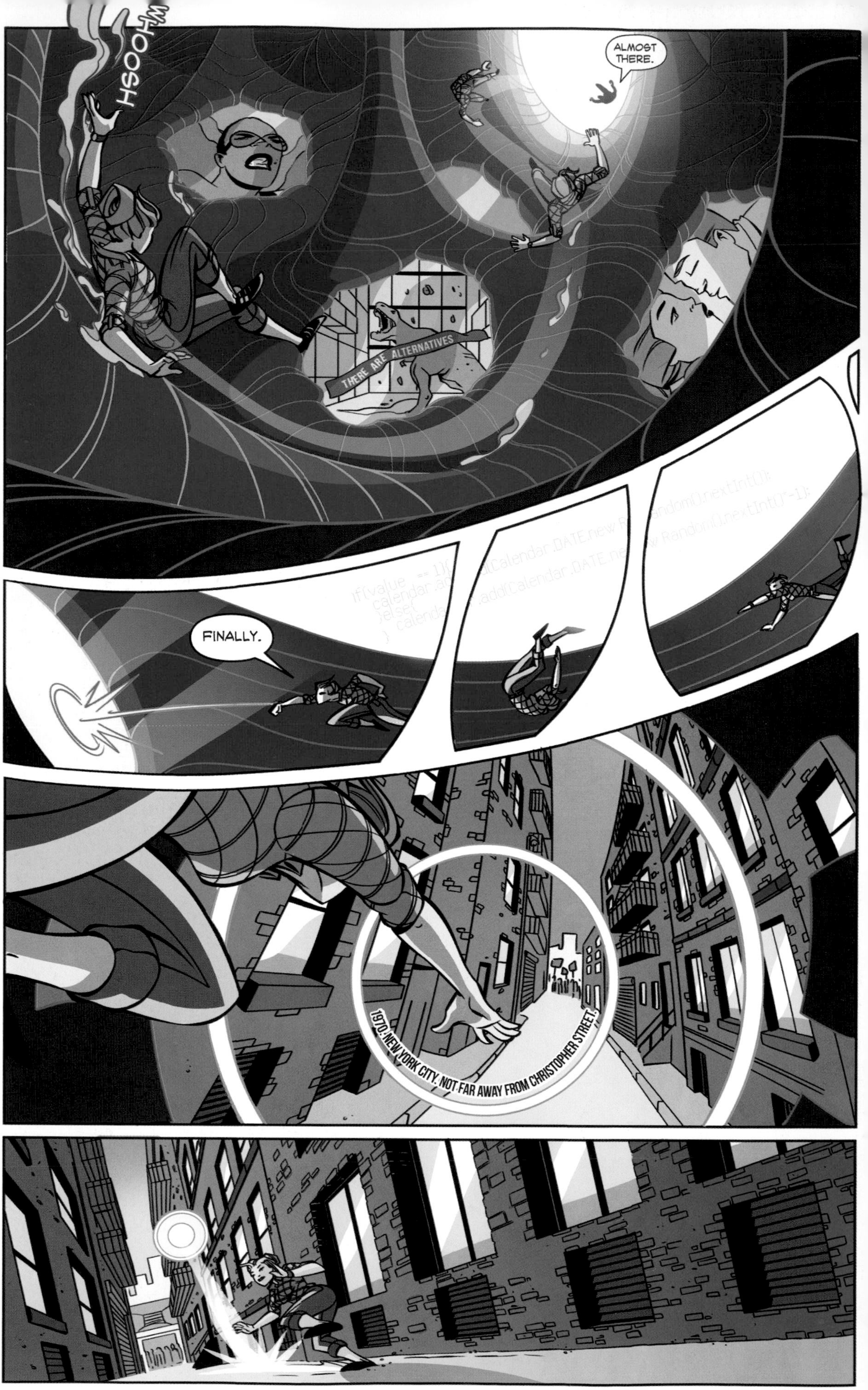
WHOOSH
ALMOST THERE.
THERE ARE ALTERNATIVES
FINALLY.
1970. NEW YORK CITY. NOT FAR AWAY FROM CHRISTOPHER STREET.

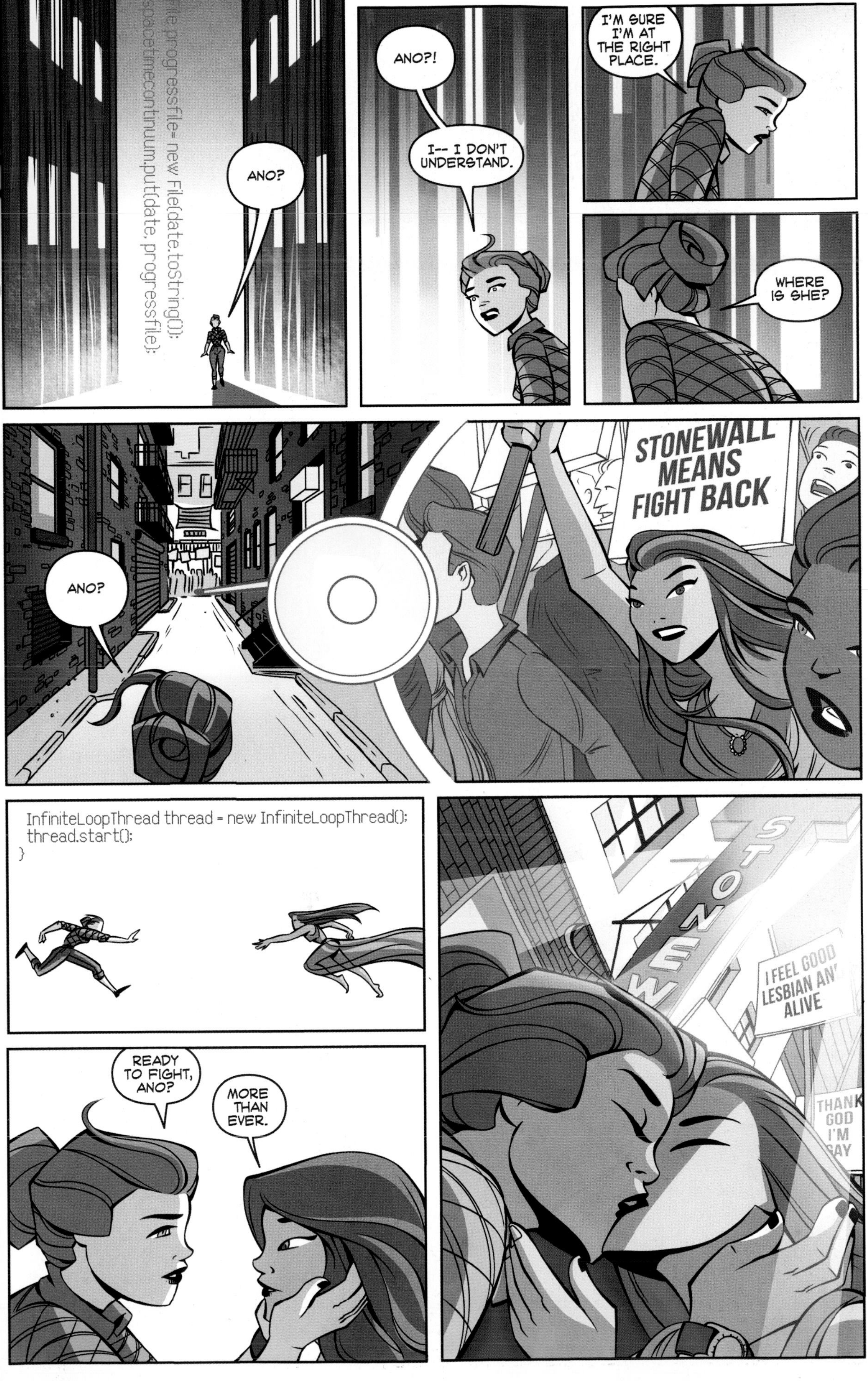
File progressfile= new File(date.toString());
spacetimecontinuum.put(date, progressfile);
ANO?
ANO?!
I-- I DON'T UNDERSTAND.
I'M SURE I'M AT THE RIGHT PLACE.
WHERE IS SHE?
ANO?
STONEWALL MEANS FIGHT BACK
InfiniteLoopThread thread = new InfiniteLoopThread();
thread.start();
}
READY TO FIGHT, ANO?
MORE THAN EVER.
STONEW
I FEEL GOOD LESBIAN AN' ALIVE
THANK GOD I'M GAY

A problem has been detected and your world has been shut down to prevent damages to the space-time continuum.

The problem seems to be caused by the following file: infiniteloop.sys

MANUALLY_INITIATED_CRASH

If this is the first you've seen this stop screen, well, Teddy, you blew it. Restart your world. Do better. If this screen appears again, it may suggest the return of The Infinite Loop. In that case, follow these steps:

1_ACT (Do not run away AGAIN to your fancy secret place.)

2_SPEAK UP (This time, listen to Ano, dammit!)

3_UNITE (You know where I'm going with this. Other Teddys, blah, blah, blah.)

4_PROTECT THE VICTIMS (All of them.)

5_TEACH TOLERANCE (Face it, THE INFINITE LOOP will come back. Be prepared.)

6_CREATE AN ALTERNATIVE ("There Is No Alternative," my ass. Prove them wrong.)

7_LOVE (You mushy unicorn lover.)

Pride up.

                                        - The Guardian of Forever

                                            Just kidding.

                                            Or am I?

                                        We'll never know.

INITIALIZING REBOOT
INITIALIZING REBOOT
INITIALIZING REBOOT
INITIALIZING REBOOT
INITIALIZING REBOOT
INITIALIZING REBOOT
INITIALIZING REBOOT
INITIALIZING REBOOT
INITIALIZING REBOOT
INITIALIZING REBOOT
INITIALIZING REBOOT
INITIALIZING REBOOT
INITIALIZING REBOOT
INITIALIZING REBOOT
INITIALIZING REBOOT
INITIALIZING REBOOT
INITIALIZING REBOOT
INITIALIZING REBOOT
INITIALIZING REBOOT
INITIALIZING REBOOT

reboot.

PRESENT. OR FUTURE. WHATEVER.
SOMEWHERE OVER THE RAINBOW. Your world has been s...
& the space-time continuum.

The problem seems to be caused by the following file: in...

MANUALLY_INITIATED_CRASH

If this is the first you've see this stop screen, well, re...
world. Do button. If this screen appears again, it mu...
Infinite Loop. In that case, follow these...

ACT (Do not run away AGAIN to your f... secret pla...

SPEAK (This time, listen to Ano. dar...

UNITE (You know ...e... in going with ... Other Tea...

PROTECT THE VICTIMS (All of them.)

TEACH TOLERANCE (Face it. THE INFINITE LOOP will come...

CREATE AN ALTERNATIVE ("There is No alternative". my...

LOVE (You must ... unicorn lover.)

...de up.

WELL, SHIT. ANO! RETIREMENT IS ALREADY OVER.

IT'S HAPPENING AGAIN.

Hill Valley Telegraph

THEY ARE NOT LIKE US.

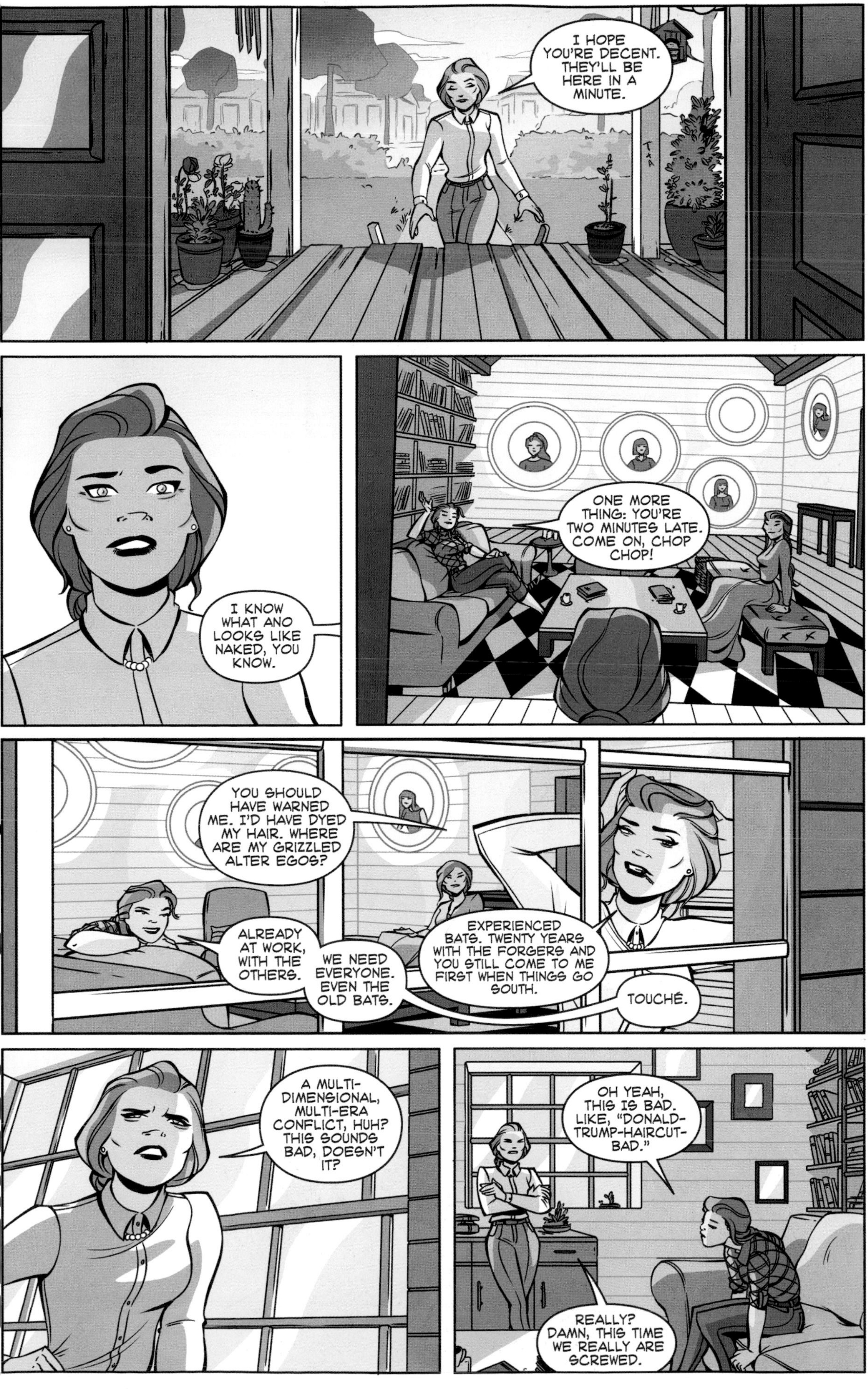
I HOPE YOU'RE DECENT. THEY'LL BE HERE IN A MINUTE.
I KNOW WHAT ANO LOOKS LIKE NAKED, YOU KNOW.
ONE MORE THING: YOU'RE TWO MINUTES LATE. COME ON, CHOP CHOP!
YOU SHOULD HAVE WARNED ME. I'D HAVE DYED MY HAIR. WHERE ARE MY GRIZZLED ALTER EGOS?
ALREADY AT WORK, WITH THE OTHERS.
WE NEED EVERYONE. EVEN THE OLD BATS.
EXPERIENCED BATS. TWENTY YEARS WITH THE FORGERS AND YOU STILL COME TO ME FIRST WHEN THINGS GO SOUTH.
TOUCHÉ.
A MULTI-DIMENSIONAL, MULTI-ERA CONFLICT, HUH? THIS SOUNDS BAD, DOESN'T IT?
OH YEAH, THIS IS BAD. LIKE, "DONALD-TRUMP-HAIRCUT-BAD."
REALLY? DAMN, THIS TIME WE REALLY ARE SCREWED.

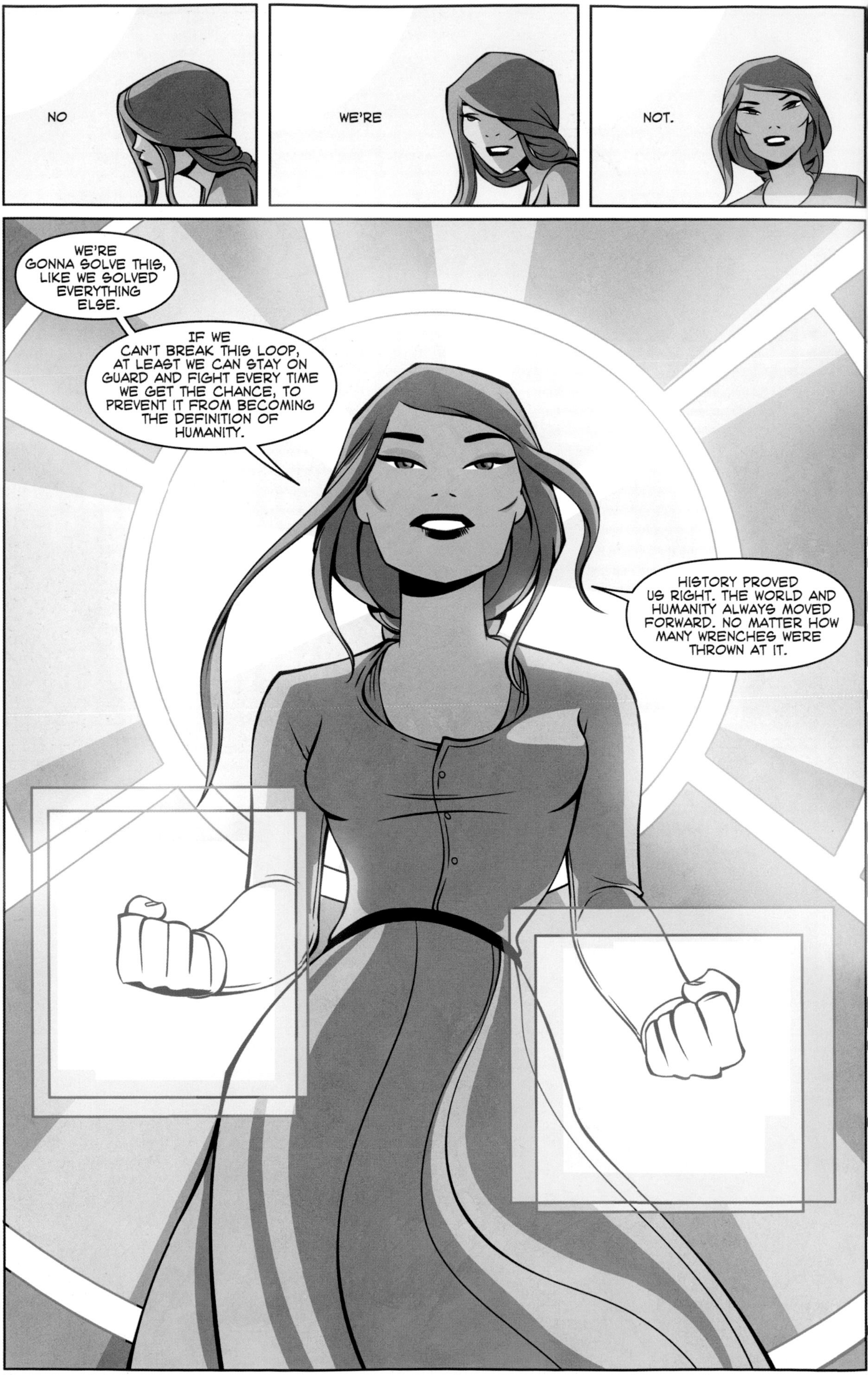
NO
WE'RE
NOT.
WE'RE GONNA SOLVE THIS, LIKE WE SOLVED EVERYTHING ELSE.
IF WE CAN'T BREAK THIS LOOP, AT LEAST WE CAN STAY ON GUARD AND FIGHT EVERY TIME WE GET THE CHANCE, TO PREVENT IT FROM BECOMING THE DEFINITION OF HUMANITY.
HISTORY PROVED US RIGHT. THE WORLD AND HUMANITY ALWAYS MOVED FORWARD. NO MATTER HOW MANY WRENCHES WERE THROWN AT IT.

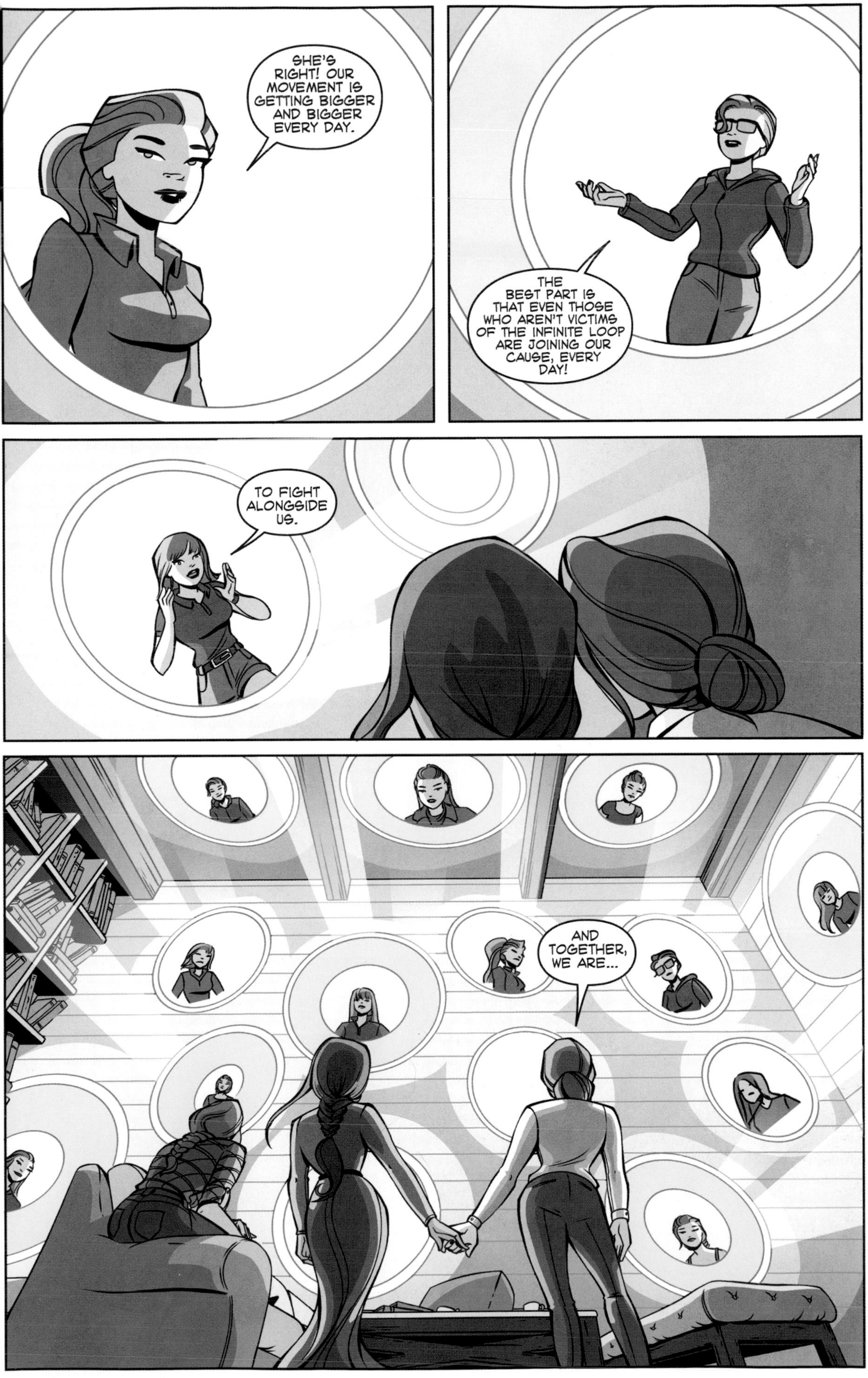
SHE'S RIGHT! OUR MOVEMENT IS GETTING BIGGER AND BIGGER EVERY DAY.
THE BEST PART IS THAT EVEN THOSE WHO AREN'T VICTIMS OF THE INFINITE LOOP ARE JOINING OUR CAUSE, EVERY DAY!
TO FIGHT ALONGSIDE US.
AND TOGETHER, WE ARE...

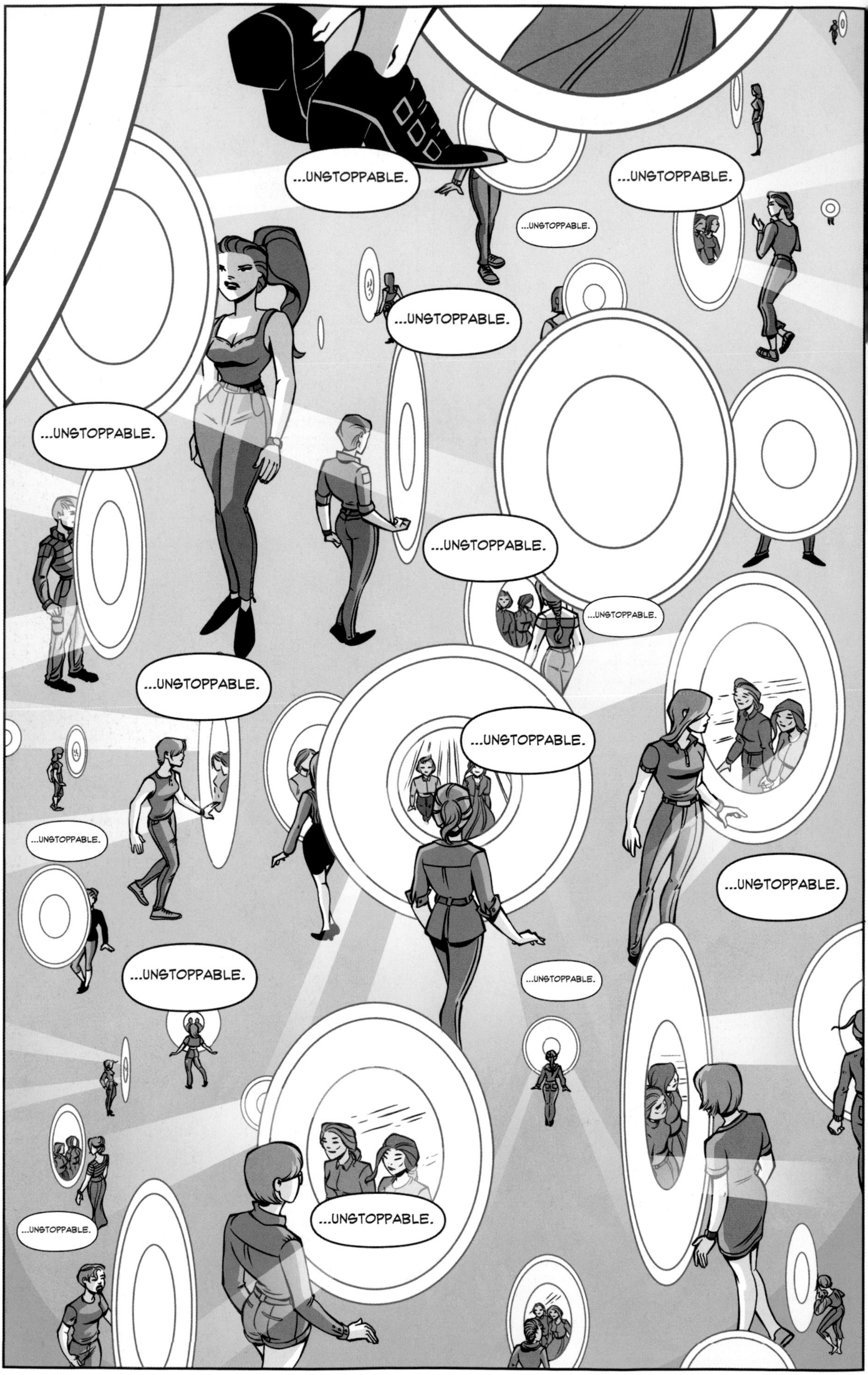
...UNSTOPPABLE.
...UNSTOPPABLE.
...UNSTOPPABLE.
...UNSTOPPABLE.
...UNSTOPPABLE.
...UNSTOPPABLE.
...UNSTOPPABLE.
...UNSTOPPABLE.
...UNSTOPPABLE.
...UNSTOPPABLE.
...UNSTOPPABLE.
...UNSTOPPABLE.
...UNSTOPPABLE.
...UNSTOPPABLE.
...UNSTOPPABLE.

Art by ELI POWELL

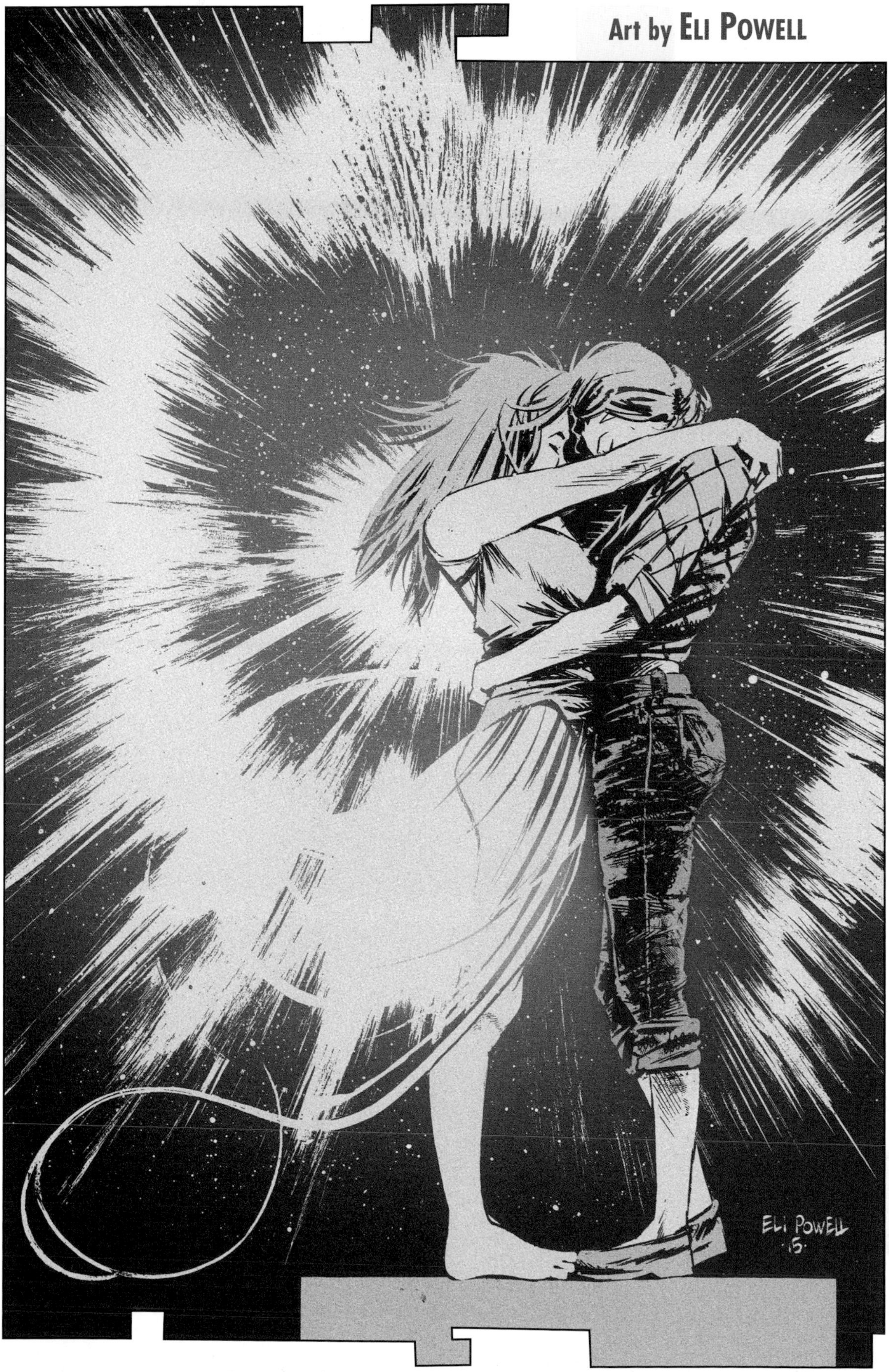
ELI POWELL
'15

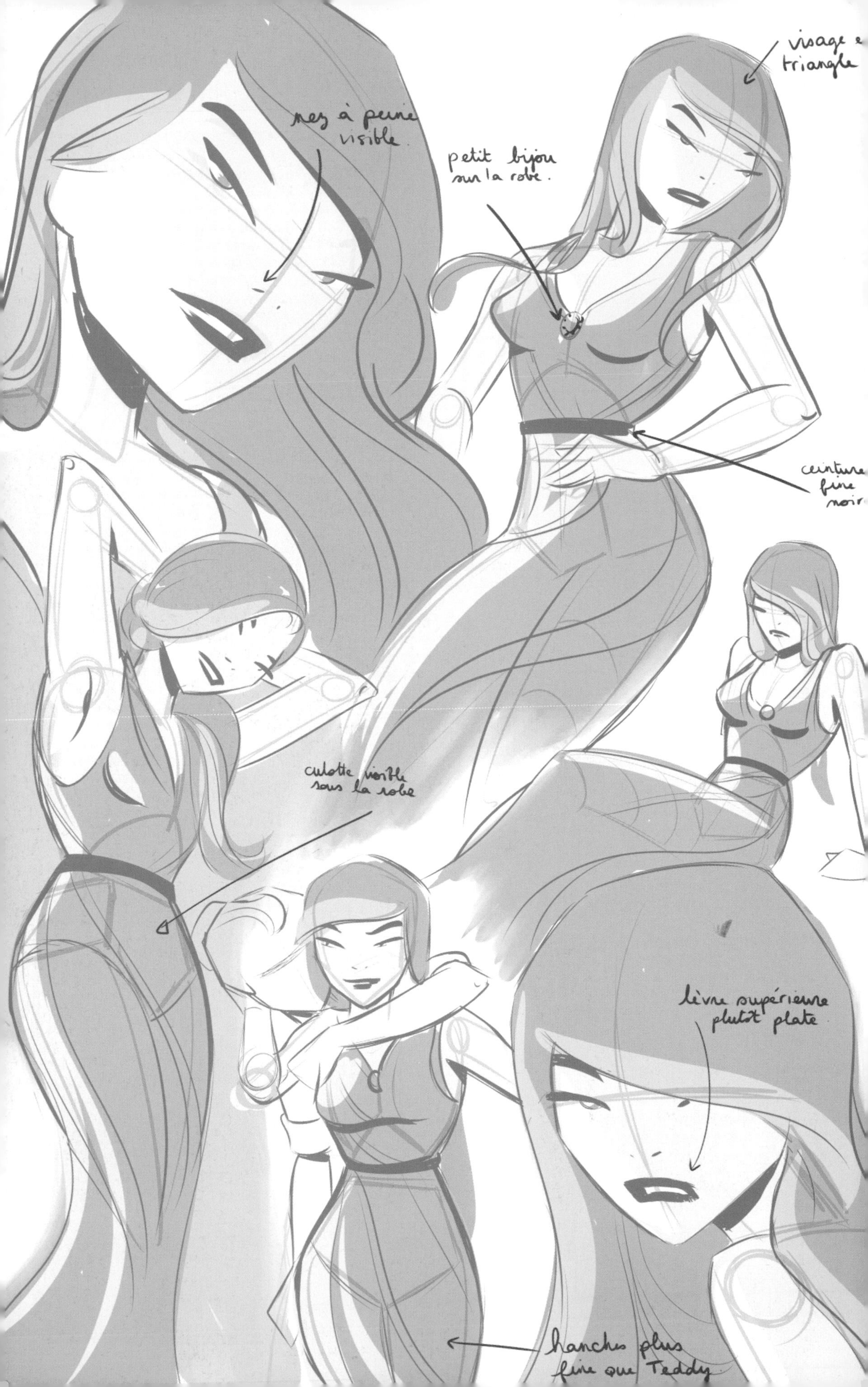
nez à peine visible.
visage e triangle
petit bijou sur la robe.
ceinture fine noir
culotte visible sous la robe
lèvre supérieure plutôt plate.
hanches plus fine que Teddy

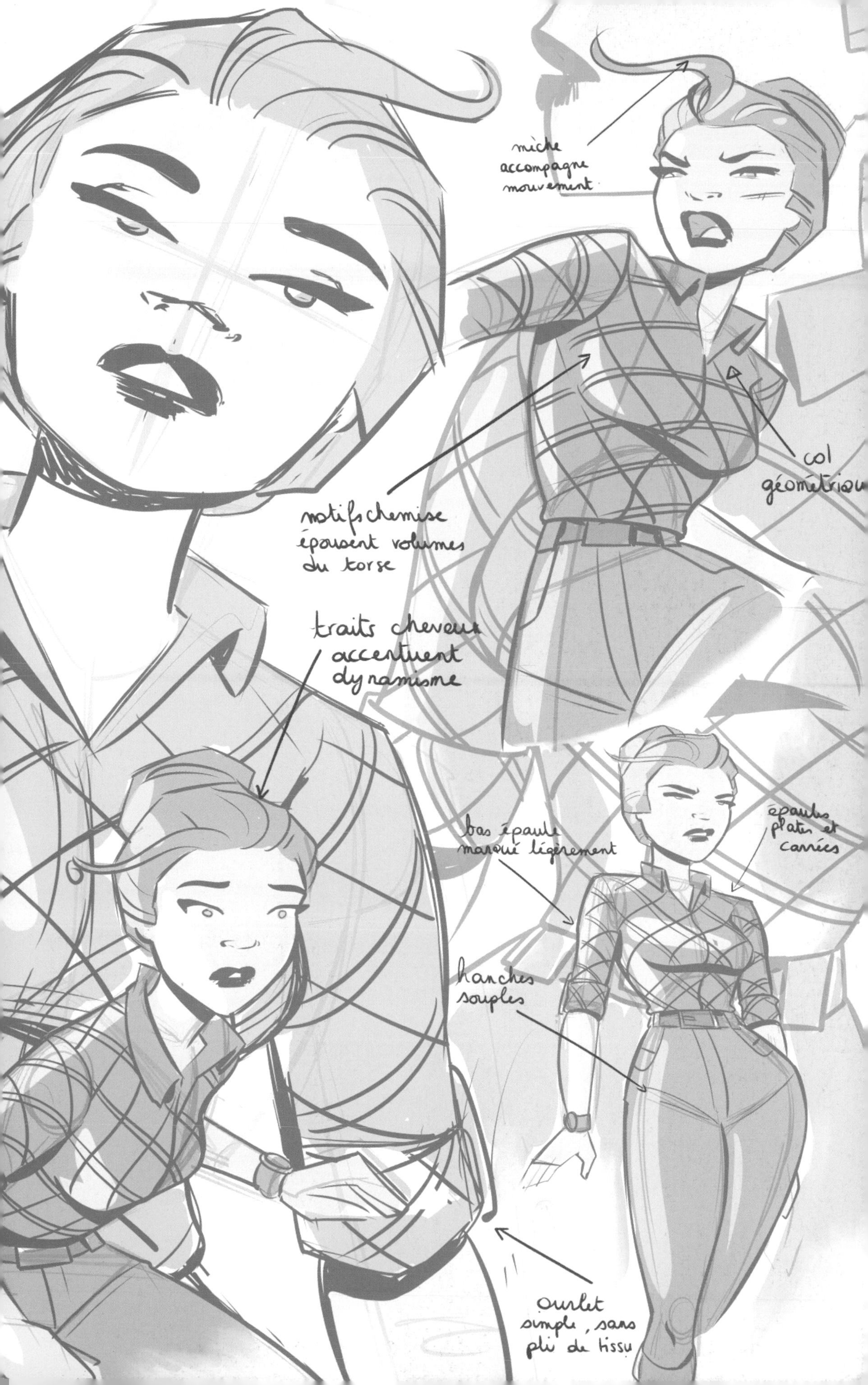

miche
accompagne
mouvement
col
géométrique
motifs chemise
épousent volumes
du torse
traits cheveux
accentuent
dynamisme
bas épaule
marqué légèrement
épaules
plates et
carrées
hanches
souples
ourlet
simple, sans
pli de tissu

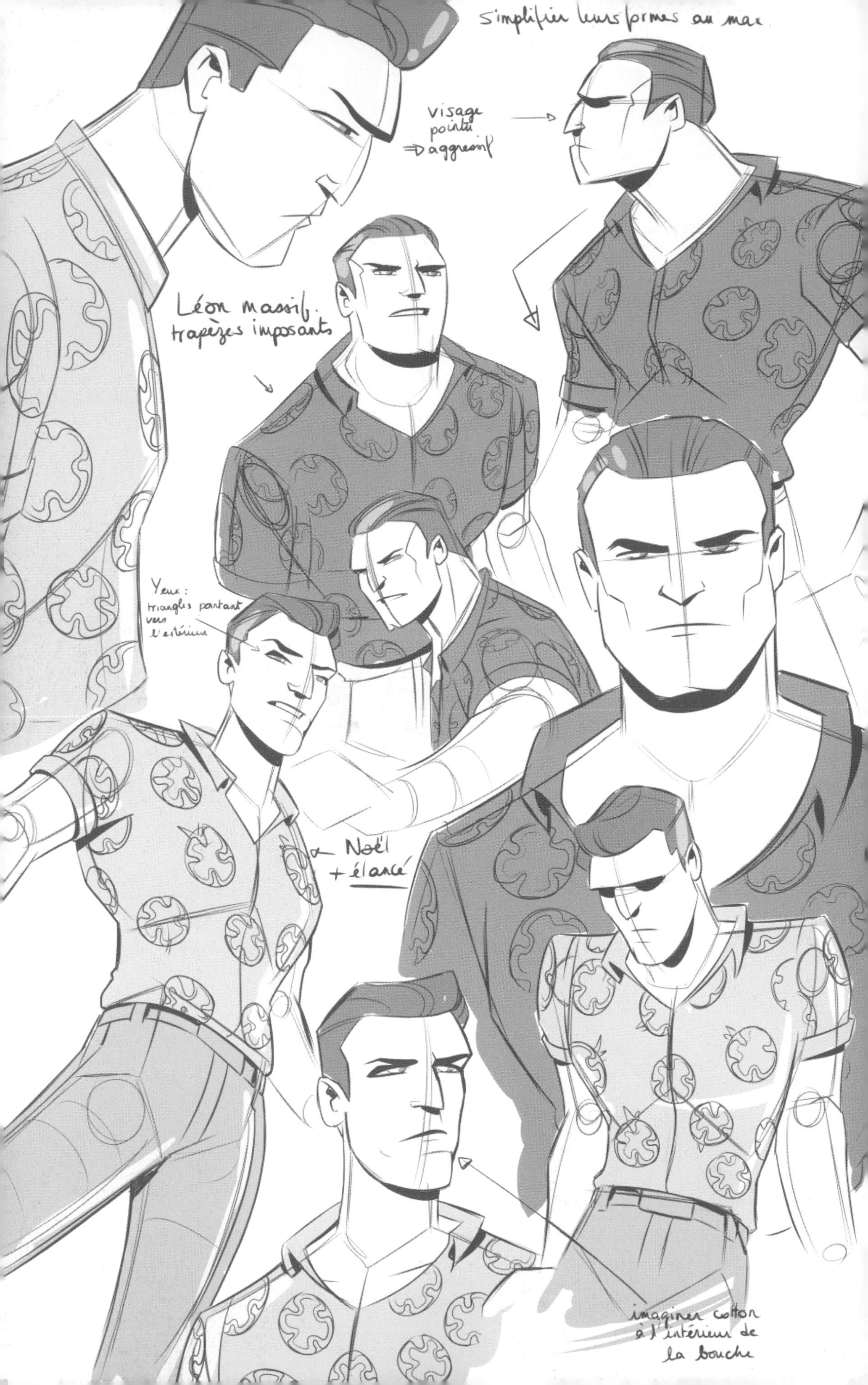
simplifier leurs formes au max
visage pointu
⇒ aggressif
Léon massif.
trapèzes imposants
Yeux : triangles pointant vers l'extérieur
Noël + élancé
imaginer cotton à l'intérieur de la bouche

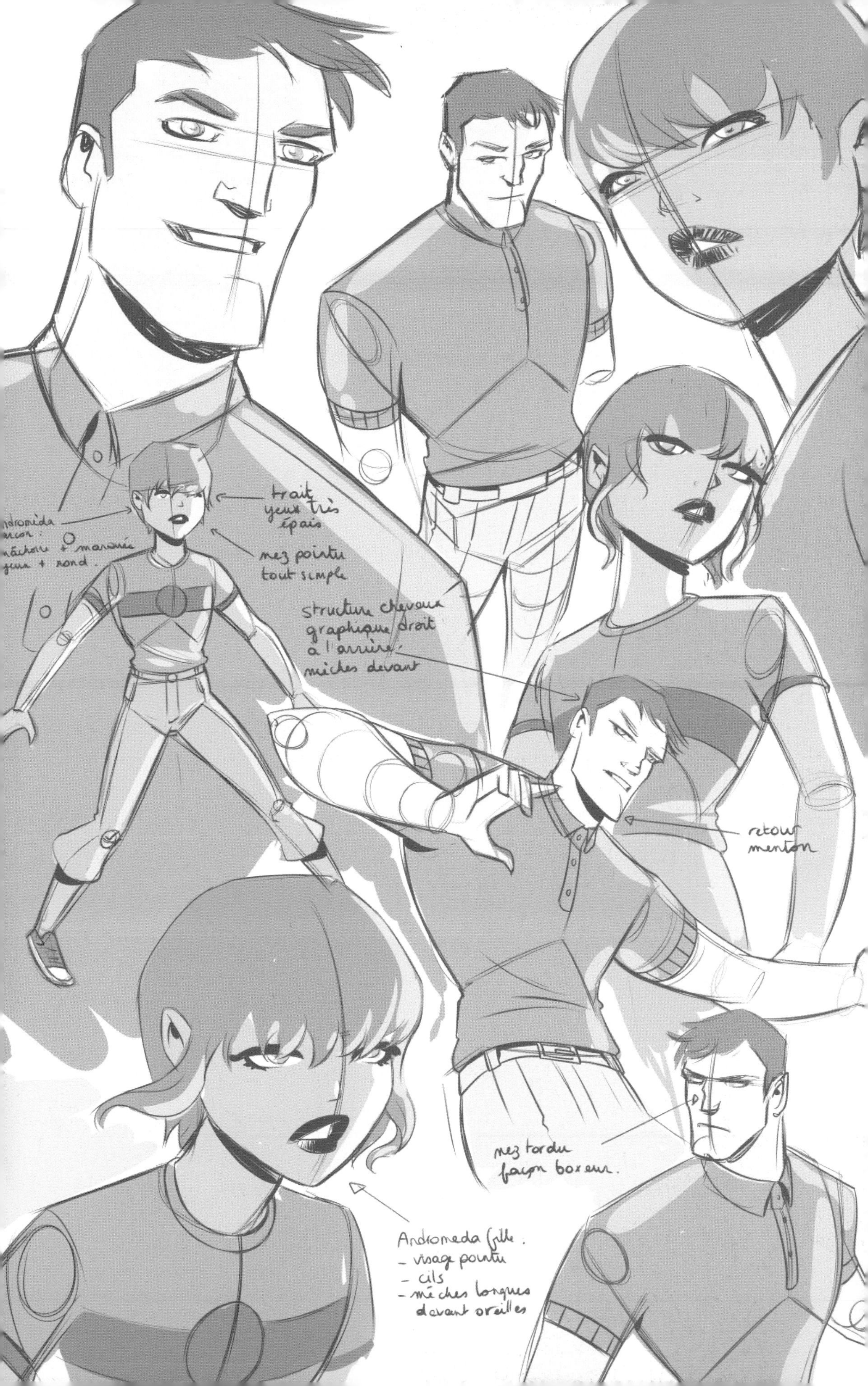

ndromeda
arçon :
mâchoire + marquée
yeux + rond.
trait yeux très épais
nez pointu tout simple
structure cheveux graphique droit à l'arrière mèches devant
retour menton
nez tordu façon boxeur.
Andromeda fille.
- visage pointu
- cils
- mèches longues devant oreilles

Layout by ELSA CHARRETIER

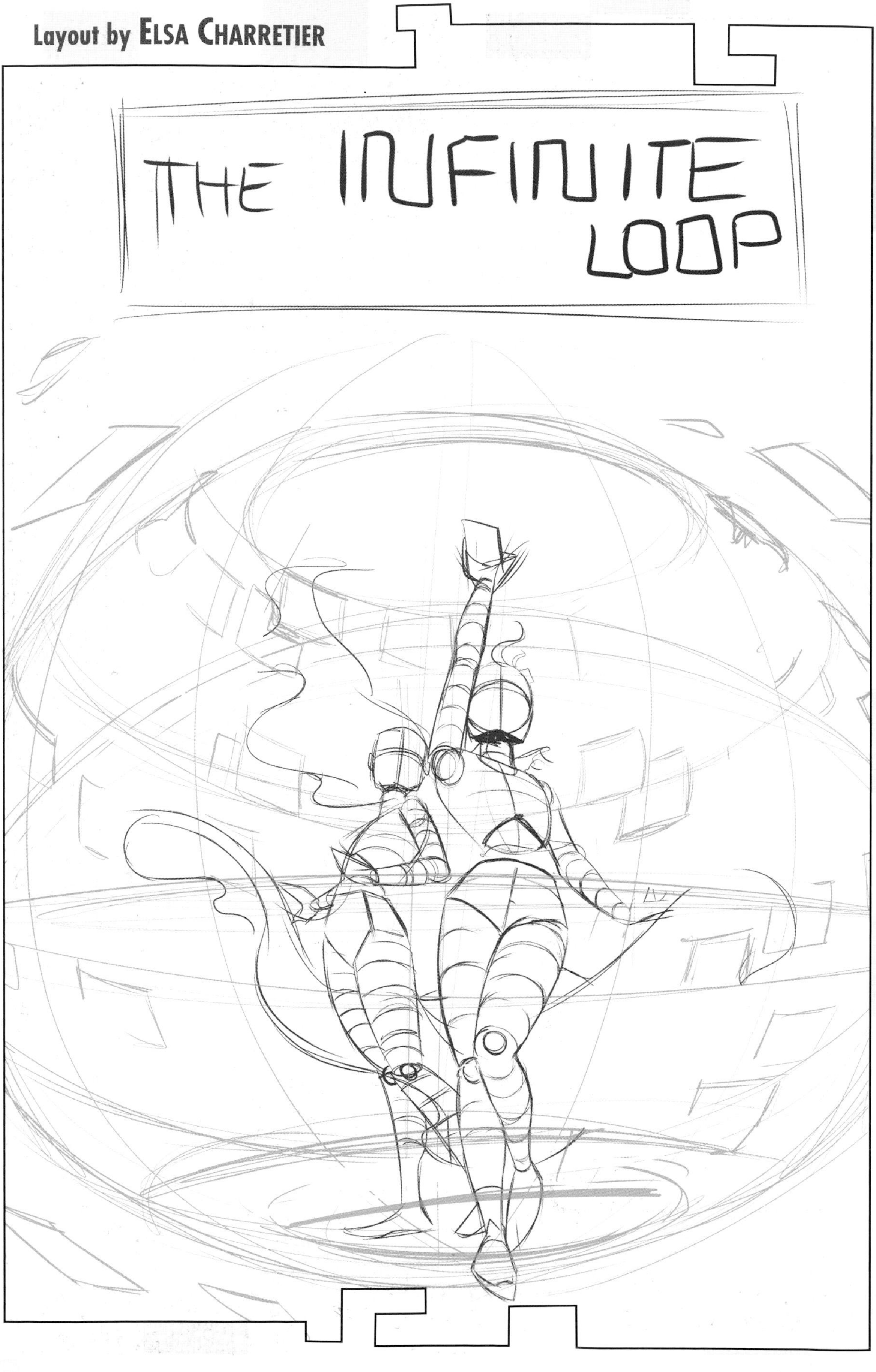
THE INFINITE LOOP

Art by ELSA CHARRETIER

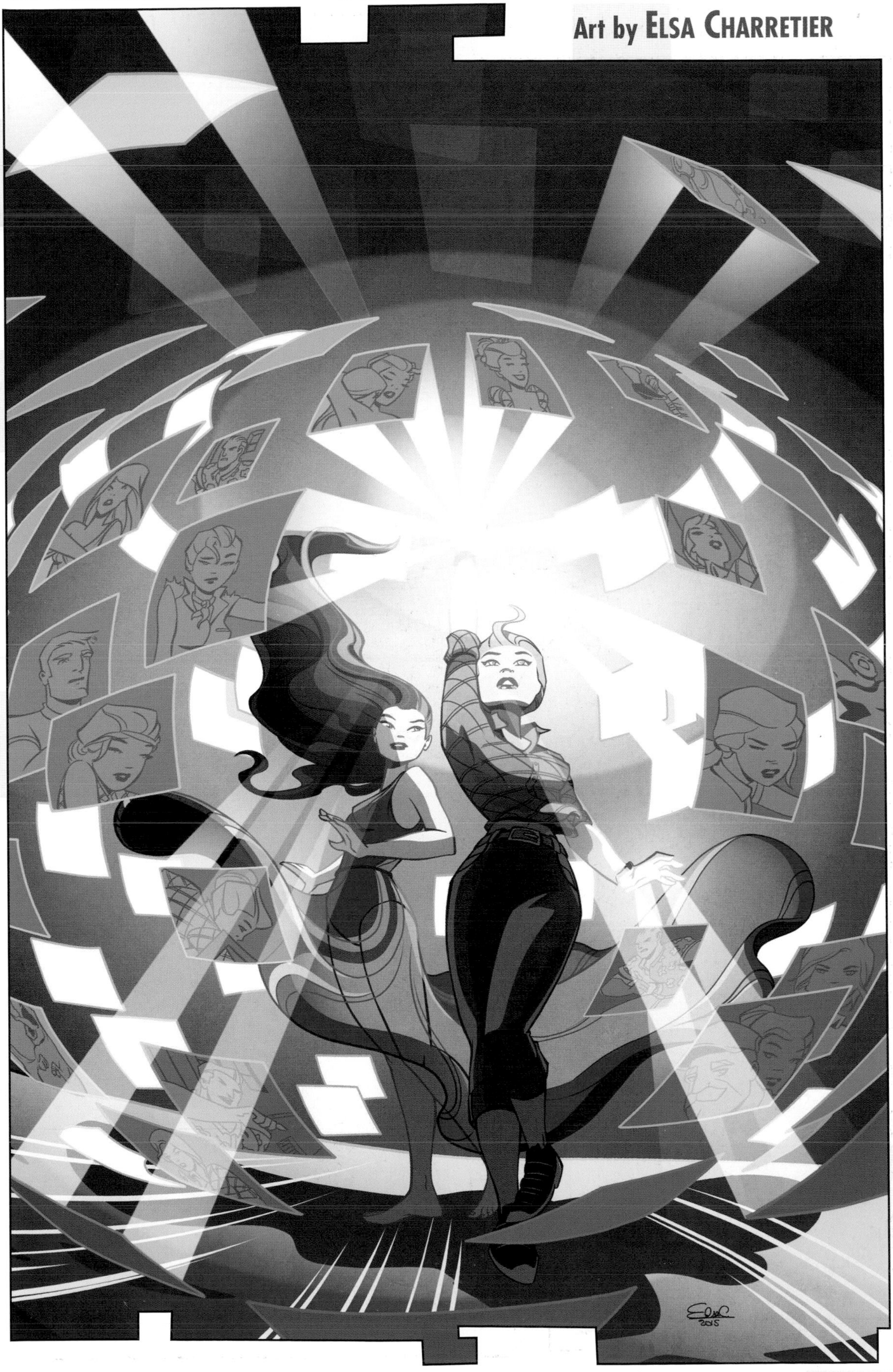

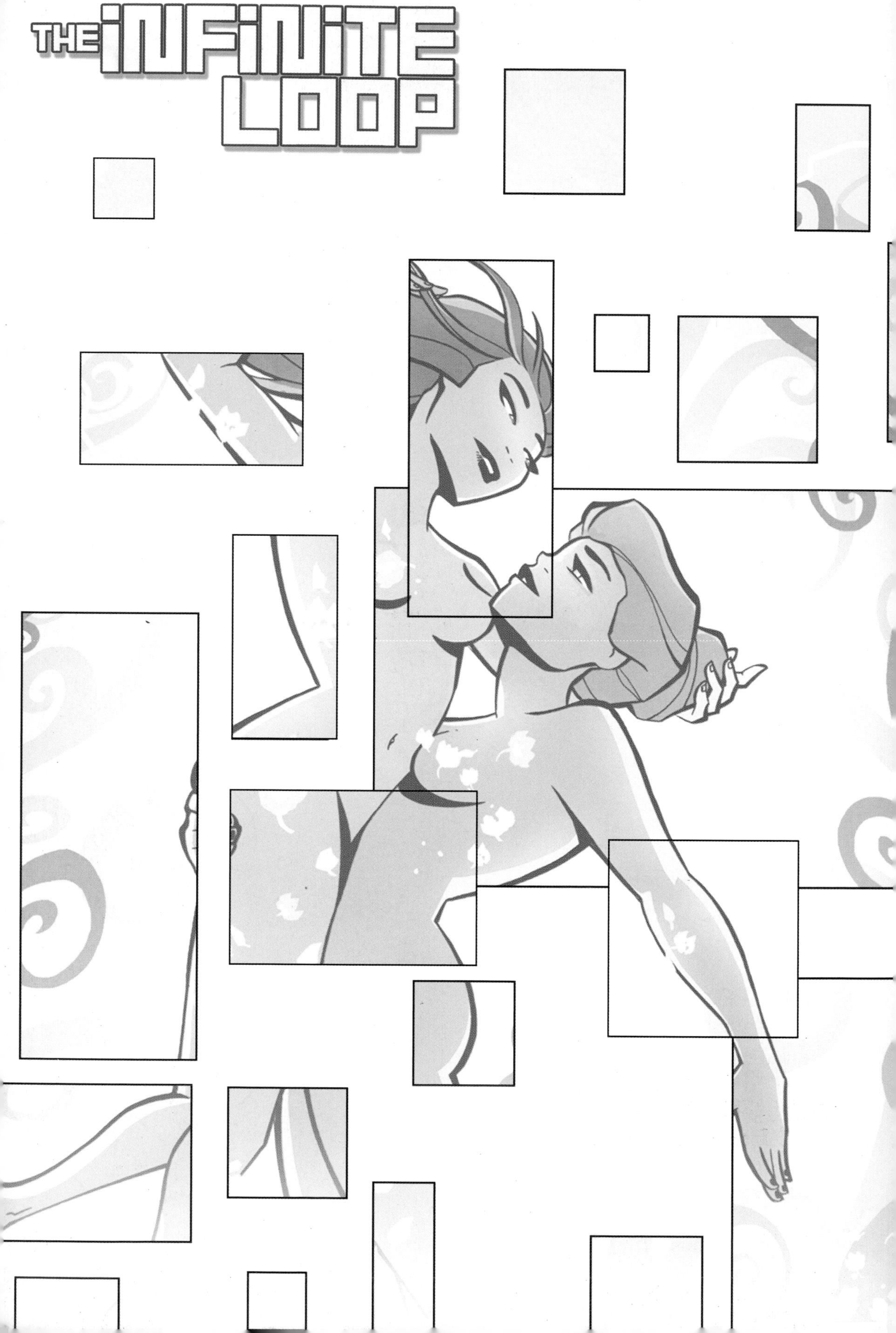
THE INFINITE LOOP